MODERN JUDGEMENTS

General Editor: P. N. FURBANK

Dickens   A. E. Dyson
Henry James   Tony Tanner
Milton   Alan Rudrum
Walter Scott   D. D. Devlin
Shelley   R. B. Woodings
Swift   A. Norman Jeffares

IN PREPARATION

Matthew Arnold   P. A. W. Collins
Freud   F. Cioffi
Marvell   M. Wilding
O'Casey   Ronald Ayling
Pasternak   Donald Davie and Angela Livingstone
Pope   Graham Martin
Racine   R. C. Knight

Milton

MODERN JUDGEMENTS

edited by
ALAN RUDRUM

MACMILLAN

Selection and editorial material © Alan Rudrum 1968

MACMILLAN & CO LTD
Little Essex Street London W C 2
and also at Bombay Calcutta and Madras
Macmillan South Africa (Publishers) Pty Ltd Johannesburg
The Macmillan Company of Australia Pty Ltd Melbourne
The Macmillan Company of Canada Ltd Toronto

Printed in Great Britain by
WESTERN PRINTING SERVICES LTD
Bristol

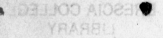

Contents

Acknowledgements

Joseph H. Summers, 'Milton and the Cult of Conformity', from the *Yale Review*, vol. 46 (1956–7) © Yale University Press; Arthur Barker, 'The Pattern of Milton's Nativity Ode', from the *University of Toronto Quarterly*, vol. 10 (The University of Toronto Press); Wayne Shumaker, 'Flowerets and Sounding Seas: A Study in the Affective Structure of "Lycidas" ', from *Publications of the Modern Language Association of America*, lxvi (1951) (The Modern Language Association of America); Stanley Eugene Fish, 'Not so much a teaching as an intangling', from *Surprised by Sin: the Reader in 'Paradise Lost'*; Arnold Williams, 'The Motivation of Satan's Rebellion in *Paradise Lost*', from *Studies in Philology*, vol. 42 (1945) (The University of North Carolina Press); Professor Murray W. Bundy, 'Milton's Prelapsarian Adam', from *Research Studies of the State College of Washington*, vol. 13, no. 3 (1945); 'Eve's Awakening', from *Essays in Honour of Walter Clyde Curry* (Professor Cleanth Brooks and Vanderbilt University Press); Professor R. L. Colie, 'Time and Eternity: Paradox and Structure in *Paradise Lost*', from the *Journal of the Warburg and Courtauld Institutes*; Lawrence A. Sasek, 'The Drama of *Paradise Lost*, Books XI and XII', from *Studies in English Renaissance Literature* (Louisiana State University Press); W. G. Madsen, 'From Shadowy Types to Truth', from *The Lyric and Dramatic Milton*, Selected Papers from the English Institute (1965), ed. J. H. Summers (Columbia University Press); M. M. Mahood, 'Milton's Heroes', from *Poetry and Humanism* (Jonathan Cape Ltd); J. B. Broadbent, 'Milton's Rhetoric', from *Modern Philology*, vol. 56 (1959) (The University of Chicago Press); William Haller, ' "Hail wedded love" ', from *English Literary History*, vol. 13, no. 2 (1946) (The Johns Hopkins Press).

General Editor's Preface

LITERARY criticism has only recently come of age as an academic discipline, and the intellectual activity that, a hundred years ago, went into theological discussion now finds its most natural outlet in the critical essay. Amid a good deal that is dull or silly or pretentious, every year now produces a crop of critical essays which are brilliant and profound not only as contributions to the understanding of a particular author but as statements of an original way of looking at literature and the world. Hence, it often seems that the most useful undertaking for an academic publisher might be not so much to commission new books of literary criticism or scholarship as to make the best of what exists easily available. This at least is the purpose of the present series of anthologies, each of which is devoted to a single major writer.

The guiding principle of selection is to assemble the best *modern* criticism – broadly speaking, that of the last twenty or thirty years – and to include historic and classic essays, however famous, only when they are still influential and represent the best statements of their particular point of view. It will, however, be one of the functions of each editor's Introduction to sketch in the earlier history of criticism in regard to the author concerned.

Each volume will attempt to strike a balance between general essays and ones on specialised aspects, or particular works, of the writer in question. And though in many instances the bulk of the articles will come from British and American sources, certain of the volumes will draw heavily on material in other European languages – most of it being translated for the first time.

P. N. FURBANK

Introduction

MILTON's fame has been so secure for two and a half centuries that it is difficult to realise that he was comparatively unknown during his lifetime, or at any rate until a few years before his death. The volume he published in 1645, containing *Comus*, 'Lycidas' and many other poems whose titles are familiar to every schoolboy, did not have a second edition until 1673. It is perhaps more surprising, in view of the great volume of politically slanted comment on Milton since the early eighteenth century, to learn that he was not a particularly well-known controversialist. There appears to be no contemporary reference to *Areopagitica*; and certainly there is no reason to believe that Milton's ideas were taken very seriously by those who controlled events.

Doubtless those ideas were often too radical to be immediately applicable. The reception given to the *Doctrine and Discipline of Divorce* is illustrative. Milton's views were a logical extension of what scores of Puritan preachers were saying about the true nature of marriage. The step to this conclusion was one which few besides Milton were prepared to take, and though the *Doctrine and Discipline* sold well it occasioned more scurrility than reasoned debate. The result was that Milton found himself unpleasantly notorious and isolated from his own side.

Disappointment at the reception of the *Doctrine and Discipline of Divorce* may have influenced Milton to collect his poems together for the volume he published in 1645. In the light of his reputation at that time, one may suppose a desire for self-justification in his printing of that encomiastic letter from Sir Henry Wotton, and those tributes from the cultivated Italians he had met on his tour, as if he were warning his readers not to dismiss too hastily one so warmly appreciated by famous and talented men. Whether or not this was the case, the poems which are now so well-known, received very little attention from Milton's contemporaries. We think of them as being intensely interested in religious matters, but the great religious verse on which our impression is partly based was less enthusiastically received by them than it has been in our own age.

There has been a tendency, ever since the establishment of Milton's great reputation as a poet, to judge his status as a political controversialist by his own high claims for himself, and to marvel in consequence that so formidable an enemy of the monarchy and the Established Church survived the Restoration. Professor William Empson has recently speculated, in a *Listener* book-review, on why Milton did not emigrate to America to escape 'almost certain death'. The truth seems to be that, while he was just sufficiently conspicuous to be imprisoned for a short time and to have two of his books suppressed by proclamation, he was so unimportant that it was not worth the Government's while to visit him with further punishment.

Milton's contemporary obscurity as a political pamphleteer is ironical, because his political opinions helped to further his poetic reputation during the years in which the Restoration of 1660 fizzled out into the Revolution of 1688. Men soon became discontented with the Stuart monarchy, and in the minds of many discontent bred nostalgia for 'the good old cause'. In 1667 Pepys thought it strange that everyone was singing the praises of Cromwell; but so it was, and to many at this time Milton became a symbol of England's freedom. Powerless to influence events during the years of Cromwell, and likewise virtually unknown as a poet, Milton then began to climb steadily into fame both as a poet and as a champion of English liberty.

And certainly in terms of purely literary history it was ironical that it was during the Restoration that Milton, as a poet, should first have found his audience, for the poetic revolution wrought by Waller and consolidated by Dryden produced an atmosphere in which *Paradise Lost* must have seemed either anachronistic or *avant-garde*. But the important fact was that the cessation of hostilities made way for the appreciation of literature, as opposed to the partisan perusal of controversial pamphlets. There are few printed allusions to *Paradise Lost* between its first publication in 1667 and its second edition of 1674; but the fact that the second edition was called for, and that Dryden, the most esteemed poet of the age, asked permission to 'tag' Milton's verses, indicates a substantial readership. Certainly, by the end of the seventeenth century – that is, within a quarter of a century of his death – Milton was an established 'classic' of English literature. A fascinating pointer to Milton's status is

Patrick Hume's edition of *Paradise Lost*, published in 1695. One doubts if the Bible itself has been annotated more obsessively, and Hume is the perfect answer to those who think that 'the Milton industry' is the recent product of twentieth-century academic professionalism. For pages together one has to read on and on to discover a single line that Hume did not think it necessary to gloss. Newton, in his edition of 1749, remarked of Hume's that 'the greater part . . . is a dull dictionary of the most common words . . . but take away what is superfluous, and there will still remain a great deal that is useful'. That was just, and remains true; only a foolhardy editor would ignore Hume.

It used to be thought that *Paradise Lost* was a little-known poem until Addison popularised it in his famous *Spectator* papers of 1712. This is not so. Milton was an established classic before Addison wrote. But there is a difference between an established classic, recognised by everyone with some genuine literary culture, and a household name. It is true, I think, that Steele in the *Tatler* (1709) and Addison in the *Spectator* made Milton a tremendously *popular* poet; and when we contemplate the Milton that Steele presented to the popular audience of the *Tatler*, we perceive another irony. From Johnson's *Life* down to our own time, there has been a tendency to deprecate Milton's attitude towards women. Johnson wrote, 'What we know of Milton's character in domestic relations is that he was severe and arbitrary. His family consisted of women; and there appears in his books something like a Turkish contempt of females, as subordinate and inferior beings.' If my own experience as a teacher is any guide, the one thing that almost every undergraduate 'knows' about Milton is that he despised women. Yet this was certainly not the prevailing view until Johnson published his *Life*. A recent thorough survey[1] of eighteenth-century periodicals shows that in those days Milton was seen as a kind of prophet of marriage. Certainly both Steele and Addison drew largely upon passages dealing with the relationship of the sexes in their attempt to improve the morals and soften the manners of their own time. The reader should see, for example, numbers 40, 79 and 114 of the *Tatler*.

In 1694 Addison, then a young man at Oxford, wrote of Milton:

> Whate'er his pen describes I more than see,
> Whilst ev'ry verse, array'd in majesty,

[1] N. L. Riffe, 'Milton in the 18th-Century Periodicals: "Hail Wedded Love"', in *Notes and Queries*, N.S. XII, no. 1 (1965).

> Bold and sublime, my whole attention draws,
> And seems above the critics' nicer laws.

Eighteen years later he set out to write a series of Saturday papers on Milton for the *Spectator*. These Saturday papers, reaching subscribers in time for them to read them on Sunday, were reserved for moral and religious topics. The motto of the first paper on Milton (*Spectator*, no. 267) was *Cedite Romani Scriptores, cedite Graii*: 'Give place to him, writers of Rome and Greece.' Much as he admired Homer and Virgil, and respected the critical *dicta* of Aristotle as understood by his age, Addison was much less in bondage to classical models and authority than most of his contemporaries. His view that Milton was if anything superior to Homer and Virgil, an opinion backed up by frequent comparisons of particular passages, was startlingly original. It is important to stress this, because it is possible, if we read Addison superficially, to see him as judging *Paradise Lost* by its adherence to, or rebellion against, classical models and doctrines. He treats his subject under the four headings of Bossu[2] – fable, character, thought and expression; and the general framework of his critique accords with critical conventions then current. But ultimately his reading is personally felt, rather than academic. As he says, 'A few general rules extracted out of French authors, with a certain cant of words' are insufficient for good criticism. One must proceed 'by entering into the very spirit and soul of fine writing, and by shewing the several sources of that pleasure that rises in the mind of the reader'. There is no space to deal adequately with Addison's essays on *Paradise Lost*. They form a considerable landmark in the progress of modern literary criticism; no one who is interested either in Milton or in the eighteenth century will be content to neglect them.

One of the curiosities of eighteenth-century Milton criticism, probably arising from the consideration that 'an . . . Heroick Poem, according to the Opinion of the best Criticks, ought to end happily' (*Spectator*, no. 369), is the view that the last two lines of *Paradise Lost*, so admired by us, are a blemish. Addison wished that Milton had omitted them:

> These two Verses, though they have their Beauty, fall very much below the foregoing Passage, and renew in the Mind of the Reader that Anguish which was pretty well laid by that Consideration:

---

[2] René le Bossu (1631–80). His *Traité du poème épique*, highly praised by Boileau, laid it down that the subject should be chosen before the characters, and the action arranged without reference to the personages.

> *The world was all before them, where to chuse*
> *Their Place of Rest, and Providence their Guide.* (*Spectator*, no. 369)

Bentley, in his notorious edition of *Paradise Lost* (1732), decided to
rewrite the last two lines of the poem:

> Why . . . does this Distich dismiss our first Parents in Anguish, and the
> Reader in Melancholy? And how can the Expression be justified, *with
> wand'ring Steps and slow*? Why *wand'ring*? Erratic Steps? Very improper:
> when in the line before they were *guided by Providence* (with much more to
> the same purpose) . . .
> Shall I therefore, after so many prior Presumptions, presume at last to offer
> a Distich, as close as may be to the Author's Words, and entirely agreeable
> to his Scheme?
>
> > Then *hand in hand* with SOCIAL steps their way
> > Through Eden took, with HEAV'NLY COMFORT CHEER'D.

Bentley's literal-minded criticism was answered by Jonathon
Richardson, in *Explanatory Notes and Remarks on Milton's Paradise Lost*
(1734):

> their Steps were *Wandring*, though Guided by Providence, for the Places
> appear'd *Unhospitable and Desert, not Knowing, nor Known by Them*, XI 305,
> and Solitarie, for though they were Company to Each Other, There was
> None that could be So to Them; Nor Man, nor Angel.

The tone of this, at once courteous, impersonal and definite, is typical
of Richardson's work, which was one of the most popular as it is still
one of the best respected of the many eighteenth-century commentaries.
The excellence of much eighteenth-century comment on Milton has been
skilfully demonstrated by Christopher Ricks in *Milton's Grand Style*
(1963). The reader who wants a fuller account will turn to Ants Oras's
Milton's Early Editors and Commentators (1931); but I shall give myself
the pleasure of copying out a paragraph from Richardson of which
many critics in recent years have discovered the truth:

> A reader of Milton must be always on duty; he is surrounded with sense, it
> rises in every line, every word is to the purpose; there are no lazy intervals,
> all has been considered, and demands, and merits observation. Even in the
> best writers you sometimes find words and sentences which hang on so
> loosely you may blow 'em off; Milton's are all substance and weight; fewer
> would not have served the turn, and more would have been superfluous.

Addison and Richardson were perhaps largely responsible for the
popular image of Milton throughout much of the eighteenth century.
An important work in the later part of the century was Thomas

Warton's edition of the *Minor Poems* (1785), bringing into prominence such poems as 'Lycidas', 'L'Allegro' and 'Il Penseroso', and enlisting them against 'wit and rhyme, sentiment and satire, polished numbers, sparkling couplets, and pointed periods'. The influence of Milton, through this edition and through the practice of poets like the Wartons, is part of the story of the decay of Augustanism and the slow development of Romanticism, a change in taste and poetic habit which Johnson deplored.

Johnson's *Life of Milton*, published in 1779, is an appraisal of Milton as man and as poet by one who set his face equally against Whiggery and Romanticism. The *Life* incurred contemporary odium for its author, famous as he was, but its influence has grown steadily, and has been of considerable importance in the formation and endorsement of hostile opinion in the twentieth century. Johnson is not entirely governed by prejudice; he can rise nobly to praise; yet it is his strictures that have been influential. He portrays Milton as a rather unpleasant human being, in an account which differs sharply from the impression given by earlier biographers, who were closer to Milton and to those who knew him. I have already quoted the well-known passage on Milton's 'Turkish contempt of females'. Equally well-known, and equally unjust, are his remarks on Milton's politics:

> His political notions were those of an acrimonious and surly republican, for which it is not known that he gave any better reason than that *a popular government was the most frugal; for the trappings of a monarchy would set up an ordinary commonwealth.* It is surely very shallow policy that supposes money to be the chief good.

As for the poems: *Comus* is 'a drama in the epick style; inelegantly splendid, and tediously instructive'. The sonnets 'deserve not any particular criticism; for of the best it can only be said, that they are not bad'. As for 'Lycidas', 'the diction is harsh, the rhymes uncertain, and the numbers unpleasing. Its form is that of a pastoral, easy, vulgar, and therefore disgusting.' *Samson Agonistes* has been too much admired: 'it is only by a blind confidence in the reputation of Milton that a drama can be praised in which the intermediate parts have neither cause nor consequence, neither hasten nor retard the catastrophe'. Many of these judgements are widely recognised to be almost ludicrously off the mark; what has persisted is the prejudice against Milton as a person (which has subtly infected what purports to be purely *literary* criticism), and the *general* indictment of Milton's style, which has been repeated in various ways from Keats through to F. R. Leavis and T. S. Eliot:

> Through all his greater works there prevails an uniform peculiarity of *diction*, a mode and cast of expression which bears little resemblance to that of any former writer, and which is so far removed from common use that an unlearned reader, when he first opens his book, finds himself surprised by a new language.

> This novelty has been, by those who can find nothing wrong in Milton, imputed to his laborious endeavours after words suitable to the grandeur of his ideas. *Our language*, says Addison, *sunk under him*. But the truth is that, both in prose and verse, he had formed his style by a perverse and pedantic principle. He was desirous to use English words with a foreign idiom . . . Milton's style was not modified by his subject; what is shown with greater extent in *Paradise Lost* may be found in *Comus*.

The three paragraphs from Johnson's *Life* which I have here abbreviated are of crucial importance; the modern reader will do well to realise that – in spite of Johnson's definite tone – they suggest questions, starting-points for research and discussion. It would be wrong to accept them as critically conclusive. Some of the *best* discussion of Milton in this century has implicitly taken Johnson's critique as its starting-point, and gone on to try to establish how far it is true, and, if true, how far it is damaging; but some of the most *influential* of our critics have written as if there were no need to go further than paraphrasing and expanding Johnson's account. One suspects that even Johnson's praise might be held against Milton, as evidence for the tendency of his verse to induce an uncritical torpor in his readers: 'such is the power of his poetry, that his call is obeyed without resistance, the reader feels himself in captivity to a higher and nobler mind, and criticism sinks in admiration'.

All interested readers will know Johnson's *Life*, but it is perhaps worth while to call attention to three of his *Rambler* articles on Milton's versification (nos. 86, 88 and 94) and two on *Samson Agonistes* (nos. 139, 140).

For most of the eighteenth century Milton was esteemed as a *religious* poet, not indeed for the exploratory quality, the personal grappling with existential problems, which some descry in his work nowadays, but for the sublimity of his expression of generally accepted religious truth: 'What oft was thought, but ne'er so well expressed.' This esteem was not confined to any one religious group; there seems to have been a tacit agreement that *Paradise Lost* expressed the universally acceptable truths of Christianity, unmarred by sectarian prejudice or eccentricity. During the nineteenth century the situation changed: appreciation was transferred to Milton's *expression*, and less concern was given to what he expressed.

The comparative unimportance of the *content* of *Paradise Lost* for the nineteenth century may be estimated by the reception of *De Doctrina Christiana*. This work, the fullest and most systematic exposition of Milton's theological position, was discovered in the Old State Paper Office in Whitehall in 1823 and published in translation in 1825. It reveals an original and highly unorthodox religious thinker, one who argued, for instance, that polygamy was not contrary to Christianity – to mention a point which even a layman would recognise as heterodox. During the twentieth century a number of studies have traced Milton's unorthodoxies through the labyrinthine ways of *Paradise Lost*; and it seems certain that if the *Christian Doctrine* had been published in 1725 rather than in 1825 it would have seriously lessened and modified Milton's reputation, which, as I have said, began to grow partly for political reasons and continued strong for (not unrelated) religious ones. Yet, although the appearance of the *Christian Doctrine* was greeted by a number of reviews (among them the well-known essay of Macaulay), it seems to have had little effect on discussion of Milton during the rest of the nineteenth century. 'Thought' and 'art' were now in separate compartments, and our forbears were on the way to the aestheticism of the nineties.

Most of the commentary on Milton during the nineteenth century represents an expansion and dilution of remarks made by the Romantic critics, who were more interested in Milton than were the 'official' critics of their time, such as Jeffrey, Gifford and Lockhart. Indeed Milton might well be taken as a focal point for discussion of the Romantic movement; and what I have said about the comparative lack of interest in Milton's thought in the nineteenth century does not apply to its first decades. Blake, whose work is seen by many as both initiation and consummation of English Romanticism, was deeply concerned with Milton, and may indeed have conceived of his own life's work as the revision, correction and re-presentation of that of his great predecessor.

It is only in the context of his own highly complex system of thought that Blake's remarks on Milton's Satan can be properly understood. But of course they have been abstracted from that context, and their place in the history of Milton criticism can be discussed without reference to it. The Romantic critics were not the first to see Satan as the hero of the poem – Dryden had done so – but it is with them that the concept of epic, with the modifications it might suggest to discussion of individual characters within the poem, began to weaken, and with them that Satan comes to be treated as a character important in his own right. Blake wrote that 'The reason Milton wrote in fetters when he wrote of angels and God, and at Liberty when of Devils and Hell, is because he was a true poet, and of the Devil's party without knowing it.' As I have said, this is not a simple statement. What Blake meant by it can be discovered only by reference to his whole system of thought; but it appealed to a contemporary mood, and was seized upon and expanded by other writers, who regarded the God of *Paradise Lost* as a tyrant and thought that Satan's revolt against him was justified. The plainest statement of this view is probably that in Shelley's *Defence of Poetry* (1821):

> Milton's Devil as a moral being is far superior to his God, as one who perseveres in some purpose which he has conceived to be excellent, in spite of adversity and torture, is to one who in the cold security of undoubted triumph inflicts the most horrible revenge upon his enemy – not from any mistaken notion of bringing him to repent of a perseverance in enmity, but with open and alleged design of exasperating him to deserve new torments.

Byron agreed that Satan was the hero of the poem. Coleridge did not, though he was fascinated by Milton's characterisation of Satan, linking it with his own conception of the character of Napoleon:

> The character of Satan is pride and sensual indulgence, finding in self the sole motive of action. It is the character so often seen *in little* on the political stage. It exhibits all the restlessness, temerity, and cunning which have marked the mighty hunters of mankind from Nimrod to Napoleon. The common fascination of men is, that these great men, as they are called, must act from some great motive. Milton has carefully marked in his Satan the intense selfishness, the alcohol of egotism, which would rather reign in hell than serve in heaven. To place this lust of self in opposition to denial of self or duty, and to show what exertions it would make, and what pains endure to accomplish its end, is Milton's object in the character of Satan. But around this character he has thrown a singularity of daring, a grandeur of sufferance, and a ruined splendour, which constitute the very height of poetic sublimity. (*Lectures* of 1818)

Since the early nineteenth century the question of Satan's status within the poem has been important to criticism. For much of the time

20   INTRODUCTION

Satan's heroism has been taken for granted rather than discussed, though
a number of critics have felt it necessary to explain away or justify
Milton's presentation. Bagehot, writing in 1859, thought it regrettable,
and asserted that 'So far from Milton having justified the ways of God
to man, he has loaded the common theology with a new encumbrance.'
Taking a hint from Blake he tried to defend Milton by suggesting that
Milton was not fully conscious of the implications of his presentation of
Satan. This notion of Milton's subconscious guiding his poem in a
direction different from what he consciously intended has rampaged
through much twentieth-century comment. So has the related idea that
from time to time in the course of writing *Paradise Lost* Milton became
uneasily aware that his art was leading him into a course at variance
with his declared aim of justifying the ways of God to men, and that he
kept on nudging the poem back onto course with authorial comments
which are discordant with the way he has presented his characters
dramatically. Both ideas are expressed by Raleigh in his *Milton* (1900),
which is probably rarely looked at now, but once had an immense
vogue. He asserted that Milton was in the devil's service before he knew
it: 'He can hardly have foreseen this chance. Although there are not
wanting signs in the poem itself that, before it was half completed, he
became uneasily conscious of what was happening, and attempted, too
late, to remedy it.' I shall not go on to discuss the Satanic controversy in
its twentieth-century phase; it is still very much alive. The reader may
follow it for himself in A. J. A. Waldock's *Paradise Lost and its Critics*
(1947) and William Empson's *Milton's God* (1961).

Whereas Raleigh had argued that in Milton's poetry 'we find ourselves in a remote atmosphere; far . . . from that wonderful analysis of
emotion which is the pastime of Shakespeare and Meredith', E. M. W.
Tillyard, in his *Milton* (1930), contended that everything in *Paradise
Lost* was meant to be subordinate to the human drama, that Milton
intended neither Satan nor anything else to detract from the struggle
that took place in the minds of Adam and Eve. Interest in Milton's
handling of the Fall, in Book ix of *Paradise Lost*, has been a major preoccupation for twentieth-century interpretation. Previously it had
rather been taken for granted, and most critics during the eighteenth
and nineteenth centuries would have felt Addison's account to be
adequate:

> The great Moral . . . which reigns in Milton is the most universal and most
> useful that can be imagined: it is in short this, *that Obedience to the Will of*

God makes Men happy, and that Disobedience makes them miserable. This is
visibly the Moral of the principal Fable which turns upon Adam and Eve,
who continued in *Paradise* while they kept the Command that was given
them, and were driven out of it as soon as they had transgressed.

Twentieth-century critics have felt that this is too simple to be true. In
an important article ('A Better Teacher than Aquinas', in *Studies in
Philology*, 1917), Greenlaw suggested that the sin which led to the Fall
was intemperance, thus connecting Milton's treatment with his known
interest in the Guyon episode in Book II of Spenser's *Faerie Queene*.
Tillyard, taking issue with Greenlaw, contended that Eve falls through
triviality of mind and Adam through gregariousness, and that Milton
tells us, in his authorial comment, that Adam fell 'fondly overcome
with Femal charm', because 'for him personally sex was the great
pitfall. And so he cannot refrain from grafting sex onto the scheme of
the Fall.' Tillyard goes further, suggesting that Milton's 'unconscious
betrayal of a personal spite against the enticements of women' is 'one of
many instances of Milton's betraying what he will not admit or does
not realize he feels'. Another, apparently, is that 'Milton did partly ally
himself with Satan . . . unwittingly he was led away by the creature of
his own imagination'. Tillyard was, I believe, the first commentator on
Milton to make something like a full-scale use of this concept of
Milton's unconscious mind; more recently Waldock has done so in
Paradise Lost and its Critics. Waldock's is an example of a dubious
interpretation that in the long run does more good than harm, since it
has forced Miltonists to a more careful consideration of Milton's technique in the presentation of Satan and of God, Adam and Eve. In my
opinion Stanley Fish's two articles in the *Critical Quarterly* for 1965
('The Harassed Reader in *Paradise Lost*' and 'Further Thoughts on
Milton's Christian Reader'[3]) represent not only the best reply to
Waldock so far, but, in adumbration at least, a complete demolishing
of Waldock's position and an important advance in our understanding
of Milton's strategy in *Paradise Lost*.

In England at any rate, two of the most influential critics of this
century have been T. S. Eliot and F. R. Leavis, both hostile to Milton.
Eliot's first major statement was his 1936 contribution to *Essays and
Studies of the English Association*. It begins with an apparently frank
statement about Eliot's antipathy to Milton the man:

[3] Fish's two essays are incorporated in '"Not so much a teaching as an intangling":
Milton's method in *Paradise Lost*', in this volume, pp. 104–35, and in *Surprised by Sin* (1967).

46286

As a man, he is antipathetic. Either from the moralist's point of view, or from the theologian's point of view, or from the psychologist's point of view, or from that of the political philosopher, or judging by the ordinary standards of likeableness in human beings, Milton is unsatisfactory.

Eliot then goes about the proper work of literary criticism, to discuss Milton in less personal terms; but the sentences I have quoted amount to something like a revival of Johnsonian prejudice. Eliot's antipathy is less formulated than Johnson's; its expression is at once confident and jejune: words like 'moralist', 'theologian', 'psychologist', 'political philosopher' and 'human being' give the statement a wholly unearned air of exactness. We must supply its content ourselves, and most of us unconsciously fall back on Johnson's *Life* in doing so: Milton was an unpleasant man, whose first wife did well to leave him, who was harsh towards his pupils and his daughters, and so on. Mr Eliot should have given his sources, and his reasons.

Eliot writes as a practising poet, concerned with the problems of writing verse in his particular time, and with the relation between the tradition of literature and the individual talent. His charge against Milton is that he subjected the language to 'a peculiar kind of deterioration' (Johnson lurks in the background again), and that not only has Milton been a bad influence; he could '*only* be an influence for the worse, upon any poet whatsoever'. The peculiar kind of deterioration to which Milton subjected the language is, in Eliot's view, to be explained by the fact that Milton was a man whose sensuousness had been withered early by book-learning, whose gifts were naturally aural, and who became blind. Eliot advances these reasons as if they had equal status as matters of established fact. It is important to remember that they have not. It is also important to remember 'what decorum is, which is the grand masterpiece to observe': both Eliot and Leavis write as if the concept, so important to Milton, had never existed. So Eliot finds it proper to compare a passage from *Macbeth* with passages from two very different *kinds* of work, *Comus* and 'L'Allegro', as if *genre* were unimportant, and to go on to observe that 'It is not a particular ploughman, milkmaid, and shepherd that Milton sees (as Wordsworth might see them)' without taking into account the very different intentions that the two poets may have had.

Eliot concludes that Milton's verse is 'in one sense of the word, *rhetoric*', that his syntax is 'determined by the musical significance . . . rather than by the attempt to follow actual speech or thought', and that 'although his work realizes superbly one element in poetry, he may still be considered as having done damage to the English language from which it has not wholly recovered'.

Eleven years later Eliot lectured to the British Academy on Milton.[4] The statement he made on this occasion has sometimes been treated as if it were an amusing recantation of the errors of Mr Eliot's greener years, but that is not so. He was no longer prepared to say that Milton's verse could *only* be an influence for the worse; otherwise his view seems substantially unaltered, so far as one can discover from what is, it seems to me, a somewhat inconsequential piece of writing. He quotes in full the three paragraphs from Johnson which I quoted earlier, saying that they express 'the essence of the permanent censure of Milton'.

In discussing versification, Eliot drew attention to one aspect of Milton's genius which had not been adequately appreciated or explored, pointing out that such studies as Bridges' *Milton's Prosody* (1893) are of limited usefulness, because 'Milton's verse is especially refractory to the yielding up of its secrets to examination of the single line':

> It is only in the period that the wave-length of Milton's verse is to be found: it is his ability to give a perfect and unique pattern to every paragraph, such that the full beauty of the line is found in its context, and his ability to work in larger musical units than any other poet – that is to me the most conclusive evidence of Milton's supreme mastery. The peculiar feeling, almost a physical sensation of a breathless leap, communicated by Milton's long periods, and by his alone, is impossible to procure from rhymed verse. Indeed, this mastery is more conclusive evidence of his intellectual power, than is his grasp of any *ideas* that he borrowed or invented. To be able to control so many words at once is the token of a mind of most exceptional energy.

F. R. Leavis, discussing Eliot's lecture (in *The Common Pursuit*, 1952), would deny 'intellectual mastery' to Milton:

> It is in the 'versification' everywhere that the essential inaptitude appears: the man who uses words in this way has (as Mr Eliot virtually says) no 'grasp of ideas', and, whatever he may suppose, is not really interested in the achievement of precise thought of any kind; he certainly hasn't the kind of energy of mind needed for sustained analytic and discursive thinking.

One or two quotations from an earlier essay, in *Revaluation* (1936), will serve to bring out the full force of Leavis's objections to Milton's verse:

[4] Both his essays are reprinted in his *On Poetry and Poets* (1957).

Even in the first two books of *Paradise Lost*, where the myth has vigorous life and one can admire the magnificent invention that Milton's verse is, we feel, after a few hundred lines, our sense of dissatisfaction growing into something stronger. In the end we find ourselves protesting – protesting against the routine gesture, the heavy fall, of the verse, flinching from the foreseen thud that comes to inevitably, and, at last, irresistibly: for reading *Paradise Lost* is a matter of resisting, of standing up against, the verse-movement, of subduing it into something like sensitiveness, and in the end our resistance is worn down; we surrender at last to the inescapable monotony of the ritual.

So complete, and so mechanically habitual, is Milton's departure from the English order, structure, and accentuation that he often produces passages that have to be read through several times before one can see how they go, though the Miltonic mind has nothing to offer that could justify obscurity – no obscurity was intended: it is merely that Milton has forgotten the English language. There is, however, a much more important point to be made: it is that, cultivating so complete and systematic a callousness to the intrinsic nature of English, Milton forfeits all possibility of subtle or delicate life in his verse.

There is nothing very new or surprising about the strictures of Eliot and Leavis. As I remarked earlier, through most of the nineteenth-century critics tended to divide Milton's achievement into 'thought' and 'expression' and to concentrate for the most part on the latter. Both Eliot and Leavis have done this. Eliot's concern with the meaning of *Paradise Lost* may be gauged from his remark, 'So far as I perceive anything, it is a glimpse of a theology that I find in large part repellent, expressed through a mythology which would have been better left in the Book of *Genesis*, upon which Milton has not improved.' As *description*, the accounts of Milton's style given by Eliot and Leavis do not differ radically from those of many nineteenth-century critics. The difference lies in their attitude to what they describe. The nineteenth-century critics on the whole admired Milton's writing, though they regarded it as unique, a sort of 'sport'. Eliot and Leavis are much less inclined to admire; Eliot because, as a poet, he had felt, as Keats had done, that Milton was a dangerous model; Leavis, it would seem, because Milton's use of language is different from that of Shakespeare and Keats.

The nineteenth century's habit of separating thought and expression in Milton's work has persisted into the twentieth century, but with the difference that there has been an upsurge of interest in his thought.

Though the old clichés are persistent, recent scholars have made serious attempts to find out what manner of man Milton really was, how his thought developed, and how his thinking and his experience of life shaped his poetry. The appearance of the great Columbia edition led, as William Haller has said, 'to the rediscovery of Milton's prose and to the rediscovery of the man himself, a poet of genuinely epic imagination and heroic temper living and writing in an age of epic significance'. In the work of such scholars as Greenlaw, Hanford, Woodhouse and Haller, Milton has been the subject of some excellent historical criticism. Yet, valuable as their work is, it cannot be said to have provided an *answer* to the fire from the other camp. The division persisted; the two sides never really met. Cleanth Brooks, an exponent of the New Criticism, has suggested a reply to Leavis from a position close to, if not within, his own area of concern. He asserts that the conventional description of Milton's verse, which led earlier critics to praise and later ones to condemn it, is simply wrong, and that Milton is much more like Donne than he has been given credit for. Brooks has enforced this view with some penetrating and convincing analyses, while Christopher Ricks, in *Milton's Grand Style* (1963), has devoted a whole book to showing that Milton's verse is as remarkable for its delicacy as for its grandeur, that the reader of Milton is in fact, as Jonathon Richardson said he was, 'surrounded with sense'. This is an excellent book. Nevertheless, the foreground of Ricks's work is taken up with Milton's local subtleties rather than with his controlling theme.

The reader will see that a *desideratum* is implied. So far, in my view, Joseph Summers, in *The Muses' Method* (1962), comes nearest to fulfilling it. That is, Summers is both 'scholarly' and 'critical' – deeply interested in the meaning of *Paradise Lost* as a whole, sensitive to the *nuances* of Milton's writing, and rigorous in relating his individual perceptions to his sense of the entire poem. This is not to ignore the fact that there has been a considerable amount of vigorously intelligent work on Milton in recent years. There has, at all events, been sufficient to have rendered the labours of making this selection both arduous and delightful.

ALAN RUDRUM

Chronology

1608	John Milton born.
1615(?)–20(?)	Entered St Paul's School at an unestablished date.
1625	Entered Christ's College, Cambridge.
1629	Graduated B.A.
	'Nativity Ode'.
1632	Graduated M.A.
	Settled at Horton.
1634	*Comus* performed at Ludlow Castle.
1637	'Lycidas'.
1638–9	Continental tour.
1641–2	The anti-prelatical pamphlets.
1642	Married Mary Powell.
1643–5	The divorce tracts.
1644	*Of Education.*
	Areopagitica.
1645	Reconciled with Mary Powell.
	Poems of Mr John Milton (his first volume of poems).
1649	*Tenure of Kings and Magistrates.*
	Eikonoklastes.
1651	*Defensio pro Populo Anglicano.*
	Milton became totally blind.
1652	Mary Powell died.
1654	*Defensio Secunda.*
1655	*Defensio pro Se.*
1656	Married Katharine Woodcock.
1658	Katharine Woodcock died.
1658–60	*De Doctrina Christiana* probably completed about this time.
1659	*A Treatise of Civil Power in Ecclesiastical Causes.*
	Considerations touching the Likeliest Means to Remove Hirelings out of the Church.

1660	*The Ready and Easy Way to Establish a Free Common-wealth.*
	At the Restoration Milton was dismissed from office, and was imprisoned for a short time.
1663	Married Elizabeth Minshull.
1667	*Paradise Lost.*
1671	*Paradise Regained* and *Samson Agonistes.*
1673	Second edition (enlarged) of early poems.
1674	Second edition of *Paradise Lost.*
	Milton died.

J. H. SUMMERS
Milton and the Cult of Conformity (1956)

IN a recent essay entitled 'A Meditation on Literary Blasphemy', Merritt Hughes, the eminent Milton scholar at the University of Wisconsin, commented on the uses and abuses of blasphemy against the literary idols of the past. It is surely as normal for each generation to revolt against the standards and literary gods of the preceding generation as it is for sons to revolt against their fathers. 'Blasphemous impulses', Mr Hughes remarked, 'are part of the instinct for self-preservation, but they are healthy only when they are spontaneous, personal, and unfashionable. Unfortunately, they are seldom any of these things.' All too soon the once-new heresy becomes the new conformity, and fashionable anti-conformity may be as crippling both to reader and writer as fashionable conformity. Mr Hughes concluded his meditation with considerable irony: 'Let us grant that . . . Milton is [not] entitled to the unqualified respect of a society that is as anti-revolutionary and as deeply committed to psychological analysis as ours.'

Early in the twentieth century Milton was attacked by a number of critics of various schools. After two and a half centuries of near literary deity, one of the three greatest English poets was attacked as a personality, as a thinker, as a religionist, and as an artist. In the mid-thirties, looking back on those years, a prominent contemporary critic remarked, 'Milton's dislodgement . . . was effected with remarkably little fuss.' Today, in the mid-fifties, that remark seems a bit premature. From the number and tone of the books and essays on Milton which have appeared in the past ten years, one must assume that, in scholarly and critical circles at least, Milton's eminence is still acknowledged. With the general public and with most writers and poets, however, one would guess that Milton is less frequently a 'creative' influence than is either John Donne or Andrew Marvell – to mention two other seventeenth-century poets. Milton's name is still associated with

'Puritanism' – vaguely confused with Blue Sundays, Prohibition, sexual repression, and the stocks – and with an oppressive grandeur and conformity of style and art, altogether forming an image of a sort of academic sacred cow, which can hardly be discussed and certainly cannot be read.

The earlier iconoclasm did a great deal of good. Milton had often been read and defended on either poor or incorrect grounds, and it was a good thing for those positions to be taken or obliterated: Milton never anticipated nor advocated the social *mores* of the days of Queen Victoria. And it is certainly true that Milton should not be widely admired in an age of conformity. His is not a clubby nor a chummy personality. He does make embarrassing demands on himself and on his audience. Many readers' dislike for Milton may be accurately based on an almost instinctive recognition that he threatens our comfort and our fashionable conformities in political and religious theory, in our assumptions about the nature of the arts and the artist, and in our personal lives. Yet it would be sad if those individuals today who are opposed to fashionable currents, who are trying to possess their own souls, should reject unread the most uncompromisingly radical individualist of all of our major poets.

There is an old Spanish proverb, 'Lord, deliver me from my friends; I can take care of my enemies myself.' That saying might be put in Milton's mouth, for his mind and his art have often suffered at the hands of his warmest admirers. Most of Milton's critics, like most of us, embrace one or another of the 'isms', and any insight or body of thought general enough to be labeled as an 'ism' has usually developed its own restrictive conformity. And it is a rare critic who can resist the tendency to reduce an admired figure to his own image. It is then, depending on one's point of view, depressing or delightful to see how Milton slips between or burns the fingers of his critics. Mr C. S. Lewis's *Preface to Paradise Lost*, for example, is surely one of the best books ever written on Milton's major poem. Yet Mr Lewis is an Anglo-Catholic, extremely aware of heresy, for whom tradition is a good thing; and he manages to impart a good deal of the Anglo-Catholic aura to his image of Milton. When one reads his persuasive book, one may hear in the background Milton's mocking definition of tradition as 'the perpetual cankerworm', and one may remember his definition of heresy: 'Truth is compared in Scripture to a streaming fountain; if her waters flow not in a perpetual progression, they sicken into a muddy pool of conformity and tradition. A man may be a heretic in the truth; and if he believe things only because his pastor says so, or the Assembly so determines, without knowing other reasons, though his belief be true, yet the very truth he holds becomes his heresy.' At the other extreme, a few Marxists took Milton up in the thirties – he was, after all, a revolutionist, a regicide, and surely something of a materialist and a determinist: yet once again one can hear the Miltonic argument that 'God determined' man to be free, or the denunciation of the tyranny of a majority which rejects freedom, or the most devastating attack in English on the mystical belief that the 'people' are the source of wisdom –

> Of whom to be disprais'd were no small praise –
> His lot who dares be singularly good.

Lest we approve too enthusiastically of Milton's rebuttal of extreme positions, let us remember how little comfort any other group can take from Milton. Nineteenth-century liberals and *laissez-faire* economists who see in the freedom *from* oppressive restraints the ultimate good of man are checked by Milton's famous distinction between liberty and license and by his scornful attack on the conception that economic prosperity – what is good for business – is the chief aim of society. Almost any religionist finds himself left behind by Milton's own constant progression to the left, from Episcopalianism to Presbyterianism, to Congregationalism, to his final position as the sole member of his own church. And on the other hand, any agnostic or atheist must surely be embarrassed by a man as God-intoxicated as Dostoyevsky who spent some of the most creative years of his life in constructing the *De Doctrina Christiana*, a radical and personal *summa theologica* which, Milton insisted, had no more authority than reason gave it. Humanists, at least those who have attempted to make a vaguely anti-democratic religion out of their own vision of selected classical authors, should be permanently estranged by Milton's political and philosophical radicalism, and mortally wounded by the fact that Milton, the greatest classicist of his age or perhaps of the entire English Renaissance, wrote the strongest denunciation in English of the assumption that classical learning was *necessary* for any man – or for Christ's church. English nationalists may be warmed by Milton's remark in *Areopagitica* that God reveals 'himself to his servants, and, as his manner is, first to his Englishmen'; but they must be chilled by Milton's later definition of an Englishman as any man 'that keeps peace with me, near or remote, of

whatsoever nation'. Milton expressed his ultimate internationalism in
the last letter he published: 'One's native land is wherever it is well with
one.'

I must indicate one other group to which Milton did not belong: the
professional non-conformist. *Épater les bourgeois* did not seem to Milton
a respectable full-time job for an adult. He did not seem to believe it was
possible or desirable to 'reject the past'. He was not a conventional
Bohemian. He would simply not admit that other people's actions or
opinions formed a respectable standard, positive or negative, for any
individual's life – a standard either for an individual to conform to or
for him to oppose. The ultimate stupidity, in Miltonic terms, was the
situation of an antagonist who allowed his values to be determined
negatively by his enemy, who gave up his freedom by automatically
embracing any position opposed to one which his enemy had already
taken. It is this which makes part of the absurdity of Satan's position in
Paradise Lost, and which leads to the satanic formulation, 'Evil be thou
my good'.

Any attempt to file away Milton's personality and thought under the
traditional labels ends with a series of paradoxes. We seem to have a
figure who was both a passionate radical and a conservative; a man who
believed that freedom was the greatest social and individual value, but
who also believed in a natural hierarchy; a 'Puritan' who placed a higher
value on sexual love than did any other figure in English literature –
with the possible exceptions of William Blake and D. H. Lawrence; an
idealist and a materialist; a 'progressive' who wrote an epic, insisting
both on precedent, antiquity, and on 'Things unattempted yet in Prose
or Rhyme'; a dramatist who wrote a play for no stage, a play which is
the nearest thing to a Greek tragedy in English and which comes close
to recapturing the spirit of the Hebrew prophets; an heroic poet who
denounced the central values of ancient heroic poetry; a fearfully
learned poet who seemed to believe that literary excellence (like human
virtue) must be spontaneous in origin.

From such a summary, we may grant that Milton cannot be reduced
to any pattern of conformity or of conformist anti-conformity, but we
might also be tempted to dismiss him as a madman, or as an hopelessly
inconsistent thinker and artist who could not possibly be relevant to our
own time. Yet, if we choose another alternative and take the trouble to
read his works, we are struck not by any sense of confusion or paradox,
but by a ferocious singleness of purpose. To attempt to trace that

singleness of purpose through Milton's writings would take a volume. Here, briefly and necessarily superficially, I wish only to indicate what I believe to be the general framework of that singleness, illuminated by a brief glance at his career, his apprenticeship for the writing of the great poems.

At an extraordinarily early age, Milton seems to have decided to be a great poet. Many other young men have had such an ambition, but few have ever worked so hard at it. Milton did not consider the simple mastery of the craft of verse, however necessary, as of major importance – after all, he had written passable Latin verse as an undergraduate. His aim was to be a great poet, in the company of Homer, Virgil, Dante, and a few others, and for this aim he conceived that a lifetime of work was necessary. He determined 'that by labor and intent study (which I take to be my portion in this life) joined with the strong propensity of nature, I might perhaps leave something so written to aftertimes, as they should not willingly let it die'. This meant that the would-be poet must begin simply by acquiring all the knowledge possible. He must, of course, know all the major languages (for Milton they were Greek, Latin, Hebrew, and Italian) and all the major literature in those languages; but he must also go beyond what we think of as 'literature': he must, if he lived in the seventeenth century, know Galileo's work as well as Tasso's, the thought of Francis Bacon as well as Virgil. History, theology, philosophy, and music were almost as important as poetry – or rather, it was impossible to separate them from poetry.

But formal knowledge was only the beginning: the heroic poet did not study the ancients in order to imitate them so much as to compete with them – and to surpass them. The business of the heroic poet was to celebrate or to create heroic action. A heroic poem in English would be, whether the poet intended it or not (although Milton assumed that any heroic poet would intend it) 'doctrinal and exemplary to a nation' just as he believed the works of Homer and the Greek tragedians had been to the Greeks and the *Aeneid* to the Romans. The great poem was inevitably didactic. And to celebrate greatness, the poet must have developed a discriminating analysis of the constituents of greatness and a coherent view of the universe and of man.

The word 'didactic' (like the word 'morality') has come to be suspect in modern literary circles, partially, I believe because it is usually associated with abstract systems of value and with impersonality: the didactic or moralist writer, we tend to think, is usually busy giving general advice to the public, presenting a morality 'for other people' which will preserve traditional taboos. We are often extremely conscious of the gap between the moralist's general rules and the actual stuff of individual experience. Milton, however, did not believe that words or moral maxims could be divorced from individual experience – could be divorced and still partake of the qualities of great poetry, that is. He scorned the fake; he insisted that the relationship between experience and significant imaginative creation must be close: the writer must 'know' what he was talking about; he must have lived an essential part of his creation. But instead, then, of insisting that really significant literature must reflect the common non-heroic experience of the average man, he came to a startlingly simple conclusion: the heroic poet must not lead the life of the average man. Milton did not share the modern assumption that one's life is largely 'given' in terms of heredity and environment and that one cannot do much about it; instead, he insisted that an essential part of the would-be heroic poet's apprenticeship must be the living of an heroic life: 'I was confirmed in this opinion that he who would not be frustrate of his hope to write well hereafter in laudable things, ought himself to be a true poem, that is, a composition and pattern of the best and honorablest things – not presuming to sing high praises of heroic men, or famous cities, unless he have in himself the experience and the practice of all that is praiseworthy.' The *experience* of a life of fantastic integrity was, Milton believed, as necessary to the creation of the poems which he wished to write as, say, Hemingway's war experiences, his hunting and fishing (and perhaps his drinking and love-making) have been for the kinds of novels and stories which he has written.

Milton's requirements seem so extreme that we may already feel with a character in Dr Johnson's *Rasselas*, 'Enough! thou hast convinced me that no human being can ever be a poet.' But I have not yet mentioned what Milton considered the most important requirement of all, a requirement which it was not in the poet's individual power to fulfill, and for which all the busy study and all the will and effort for the heroic life were more or less irrelevant. Milton believed that the abilities to compose the greatest poetry, 'wheresoever they be found, are the inspired gift of God rarely bestowed, but yet to some (though most abuse) in every nation'. This belief, for Milton, went beyond a Christian version of 'the poet is born and not made'; it concerned not merely natural sensitivity to rhythm and image and form. The composition of a major work, a work which would live for centuries, was, Milton believed, beyond the simple will of any poet, however 'naturally' endowed and however learned, and however 'heroic' his personal life. It required divine inspiration, and for that the poet could only pray. It was 'a work not to be raised from the heat of youth, or the vapours of wine, like that which flows at waste from the pen of some vulgar amourist, or the trencher fury of a rhyming parasite, nor to be obtained by the invocation of Dame Memory and her Siren daughters, but by devout prayer to that eternal Spirit who can enrich with all utterance and knowledge, and sends out his seraphim with the hallowed fire of his altar, to touch and purify the lips of whom he pleases'.

The decision to attempt to write heroic poetry was not, then, to be undertaken by anyone who insisted on a 'sure thing', a guaranteed return on his investment; it was to gamble on a very long shot indeed. And the chances against a poet's success were increased, not only by possible failures of natural ability, or of the heroic individual life, or of divine inspiration, but also by what we would call the forces of history and civilization. The nineteenth century did not invent the idea that great literary achievements were in some sense determined by matters of history and of climate. After all, Aristotle had remarked that northern Europeans lacked intelligence and skill, and Milton and his contemporaries tended to believe that climate might be partially responsible for the fact that no great epic which they admired had ever been written outside the Mediterranean region: 'natural endowments' might be worse for 'two and fifty degrees of northern latitude'. And however seriously one might accept the decay of nature as a theological or scientific proposition (or however one might rejoice at the fruits of the Renaissance), the examples of Greek and of Roman literature were always present to remind the modern poet that, so far as literature was concerned, regress rather than progress had been the general tendency for approximately two thousand years. The idea of the decay of nature and of human abilities was at least as oppressive for a seventeenth-century poet as our current theories concerning the decline and fall of civilizations are for many moderns.

Milton never rejected the idea that the general conditions of his own time and place might make the fulfillment of his ideal impossible. He was, at least at certain times in his life, as convinced that he lived in a time of decadence, in a 'non-heroic' age, as have been any number of modern writers. And yet only history provided the final judgment on history: it is easy for an historian with hindsight to say of an age when greatness did not appear that it was then impossible – or, when it did appear, that it was then inevitable. The individual while alive could not afford to wait for that sort of historical judgment. He could not give up his heroic ambitions and simply accept a lesser stature in a lesser age unless he was willing also to give up a large degree of his significant freedom. Although the prophets of collective degeneration and doom might well be right, the poet must act as if they might be wrong, else there was no possible chance of fulfilling his deepest desires, his highest aims. Milton seems never to have found the idea of life on a second-rate level at all attractive. Although his decision was made somewhat simpler by the fact that he considered it the duty of an artist to illumine his age rather than to mirror it, the attempt to write an heroic poem required for Milton, too, a decision which was itself heroic. It meant that he had discovered a great action which he desired to do so much that he was willing to devote his life to it, whatever the costs and however likely his failure – in his own eyes as well as in those of his contemporaries. And failure in such an enterprise might imply not simply a lack of a sense of 'success' but the fate of Bellerophon, to 'fall' in the waste land, 'Erroneous there to wander and forlorn' in madness.

The role of a man who had committed himself to such a goal would seem to be obvious: he should shut himself into his tower, become an exile from the ordinary social world, and proceed to write. But this was exactly what Milton's ambition and determination would not allow. The poet could achieve greatness only if he believed that there were some things more important than poetry. The heroism which Milton wished to celebrate could not be conceived apart from the passion for freedom and for love. If the heroic poet sought (or hoped he sought) predominantly the glory of God rather than his own glory, he might discover that his very single-minded devotion to poetry required him to become 'engaged' in the social struggles of his time to a degree shocking even to most contemporary French existentialists.

It was in Italy in 1639, when he was thirty years old, that that issue was presented most dramatically to Milton. When he had left England in the previous year, he had gone far in his apprenticeship for his life-time's work. He had already 'enjoyed an interval' of five years 'of uninterrupted leisure' on his father's estate, 'which I entirely devoted to the perusal of the Greek and Latin classics', with occasional visits to London 'either for the sake of purchasing books, or of learning something new in mathematics or in music'. He had, moreover, with the publication of *Comus* and 'Lycidas', already shown himself to be the best poet then living in England. He was now ready for the grand tour, particularly for Italy, 'the seat of civilization and the hospitable domicile of every species of erudition'. The trip had been an immense success. Armed with a letter from his elegant and learned friend Sir Henry Wotton, the former English ambassador to Venice, he had met Thomas Scudamore, the English ambassador at Paris, and Hugo Grotius, Queen Christina's ambassador at the French court. He had traveled by boat from Nice to Genoa, then to Leghorn, Pisa, and Florence, where his ability to compose both Latin and Italian verse helped him to enjoy something of a triumph and where he 'was a constant attendant at their literary parties' for two months. Then to Siena and Rome, where the Librarian of the Vatican, Lucas Holstein, showed him unusual courtesies; and finally to Naples, where Manso, Marquis of Villa, the illustrious patron of the poet Tasso, received him. He was not only seeing the fabulous classical and Renaissance world, but he was being seen and admired as one of its prospective luminaries. It was just at this rather heady moment when he was getting ready to go to Sicily and Greece (the next inevitable stages of such a journey) that 'the melancholy intelligence which I received of the civil commotions in England made me alter my purpose; for I thought it base to be travelling for amusement abroad, while my fellow-citizens were fighting for liberty at home'.

What called Milton back to England was the short-lived First Bishops' War in Scotland, which was over before he returned. But with the meeting of the Long Parliament in the next year, Milton put aside his larger projects in order to take part in the pamphlet war on ecclesiastical and political issues. Thus Milton began the writing of the prose works, which was to take most of the next twenty years of his life. He temporarily abandoned poetry, except for the occasional – and magnificent – heroic sonnets, and he abandoned it during exactly those years, from the age of 31 until the age of 52, which in the normal course of events might have been his most productive as a poet. He abandoned poetry for the sake of what he admired most about the particular kind of poetry to which he was devoted. He engaged in the controversies of his time not from any natural love of controversy but because he could not see what he thought was the cause of liberty threatened without acting.

Although they contain magnificent passages, most of Milton's prose works are not as wholes literary masterpieces – and Milton knew that they were not. 'I should not choose this manner of writing, wherein knowing myself inferior to myself, led by the genial power of nature to another task, I have the use, as I may account it, but of my left hand.' The controversial pamphlets of the time required even of Milton, the man who remarked 'I hate a pupil teacher', that he cite authorities and precedents. It was distasteful, but it was, Milton believed, necessary when one argued with people who trusted authority and precedent more than their own reason. Yet he wished his readers to understand 'with what small willingness I endure to interrupt the pursuit of no less hopes than these [his hopes to be an heroic poet], and leave a calm and pleasing solitariness, fed with cheerful and confident thoughts, to embark in a troubled sea of noises and hoarse disputes, put from beholding the bright countenance of truth in the quiet and still air of delightful studies to come into the dim reflection of hollow antiquities sold by the seeming bulk, and there be fain to club quotations with men whose learning and belief lies in marginal stuffings, who, when they have like good sumpters laid ye down their horse-load of citations and fathers at your door, with a rhapsody of who and who were bishops here or there, ye may take off their packsaddles, their day's work is done, and episcopacy, as they think, stoutly vindicated. Let any gentle apprehension that can distinguish learned pains from unlearned drudgery imagine what pleasure or profoundness can be in this, or what honor to deal against such adversaries. But were it the meanest under-service, if God by his secretary conscience enjoin it, it were sad for me if I should draw back.'

In his first ten years as a prose writer 'in the public interest', Milton did not confine himself to matters of church government. The army and the parliament between them were, he believed, taking care of the most pressing issues concerning religious and civil liberty, so Milton, individualist still even in the midst of collective revolutionary activity, turned 'to the promotion of real and substantial liberty, which is rather to be sought from within than from without, and whose existence depends, not so much on the terror of the sword as on sobriety of conduct and integrity of life'. Milton's own account in *The Second Defense of the English People* of his efforts for 'domestic' liberty cannot be improved on: 'As this seemed to involve three material questions, the conditions of the conjugal tie, the education of the children, and the free

publication of the thoughts, I made them objects of distinct consideration. I explained my sentiments, not only concerning the solemnization
of the marriage, but the dissolution, if circumstances rendered it
necessary . . . for he in vain makes a vaunt of liberty in the senate or in
the forum, who languishes under the vilest servitude, to an inferior at
home. . . . I then discussed the principles of education in a summary
manner, but sufficiently copious for those who attend seriously to the
subject; than which nothing can be more necessary to principle the
minds of men in virtue, the only genuine source of political and
individual liberty, the only true safeguard of states, the bulwark of their
prosperity and renown. Lastly, I wrote my Areopagitica, in order to
deliver the press from the restraints with which it was encumbered;
that the power of determining what was true and what was false, what
ought to be published and what to be suppressed, might no longer be
entrusted to a few illiterate and illiberal individuals, who refused their
sanction to any work which contained views or sentiments at all above
the level of vulgar superstition.'

Up to this point Milton was, as he expressed it, 'recompensed by
nothing but impunity'. When he was appointed Secretary for Foreign
Tongues to the Council of State in 1649, he accepted the position
because he believed in the government which he served. Although the
most important of the later pamphlets in defense of the regicide were
written at the request of the government, they represent unmistakably
the opinions of Milton. In view of the violent criticisms which those
pamphlets still excite, we might remember Milton's remark, 'I did not
insult over fallen majesty, as is pretended; I only preferred queen Truth
to King Charles.' Milton's eyesight had been failing for some years, but
it was the work on *The Defense of the English People* which caused his
final blindness in 1651. His enemies immediately seized upon the fact of
his blindness as proof of the judgment of God against a defender of
regicide. That charge itself is of little interest to us today, but in his
rebuttal to it, Milton provided us with a description of another heroic
decision which he was forced to make: the decision of a poet, an artist
of images, to sacrifice his sight: 'Since my enemies boast that this
affliction is only a retribution for the transgressions of my pen, I . . .
invoke the Almighty to witness, that I never, at any time, wrote anything which I did not think agreeable to truth, to justice, and to piety.
This was my persuasion then, and I feel the same persuasion now. Nor
was I ever prompted to such exertions by the influence of ambition, by

the lust of lucre or of praise; it was only by the conviction of duty and the feeling of patriotism, a disinterested passion for the extension of civil and religious liberty. Thus, therefore, when I was publicly solicited to write a reply to the Defense of the royal cause, when I had to contend with the pressure of sickness, and with the apprehension of soon losing the sight of my remaining eye, and when my medical attendants clearly announced, that if I did engage in the work, it would be irreparably lost, their premonitions caused no hesitation and inspired no dismay. I would not have listened to the voice even of Esculapius himself from the shrine of Epidaurus, in preference to the suggestions of the heavenly monitor within my breast; my resolution was unshaken, though the alternative was either the loss of my sight, or the desertion of my duty. . . . I resolved, therefore, to make the short interval of sight, which was left me to enjoy, as beneficial as possible to the public interest.'

It was not until 1660, after an extraordinary last-ditch plea for 'liberty' in the face of the almost universal desire for the return of the Stuart king, that Milton, blind and aged 52, turned again to devote his full time to what he considered the chief business of his life. There was no longer any question of his being 'needed' in the struggle for liberty; the struggle had been lost, and Milton believed the majority of the English people had shown themselves 'worthy . . . to be for ever slaves'. There was no political way to force freedom on people who did not desire it. But the political defeat involved for Milton the regaining of his artistic freedom. As an intellectual leader of a defeated revolutionary group, Milton did not recant, nor did he spend his time on apologetics for the cause or justifications for his actions; instead, he wrote books on grammar, logic, and history; he completed an epic, and he wrote a brief epic and a tragedy.

Those last poems are the basis of Milton's international reputation, and they provide the most just measure of Milton's vision of freedom. True freedom, as Milton conceived it, was not inherited; it must be achieved by the individual. The heroic poet, like any other free man, must avoid enslavement to contemporary conformities in thought and action, but he must also escape enslavement to the past and enslavement to his own blindnesses and weaknesses and prejudices. A man was truly free when he was able in some manner to create, and thus achieve value beyond his own poor status as a mere mortal animal, either isolated or in the herd. To do this, he could escape neither the present nor the past; he must know both, use both, and go beyond both.

So in *Paradise Lost, Paradise Regained*, and *Samson Agonistes*, Milton used much of the traditional material from the greatest literature of the Western world, but he infused it with his own vision and he re-created the traditional values of heroism, freedom, and love. Instead of a vision of a capricious fate (whether Greek or Calvinistic), he celebrated a vision of human freedom. Instead of celebrating the providential history of one nation, he celebrated the providential history of mankind. He rejected completely the epic tradition that military heroism was one of the highest goods. Such an opinion was worthy of a degenerate age:

> For in those days Might only shall be admir'd,
> And Valour and Heroic Virtue call'd;
> To overcome in Battle, and subdue
> Nations, and bring home spoils with infinite
> Man-slaughter, shall be held the highest pitch
> Of human Glory; and for Glory done,
> Of triumph, to be styl'd great Conquerors,
> Patrons of Mankind, Gods, and Sons of Gods,
> Destroyers rightlier call'd and Plagues of men.

He confused numbers of readers unutterably by giving one character most of the 'archetypal' 'heroic' attributes and then calling him Satan, the King of Hell. He did that, I believe, to dramatize his own perception that no single human attribute is either good or bad, has any moral significance at all, except as it is related to absolute value and the love of the good – or the love of God. He changed the setting of the significant heroic action from the external world of public events to the interior world of the individual's mind and soul. *His* heroism concerned 'deeds/ Above Heroic, though in secret done'. The highest heroic act, as Milton conceived it, was the free acceptance of suffering for the love of another, typified by the offer of the Redeeming Hero, the Son of God:

> Behold mee then, mee for him, life for life
> I offer, on mee let thine anger fall;
> Account mee man; I for his sake will leave
> Thy bosom, and this glory next to thee
> Freely put off, and for him lastly die
> Well pleas'd, on me let Death wreck all his rage.

Also heroic was simple faithfulness in the middle of a corrupt society to the good and the true – another act of love:

> . . . the Seraph *Abdiel* faithful found,
> Among the faithless, faithful only hee;
> Among innumerable false, unmov'd,
> Unshak'n, unseduc'd, unterrifi'd
> His Loyalty he kept, his Love, his Zeal;
> Nor number nor example with him wrought
> To swerve from truth, or change his constant mind
> Though single.

No one could consciously seek occasions for this kind of heroism as the knightly hero could go out in search of a dragon or a human antagonist. The 'fortitude/ Of Patience' was essential: 'Trial will come unsought.' The Miltonic hero must wait upon time and the will of God.

Each of the major poems concerns temptation or the significant trial of a hero, for it is only such trial which makes heroism necessary; it is only by means of such trial that the nature of heroism can be made manifest. The nature of the heroic action is always clear, whether the individual fails or succeeds in achieving it. And each of the poems embodies in its very structure and the movement of its verse Milton's conviction of Providence. The concept of Providence did not imply for Milton a shallowly optimistic belief in progress nor a belief in any easy triumph of good. Nor did the poet's belief in Providence mean that he could afford to rule out any subject matter or any experienced human emotion. (In Samson's lament, Milton provided as moving a realization of human suffering and despair as we can find in English poetry.) The conception of Providence which underlies the poems represents the discovery of value within the process of living, within movement, within a total pattern which includes descent as well as ascent, 'grateful vicissitude' – within even the vision of degradation and death for the man who could come to recognize reality (which Milton identified with the will of God) and to act in accordance with it, freely and with love.

Perhaps the most remarkable thing about the poems, as well as about Milton's life, is the sense of energy and creative strength which we get from each. Milton came near to identifying energy and strength with the grace of God – 'All wickedness is weakness,' Samson remarked. His undeviating insistence on the strong, the heroic, is occasionally unnerving. It refuses to take seriously the smaller concerns of our busy lives or our assumptions that we cannot achieve significant freedom. Reading him today, one finds it hard to believe that Milton, a poet who rarely allowed his readers to nod and who never flattered them, could in any age have been truly 'popular'. Perhaps the chief difference between the general attitudes toward Milton in the twentieth century and those in the past lies simply in the fact that it is no longer fashionable for literate readers to pretend to like him. That may actually provide an advantage for the independent reader of Milton today: he may have a chance to read the poetry directly, undistracted by the incense of official praise. However much we may disagree with or disbelieve in specific items in Milton's cosmos, the major poems provide as exciting and challenging literary experiences as we are likely to discover in an age which has been justly labeled both 'the age of anxiety' and 'the age of conformity'.

ARTHUR BARKER

The Pattern of Milton's 'Nativity Ode'(1940)

I

'THE Puritans', writes Professor Woodhouse, '(though in different degrees) were men who had undergone a religious experience, whose effect was to bestow a new unity of feeling upon their thoughts.'[1] As he observes, this experience of a sudden renewal of spirit, mind and purpose, after confusion and paralysis of will, animated the apparently cold formulations of Puritan theology. Indeed, so important was it in the Puritan scheme that it inevitably received its own formulation, patterned on the experiences of Moses, Elijah, and St Paul, and vividly, yet still typically, presented in Bunyan's *Grace Abounding to the Chief of Sinners*. After a life of cynical carelessness, the sinner was oppressed by a terrifying sense of human corruption and of his own especial depravity; he contemplated with horrified fascination the torments to which he felt himself justly damned – a symbol of his torturing mental paralysis; he then began hopelessly to desire peace through God's mercy and to shift the weight of his oppression by striving to accept the divine will, whatever it might be; ultimately, if he were one of the chosen, the weight was removed by his recognition of the significance of Christ's incarnation and vicarious suffering, and he experienced a transporting illumination of spirit which neutralized his self-accusation and produced the calm certainty and the unity of purpose which made the Puritan a dangerous and inflexible opponent. From the moment of his illumination he dated his spiritual rebirth; and he might prove his claim to saintship (or be called upon to prove it) by giving an account of his experience and of the precise occasion on which he was illuminated.

Like so much in Puritanism, this process merely intensified an experience common in the seventeenth century. At a time of religious, intellectual, political, economic confusion, when the aspiring enthusiasm of the Renaissance had given place to the feeling (expressed by Donne) that man's world was 'all in peeces, all cohaerance gone, All just supply, and all relation', it was natural that many should escape from their oppressive sense of frustration by turning for reassurance and direction to a power beyond themselves, and that they should describe the renewal and re-integration of their energies in the terms employed by others during the decline of Jewry and later of Rome. If the experience was not always as sharply defined as the Puritan's conversion, it was nevertheless common to men as different as Bunyan and Donne himself. Donne's poetry is a record of his conversion; Walton took pains to emphasize the same pattern in the *Life of Herbert*; Henry Vaughan presented his variation in the preface to *Silex Scintillans*; the process carried Richard Crashaw to Rome. With the metaphysical poets, no less than with Bunyan, the experience was the prime source of inspiration; and it would not be too much to say that a conversion, in one form or another, lay behind most of the important literary products of the middle years of the century.

It is obvious that the greatest of the seventeenth-century poets shared this experience to some degree. Is it possible to be more precise and to point to some particular occasion when Milton experienced an illumination corresponding to the typical exaltation of the Puritan? Professor Haller thinks not: 'We are not told in Milton's spiritual autobiography the precise moment when he first felt the conviction of grace. The sense of personal election seems to have been his from the start.'[2] Certainly Milton seems never to have doubted his own importance; yet there is nothing in his poetry or prose before his twenty-first year which suggests that he found a deeply personal significance in the Puritan theory of election. In the prose of his middle period, however, he constantly uses the doctrines in which the Puritan formulated his experience, writing of the glorious privileges of the saints with enthusiasm, and (in the pamphlets of 1659 especially) of the 'far surpassing light' of the Spirit with a depth of conviction comparable to Bunyan's. How were the formulae of theology thus animated for him? He nowhere describes an experience precisely like the typical conversion of the tinker. Nothing in his youth exactly corresponds to the depravity Bunyan emphasized; it is difficult to believe that he ever trembled at the thought of the punishments of the damned; and, however else his self-esteem was expressed, he never described himself, with Bunyan and Cromwell, as 'the chief of sinners'. Yet he repudiated (though he printed) the more sensuous of his early poems;[3] and the Hell of *Paradise Lost* is the product of a vivid sense of evil which expresses itself throughout his works. His life was no fugitive and cloistered serenity, but a series of frustrations both private and public. His Puritan contemporaries found a constant source of reassurance in the fruits of their religious experience; he found a similar source in the genius which enabled him to rise imaginatively above despair. In that fact lies the explanation of the sense of personal election which he shared with them.

The autobiographical passages Professor Haller seems specially to have in mind are those in the pamphlets of 1641 and 1642 in which Milton defends his right, though a layman, to meddle in ecclesiastical matters.[4] Somewhat incongruously, they deal chiefly with his poetical development and plans; but the incongruity is only apparent since he regarded himself by then as a poet-prophet of special calling, whose inspiration was from God. This conviction is, as Professor Hanford remarks, 'the centre of his spiritual biography'.[5] But it was not his from the start; it is not suggested in his poetry or prose before 1629; and its impact on his imagination is the experience which corresponds to the conversion of his Puritan associates. The moment of impact is fixed by his 'Ode on the Morning of Christ's Nativity', composed in December, 1629, near his twenty-first birthday. This poem strikes a note altogether new in his poetry, includes an implied rejection of his earlier manner,[6] and records a vision which produced a confident and harmonious purposefulness by overcoming the forces of gloom and confusion. It is to be regarded as the testimony of Milton's religious experience, but with this difference, that he thenceforth thought of himself not simply, like Bunyan, as a saint but as a poet sacred to the gods and their priest, whose inmost soul and lips breathe out Jove.[7] For the experience which produced the 'Ode' was unlike Bunyan's in being essentially aesthetic. I propose to show that the recognition of the significance of Christ's incarnation and sacrifice recorded in the 'Ode' was coupled with a recognition of the potentialities of a peculiarly complex poetical symbol, and that these recognitions together bestowed a new unity of feeling upon both Milton's thought and his art.

II

Milton emphasized the importance of his 'Ode' by setting it at the beginning of the section devoted to English verse in the *Poems* (1645). 'Lycidas' (November 1637) concluded this section, and clearly marks the end of a period in Milton's development of which the 'Ode' is the beginning. Hitherto Ovid had been his chief model; after 1629 his tone was more severe. He noted this departure in an account of his development written in 1642,[8] and more significantly in *Elegia Sexta*, composed shortly after the 'Ode', when he spoke for the first time of the rigorously disciplined virtue required of the poet who would write of cosmic and epic themes, and referred to his Nativity poem as, by implication, an earnest of his intentions.[9]

The self-dedication of the 'Ode' and the 'Elegy' have often been noted;[10] the nature of this dedication has not, I think, been precisely explained because the quality of Milton's art in the 'Nativity Ode' has not been fully comprehended. Its charm and freshness have been praised, but (apart from a few lines of swelling grandeur) it has been said to lack the distinctively Miltonic excellences so fully apparent in 'Lycidas'. Mr Tillyard, for example, thinks 'Lycidas' 'one of the greatest poems in English'; but he finds the 'Ode' less satisfactory since, though it has a 'beautiful diversity', its heterogeneous elements are only 'harmonized by a pervading youthful candour' and superficially unified by the fact that at the beginning Milton hastens to prevent the Wise Men whose arrival (as he thinks) is indicated at the end.[11] The impression made on my mind by the 'Ode' has, however, a unity which could not be produced simply by a pervasive charm or the provision of a frame for the picture. In this respect it is not unlike the impression created by 'Lycidas'. I believe one can show how Milton's architectonic power is exerted with impressive results in both poems, and how in the case of the 'Ode', as more obviously in 'Lycidas', its influence helps to define mood and significance.

Since 'Lycidas' is in many respects the type in little of Milton's peculiar genius, it provides a suitable standard for judging the earlier 'Ode'. As Mr Tillyard has made clear, the elegy is essentially a personal poem, the ostensible subject making possible the resolution of the emotional problems created by Milton's disciplined devotion to poetry.[12] Like his great poems, it performed a cathartic function for the poet himself, was indeed the very process through which a balanced calm was brought out of emotional disquiet. The achievement of this calm is expressed through the poem's achievement of a symmetry of structure which Mr Tillyard might have emphasized more heavily. Dr Johnson recognized the excellence of 'the design' in *Paradise Lost*, but he was prevented from discerning the same quality in 'Lycidas' by what seemed to him the trivial character of the pastoral fiction. It is just Milton's balanced manipulation of this convention to throw into relief the resolution of his own problems, which gives the poem its serene power.

'Lycidas' consists of an introduction and conclusion, both pastoral in tone, and three movements, practically equal in length and precisely parallel in pattern. Each begins with an invocation of pastoral muses (15, 85, 132), proceeds with conventions drawn from the tradition of the pastoral elegy (the association of the lamented and the poet as shepherds, the mourning of nature, the questioning of the nymphs, the procession of mourners, a flower passage,[13] and the reassurance), and ends with the formulation and resolution of Milton's emotional problem. The first movement laments Lycidas the poet-shepherd; its problem, the possible frustration of disciplined poetic ambition by early death, is resolved by the assurance, 'Of so much fame in heaven expect thy meed.' The second laments Lycidas as priest-shepherd; its problem, the frustration of a sincere shepherd in a corrupt church, is resolved by St Peter's reference to the 'two-handed engine' of divine retribution. The third concludes with the apotheosis, a convention introduced by Virgil in *Eclogue* v but significantly handled by Milton. He sees the poet-priest-shepherd worshipping the Lamb with those saints 'in solemn troops' who sing the 'unexpressive nuptial song' of the fourteenth chapter of Revelation. The apotheosis thus not only provides the final reassurance but unites the themes of the preceding movements in the ultimate reward of the true poet-priest.

It is the cumulative effect of its three parallel movements which makes 'Lycidas' impressive; the return to the pastoral at the beginning of each makes possible three successive and perfectly controlled crescendos. The gathering up of the first two in the last gives the conclusion its calm finality; and the balanced unity of the design appropriately represents the calm achieved through the resolution of emotional conflicts. The problems are solved for Milton by the apotheosis because he regards himself as a poet-priest who can hope that his 'destin'd urn' will bring the same reward.

The 'Nativity Ode' resolves no pressing problems, but it expresses profound feeling and calm determination in much the same way as 'Lycidas'. It seems architectonically inferior because its parts are not held together by the same strictness of formal design. But it produces a unified impression because it is built upon another kind of design. The four introductory stanzas apart, and the brief conclusion, it too consists of three equal movements, held in relation, not by the repetition of a structural pattern, but by the variation of a basic pattern of imagery. The first eight stanzas of the 'Hymn' describe the setting of the Nativity, the next nine the angelic choir, the next nine the flight of the heathen gods. The conclusion, the last stanza, presents the scene in the stable. A brief analysis will show that the three movements each present a single modification of the simple contrast, preserved throughout the poem, between images suggesting light and harmony and images of gloom and discord.

The Nativity setting is described in a series of negatives whose effect is to reduce light and sound to a minimum while subduing all discordant elements. There is no colour because Nature has 'doffed her gaudy trim' and covered her face with 'a veil of maiden white'.* Peace has stilled the din of war; the air is 'gentle'; the winds 'smoothly the waters kiss't' while 'birds of calm sit brooding on the charmed wave'. The scene is dimly lit by the 'glimmering orbs' of the stars standing 'fixt'; the sun (as we are told in the first and seventh stanzas) withholds his 'inferior flame'. The eighth stanza completes this peacefully hushed and faintly illuminated scene by introducing the shepherds 'simply chatting in a rustic row'. It also serves as a link with the second movement, for there breaks upon their ears, with a suddenness for which the poet has carefully prepared, the enrapturing harmony of the angelic choir:†

> When such music sweet
> Their hearts and ears did greet,
>   As never was by mortal finger strook,
> Divinely-warbled voice
> Answering the stringed noise,
>   As all their souls in blissful rapture took:
> The air such pleasure loath to lose,
> With thousand echoes still prolongs each heav'nly close.

The harmony is such as might bind heaven and earth 'in happier union'; and it is accompanied by an intense but not formless brilliance – 'a globe of circular light' – revealing the angels 'in glittering ranks'. This association of light with harmony and order is emphasized in the succeeding verses with reference first to Job xxxviii 7, and then to the Pythagorean music of the spheres. The music is such as was heard 'when

* The unhappy personifications of Peace and Justice contain the only touches of colour in the first two movements.

† Milton wisely omits the announcement of Luke's single angel which would have reduced the sharpness of the contrast.

of old the sons of morning sung' and God, setting his constellations in the heavens, brought order out of chaos in creating the 'well-balanc't' world. The 'crystal spheres', representing the order of nature, are urged to ring out their ninefold 'silver chime' to 'make up full consort to the angelic symphony'. The possible effect of the harmony on men is elaborated by the two following verses in terms of light: 'the age of gold' may return, and 'speckl'd vanity' and 'leprous sin' give place to Mercy, 'thron'd in celestial sheen', and Justice, wearing 'th' enamel'd arras of the rainbow'.

This vision is dissipated by the thought of the Cross, and the movement comes to an end with a reference to the last judgment which prepares for the third movement by introducing ideas of dissonance and gloom in sharp contrast with the harmony and order of the second. The trump of doom must 'thunder' with 'a horrid clang' such as was heard amid the 'smouldering clouds' of Sinai, and with a 'blast' shaking the earth 'from the surface to the centre'.

The last movement is full of discordant sounds, distorted forms, and shadows. The old dragon thrashes with his 'folded tail'; one hears the 'hideous hum' and 'hollow shriek' of the oracles, and 'a voice of weeping' and 'loud lament'; with 'flow'r-inwoven tresses torn' the nymphs sorrow in 'twilight shade of tangled thickets'; the lars and lemurs 'moan with midnight plaint'; 'a drear and dying sound' affrights the flamens; Moloch leaves his 'shadows dread' and 'burning idol all of blackest hue'. 'The rays of Bethlehem' blind the gods, and the Babe can 'control the damned crew'.

Light and order return with these phrases, and gloom and confusion make way for them as the 'shadows pale' disperse and the fairies leave 'their moon-lov'd maze'. The poet strives for striking brilliance through the unhappy image of 'the sun in bed' which, if less clumsy, would have reminded the reader that day-break was withheld in the opening movement. Even so, the verse prepares for the final picture of the nativity:

> But see! the Virgin blest,
> Hath laid her Babe to rest.
>   Time is our tedious song should here have ending;
> Heav'n's youngest teemed star
> Hath fixt her polisht car,
>   Her sleeping Lord with handmaid lamp attending:
> And all about the courtly stable,
> Bright-harness'd angels sit in order serviceable.

This scene has often been compared with the simply but definitely composed fifteenth-century nativities; but its effectiveness depends on more than its own composition. It catches up the pattern underlying the preceding movements, bringing order after confusion and reflecting the peaceful hush and the brilliant harmony of the first two movements. It is pervaded by the clear and steady brilliance of the new star's 'handmaid lamp', and enclosed by the 'order serviceable' of the 'bright-harness'd angels'. Its static quality fixes with appropriate firmness the pattern of light and harmony on which the poem has been composed.

The effect of the 'Nativity Ode' is thus produced by its reiteration of a pattern of imagery, variously presented in the three movements, and impressed with finality in the concluding verse. The balanced contrast between the first and third movements serves to throw the central movement into sharp relief. This emphasis defines the poem's significance for Milton. It was at about this time that he was, in his own phrase, 'confirmed in this opinion, that he who would not be frustrate of his hope to write well hereafter in laudable things ought himself to be a true poem; that is, a composition and pattern of the best and honourablest things. . . .'[14] The 'Nativity Ode' is his first achievement of composition and pattern in the full Miltonic sense, and it is so because it expresses his achievement of composition and pattern in himself through the harmonious illumination resulting from his recognition of the significance of the Incarnation. It is the first of Milton's inspired poems; and the angelic choir is the symbol of his inspiration.

III

The imagery of the 'Ode' is of course no more original than the pastoral conventions of 'Lycidas'.[15] The effect again depends on Milton's handling of traditional elements. The emphasis on the intense brilliance and divine harmony of the angelic choir has in itself no peculiar personal significance, for it was a commonplace in seventeenth-century poetry – to go no farther. Milton knew, for example, Giles Fletcher's reference, in 'Christ's Victorie in Heaven', to the time

> When, like the starres the singing angels shot
> To earth, and heav'n awaked all his eyes
> To see another sun at midnight rise
> On earth.

Nearly the whole of Milton's conception is implicit in these unmusical lines; but they are not a source, for the ideas were simply part of the consciousness of a century whose metaphysics were shot through with symbolic light. They occur repeatedly in the work of poets who neither knew Milton nor were known to him in 1629. George Herbert concluded his second 'Christmas' with a typically metaphysical association of the sun and harmony:

> His beams shall cheer my breast, and both so twine,
> Till even his beams sing, and my music shine.

His mystically-minded disciple, Henry Vaughan, used the idea of nature's harmony in 'The Morning Watch':

> Thus all is hurl'd
> In sacred hymns, and order, the great chime
> And symphony of nature. Prayer is
> The world in tune.

Richard Crashaw made the idea that the Nativity was the 'bright dawn of our eternal day' the centre of 'In the Holy Nativity', and his 'In the Glorious Epiphany' associated harmony with light through the idea that the sun is symbolic of the sin which prevents man from hearing the heavenly music:

> This daily wrong
> Silenc't the morning-sons, & dampt their song.
> Nor was't our deafness, but our sins, that thus
> Long made th'harmonious orbes all mute to us.

These examples will suffice to indicate that Milton's imagery is not unique, and also to suggest what I believe could be proved by an extensive examination of seventeenth-century poetry, that none of his contemporaries developed the idea and its varied associations with anything like the controlled complexity of the central passage of the 'Ode'. Behind the symbol of the choir and the spheres lies an intricate fusion of traditions. The connection of angels with stars is suggested by such passages as Revelation ix 1, 11; xii 4; 1 Kings xxii 19; Judges v 20. It also owes much to the Greek idea, recorded by Plato (*Republic* 621B) and Aristotle (*Nicomachean Ethics* vi 7), and frequently employed by Milton's former model Ovid, that the stars are divine beings. This leads inevitably to the association of the songs of praise sung by the angels in heaven with the music of the spheres (as in Crashaw), the bringing together of passages like Job xxxviii 7, and the Pythagorean doctrine expressed, for example, by Plato (*Republic* 617) and by Cicero (*De re publica*, VI 17, 18). Nine was the number of spheres usually given (as by Cicero). This is the number of the Muses, identified by Plutarch with the spheres (*Symposium* 9). The Muses can thus be connected with the angels, who (according to Pseudo-Dionysius the Areopagite) are divided into nine orders. Moreover, the music of the spheres is represented by the pipe of Pan, who is in love with Echo, another symbol of the music. Pan is sometimes identified with the universe, sometimes with the sun; and he is a shepherd who controls the flocking stars and preserves their harmony. The early Christians associated Pan with Christ, as does Milton in the eighth stanza of the 'Ode'; but the full significance of Milton's association is only apparent from the description of the choir which follows. Christ is the reason for the angelic music and the source of the music of the spheres, which, at his birth, should harmonize with the choir and produce in men the harmony of their first perfection. These harmonies are not only described but echoed in Milton's verse. Of the music of the spheres Cicero wrote: 'Some learned men, by imitating this harmony with strings and vocal melodies, have opened a way for their return to this place; as all others have done who, endued with pre-eminent qualities, have cultivated in their mortal life the pursuits of heaven.'[16] This becomes the function of Milton's verse for the first time in the 'Nativity Ode'; and the incarnate Christ is not only the subject of his poem, but the source of his inspiration.

It is thus the symbol of illumination and harmony provided by the choir and the spheres which fuses the heterogeneous particles of the 'Ode' and gives it its controlled power. It does so because it enables the poet to draw on a vast reservoir of pagan and Christian suggestion while transcending the conflict between the two traditions, and consequently to express something approaching the totality of his literary experience. The fruit of this experience is his sense of divine inspiration. From 'the Samian teacher'[17] he had learned of the stern discipline required of the poet who would reproduce the music of the spheres; for the Christian the aim of such discipline must be to echo the angelic hymn of communion with God through the incarnate Christ. The central symbol of the 'Ode' represents the achievement of this inspiring communion.

IV

It is significant that there is no reference to the celestial music in
Milton's poetry before 1629. His attention seems to have been drawn to
it when he had to compose his second academic prolusion. Here he
examines the opinions of Plato and Aristotle on the Pythagorean
allegory, and observes: 'Hence arose the story . . . of how the Muses
dance before Jove's altar day and night; hence too the attribution to
Phoebus . . . of musical skill. Hence the belief . . . that Harmonia was
the daughter of Jove and Electra, and that at her marriage to Cadmus all
the choirs of heaven sang in concert.'[18] The mythological references to
God, the sun, harmony, and light, suggest that this is the germ from
which the 'Ode''s pattern developed; its significance is indicated by the
assertion that man cannot hear the music because 'the presumption of
that thief Prometheus' has left him 'buried in sin', though 'if our souls
were pure, chaste, and white as snow . . . then indeed our ears would
ring and be filled with that exquisite music of the stars in their orbits;
then would all things turn back to the age of gold, and we ourselves,
free from every grief, would pass our lives in a blessed peace. . . .'

The force with which this idea struck Milton's imagination is
indicated by the fact that from the 'Ode' to 'Lycidas' he was almost
incapable of writing on a serious subject without introducing the music.
'Il Penseroso' echoes the phrasing of his prolusion; 'The Passion' and
'Upon the Circumcision' begin with references to the music of the
'Ode'. 'At a Solemn Music' is constructed upon its central conception,
with this significant variation, that the place of the Nativity angels is
taken by the hundred forty and four thousand 'not defiled with
women', who sing before the Lamb in Revelation xiv. In 1642 Milton
recorded the impression made on his youthful mind by this passage.[19]
Its song provided a more suitable angelic counterpart for the music of
the spheres than the Nativity choir since the latter belonged to a particular occasion while the former was constant. In 'Arcades' 'the celestial
siren's harmony' marks the climax of the speech of the Genius, though
there is no reference to its scriptural counterpart. Superficially this is
also true in *Comus*; but the Renaissance habit of speaking of God and
Christ in mythological terms indicates the significance of the prologue's
opening lines and of the epilogue's exhortation to love virtue since

> She can teach you how to climb
> Higher than the sphery chime.

Finally in 'Lycidas' the destiny of the poet-priest is fulfilled as he hears 'the unexpressive nuptial song' sung by

> all the saints above,
> In solemn troops, and sweet societies,
> That sing, and singing in their glory move.

This is the appropriate resolution of the problems involved in the elegy's lament; for in his youthful defence of poetry, *Ad Patrem*, Milton envisaged for himself and his musical father the same reward: 'When we return to our native Olympus . . . we shall walk . . . through the temples of the skies, and with the harp's soft accompaniment we shall sing sweet songs to which the stars shall echo and the vault of heaven from pole to pole. Even now the fiery spirit who flies through the swift spheres is singing his immortal melody and unutterable song in harmony with the starry choruses.'[20]

This is the reward of the poet who seeks his inspiration from the 'Heav'nly Muse' of the 'Ode''s introductory verses.[21] Here Milton calls on his muse to present a gift to the Christ who has laid aside 'that glorious form, that light unsufferable', and to prevent with her offering the star-led wizards:

> Have thou the honour first, thy Lord to greet,
> And join thy voice unto the angel quire,
> From out his secret altar toucht with hallow'd fire.

This hallowed fire from God's altar, about which the angelic muses eternally sing and singing in their glory move like stars, is the fire with which the seraph touched the lips of the prophet Isaiah.[22] The product of this inspiration is the glorious form and light unsufferable of the symbol thrown into relief by the patterning of the 'Ode' whose beauty surpassed anything Milton had hitherto written because it expressed with perfect adequacy and complete control a new and profound religious emotion. Like that Englishman of whom Bede tells 'a marvellous and very pleasant anecdote', Milton 'suddenly by an act of God became', not simply 'a poet', but a poet with a peculiar purpose and peculiar gifts.[23]

It was this experience, at once aesthetic and religious, which crystallized Milton's conviction of special poetical calling and provided him with a definition of his function. Its effects correspond in general to the effects of the Puritan conversion. He then determined to forsake the ways of his youth and (as *Elegia sexta* implies) the masters of the *elegia levis*; the new pattern imposed on his thought and feeling drove out these masters as the Babe drove out the pagan gods. But as his experience was essentially aesthetic and immediately produced the harmonies of the 'Ode', so it differed from the experience of his Puritan contemporaries in involving a recognition, not only of the personal significance of the Incarnation, but also of its relationship to the classical and humanistic doctrine of harmonious perfection symbolized by the music of the spheres. Of this perfection divinely inspired poetry seemed to him the supreme expression. Thus the 'Ode' helps to explain the enthusiasm with which he found in the Calvinistic doctrine of grace a satisfactory expression of his sense of peculiar calling, and also his devotion to the ideal of a harmonious society reproducing 'the old and elegant humanity of Greece'. The delicate balance represented by the 'Ode''s central symbol was difficult to preserve; but the main effort of his life was directed towards its preservation in himself and its reproduction through poetry and in the life of men. When his efforts for society were frustrated and he himself was cut off by blindness, it was to the far surpassing light of his inspiration that he turned for the harmony of spirit expressed in the Christian doctrines and the classic composition and pattern of his great poems.

NOTES

1. *Puritanism and Liberty*, ed. A. S. P. Woodhouse (1938) p. 38.
2. William Haller, *The Rise of Puritanism* (New York, 1938) p. 297.
3. In the lines appended to *Elegia Septima* in the 1645 edition of his *Poems*.
4. Especially *Reason of Church Government*, in *Complete Works of John Milton*, Columbia edition, 18 vols (1930-40) III 235-9; and *Apology*, in *Works*, III 301-7.
5. 'Milton's Mosaic Inspiration', in *University of Toronto Quarterly*, VIII p. 147.
6. The first stanza of 'The Hymn' clearly refers to the sensuous imagery of *Elegia quinta, In adventum veris*.
7. *Elegia Sexta*, 77-8, translated.
8. *Apology*, in *Works*, III 303.
9. *Elegia Sexta*, 55 ff. He had already expressed his ambition to write upon such themes in *At a Vacation Exercise*, but without speaking of the required discipline.
10. See J. H. Hanford, 'The Youth of Milton: an interpretation of his early literary development', in *Studies in Shakespeare, Milton, and Donne*, by members of the English Department of the University of Michigan (New York and London, 1925); E. M. W. Tillyard, *Milton* (1930) pp. 35-42; Haller, op. cit.
11. Op. cit. pp. 37, 85. Similarly G. W. Knight – *The Burning Oracle* (1939) p. 64 – thinks the 'Ode' 'somewhat fluid in its addition of stanza to stanza: there is no complex inter-knitting, that is, of central action with design, nor is such necessary'. A similar failure

to recognize the design of 'Lycidas' leads Professor Knight to describe that poem as 'an accumulation of magnificent fragments' (p. 70).

12. Op. cit. pp. 80–5.

13. Mr Tillyard, finding it 'difficult to describe the function' of this passage (133–64), regards it as a transitional interlude, the third movement of the poem beginning with line 165. But the invocation of Alpheus in line 132 clearly marks the beginning of a third movement, and the flower passage performs for this movement exactly the same function as the similarly conventional passages of the preceding movements.

14. *Apology*, in *Works*, III 303.

15. See the annotations by A. W. Verity in *The Cambridge Milton for Schools*, 11 vols (Pitt Press series: Cambridge, 1891–9), by Merritt Y. Hughes in *Paradise Regained, The Minor Poems and Samson Agonistes* (New York, 1937), and by A. S. Cook in *Transactions of the Connecticut Academy of Arts and Sciences*, xv 307–68.

16. *De re publica*, VI 17; see S. G. S. Spaeth, *Milton's Knowledge of Music* (1963) app. v.

17. Pythagoras, *Elegia Sexta*, 59.

18. *Milton: Private Correspondence and Academic Exercises*, trans. P. B. Tillyard (1932) p. 66. The prolusion cannot be dated, but since Milton placed it second in the group it probably belongs to the beginning of his Cambridge career. Its connection with the 'Ode' leads E. M. W. Tillyard to place it about 1629 (ibid. pp. xxvi–xxix).

19. *Apology*, in *Works*, III p. 306.

20. Merritt Hughes's translation, 30–7. Cf. the apotheosis of Diodati in *Epitaphium Damonis*.

21. On the Renaissance identification of the muse of astronomy with the Holy Spirit as the inspirer of Christian poets, and on the place of Milton's *Paradise Lost* invocations in this tradition, see Miss L. B. Campbell, 'The Christian Muse' (in *Huntington Library Bulletin*, 8).

22. Cf. *Reason of Church Government*, in *Works*, III 241.

23. Translation of a Latin note in Milton's Commonplace Book, in *Works*, XVIII 139.

J. B. LEISHMAN

'L'Allegro' and 'Il Penseroso' in their Relation to Seventeenth-century Poetry (1951)

My only reason for not describing 'L'Allegro' and 'Il Penseroso' as the most typically seventeenth-century of Milton's shorter poems is that I cannot conceive how any other seventeenth-century poet could possibly have written them. What, though, may be safely asserted is that many of the most delightful characteristics of seventeenth-century poetry in general are there more perfectly exhibited than elsewhere.

It is not an accident that they are written in that octosyllabic couplet which various poets of the earlier seventeenth century brought to perfection: it was precisely the right form both for Milton's subject-matter and for his attitude towards it; and both subject-matter and attitude (or tone) are here further from Spenser (who never used this metre) and nearer to some of the best seventeenth-century poets than anywhere else in what may be called Milton's major minor poems. There is more wit here than elsewhere in his serious poetry – wit, not in the narrower sense of ingeniousness and the devising of ingenious analogies and comparisons (although there are some traces of this), but wit in the wider sense, as denoting a certain flexibility of mind and mood, a certain balance between seriousness and light-heartedness.

There is also some trace in them of that dialectical, argumentative, and debating strain which is so strong in Donne and in some of his successors.

How strong is this debating strain, and what exactly is the debate about? Most of us, I suppose, have always assumed that it was about Mirth and Melancholy, but Dr Tillyard, partly perhaps because he was looking for evidence to support his belief that the two poems, because they do not appear in the Trinity College Manuscript, must have been written before Milton left Cambridge, has declared that they grew out of Milton's *First Prolusion*, a semi-serious academic exercise, delivered not later than July 1628, on the subject 'Whether Day or Night is the more excellent'. Noticing, in his lecture[1] on the two poems, Dr Johnson's objection that the cheerful man and the meditative man are too much alike, Dr Tillyard declares:

> Nevertheless, the two poems *are* sharply contrasted, and the contrast is that between day and night. *L'Allegro* written in praise of day corresponds to the *First Prolusion*; *Il Penseroso* written in praise of night corresponds to what Milton would have said had he been called to take the other side.

To this it may be shortly replied that 'L'Allegro' cannot be described either as a poem about day or as a poem in praise of day, and the 'Il Penseroso' cannot be described either as a poem about night or as a poem in praise of night. In each poem, as Warton observed long ago, there is a day piece and a night piece; both the cheerful man and the pensive man have their characteristic day-time and their characteristic evening pleasures, although, as might be expected, in 'L'Allegro' it is the day-time and in 'Il Penseroso' the evening pleasures that preponderate; and while the list of pleasures in 'L'Allegro' begins at dawn, with the lark, that in 'Il Penseroso' begins at night, with the nightingale. L'Allegro's evening pleasures begin after the rustic company have heard tales of Robin Goodfellow and gone to bed: he then goes to town ('Towred Cities please us then, And the busie humm of men'), sees tournaments, masques and comedies and hears soft Lydian airs. And just as L'Allegro has his evening pleasures, Il Penseroso has his day-time ones: his dawn is ushered in by a shower; he goes for a solitary walk in the woods; meditates, sleeps and dreams beside a stream, paces the studious cloister, hears organ and choir in a cathedral or in a college chapel. If, then, there is a contrast between the two poems, it is not that between day and night, and if there is a debate, it is not on the respective merits of day and night. In spite of Dr Tillyard, we may be content to believe that when Milton exorcised Melancholy and invoked Mirth he supposed himself to be writing a poem about Mirth; that when he exorcised Mirth and invoked Melancholy he supposed himself to be writing a poem about Melancholy; and that mirth and melancholy did not mean precisely the same to him, in spite of Dr Johnson's complaint that the two characters were not kept sufficiently apart.

The question, what exactly did Milton mean by melancholy? is complex and interesting and will detain us for some time. First, though, it is worth observing that for the idea of two contrasted poems, one

praising the pleasures of mirth and the other praising the pleasures of
melancholy, there existed far better and more obvious precedent than
his own early prolusion on the superiority of day to night. It was, I
think, Sympson, one of the co-editors of the edition of Beaumont and
Fletcher's plays published in 1750, who was the first to point out certain
obvious resemblances between 'Il Penseroso' and Fletcher's song in *The
Nice Valour* beginning 'Hence, all you vaine Delights'. Both play and
song were first printed in the folio of 1647, but long before that date the
song had become very popular, and it appears in several manuscript
collections from about 1620 onwards. In one of these, MS Malone 21 in
the Bodleian, it is followed by a reply entitled 'Against Melancholy' and
ascribed to 'Dr Strode', that is, to William Strode (1602–45), Canon of
Christ Church, Chaplain to Bishop Corbet, and Public Orator at
Oxford. Both Fletcher's poem and Strode's reply to it were printed in
the Miscellanies *Wits Interpreter* (1655) and *Wit Restor'd* (1658).

After having dismissed, rather summarily perhaps, Dr Tillyard's
hypothesis, I rather hesitate to advance one of my own. I will, though,
venture to suggest that someone may have shown Milton a manuscript
of Fletcher's poem and Strode's reply and that this may have started him
off. This hypothesis has four great merits: it is simple; it conflicts with
no existing facts; it involves no new interpretation of Milton's poems;
no one can prove that it is untrue.

Let us, before proceeding, have the two poems before us. Here is
Fletcher's:

> Hence, all you vaine Delights,
> As short as are the nights,
> > Wherein you spend your folly.
> Ther's nought in this life sweet,
> If man were wise to see 't,
> > But onely Melancholy,
> > O sweetest melancholy.
> Welcome, folded Armes and fixed eyes,
> A sigh that piercing mortifies,
> A look that's fastned to the ground,
> A tongue chain'd up without a sound.
>
> Fountaine heads, and pathlesse Groves,
> Places which pale passion loves:
> Moon-light walkes, when all the fowles
> Are warmly hous'd, save Bats and Owles;

> A mid-night Bell, a parting groane,
> These are the sounds we feed upon;
> Then stretch our bones in a still gloomy valley,
> Nothing's so daintie sweet as lovely melancholy.

Strode's reply, though not without merit, is far less memorable and distinguished. It is also less romantic and less pictorial than Fletcher's poem, and nearer to some of Jonson's more epigrammatic lyrics.

> Returne my joyes and hither bring
> A heart not taught to speak but sing,
> A jolly spleen, an inward feast,
> A causelesse laugh without a jest;
> A face which gladnesse doth anoint,
> An arme for joy flung out of joynt;
> A sprightfull gate that leaves no print,
> And makes a feather of a flint;
> A heart that's lighter then the aire,
> An eye still daunceing in its spheare;
> Strong mirth which nothing can controule,
> A body nimbler than a Soule;
> Free wandring thoughts not ty'de to muse,
> Which thinke on all things, nothing choose,
> Which ere wee see them come are gone:
> These life itselfe doth live upon.
>   Then take no care, but only to be jolly:
>   To be more wretched then we must is folly.

I may, perhaps, be too confident in my hypothesis, but it seems to me almost self-evident that it was Fletcher's

> Hence, all you vaine Delights

which suggested

> Hence vain deluding joyes

and the rest of the elaborate abjuration at the beginning of 'Il Penseroso', and that it was Strode's catalogue of the qualities which his returning joys were to bring with them which suggested the various personified qualities and moods which Mirth and Melancholy are exhorted to bring with them in Milton's poems. It also seems to me that the luxurious, or, as a seventeenth-century writer might have called it, the humorous and self-pleasing, the on the whole very agreeable,

melancholy of Fletcher's poem is much like the kind of melancholy
which Milton invokes and describes in 'Il Penseroso', as distinct from
the kind which he abjures at the beginning of 'L'Allegro'.

There is a further and rather important resemblance between Milton's
poems and the pair which I think may have suggested them. Fletcher
and Strode do not *argue* as Donne would have done had he chosen to
exert himself upon this topic; they merely *describe*. Fletcher says in
effect: 'Melancholy's a delicious thing: feel, look, listen'; Strode says in
effect: 'Mirth's the thing I want – makes you feel like this'. This is very
different from Donne's method, when, in 'The Anagram', he sets himself to persuade an imaginary friend that it is in all respects better and
wiser to marry an old and ugly woman than a young and handsome
one, or when he argues with an imaginary mistress that she is refusing to
him what she has permitted to a flea. There is *something* of argument, of
debate, of paradox, of hyperbole in these poems of Fletcher and Strode
and Milton, but not that mock-serious application of close and ingenious
argument to the maintenance of monstrously absurd paradox which we
often find in Donne. Their poems are also, though far from solemn,
more serious than those two of Donne's which I have mentioned. They
take their subject more seriously and they treat it more seriously; their
subject, one may say, *means* more to them. Milton's poems, as I need
scarcely insist, are more serious and elaborate and important than those
of Fletcher and Strode, which, in comparison, are almost trifles; nevertheless, Milton's poems too are, partly at least, in the same tradition, the
same fashion, the fashion of serious, and yet at the same time light-
hearted, poetical debate.

There is indeed a relation between Milton's First Prolusion and his
'L'Allegro' and 'Il Penseroso', but it is very much slighter and more
distant than Dr Tillyard seems to suppose. For the fact is that the relation
between these two poems and Milton's First Prolusion is no more and
no less intimate than that between these poems and several of Milton's
other prolusions, or, for that matter, between these poems and the
whole tradition of academic paradox and debate. Something of the
same kind of wit, something of the same kind of intention, namely, to
show your wit, to show what you could do, is present both in the
poems and in the prolusions. Something, but only something. For, after
the abjurations with which each poem begins, the purely paradoxical or
hyperbolic element in Milton's poems ceases, if it is present at all, to
be felt as paradox or hyperbole. In this respect 'L'Allegro' and 'Il

Penseroso' differ greatly, not only from some of the outrageously and quite unseriously paradoxical poems of Donne, but even from such a poem as Marvell's 'The Garden'.

> No white nor red was ever seen
> So am'rous as this lovely green.

Throughout Marvell's praise of the garden we are delightfully aware of the element of hyperbole and paradox, whereas Milton's praise of the pleasures of mirth and of melancholy is, in comparison, as unhyperbolical as, let us say, Ben Jonson's Virgilian and Horatian praise of a country life in his epistle To Sir Robert Wroth.

Each of Milton's poems might almost be described as a Catalogue of Delights, a formula which relates them, not merely to the two poems of Fletcher and Strode, but also to Marlowe's 'Passionate Shepherd', Ralegh's reply thereto (both printed in *Englands Helicon*), and to the many imitations (including Donne's 'The Baite') which those two poems provoked. Todd, indeed, in his introductory remarks to 'L'Allegro', says that it has been observed (he does not say by whom) that the concluding lines of Marlowe's and Ralegh's poems,

> If these delights thy mind may move,
> Then live with me, and be my love,

'seem to have furnished Milton with the hint for the last lines both of his "Allegro" and "Penseroso"'.[2]

II

The subject of the two poems, then, is the contrast between the pleasures of mirth and the pleasures of melancholy, and they have some relation, though not, perhaps, a very close one, to a well-established academic and poetic tradition of witty and paradoxical debate. Let us now return to Dr Johnson's complaint that the contrast between the two poems and the two kinds of pleasure is not great enough, and to the question of what exactly Milton meant by melancholy.

'I know not', Johnson remarked, 'whether the characters are kept sufficiently apart. No mirth can, indeed, be found in his melancholy; but I am afraid that I always meet some melancholy in his mirth.' In a sense Johnson was right. He was aware of some apparent inconsistency, and it lies, I think, in a certain disparity between programme and performance, between what we are led to expect and what we actually get: that is to say, the melancholy abjured in the introductory stanza of 'L'Allegro' as

> loathed Melancholy
> Of *Cerberus*, and blackest midnight born,

is not the kind of melancholy which is invoked and of which the pleasures are described in 'Il Penseroso'; and the heart-easing mirth invoked at the beginning of 'L'Allegro', together with

> Jest and youthful Jollity,
> Quips and Cranks, and wanton Wiles,

and so forth, has only the very slightest connexion with the mood or moods whose pleasures are actually described in the course of the poem. The mood of 'L'Allegro' is not really the mood of Strode's lines against melancholy, although, as I have suggested, it was probably Fletcher's praise of melancholy and Strode's reply to it which suggested to Milton the idea of his two companion poems. Milton's two poems are less antithetical than Fletcher's and Strode's. The mood of Strode's poem,

> Returne my joyes and hither bring
> A heart not taught to speake but sing,
> A jolly spleen, an inward feast,
> A causelesse laugh without a jest,

and so forth, is indeed the mood of the opening lines of 'L'Allegro', of the invocation of 'heart-easing Mirth' and of 'Laughter holding both his sides'; but although Milton can abstractly approve of such a mood and abstractly personify it, he is, of course, quite incapable of evoking, with pleasure to himself and to his readers, a succession of scenes in all of which he shall appear laughing and holding both his sides, tripping on light fantastic toe, and otherwise joyfully jollificating. Therefore, as soon as the invocation is finished, as soon as personification gives place to exemplification, as soon as L'Allegro himself appears and proceeds to go through his round of day-time and evening pleasures, there is a very considerable sobering down. As Warton observed:

There is specifically no mirth in contemplating a fine landscape. And even his landscape, although it has flowery meads and flocks, wears a shade of pensiveness; and contains *russet* lawns, fallows *grey*, and *barren* mountains, overhung with *labouring* clouds. Its old turreted mansion peeping from the trees, awakens only a train of solemn and romantic, perhaps melancholy, reflection. Many a pensive man listens with delight to the milk-maid *singing blithe*, to the mower *whetting his scythe*, and to a distant peal of village bells. He chose such illustrations as minister matter for true poetry and genuine description. Even his most brilliant imagery is mellowed with the sober hues of philosophic meditation.[3]

And just as the exemplifications of cheerfulness in 'L'Allegro' are very different from the personifications of it, so too both the personifications and exemplifications of melancholy in 'Il Penseroso' have nothing in common with the 'loathed Melancholy' abjured at the beginning of 'L'Allegro', and much in common with the rather attractive, romantic, and luxurious melancholy exemplified in Fletcher's poem. Indeed, one may say that Strode, whose poem does not get beyond personifying various aspects of cheerfulness, suggested to Milton the idea of personi- fication, while Fletcher, who exemplifies what he means by melancholy

> Foutaine heads, and pathlesse Groves,
> Places which pale passion loves,

suggested to him the idea of exemplifying, as distinct from merely personifying, the two moods; although, when he actually got to work, Milton found that he could follow Fletcher more closely than he could follow Strode. He could, that is to say, amplify and diversify and sublimate Fletcher's exemplifications of melancholy, but he could not exemplify, as distinct from merely personifying, the boisterousness of Strode's reply. And exemplification rather than personification was to provide the main substance of his poems, if only because they were to be very much longer than the pair which suggested them.

Nevertheless, although the moods of 'L'Allegro' and 'Il Penseroso' are less sharply contrasted than in the poems of Fletcher and Strode, although it is only in the rhetorical introductory abjurations and in the personification of Mirth and her companions that anything of the originally crude antithesis appears, and although even Warton, a great admirer of these poems, agrees with Johnson in finding some mixture of melancholy in Milton's mirth, there still remains a contrast between the moods of the two poems which is both greater and subtler than has commonly been noticed, if not by readers, at any rate by critics. Perhaps I can best indicate the nature of this contrast by remarking that while L'Allegro's pleasures, though far from boisterous, nearly all have some admixture or suggestion of human society and are of the kind

which, in some degree, take one, as the saying is, out of oneself, the
pleasures described in 'Il Penseroso' are more solitary, more introspective, more purely the pleasures of reverie and of solitary contemplation
and imagination. L'Allegro, although he scarcely, perhaps, takes any
very active share in them, is still fairly continuously aware of the doings
of his fellow-men, and reflections of their activities and pleasures largely
determine and largely colour his moods. What would his morning walk
be without the sound of the huntsman's horn, the whistling ploughman,
the singing milkmaid, the scythe-whetting mower, and the counting
shepherds? Later he approaches the smoking cottage chimney of Thyrsis
and Corydon and closes his round of day-time pleasures among country-
dancers and story-tellers. His evening pleasures are essentially sociable:
tournaments, masques, and comedies. And even when he is alone he
looks around him with delighted attention and is taken out of himself
by what he sees: nibbling sheep, labouring clouds, daisy-pied meadows,
brooks and rivers, romantically embowered towers. The pleasures of
Il Penseroso are much more brooding and solitary. Indeed, only once is
there any suggestion of human society, when, at the very end of the
poem, he hears organ and choir in some cathedral or college chapel. He
begins his night (for apparently he does a good part of his sleeping by
day) with a stroll in some lonely wood, listening to the nightingale,
gazing at the wandering moon, hearing the distant curfew – sights and
sounds more likely to prolong than to interrupt his reverie. He then
sits alone by the glowing embers of his hearth and ascends to his lonely
tower, where he reads Plato, Greek tragedies (L'Allegro did not read,
but visited, comedies) and various romantic poems. When day comes
he again repairs to his wood to rest and dream by a brookside, and then,
after pacing the studious cloister, first encounters his fellow-beings at
divine service.

During the seventeenth century the word melancholy had many
different senses and shades of meaning. The noun, in what may be called
its strict or proper sense, denoted that dark and dangerous mental
disease of melancholia, produced partly by physical causes, such as lack
of exercise or ill-regulated diet, and partly by indulgence in certain
mental habits, which Burton describes and for which he suggests
remedies in his famous book.

Loathed Melancholy
Of *Cerberus* and blackest midnight born.

In Shakespeare the word nearly always denotes a disposition which is regarded as unpleasant, unfortunate, or deplorable: Viola's imaginary sister fell into a green and yellow melancholy, and Hamlet feared that the ghost might be a devil which, out of his weakness and his melancholy, was abusing him to damn him. And in Elizabethan usage generally the word denoted, if not the actual disease of melancholia, at any rate a mood of habitual sadness and depression, true though it be that the mood was often affected by persons with pretensions to superior refinement. It was, characteristically, during the more analytic and introspective seventeenth century that the word came to be used to denote a certain tender and pensive sadness which, at times perhaps not without some sense of guiltiness and of playing with fire, was regarded as positively agreeable. William Drummond, for example, declared in one of his madrigals that when his mistress wept

> A sweet Melancholie my Senses keepes;[4]

Fletcher declared that

> Nothing's so daintie sweet as lovely melancholy;

while Milton in '*Il Penseroso*' invokes 'divinest Melancholy', and in *Comus* (545) makes the Attendant Spirit describe himself as having been

> Wrapt in a pleasing fit of melancholy.

The history of the adjective is similar. Shakespeare's 'melancholy Jaques' is saturnine rather than sweetly pensive; when Capulet, after the discovery of the supposed death of Juliet, declares

> All things that are ordained festival
> Turn from their office to black funeral,

and speaks of 'melancholy bells' (IV v 86), he means sad, gloomy, dismal bells, and when Orlando in *As You Like It* exclaims to the banished Duke and his company

> But whate'er you are
> That in this desert inaccessible
> Under the shade of melancholy boughs
> Lose and neglect the creeping hours of time,

he means that he finds their situation gloomy and depressing, rather frightening, perhaps a little pathetic; certainly not that he finds it agreeably romantic. Nevertheless, some forty years later (8 October 1641) Evelyn thus described the royal park at Brussels:

> From hence we walked into the Parke, which for being intirely within the walls of the Citty is particularly remarkable; nor is it less pleasant than if in the most solitary recesses, so naturally is it furnish'd with whatever may render it agreeable, melancholy, and country-like.

In the early part of 1659 Anthony à Wood was taken by a friend to visit one Hannibal Baskervyle who inhabited 'a private and lone house in or neare Bagley Wood', 'an old house situated in a romancey place'. This Mr Baskervyle was very civil, 'but A. W. found him to be a melancholy and retir'd man'; nevertheless

> A. Wood afterwards frequented the house, especially in the time of his son Thomas Baskervyle, to refreshe his mind with a melancholy walke, and with the retiredness of the place.[5]

Thus, while Wood found the melancholy and retiredness of the elder Baskervyle rather depressing, he found the melancholy and retiredness of his grounds, with their 'romancey' situation, rather refreshing. And the fact that Wood calls the situation of the place where he took these refreshingly melancholy walks 'romancey' suggests that 'melancholy' might well have been added to those 'Four Words' of which Logan Pearsall Smith so delightfully and illuminatingly investigated the sense-history, and that, accordingly, the origin of romanticism, the romantic mood, and even of the romantic movement might have been taken yet a little further back. For it has often been remarked that something like a new taste had been formed when, shortly after 1650, the words 'romancy' and 'romantic' began to be commonly applied to scenes which recalled those in old romances, 'old castles, mountains and forests, pastoral plains, waste and solitary places'.[6] It is true that it is not until the eighteenth century that we hear, from Thomson, of a 'fine, romantic kind of melancholy',[7] but already in 1659 we find Wood enjoying a refreshing melancholy in a romancy place, and more than forty years before that Fletcher had discovered the sweetness of melancholy and of scenes where that sweetness could be most luxuriously savoured. It is appropriate that the romantic discovery of the sweetness of melancholy should have been made during the seventeenth century, when so many other important discoveries were made, and when so many characteristically modern movements, including, for all I know, the Romantic Movement, began. Fletcher, perhaps, was the first romantic. Donne was not of the movement, nor, I think, was Jonson, but Milton, the Milton of 'Il Penseroso', certainly was, and, as I shall insist in a moment, it is significant that the Wartons and Hurd and other unimpeachable eighteenth-century romantics, revolting, as school-children say, against the Age of Prose and Reason, should have con-tinually praised his 'romantic' scenes and descriptions.

Before leaving this topic of the kind of melancholy exemplified in 'Il Penseroso', I will notice a conjecture advanced by Thomas Warton in his edition of Milton's Shorter Poems, from which I have already quoted. Neglecting Fletcher and Strode, Warton believed that Milton's two poems had been suggested by a poem of Burton's:

> He seems to have borrowed the subject of *L'Allegro* and *Il Penseroso*, together with some particular thoughts, expressions, and rhymes, more especially the idea of a contrast between these two dispositions, from a forgotten poem prefixed to the first edition of Burton's *Anatomie of Melancholy*, entitled 'The author's abstract of Melancholy or a Dialogue between Pleasure and Pain'. Here Pain is Melancholy.[8]

Now although it seems to me more than likely that Milton knew both Burton's poem and Burton's book, and that he took some suggestions from both, I must insist that Burton's poem is not what Warton says it is. It is not really a dialogue between Pleasure and Pain, and certainly not a debate between Mirth and Melancholy, but a series of alternate representations of the pleasures and pains of melancholy in the serious Burtonian sense: of those oscillations between exaltation and dejection which attend the unrestrained indulgence of solitary imagination, and which, if not checked, may finally unhinge the mind. Here is a repre-sentative passage:

> When to my selfe I act and smile,
> With pleasing thoughts the time beguile;
> By a brooke side or wood so greene,
> Vnheard, vnsought for, or vnseene,
> A thousand pleasures doe me blesse,
> And crowne my soule with happinesse.
>   All my ioyes besides are folly,
>   None so sweete as Melancholy.
> When I lie, sit, or walke alone,
> I sigh, I grieue, making great moane.

> In a darke groue, or irkesome denne,
> With discontentes and Furies then,
> A thousand miseries at once,
> Mine heauy heart and soule ensconce.
> All my griefes to this are iolly,
> Nine so soure as Melancholy.*

Burton's poem might, in fact, be regarded as a series of alternate representations of Fletcher's 'sweetest Melancholy' and Milton's 'loathed Melancholy', that melancholy into which, as Burton insists, sweetest melancholy, if excessively indulged in, may easily turn. For Burton sweetest melancholy is a dangerous thing, and it is against such 'pleasing melancholy and vaine conceits' that, in his chapter 'Exercise rectified of Body and Minde', he recommends sight-seeing, recreation and study. I will quote some scattered sentences from the chapter, for it contains, as Warton observed, many parallels with Milton's poems.

> To walke amongst Orchards, Gardens, Bowers, and Arbors, artificiall Wildernesses, and greene thickets, Arches, Groues, Pooles, Fishponds, betwixt wood and water in a faire Meddowe, by a riuer side, to disport in some pleasant plaine, or runne vp a steepe hill, or sit in a shady seat, must needs bee a delectable recreation . . . To see some Pageant, or sight go by, as at Coronations, Weddings, and such like solemnities, to see an Embassadour or a Prince met, receaued, entertained with Masks, shews, fire-works, &c. . . . The Country hath it's recreations, the Citty it's seuerall Gymnicks and exercises, Maygames, Feasts, Wakes, & merry meetings to solace themselues . . . *Dancing, Singing, Masking, Mumming, Stage-playes*, howsoeuer they be heauily censured by some seuere *Catoes*, yet if opportunely and soberly used, may iustly be approued . . . To read, walke and see Mappes, Pictures, Statues, old Coynes of severall sorts in a fayre Gallery, artificiall perspectiue glasses, old reliques, Roman antiquities, variety of colors.[9]

Burton is here recommending to the man carried away with 'a pleasing melancholy and vaine conceits' various things that will 'take him out of himself', make him less introspective and more extravert. And if anyone positively insists on somehow bringing Burton into 'L'Allegro' and 'Il Penseroso', I think we might at least allow him to maintain that in 'L'Allegro' Milton has exemplified various pleasures and activities (many of them mentioned by Burton) which will correct the pleasing,

* I quote from the poem as it was first printed, in the third edition, 1628. Warton wrongly supposed that it had appeared in the first edition, 1621.

the sweetest, the divinest melancholy of 'Il Penseroso', and prevent it from turning into Melancholia. Not that Il Penseroso lives entirely in his own solitary imagination; he does, after all, spend a considerable time reading in his lonely tower and he regularly attends divine service. Even when Milton is most characteristically seventeenth century he nearly always is so with a difference. His divinest melancholy is less paradoxical than Fletcher's sweetest melancholy, less illicit, less a kind of secret indulgence. Milton, after all, identifies himself, at least to a considerable extent, with the two characters, and he just cannot imagine himself as indulging in any mood or pleasure that is at all reprehensible.

III

Having now seen more clearly what is the real nature of the contrast between the two poems and what Milton meant by melancholy, let us proceed to consider 'L'Allegro' and 'Il Penseroso' as descriptive poems.

It will be well to apply first the method of comparison and to decide in what sense they are not descriptive, and then to apply the method of analysis, and, proceeding from the more general to the more particular, to decide precisely in what sense they are. Let us begin with Warton's statement that they may be called 'the two first descriptive poems in the English language'. What Warton and his contemporaries meant by a descriptive poem was one where description was not merely incidental or illustrative but essential, a poem which existed purely for the sake of its descriptions, and whose descriptions were mainly of natural sights and sounds, not of individual human beings, though sometimes, perhaps, of typical human activities. Milton's poems, it is true, are not purely descriptive in this sense, since they are controlled by an idea, that of the exemplification of the pleasures appropriate to two contrasted but complementary moods; nevertheless we may be content without quibbling to regard them as examples of what is ordinarily meant by descriptive poetry.

Have they any predecessors? They are obviously different from, on the one hand, the purely topographical or guide-book description of Drayton's *Poly-Olbion* and, on the other hand, from the almost purely witty description of Donne's two verse-letters entitled 'The Storme' and 'The Calme'. The Donne who wrote these two poems may perhaps be regarded as the originator of a kind of descriptive, or professedly descriptive, poetry which became very popular during the seventeenth century, and of which the formula would seem to be: to how many other things, ideas, experiences can this particular experience, or this particular object in front of me, be related? The chief characteristic of this kind of poetry is the ingenious simile, and the poet is far less concerned with his professed subject, which may be almost completely indifferent to him, than with the ingenious things he can find to say about it, the number of apparently unlikely things and ideas to which he can somehow succeed in relating it. Clearly, 'L'Allegro' and 'Il Penseroso' are quite outside this tradition, although they do contain one or two ingenious similes. So far from being indifferent to what he is describing, Milton is pre-occupied with it, fascinated by it, in love with it. His two poems, then, are descriptive neither in the topographical manner of Drayton nor in the purely witty manner of Donne. Their only predecessors or proto-types are certain 'Catalogues of Delights' (if I may repeat my own phrase) and certain descriptive exemplifications of more or less romantic moods – Fletcher's lines on melancholy, Burton's poem prefixed to the *Anatomy*, some of the descriptions in Beaumont and Fletcher's plays, notably, perhaps, those of and by the wronged Aspasia in *The Maid's Tragedy*.

What, then, of their successors? How do they stand in relation to later poems which may be classified as descriptive? An interesting piece for comparison is that long and rather rambling poem on Appleton House which Marvell wrote sometime in 1651 or 1652, after, I cannot but think, he had bought and read Milton's 1645 volume. For 'Appleton House' stands somewhere between the purely witty manner of Donne and Milton's manner in 'L'Allegro' and 'Il Penseroso': Marvell is as witty and ingenious as Donne, but, like Milton, he is also in love with what he is describing:

> And now to the Abbyss I pass
> Of that unfathomable Grass,
> Where Men like Grashoppers appear,
> But Grashoppers are Gyants there:
> They, in there squeking Laugh, contemn
> Us as we walk more low then them:
> And, from the Precipices tall
> Of the green spir's, to us do call.
>
> To see Men through this Meadow Dive,
> We wonder how they rise alive,

> As, under Water, none does know
> Whether he fall through it or go.
> But, as the Marriners that sound,
> And show upon their head the Ground,
> They bring up Flow'rs so to be seen,
> And prove they've at the Bottom been.

Milton is obviously far less witty than Marvell, but, on the other hand, he is far wittier in the seventeenth-century sense than the almost professional nature poets of the eighteenth and nineteenth centuries. 'L'Allegro' and 'Il Penseroso' are not descriptive poetry in the sense in which Thomson's *Seasons*, or Wordsworth's *Poems on the Naming of Places*, or many famous things by Tennyson are descriptive poetry. Milton does not set out to give minute descriptions of natural scenes and natural objects, but to give precise descriptions, precise exemplifications, precise evocations of the pleasures appropriate to two contrasted moods. His outlines, the directions he gives to our imagination, are as precise and concise as possible, but he generally leaves us to fill in the visual detail for ourselves.

> Or let my Lamp at midnight hour,
> Be seen in some high lonely Towr –

that example will do as well as any: a *seen* lamp in a tower that is high and lonely. Whether the tower be old and grey, round or square, ruinous, ivy-mantled, moss-grown or lichenous, we may decide for ourselves. This very important distinction between precision of outline, or of imaginative direction, achieved mainly by the use of most carefully chosen adjectives, and minuteness of visual detail, is one that has been completely overlooked by Mr Eliot in perhaps the most unfortunate of all his writings on Milton:[10] after declaring that, for his purposes, the most important fact about Milton is his blindness, he there complains that 'the imagery in *L'Allegro* and *Il Penseroso* is all general', and that, among other things, the whistling ploughman is not individualized. Was Mr Eliot, I wonder, like Irving Babbitt, recoiling from what seemed to him a symptom of romanticism? For there can, I think, be little doubt that it was the essentially evocative nature of Milton's descriptions which led many of his eighteenth-century admirers to call them romantic. Thomas Warton, for example, in the Preface to his edition, sees in Milton's shorter poems 'fiction and fancy ... picturesque description and romantic imagery'. Consider, as a description that

would probably have seemed to Warton and his contemporaries
especially romantic, this from 'Il Penseroso':

> And missing thee, I walk unseen
> On the dry smooth-shaven Green,
> To behold the wandring Moon,
> Riding neer her highest noon,
> Like one that had bin led astray
> Through the Heav'ns wide pathles way;
> And oft, as if her head she bow'd,
> Stooping through a fleecy cloud.

What, especially the third of those couplets, could be more 'romantic'?
Shelley might almost have written it, the Shelley of 'Art thou pale for
weariness . . .?' It is true that Shelley dwells on the imagined loneliness
of the moon more lingeringly and emphatically than Milton, but the
two descriptions, the two ways of seeing it, even the two ways of saying
it, still remain strikingly similar. Critics have often complained of a lack
of mystery in *Paradise Lost*, but both there and in Milton's shorter poems
there is no lack of a suggestiveness that may not inappropriately be
called romantic. Milton is commonly regarded, and perhaps rightly, as
the most classical of our poets, and yet, as I have observed, we find many
eighteenth-century precursors of the so-called Romantic Revival continually praising what seem to them his romantic descriptions, his
romantic wildness, his romantic fancy. One could quite plausibly
maintain that the classical Milton is the most romantic of seventeenth-
century poets. One could also maintain that the official romantics (if I
may so describe them) tended to exploit and overemphasize what in
Milton remain elements in a balanced whole. The wandering moon and
the sound of the far-off curfew,

> Over some wide-water'd shoar,
> Swinging slow with sullen roar,

occupy only a few lines of 'Il Pensoroso', whereas with a full-blown
romantic each might well occupy a whole poem. We have already noticed
some interesting differences and resemblances between 'L'Allegro' and
'Il Penseroso', as descriptive poems, and Marvell's 'Appleton House':
compare them with those two indisputably beautiful and indisputably
romantic poems, Collins's 'Ode to Evening' and Keats's 'Ode to
Autumn'. In comparison with Milton, Collins and Keats (I do not say
it in any pejorative sense) are much more monotonous, much more

willing to linger and luxuriate in single images and single moods. I will
leave the subject with a pregnant observation of W. P. Ker's: 'Romance
is often near its best with authors who are not thinking about it, or who
think other things more important.'[11]

The precisely evocative descriptions in these two poems sometimes
have a touch (it is no more) of that wit which is still popularly and, as it
seems to me, inappropriately, termed 'metaphysical'.

> Towers and Battlements it sees
> Boosom'd high in tufted Trees,
> Wher perhaps som beauty lies,
> The Cynosure of neighbouring eyes.

Here there is a truly remarkable combination of romantic suggestiveness
(what precision and concentration in that second line, where every
word counts!), of characteristically seventeenth-century wit, and of
characteristically Miltonic scholarship. The Cynosure is the Dog's Tail
or Lesser Bear, the star by which the Phoenician sailors steered, and the
wit, the conceit, is reminiscent of Marvell, although the word itself, like
the epithet Hippotades for Aeolus in 'Lycidas', is Miltonically recondite.
There are a few other examples of such conceits in these poems. The
description of sunrise in 'L'Allegro':

> Right against the Eastern gate,
> Where the great Sun begins his state,
> Roab'd in flames, and Amber light,
> The clouds in thousand Liveries dight.

The sun, that is to say, begins his royal progress or 'state' from the
eastern gate, attended by courtier-like clouds in robes of a thousand
different colours. This, though far more appropriate and decorous, has
perhaps some affinity with the description of

> the Sun in bed
> Curtain'd with cloudy red,
> Pillowing his chin upon an Orient wave

in the Nativity Ode, a conceit in the manner of Sylvester or of Crashaw
rather than of Donne or Marvell. For what distinguishes Crashaw's
conceits from Donne's and from those of many of Donne's imitators is
their picturesqueness, their bright visual images. Indeed, the picturesqueness is often more striking than the ingenuity, although the ingenuity,

the wit, prevents the images from being just conventionally pretty.
Todd compares with Milton's image of the sun beginning his state some
lines from a poem in Drummond's *Flowres of Sion* (1623). Drummond
is freely translating from a poem of Sannazaro's, and in this passage he
greatly elaborates his original. Sannazaro merely says:

> E se vedendo il Sol dall' Oriente
> Venir di' rai vestito,

'and if, seeing the sun from the East come clad with rays' – a passage
which Drummond expands and elaborates as follows:

> If, when farre in the East yee doe behold
> Foorth from his Christall Bed the Sunne to rise,
> With rosie Robes and Crowne of flaming Gold.[12]

From Petrarch onwards Italian poetry, of which Drummond was a
devoted admirer and imitator, abounds with such images, and so too
does Spenser's. It is such essentially picturesque, Italianate, or Spenserian
imagery that Crashaw's wit generally combines and permeates. And
when such imagery (quite unlike Donne's) is presented in some
strikingly ingenious or epigrammatic or antithetical way we call it a
conceit, or even (inappropriately, as I think) metaphysical. What exactly
is the difference between a characteristically Italianate or Spenserian
personification and a characteristic early seventeenth-century conceit?
Is it a difference of kind, or merely one of degree? Perhaps it is like the
point where day passes into night, of which Burke said that, although no
one could define it exactly, everyone knew when it had taken place.
The chief difference between Milton's personification of the sun and
Drummond's is that in Milton's the implied comparison of the sun to an
earthly monarch is several degrees more particularized. Drummond's
sun only resembles an earthly monarch in having robes and a crown.
Earthly monarchs do not rise from crystal beds. In other words, in
Drummond's personification the resemblance is not more insisted upon
than the difference. But Milton's sun resembles an earthly monarch in
setting out on a progress and in being attended by courtier-like clouds,
although it is true that these detailed resemblances are rather fleetingly
suggested than insisted upon and, as it were, underlined, as they might
have been by Cowley in the *Davideis*. Nevertheless, there is in Milton's
personification an ingenuity, a wit, a quaintness (as we might be
inclined to call it) which there is not in Drummond's, or in the nine-

teenth Psalm, where the sun 'is as a bridegroom coming out of his
chamber, and rejoiceth as a strong man to run a race', or in Spenser's
famous personification which that passage in the nineteenth Psalm
partly suggested:

> At length the golden oriental gate
> Of greatest heaven gan to open faire;
> And Phoebus, fresh as bridegroome to his mate,
> Came dancing forth, shaking his deawy haire.[13]

What needs to be insisted upon is that the ingenious comparison, which,
although it is only one element, and by no means the most important
one, in Donne's poetry, has so often been regarded as *the* characteristic
of so-called metaphysical poetry in general, can, and often does, take as
its substance or subject-matter precisely that picturesque, Italianate,
Spenserian, or, as one might be inclined to say, typically Elizabethan
imagery which Donne seems to have deliberately rejected. Such witty
or ingenious combinations of traditional and picturesque imagery are
very frequent in certain sixteenth- and seventeenth-century Italian poets,
Guarini, Marino, and the rest, poets whom Crashaw seems to have
admired; and in Milton's early poems the kind of ingenuity so assi-
duously cultivated by most of his academic contemporaries is sometimes applied, not always successfully, to his predominantly Spenserian
or Italianate imagery. Wit, though, except in the wide sense, was never
more than a very occasional intruder into Milton's poetry. It is above all
in Marvell, a poet in some respects even more eclectic than Milton, that
we may observe how wit and ingenuity can be combined in all manner
of ways with traditional imagery, traditional forms, and traditional
themes. Too much tidy-mindedness and love of classification have
prevented readers from seeing in what a variety of ways the manners of
Spenser, of Jonson, and of Donne, poets commonly regarded as the
founders of distinct schools, could be combined.

While, then, 'The Cynosure of neighbouring eyes' is the kind of
conceit one might almost expect to find in Marvell, that about the sun
beginning his state is more like what one might expect to find in
Sylvester or Crashaw. Much more like Marvell is the astrological
metaphor in

> store of Ladies, whose bright eies
> Rain influence, and judge the prize
> Of Wit, or Arms.

Here too, though, the wit is no more than the lightest of flashes, and
how much more appropriately might this passage, like so many others
in these poems, be called an evocation rather than a description! There
are a few other flashes or gleams of this ingenious and surprising kind of
wit that was so popular with many of Milton's contemporaries, but in
every case the ingenious or surprising comparison is merely implied,
never elaborated or insisted upon. There is the Platonic conceit, as one
might call it, in

> Untwisting all the chains that ty
> The hidden soul of harmony,

where the soul of harmony is conceived of as a kind of sleeping beauty,
a mere potentiality, first actualised, awakened into life, by the singer and
the instruments. There is some likeness between this conceit and a very
famous one at the beginning of Michelangelo's sixteenth sonnet:

> Si come nella penna e nell' inchiostro
> È l'alto e basso e l'mediocre stile,
> E ne' marmi l'imagin ricca e vile,
> Secondo che 'l sa trar l'ingenio nostro –

As in pen and ink is the high and the low and the middle style, and as in
marble the image rich or mean according as our genius is able to extract it.

There is the almost Shakespearean conceit in

> While the Cock with lively din,
> Scatters the rear of darkness thin

– scatters, that is, like a routed army the last thin wreaths of dark mist
that linger after sunrise. The praise of Melancholy's blackness in 'Il
Penseroso' has something, if only a little, in common with many
paradoxical praises of dark or 'black' beauty by seventeenth-century
poets,[14] and even with Donne's praise (greatly wanting in propriety and
decorum though, for the most part, it is) of the 'autumnal' beauty of Mrs
Herbert:

> Hail divinest Melancholy,
> Whose Saintly visage is too bright
> To hit the Sense of human sight;
> And therefore to our weaker view
> Ore laid with black staid Wisdoms hue.

> Black, but such as in esteem,
> Prince *Memnons* sister might beseem,
> Or that starr'd *Ethiope* Queen that strove
> To set her beauties praise above
> The Sea Nymphs, and their powers offended.

One may also, perhaps, recall one of the items in Sir Thomas Browne's 'Musaeum Clausum', that imaginary and characteristic descriptive catalogue of 'some remarkable Books, Antiquities, Pictures and Rarities of several kinds, scarce or never seen by any man now living':

> a fair English Lady drawn *Al Negro*, or in the Aethiopian hue excelling the original White and Red Beauty, with this Subscription,

> *sed quandam volo nocte Nigriorem.*[15]

In his later exhortation to Melancholy,

> There held in holy passion still,
> Forget thy self to Marble,

Milton is using in what one might almost call a normal and Petrarchan manner a conceit which seems ultimately to derive from Petrarch's declaration, in sonnet cxxxi, that the pure ivory of Laura's face turns to marble whoever gazes at it from anear. Thomas Tomkyns, in a comedy acted before King James at Trinity College Cambridge, used this conceit in the simple Petrarchan manner when he made a character exclaim:

> Marvaile thy selfe to Marble at these engines;[16]

but William Browne exercised his ingenuity upon it, and in the second stanza of his Epitaph on the Countess of Pembroke declared that grief would transform some future reader of his lines not merely into a marble statue but into a marble tomb; and Milton himself, in his lines on Shakespeare, had been still more elaborately ingenious when he declared that Shakespeare possessed in his readers an everlasting funeral monument, or rather, forest of monuments, since admiration for him transformed each of them into the likeness of a marble statue, within which, as in a marble tomb, his lines were buried. By the time he came to write 'L'Allegro' and 'Il Penseroso' Milton had left this kind of extravagance behind him. In comparison with that of many of his contemporaries, his wit is now as unextravagant, as decorous, as Pope's, when (no doubt with this passage in 'Il Penseroso' in mind) he makes Eloisa exclaim

> Tho' cold like you, unmov'd, and silent grown,
> I have not yet forgot my self to stone.

In every one of these passages the wit, the ingenuity, is strictly subordinated to the purpose of illuminating or sharpening the particular delight Milton is evoking, just as each delight is dwelt upon not a line longer than his conception of his subject and the plan of his poem require. We never feel that any of these not very extreme examples of ingenuity is there merely *because* it is ingenious. Indeed, the strict *decorum* which in these two poems Milton observes even in his wit seems to me one of the strongest arguments for assuming that they were written during the Horton period, for several times in his Cambridge poems we find him elaborating conceits in the inappropriate and indecorous manner of his academic contemporaries.

IV

In the introduction to 'Il Penseroso', which is largely an appropriation and transformation of phrases in the description of the Cave of Sleep in Sylvester's Du Bartas, one might regard 'The fickle Pensioners of *Morpheus* train' as a conceit. Elizabeth, like Henry VIII, had a bodyguard of tall, handsome young men called pensioners, to whom Mrs Quickly alludes in *The Merry Wives of Windsor* (II ii 79): 'And yet there has been earls, nay, which is more, pensioners'. The only figurative use of the word before Milton recorded by the Oxford Dictionary is in *A Midsummer Night's Dream* (II i 10): 'The cowslips tall her pensioners be'. This is by no means the only place in these two poems where Milton is indebted to 'sweetest *Sheakespear* fancies childe'. The 'fresh-blown Roses washt in dew' at the beginning of 'L'Allegro' were almost certainly suggested by Petruchio's

> Say that she frown, I'll say she looks as clear
> As morning roses newly wash'd with dew

in *The Taming of the Shrew* (II i 173–4). The 'dappled dawn' in line 44 was probably suggested by

> And look! the gentle day . . .
> Dapples the drowsy east with spots of gray

in *Much Ado About Nothing* (v iii 25); and the 'nibling flocks' in line 72 by 'The turfy mountains where live nibbling sheep' in *The Tempest* (IV i 62). The 'Chequer'd shade' in 'Dancing in the Chequer'd shade' almost certainly owes something to the lines which so incongruously appear in Queen Tamora's seductive speech to Aaron the Moor in *Titus Andronicus* (II iii 14–15):

> The green leaves quiver with the cooling wind
> And make a chequer'd shadow on the ground.

Only twice more did Shakespeare use the verb *chequer*, and then still only in its participial forms: the present participle in *Romeo and Juliet* (II iii 2), 'Chequering the eastern clouds with streaks of light', and the past participle once again, this time in a context with which numerous contemporary parallels could be produced, in *Venus and Adonis* (1168), 'A purple flower sprang up, chequer'd with white'. He was, I think, the first to describe, and perhaps also, in what might be called the Wordsworthian sense, to notice, the pattern made by sunlight and shadow on the grass beneath trees. Of the many writers who have described it since, most, I believe, consciously or unconsciously, have used the word which he used, which Milton used after him, and which Pope used in 'Windsor Forest':

> Here waving groves a chequer'd scene display,
> And part admit, and part exclude the day.

How many later poets Shakespeare taught not merely to write but to see! Of the following lines in 'Il Penseroso',

> Far from all resort of mirth,
> Save the Cricket on the hearth,

Warton remarked that

Shakespeare, the universal and accurate observer of real Nature, was the first who introduced the crying of the cricket, and with the finest effect, into poetry.

He was thinking of a famous scene in *Macbeth*:

> 'I have done the deed. Didst thou not hear a voice?'
> 'I heard the owl scream and the crickets cry.'

Dr Johnson said of Milton:

He saw Nature, as Dryden expresses it, *through the spectacles of books*; and on most occasions calls learning to his assistance.

However that may be, it is certainly true that when in these poems there appears in Milton's precise evocations (evocations rather than descriptions) some more than usually arresting detail, it will often be found that he is looking at nature through the eyes and through the language of Shakespeare.

There is, though, at least one example of what Wordsworth would have called a new image from external nature for which Milton does not seem to have been indebted either to Shakespeare or to anyone else – in that passage where he declares that, after one of his studious vigils, he would have dawn ushered in with a shower,

> Ending on the russling Leaves,
> With minute drops from off the Eaves.

'Minute drops', drops, that is to say, falling at intervals of a minute, a phrase formed on the analogy of minute-gun, minute-bell, and so forth, is a precise expression of a hitherto unrecorded phenomenon which is not unworthy of the wild woodnote warbler himself. (That famous phrase, by the way, seems, as Todd observed, to be a free translation of one in Tasso's *Gerusalemme Liberata* – VII 6 – where Erminia hears a sound

> di pastorali accenti
> Misto, e di boscareccie inculte avene
>   commingled
> Of shepherd accents and rude woodland reeds.)

'Minute drops', both as a phrase and as an observation, is original, although it is possible that in admitting into his catalogue of delights that of listening to the sound of rain upon one's roof Milton may, as Todd suggested, have been remembering a fragment of Sophocles quoted by Cicero in one of his letters to Atticus (II vii):

> I had grown weary of piloting the state even while I was allowed to do so. Now, though, that I have been turned out of the boat, and have not abandoned the tiller but had it snatched out of my hands, my desire is to watch their shipwreck from the shore; my desire, as your friend Sophocles says, is
>
> > beneath my roof
> > To hear with drowsing mind the frequent drop.*

But to return to Shakespeare: Milton, like so many of his predecessors

*πυκνᾶς ἀκούειν ψεκάδος εὐδούσῃ φρενί.

and contemporaries, was indebted to him not merely for new images from external nature but for his fairy-lore. In his notes on the passage in 'L'Allegro' about Mab and Robin Goodfellow, Warton prefaces his numerous illustrations with the remark that 'All this is a part of the pastoral imagery which now prevailed in our poetry.' He might have added that it was a part which came to prevail through the example of Shakespeare, for Shakespeare in *A Midsummer Night's Dream* seems to have been the first to exploit the poetic possibilities of popular superstition, seems, in fact, to have started a new fashion, in which he was soon followed by Ben Jonson (*The Satyr*, 1603), William Browne, Drayton (*Nimphidia*), Herrick ('Oberon's Chapel', 'Oberon's Feast', 'Oberon's Palace', etc.), and many others.

This, though, is by no means the end of Milton's indebtedness to Shakespeare, both here and elsewhere. Shakespeare taught him not merely to see but to say, and even in passages of a much more general and figurative kind we often find him appropriating Shakespeare's diction – almost, I might say, his 'poetic diction'.

Milton's indebtedness to Shakespeare's diction is sometimes direct and sometimes indirect: sometimes, that is, he appropriates Shakespearean phrases without, or with only slight, modification; sometimes, especially in personifications, he uses phrases and images which, although one cannot positively assert that they *must* have been suggested by particular passages in Shakespeare, are yet thoroughly Shakespearean and without Shakespeare's example, would almost certainly have been different. 'Weeds of Peace' in 'L'Allegro',

> Where throngs of Knights and Barons bold,
> In weeds of Peace high triumphs hold,

is from *Troilus and Cressida* (III iii 239): 'To see great Hector in his weeds of peace.' 'Hit the Sense' in 'Il Penseroso',

> Whose Saintly visage is too bright
> To hit the Sense of human sight,

is from *Antony and Cleopatra* (II iii 216–17):

> From the barge
> A strange invisible perfume hits the sense.

'Civil-suited Morn' in 'Il Penseroso' is almost certainly a re-combination of epithets which Shakespeare in *Romeo and Juliet* (IV ii 10–11) had applied to night:

> Come, civil night,
> Thou sober-suited matron, all in black.

But Milton was also, I think, though less directly, indebted to that same speech of Juliet's, as well as to the general imagery of the play, when in 'Il Penseroso' he wrote of Philomel

> Smoothing the rugged brow of night.

He was also very probably, and, at first sight, more deeply indebted, as Todd suggested, to some lines in Spenser's sonnet to Sir Christopher Hatton, prefixed to *The Faerie Queene*:

> So you, great Lord, that with your counsell sway
> The burdeine of this kingdom mightily,
> With like delights sometimes may eke delay
> The rugged brow of carefull Policy,

where the obsolete verb *delay* (derived, unlike the verb meaning 'retard', 'defer', from *dis-ligare*, unbind) means to smooth. Nevertheless, although the diction here is partly Spenserian, it is also partly Shakespearean, and the image itself is as characteristically Sheakespearean as that in Comus's description of the Lady's singing:

> How sweetly did they float upon the wings
> Of Silence, through the empty-vaulted night
> At every fall smoothing the Raven doune
> Of darkness till it smil'd –

a passage where, as Miss Ethel Seaton has lately demonstrated, 'from many lines and images in *Romeo and Juliet* Milton has woven a fresh pattern of meaning and melody'.[17]

There are at least three other places in these poems where Milton seems to have combined the diction of Shakespeare with that of other Elizabethans.

> Com, and trip it as you go
> On the light fantastick toe

– in these lines it is hard not to suppose that the phrase 'Come, and trip it' and the rhyme 'go – toe' are recollections, or even deliberate imitations, of Ariel's

> Before you can say 'come' and 'go'
> And breathe twice and cry 'so, so',
> Each one, tripping on his toe,
> Will be here with mop and mow,

just as it is also hard not to suppose that the combination 'light fantastick',
both here and in *Comus*,

> Com, knit hands, and beat the ground,
> In a light fantastick round,

was not remembered, or imitated, from Drayton's *Nimphidia*, 'My
pretty light fantastick maid'. Similarly, in the 'Meadows trim with
Daisies pide' of 'L'Allegro', it would surely have been impossible for
Milton or any other poet to write of 'Daisies pide' without reminding
his readers of Shakespeare's famous song, even if the phrase had occurred
to him quite spontaneously; nevertheless, it is interesting to learn from
Todd that the phrase 'trim meadow' actually occurs in Bartholomew
Yong's translation of Boccaccio's *Amorous Fiametta* (1587): 'I went
singing vp and downe in this pleasant and trym meadowe', and it is
difficult to suppose that *both* phrases could have come to Milton, as
children say, 'out of his own head'. In 'Hide me from Day's garish eie'
Milton seems to have been recollecting both Juliet's exclamation that
the 'starred' Romeo

> will make the face of heaven so fine
> That all the world will be in love with night,
> And pay no worship to the garish sun

and, as Todd suggested, the phrase 'a woman's garish eye' from Barnaby
Riche's *Adventures of Simonides* (1584). (Examples of such phrases as 'the
great eye of heaven', 'the heaven's bright eye', 'day's glorious eye' in
Spenser, the Elizabethan Song-Books, Drayton, Browne, Shakespeare,
Sylvester, etc., are too numerous to mention.)

v

For both here and elsewhere Milton reveals a very considerable
indebtedness, not merely to the diction of Shakespeare, but to that of
many other sixteenth- and seventeenth-century poets, some of them
very minor ones. Some of his most memorable phrases are often
appropriations, with certain additions and modifications of his own, of
what were almost clichés. Examples are so numerous that it is hard to
suppose that it can have been a matter of mere memory, conscious or
unconscious. Milton's 'industrious and select reading' embraced, one
must assume, English as well as classical and Italian poets, and almost

certainly demanded the companionship of a notebook (would it had
been preserved!) into which he copied any passage or phrase, any
'elegances or flowers of speech', which happened to take his fancy and
of which he felt that he might at some time be able to make good use
himself. He had been taught to write Latin verse with the aid of a *Gradus*
and a *Flores Poetarum*, and even after he had become able to dispense
with such aids he remained continuously careful of Virgilian and
Ovidian precedent. When he turned to English poetry he wrote it on,
so to speak, the same principles as those on which he had written his
Latin poetry. He sometimes complied with the contemporary academic
taste for the ingenious comparison, but it would no more have occurred
to him to cultivate in his English poetry that out-of-one's-own-head
kind of originality which Carew praised in Donne than it would have
occurred to him to try to write Latin poetry as though no one had ever
written it before. The only difference was that, while in Latin poetry,
'best example' was not a matter of dispute, in English poetry it was a
matter upon which Milton had to decide.

As an example of what I mean by the appropriation and transformation (whether by addition, modification, or context) of phrases that
were almost clichés, I will mention 'L'Allegro's 'bucksom, blith, and
debonair'. That *buxom* and *blithe* had been keeping company for some
considerable time is suggested by their appearance in the slightly ludicrous context of Gower's Prologue to the first act of *Pericles*:

> This king unto him took a fere,
> Who died and left a female heir,
> So buxom, blithe, and full of face,
> As heaven had lent her all his grace.

It also seems possible that *buxom* and *debonair* may long have been
accustomed to hunt in couples, for in James Bell's *Answer Apologetical
to Hierome Osorius*, 1581 (quoted by *O.E.D.*) we find: 'The Consuls
should . . . sweare faythfully to become bonnaire and buxome to the
Pope', although it is true that *buxom* is here used in the more restricted
sense of 'obedient'. At any rate, when Milton's Cambridge contemporary, Thomas Randolph of Trinity, writes in his comedy of *Aristippus*
(1630)

> A bowl of wine is wondrous boon cheer,
> To make one blithe, buxome, and deboneer,

it does not seem absolutely necessary to assume that either he must have been borrowing from Milton or Milton from him. If one of them was borrowing, it is rather more likely to have been Milton, who, as his manner was, had entered the phrase in his notebook; but it seems possible that each of them, quite independently, was, as it were, telescoping two time-hallowed and traditional phrases. The point is, though, that but for Milton the phrase (or combination of two phrases), however often it had been used by earlier poets, would have died a natural death. The mere words themselves might well have appeared together in a line in one of those painfully undistinguished poems in Poulter's Measure which make up the greater part of *Tottel's Miscellany*, and there they would have been as unlikely to arrest the attention of any but philologists or lexicographers as in the line from Randolph's *Aristippus*. Milton, by means of context and rhythm, has conferred upon them a modest immortality: in their place in his poem they have struck, and will long continue to strike, most readers as being exquisitely original and right.

One might say almost the same of

> Com pensive Nun, devout and pure,
> Sober, steadfast, and demure.

The combination 'sober and demure' seems to have been almost as much of a fixed phrase as were 'fair and free' and the like in those metrical romances parodied by Chaucer in 'Sir Thopas': in Skelton's 'Philip Sparrow' we have

> Goodly Mistress Jane,
> Sober, demure Diane;[18]

in the old *Chronicle History of King Leir* Ragan says of Cordella:

> Besides, she is so nice and so demure;
> So sober, courteous, modest, and precise;[19]

and in the Catholic devotional manual *Partheneia Sacra* (1633, p. 209) occurs the invocation 'most sober and demure Virgin'. Here again by means of rhythm and context Milton has transmuted copper currency into gold. And when I say 'by means of context', I mean very largely that, because of the extreme economy and *decorum* which Milton observes in these two poems, every detail receives the maximum emphasis and produces the maximum effect: everything stands out clearly, nothing gets lost in the crowd.

The line 'Nods, and Becks, and Wreathed Smiles', which has

probably struck most readers as delightfully original (as indeed, in the most valuable sense, it is), seems to have been compounded from a ballad-like translation of a passage from Musaeus's *Hero and Leander* in Burton's *Anatomy of Melancholy*:

> With becks and nods, he first beganne
> To try the winches minde,
> With becks and nods and smiles againe,
> An answere he did finde.[20]

The exquisite use of the verb *ride* in

> To behold the wandring Moon,
> Riding near her highest noon,

may well have been inspired, as Todd suggested, by a passage in Archbishop Parker's translation of *The Whole Psalter* (?1567, p. 199):

> Sweet peace shalbe on every side,
> As long as moone her sphere doth ryde.[21]

Poets who had used such phrases before him did not, one might say, know what to do with them; they fumbled, they dropped their catches. Milton picked them up, and phrases which might otherwise have quietly disappeared from the language are now among the most memorable in these two poems – or rather, perhaps I should say, as memorable as any, since the distinction of 'L'Allegro' and 'Il Penseroso' is that nearly all their phrases are memorable. Nowhere do we find such striking confirmation of that hard saying:

> Unto every one that hath shall be given, and he shall have abundance: but from him that hath not shall be taken away even that which he hath.

VI

At least twice in these poems not just a phrase or a metaphor but an extended passage seems to have been suggested to Milton by something he had remembered (or transcribed into his notebook) from earlier poets. In *Britannia's Pastorals* (1616) William Browne, with a touch of epigrammatic wit, had written of Spenser:

> He sung the heroicke nights of fairery land
> In lines so eloquent, of such command;

> That had the Thracian plaid but half so well
> He had not left Eurydice in Hell (II i 991–4).

It was perhaps the possibility he saw of exquisitely refining and pointing this touch of epigrammatic wit which led Milton to bring Orpheus and Eurydice into the last lines of '*L'Allegro*', and to express the wish that from the marriage of Lydian airs and immortal verse he might hear such strains as would move even Orpheus in Elysium to listen

> and hear
> Such strains as would have won the ear
> Of *Pluto*, to have quite set free
> His half regain'd *Eurydice*.

Nowhere else in these poems is Milton's power of compressed statement so brilliantly and astonishingly revealed as in the last two lines of this passage. 'Quite set free' – that is, without any conditions, since, as it was, Orpheus only 'half-regained' her, regained her subject to the condition of not looking back until they had reached the upper world.* The monosyllables 'quite' and 'half' are not only unimprovably and magisterially right, but each is so placed in its line that it receives the maximum emphasis and performs the maximum amount of work. One might almost say that the 'wit' which so many of his contemporaries expended upon the devising of ingenious similes, Milton came more and more to spend upon the rightness and economy of his choice of words. Most of the poets he borrowed from habitually used far too many words, and when they did hit upon a good phrase or a good idea its potential energy was nearly always damped or dissipated by an undistinguished context.

The other example of such extended imitation (or transmutation) is less remarkable. Drayton had written in *The Owle* (1604 and 1619, lines 117–21),

> See the small brookes as through their Groves they travell . . .
> With the smooth cadence of their murmuring.
> Each Bee with Honey on her laden thye.

It was almost certainly with these lines in his memory (or in his notebook) that Milton begged Melancholy to hide him from day's garish eye by some shady brook,

---

* Milton then reintroduced Orpheus and Eurydice into what may be called the corresponding place in '*Il Penseroso*', 105–8.

> While the Bee with Honied thie,
> That at her flowry work doth sing,
> And the Waters murmuring
> With such consort as they keep,
> Entice the dewy-feather'd Sleep★

'Flowry work' is the translation of a phrase (*laboris floriferi*) from Lucan's *Pharsalia* (IX 289–90), in a description of how bees, at the sound of beaten brass,

> Attonitae posuere fugam, studiumque laboris
> Floriferi repetunt et sparsi mellis amorem.

In his translation (1627) Thomas May rendered it as 'flow'ry taskes', a phrase which Milton may possibly have remembered and improved upon. Such periphrases – 'watery plain', 'heavenly round', 'finny tribe', 'feathered choir', etc. – which are still popularly supposed to constitute almost the sum total of 'poetic diction' and to have been introduced by Pope, are very numerous in the work of the seventeenth-century translators, from Sylvester's Du Bartas onwards. They are generally translations of more or less equivalent Latin phrases, but where he speaks in 'L'Allegro' of the lubber fiend's 'hairy strength', Milton seems to have coined one of his own.

But just as such periphrases constitute only a small and rather specialised portion of what may properly be called poetic diction, they also constitute only a small portion of Milton's Latinisms, of those phrases which he has either adapted directly from Latin authors or into which, although they had been used by his English predecessors, he has re-injected some of their original virtue. There are two very notable examples in four consecutive lines of 'L'Allegro':

> And ever against eating Cares,
> Lap me in soft *Lydian* Aires,
> Married to immortal verse
> Such as the meeting soul may pierce.

'Eating cares' is a translation of the phrase *edaces curae*, which occurs several times in Horace's Odes, e.g. II xi: 'Dissipat Euhius curas edaces'.

★ 'Dewy-feather'd' is but one of the dozens of compound epithets scattered through his shorter poems which Milton seems to have coined. Both Spenser and Shakespeare use a fair number of such epithets, and Sidney abounds with them, both in the *Arcadia* and in his poems. Milton, like Sidney, seems to have been deliberately trying to introduce into English one of the beauties of Greek.

'Meeting', in the phrase 'meeting soul', is an anglicization of Latin *obvius*, in the sense of 'coming forward in response or welcome', as in Virgil, *Aeneid* I 314, 'cui mater media sese tulit obvia silva', 'to whom in the midst of the forest rose meetingly his mother'. The only pre-Miltonic example cited by *O.E.D.* is from Udall's translation of Erasmus's *Paraphrase upon the First Epistle to Timothy*, 1548, where the phrase *obviis, ut aiunt, ulnis amplectendum* is rendered 'to be embraced (as they saye) with meeting armes'. Nevertheless, it would seem that by Milton's time the word had become, and for some time remained, quite current English: Saltmarshe, 1639, has 'Be not too meeting, and seem not too hasty in accepting graces and favours', and South in a sermon speaks of 'all the meeting readiness of appetite and desire'. Dr Johnson declared that both in prose and verse Milton had 'formed his style by a perverse and pedantick principle', and that he was 'desirous to use English words with a foreign idiom'; very often, though, investigation will reveal that what seems Latin or 'foreign' idiom now was good English idiom at the time when Milton wrote, although it is true that, by means of context and emphasis, he not infrequently injected into such Latinate phrases a new dose of their original virtue. 'Decent' in '*Il Penseroso*' is an excellent example:

> And sable stole of *Cipres* Lawn
> Over thy decent shoulders drawn.

Latin *decens* means either 'seemly' or 'becoming', sometimes both, and the word 'decent' was similarly used by Milton's predecessors and contemporaries. Here, though, by means of context and emphasis, he has contrived to give it a depth of meaning such as Horace often achieves: Odes III xxviii (Europa speaking): 'antequam turpis macies decentis/ occupet malas' ('Before hideous wasting seizes upon my comely cheeks'); or I iv: 'iunctaeque Nymphis Gratiae decentes'; or IV i: 'namque et nobilis et decens' ('a youth noble and comely'); or IV xiii: 'quo fugit Venus, heu, quove color? decens/ quo motus?' ('Whither, alas, has fled thy grace, whither thy bloom? Whither thy decent carriage?') Collins, undoubtedly imitating Milton, used the same word to achieve precisely the same effect in the 'Ode to Simplicity' (where he has also borrowed the phrase 'meeting soul'):

> Thou, who with Hermit Heart
> Disdain'st the Wealth of Art,

And Gauds, and pageant Weeds, and trailing Pall:
But com'st a decent Maid
In *Attic* Robe array'd,
O chaste unboastful Nymph, to Thee I call!

Neither here nor elsewhere in these two poems is there anything perverse or pedantic, odd or eccentric, startling or stunning about Milton's 'originality', which in almost every one of its manifestations consists simply in doing better, more economically, more tellingly, things which other poets had done, or had tried to do, before. All his materials, one might almost say, lay ready to his hand, and his whole art and power consists in his judicious selection and combination of them. The observance of *decorum*, the subordination of the parts to the whole, the placing of words in a line, of lines in a passage, of passages in a poem – nowhere, perhaps, is that sheer craftsmanship which is the foundation of all great poetry so apparent as in 'L'Allegro' and 'Il Penseroso'. Almost everything that is commonly understood by 'originality', almost everything that Carew meant when he praised the originality of Donne, is missing: Milton's originality in these two poems consists almost entirely in his manipulation and craftsmanship – in his style, which, 'by certain vital signs it had, was likely to live'.

NOTES

1. Published by the English Association, July 1932, and reprinted in *The Miltonic Setting* (1938). Dr Tillyard believed that the two poems had been written in the summer of 1631, during Milton's last Long Vacation. More recently Mr F. W. Bateson – *English Poetry* (1950) pp. 155–6 – has argued (unconvincingly, as it seems to me) in favour of a still earlier date, and would persuade us that the two poems preceded the Nativity Ode and were written during the late summer or autumn of 1629.
2. *Poetical Works of John Milton*, ed. H. J. Todd (2nd ed. 1809) VI 69.
3. *Poems upon Several Occasions by John Milton*, ed. T. Warton (2nd ed. 1791) p. 97.
4. *Poetical Works*, ed. L. E. Kastner, 2 vols (1913) I 35.
5. *The Life and Times of Anthony à Wood*, ed. Llewelyn Powys (1932) pp. 64–5.
6. L. Pearsall Smith, 'Four Romantic Words', in *Words and Idioms* (1928) p. 79.
7. Op. cit. p. 76.
8. *Poems* (ed. 1791) p. 94.
9. Part 2, sect. 2, memb. 4 (1621 ed.) pp. 341–51.
10. 'A Note on the Verse of John Milton', in *Essays and Studies*, XXI (1935).
11. *Collected Essays* (1925) II 318.
12. *Poetical Works*, ed. Kastner, II 14.
13. *Faerie Queene*, I v 2.

14. e.g. Walton Poole's 'On Black Hayre and Eyes' (in *Poems of John Donne*, ed. H. J. C. Grierson, 2 vols (1912) I 460), 'On his Black Mistress', in *Wits Interpreter* (1655) p. 76.

15. *Works*, ed. C. E. Sayle, 3 vols (1904–7) III 359.

16. *Albumazar*, 325.

17. '*Comus* and Shakespeare', in *Essays and Studies*, XXXI (1945) 70.

18. *Poems*, ed. Philip Henderson (1931) p. 95.

19. ed. Sidney Lee (1909) I ii 9–10.

20. Part. 3, sect. 2, memb. 2, subs. 4 (Allurements of Loue) 1621 ed., p. 583.

21. Cf. also *PL* I 796: 'In spring-time, when the Sun with Taurus rides'. *O.E.D.* quotes no earlier examples of the application of the verb to the heavenly bodies: its later examples all seem to have been imitated from Milton.

WAYNE SHUMAKER

Flowerets and Sounding Seas: a study in the affective structure of 'Lycidas' (1951)

MORE insistently, perhaps, than any other poem in English, 'Lycidas' raises the purely æsthetic problem of how the emotions may be stirred by lines which at first are much less than perspicuous to the intellect and even after many readings remain obscure at two or three points. Johnson's attack to one side, 'Lycidas' has received all but universal praise, couched often in language so high-pitched that it absorbs easily adjectives like 'exquisite', 'thrilling', 'tremendous', and 'supreme'. Why is the emotional impact so powerful? A reply must be sought (I think) in the affective connotations of words, phrases, and images in formal combination; and it is worth finding because if in one of its aspects literature is history, in another, and not unimportant, aspect it is immediate experience.

In the present paper I shall attempt to make only a small contribution to the complete explanation. I propose, specifically, to extract two of a large number of formal strands and discuss them as musical themes which blend into a total emotional harmony both massive enough and piercing enough to be overpowering.

I must begin by discussing the place of the two strands in the large structure. Three movements are enclosed within a pastoral introduction and conclusion, each movement in turn depending to some extent on pastoral machinery for its organization. I cannot improve on a summary given by Arthur Barker.

> The first movement laments Lycidas the poet-shepherd; its problem, the possible frustration of disciplined poetic ambition by early death, is resolved by the assurance, 'Of so much fame in heaven expect thy meed'. The second laments Lycidas as priest-shepherd; its problem, the frustration of a sincere shepherd in a corrupt church, is resolved by St Peter's reference to the 'two-handed engine' of divine retribution. The third concludes with the

apotheosis, a convention introduced by Virgil in *Eclogue* V but significantly handled by Milton. He sees the poet-priest-shepherd worshipping the Lamb with those saints 'in solemn troops' who sing the 'unexpressive nuptial song' of the fourteenth chapter of Revelation. The apotheosis thus not only provides the final reassurance but unites the themes of the preceding movements in the ultimate reward of the true poet-priest.

Barker is almost certainly right in assigning a large part of the poem's impressiveness to the 'three successive and perfectly controlled crescendos', culminating in a second triumphal resolution of tensions already half-released in their appropriate sections. The two strands with which I am presently concerned – thematic strands, as will appear shortly – help prepare in the first and second movements for the final resolution in the third.

The third movement begins with the celebrated catalogue of flowers. One function of this passage is to modulate between St Peter's angry speech about the corruption of the English Church and the exultant description of Edward King's reception into Paradise. The catalogue interposes a little ease, as Milton himself says, which is to lead ultimately into the fuller and less deceptive comfort accessible through the realization that in its largest implications the drowning has not been tragic. It cannot have been tragic, for earthly life is continuous with eternal, in which temporal misfortunes are recompensed. But the image of flowers banking a drowned man's hearse cannot develop immediately into ecstatic and thrilling joy. The notion is too pretty-pretty, too conventionally poetic to carry a heavy emotional weight. Moreover, in this context the thought of floral offerings is consciously and deliberately delusive. Accordingly the next mood is one of profound spiritual depression; and this, by a natural emotional rhythm, illustrated on the abnormal level by the familiar manic-depressive pattern, passes into the final rapture. The three parts of the final movement are thus organically related, the first being emotionally causal to the second, and the second, and through it the first, emotionally causal to the third. The structure is not logically but emotionally inductive. Much of the value of the first two of the three parts lies in their power to entail the third. The first two parts, however, in their turn have been implied by everything that has gone before. The catalogue of flowers that 'sad embroidery' wear picks up and utilizes many preceding references to a blight that has been placed on vegetative nature by King's death, and the description of the sounding seas which hurl his body to and fro is the poetically inevitable culmination of many earlier references to water.

I do not know how many readers have noticed the remarkable consistency with which Milton has made every mention of vegetation in the first 132 lines of the elegy suggest a sympathetic frustration in nature to balance the human frustrations about which the poem is built. The technique goes far beyond the use of simple pathetic fallacies. It extends to descriptions of objects which seem not to be conscious of any involvement in the death of the poet-priest-shepherd.

The theme appears at the very beginning and is resumed several times, usually quite briefly and often glancingly, before the climactic enumeration of mournful flowers. The laurels and myrtles invoked in lines 1–5 have berries which are *harsh* and *crude*. The leaves of both laurels and myrtles are to be *shattered* by Milton's singing before they have an opportunity to reach mature exuberance ('before the mellowing year'). The emphasis now shifts to other matters; but when in the fourth verse-paragraph vegetation again comes momentarily into focus, the connotations are similarly depressing. The woods and caves that lament the accident are overgrown with *wild* thyme and *gadding* vines, the adjectives implying, perhaps not quite rationally, a desperate and uncontrolled abandon to grief. The willows and hazel copses have ceased to react with joyous activity to pastoral songs; their leaves, having left off their 'fanning', presumably droop in dejection. The rose is subject to canker; early flowers (Lycidas was a young man) succumb to frost. The tree-covered island of Mona mentioned a few lines later is not verdant but *shaggy*. The sixth paragraph offers a slight touch of relief: the *shade* in which the poet contemplates sporting with Amaryllis is thought of as a cool retreat. But Camus, when he appears, is described as wearing a bonnet of inelegant sedge variegated along the borders by figures which resemble 'that sanguine flower inscrib'd with woe', and no further relief is offered. The regularity with which natural growth is made to carry lugubrious associations in the introduction and first two movements is remarkable. So pervasive is the blight that as early as line 78, when Phoebus wishes to praise true fame, he is able to do so effectively by simply dissociating it from plants that grow on mortal soil.

All this would seem easily accountable if it were not for the fact that paragraph three recalls the happier times before King's death. Here one might expect attention to be diverted from gloom sufficiently to permit an avowal that for man's gayer hours (as Bryant said) nature has a voice of gladness and a smile and eloquence of beauty. The avowal is there, but it is phrased in terms of sunlight, the sounds of insects, stars, and other nonbotanical phenomena. The only exception is in the mention of 'high Lawns' in the first line of the description. For the rest, there is a studious avoidance of precisely those faces of nature which one would imagine to be most important to a shepherd. The comparative lightness of the paragraph depends not at all on images of energetic or brilliant growth. The opening eyelids of the morn carry the suggestion of an awakening, a stirring in preparation for the day's chores; the winding of the grayfly's sultry horn is associated with a genially warm air; the brightness of the evening star implies fine weather; the dancing of the satyrs and fauns is indicative of high spirits. The green of the pasturage, however, is hinted only by the single word 'lawns', and nothing whatever is said at this point about shade trees or flowers. The flocks, which anywhere else would eat grass, in this setting batten themselves on 'the fresh dews of night'. The association of plants with depression of the spirit is not compromised.

Against this background the catalogue of flowers takes on strong emotional meanings. It resumes and develops an established theme, which, however, is now partly inverted. Although the emotional connotations set up earlier are not exactly denied, they are subdued to provide a poignant contrast to the ease the poet has announced himself to be seeking. The primrose, we are reminded, dies forsaken; the cowslips hang their pensive heads; the daffodils fill their cups with tears. The floral offerings are in fact meant to include 'every flower that sad embroidery wears'. On the other hand, the coloring is no longer somber. The myrtles addressed in line 2 were *brown*, and throughout the first two of the three movements the visual imagery has been prevailingly dull. The whiteness of the thorn which blows in early spring and the redness of the sanguine flower have only deepened the general murkiness by contrast. Now, suddenly, we are asked to imagine bells and flowerets *of a thousand hues*. Certain colors are specified – the *purple* of enameled eyes, the *green* of the turf, the *paleness* of the jasmine, the *whiteness* of the pink, the *jet* of the pansy, the glowing *violet* – and others are evoked by the names of flowers like the daffodil, which can hardly be visualized in more than one way. The result is that the grief, while remaining grief, is lifted and brightened. For the moment it is made tolerable by association with beautiful objects. At the same time the reader feels relief of another kind. Up to the present he has been

under a constraint to imagine nature in only one of its moods; he has
been forced, as it were, to consent to a perversion of what he knows to
be the full truth. His conscious mind, which is aware of Milton's
elegiac purpose, has assented to the fiction that a human death has
lessened the objective beauty of woods and fields. But there is a part of
his mind which is not controlled by his will, and this part has perhaps
been, hardly perceptibly, uncomfortable, like the part of a father's mind
which feels guilty about the answers he has given to his child's questions
about the wind and the moon. The injustice is now partly rectified. In
the catalogue of flowers Milton says not only, 'There is brilliance as well
as dullness in nature', but also, more indirectly, 'The flowers named
here are those poetically associated with sadness. I have made a selection
to suit my elegiac theme.' He is not, then, unhinged by his grief. He
does not really distort. The largeness of his mind permits him to
acknowledge a partiality in his descriptions; and his reward is the
conquest of a tiny but not wholly insignificant scruple.

The second theme is somewhat less peripheral than the first, though
it also lies to one side of the poem's exact center. The description of
King's body as it is washed far away by the sounding seas, whether
northward, toward or beyond the Hebrides, or southward, toward
Cornwall, has been even more elaborately prepared for in advance. The
first visual image of the dead poet-priest-shepherd is that of a corpse
rocked to and fro on ocean swells swept by a dry wind. From the
beginning, accordingly, the sea is in the background of the reader's
consciousness. Images of water have considerably greater prominence
than images of trees and plants and have frequently been noticed by
critics. Sometimes the water moves forward into clear focus; again it
flashes rapidly across the margin of attention, half-unnoticed and
significant chiefly because the glimpses sustain a theme that must not be
allowed to lose continuity.

Some of the references to water carry only a very indirect reminder
of the sea, and, with it, the manner of King's death. For example, the
invocation in the second paragraph calls up the image of a well: 'Begin
then, Sisters of the sacred well,/ That from beneath the seat of *Jove* doth
spring.' The well is not, however, quiescent; the word 'spring' suggests
movement, and the movement of water, though now on a small scale,
both carries on the visual motif and, by reducing the image's physical
and emotional dimensions, modulates into the calmer passage which
follows. A somewhat analogous technique is used at five other points:

in the mention of Deva's wizard stream, in the apostrophe to the Fountain Arethuse and smooth-sliding Mincius, in the personification of the River Cam, in the description of St Peter as pilot of the Galilean lake, and in the reassurance addressed to the River Alpheus. Each of these glancing evocations of water helps keep the theme alive by giving the reader's memory of it a little fillip. In a similar way the fountain, the three rivers, and the Sea of Galilee, by faintly echoing the water motif, prevent the reader from ever quite losing sight of the fact that King died by drowning.

I should like to dwell for a moment on a representative passage, that which contains – and surrounds – the laments of the University and the Church. At the beginning of the paragraph the University is represented, appropriately enough, by the personified figure of the leisurely, rush-lined Cam. I should not like to pretend that every reader has a momentary glimpse of a river sliding among reeds when he comes to these lines; nevertheless the complete dissociation of the river from the figure would be difficult. St Peter next appears as the 'Pilot of the *Galilean* lake', the description providing an ironic contrast to the reader's knowledge that King was *not* rescued from the sea. After this introduction comes a thunderous attack on the state of the English Church; but the attack has no sooner ended in the climactic prediction of the two-handed engine than the water theme is again stated: 'Return *Alpheus*, the dread voice is past,/ That shrunk thy streams.' The transition could hardly be more apt. The hint of timidity in the stream lowers the key from indignation at the same time the words 'dread voice' carry the last reverberations of anger. Moreover, the ideas of water and fright have been associated before and will be associated again. The relationship in the present passage is curious, however, for now it is the water that is frightened by the man. The effect is somewhat like that of an inverted musical phrase, which remains recognizable despite the fact that it has been turned upside down.

The address to the Fountain Arethuse and smooth-sliding Mincius performs a somewhat analogous function a little earlier. It too uses water imagery to reassert the pastoral medium just when the need for a reassertion is felt. The mention of Deva's wizard stream is incidental to the fixing of a geographical location, but the motor quality of the verb 'spread' adds vividness by making the movement seem the result of an act of will. The Dee spreads its waters as a housewife might spread a tablecloth or a bird its wings.

We have seen, then, that there are six muted statements of the water theme besides the more resonant ones to be noted presently. The sacred well, the River Cam, the Galilean lake, the River Alpheus, the Fountain Arethuse and smooth-sliding Mincius (I count them as one because they occur in such close juxtaposition), and the River Dee prevent the Irish Sea from ever quite slipping out of the reader's consciousness. Milton's awareness of the manner in which King died is not wholly suppressed even in parts of the elegy in which he is mainly occupied in talking about something else. Formally, the six passages contribute to a massive harmony without themselves being very distinctly heard. It will be approximately accurate to say that their structural function is similar to that of the middle notes of triads struck on the piano. Only the analytic listener pays careful heed to them, but anyone would feel a slight decrease of tonal richness if they were omitted.

The more resonant statements of the theme begin in the description of Lycidas on his watery bier and continue at lines 50, 62, 89, and 154. At each of these points the drowning is specifically mentioned or water is in some other way made to appear menacing. There are also two later passages, at lines 167 and 183, which perform for the water theme the function performed for the flower theme by the catalogue.

The first statement, already once referred to, has evoked the image of a body rocking helplessly on ocean swells. The second is less grisly but in a way even more distressing, for it recreates briefly the exact instant at which a human life succumbed to an indifferent natural force: 'Where were ye Nymphs when the remorseless deep/ Clos'd o'er the head of your lov'd *Lycidas*?' The visual image is that of a face sinking for the last time beneath water, the motor image that of a rejoining of fluid edges; and there is perhaps induced also a slight muscular strain, as of an effort to fight one's way upward toward air. To describe small things by large, the effect is now rather that of fright than of nausea. (I hope the reader will understand that the only way in which I can make some of my points at all is by overstating them.)

The third statement picks up the nausea and drops the fright – for I should suppose no one to feel personal danger in the sight of a severed and bleeding head being tumbled down a precipitous river bed by the current. The head is that of Orpheus, who, like Lycidas, was a singer.

> by the rout that made the hideous roar,
> His goary visage down the stream was sent,
> Down the swift *Hebrus* to the *Lesbian* shore.

The cold passivity of the second image has been replaced by the movement of the first; but there are in addition angry sounds and the blood that is so frequently an accompaniment of violence. The association of water and death, however, has remained constant.

The same association is present in the fourth statement, which recurs to the passivity of the second image and develops it in considerable detail. The herald of the sea

> ask'd the Waves, and ask'd the Fellon winds,
> What hard mishap hath doom'd this gentle swain? . . .
> And sage *Hippotades* their answer brings,
> That not a blast was from his dungeon stray'd,
> The Ayr was calm, and on the level brine,
> Sleep *Panope* with all her sisters play'd.

The drowning and its circumstances are again set in contrast; death is described as having occurred in a peaceful setting. On the other hand, the feeling appropriate to this statement is neither fright nor nausea but perplexity. Within limits, variations in the emotional demands made on the reader increase the affective pull by activating dormant parts of the psyche. At the same time continuity is provided by the maintenance of the association of water and death.

Up to this point the Irish Sea has been described once as weltering and twice – if I do not misread the connotations of lines 50–1 – as tranquil. The tranquillity has been insisted on at greater length than the movement and is probably more vividly present in the reader's imagination. Yet the possibility of movement in the Sea has been strongly asserted by the verb 'welter' and implied by the swift motion of the Hebrus. In the longest, and climactic, development of the water theme the vastness of the Sea is brought together with the swiftness of the river to produce an impression of great violence.

> Ay me! Whilst thee the shores, and sounding Seas
> Wash far away, where ere thy bones are hurld,
> Whether beyond the stormy *Hebrides*,
> Where thou perhaps under the whelming tide
> Visit'st the bottom of the monstrous world . . .

The Irish Sea has become a resistless, unsympathetic force which deals with the body of the poet-priest-shepherd exactly as the Hebrus has dealt with the severed head of Orpheus, tossing it about with the indifference with which it would toss a plank broken from the hull of the wrecked ship. The effect is overwhelming (the word is suggested by the passage), and more than one critic has testified that for him this is the most powerful part of the elegy.

Relief, however, is at hand, for the depressing thought of a tossed and ruined body generates immediately, by contrast, that of a redeemed and joyous soul. The flower and water themes, in direct juxtaposition, thus lead directly into the apotheosis, in which all the tensions are finally resolved. Little more needs to be done with the flower theme. It has served its purpose and will appear only once more, disguised almost beyond recognition, in the last line of all: 'To morrow to fresh Woods, and Pastures new.' The water theme, on the other hand, has carried a much heavier emotional weight and cannot be so easily dropped. Moreover, growing nature has already been adequately purged of blight, whereas the sea continues to hold a menace. It too must be purified. The mourners must be reconciled to the physical world as well as to the turnings of human destiny.

Accordingly the transition from despair to hope is made by images drawn from the very water that we have just been led to believe coldly and impersonally fearful:

> So sinks the day-star in the Ocean bed,
> And yet anon repairs his drooping head,
> And tricks his beams, and with new spangled Ore,
> Flames in the forehead of the morning sky:
> So *Lycidas* sunk low, but mounted high,
> Through the dear might of him that walk'd the waves . . .

The sun is not harmed by the sea. Christ walked on its waves. Indeed, the very man who was killed by water on earth can seek out its Heavenly equivalent as a comfort: 'other groves, and other streams along,/ With *Nectar* pure his oozy Lock's he laves.' Even this is not all. The element *water* has been purified, but the Irish Sea must be especially cleared of threat. Hence we are told that travelers on the Sea will gain composure by recalling the 'large recompense' which we now realize to have followed the brief torment of drowning.

> Now *Lycidas* the Shepherds weep no more;
> Hence forth thou art the Genius of the shore,
> In thy large recompense, and shalt be good
> To all that wander in that perilous flood.

For myself – I do not pretend to speak for others – there is a slight dissatisfaction in the reading of these lines. If the source of composure is to be an understanding of the total meaning of King's death, the word *all* provokes resistance. Calmness of mind will be accessible only to voyagers who, having known King, have been led by reflections on his fate to an acceptance of death similar to that expressed in the poem. If, on the other hand, we are to imagine King's spirit as extending physical protection to voyagers on the Sea, the implication that death is to be avoided as significantly bad contradicts the whole drift and meaning of the elegy. The structural function of the passage, however, is clear. A *formal* means of escape from the last tension has been provided. Not only is the poet-priest-shepherd living after all; the mourners can again face nature courageously and take delight in its external beauty. Everything is as it should be, and daily activities can be taken up at the point where they were dropped.

The two minor themes, then, come into prominence at various places in the first and second movements and at other places are hinted in ways that have been described. In the third movement they are developed side by side in preparation for the apotheosis, in which sorrow is finally transcended and the mind restored to peace. There is a difference, however, both in their intrinsic importance and in their usefulness in preparing for the resolution. The flower theme shows a temporary effect of profound grief, the water theme is intimately related to the cause. The distortion of vision must wear off before adjustment to the irremedial cause becomes possible; hence it is altogether proper that the former of the two themes should be resolved a little in advance of the latter. Yet each has its function, and the emotional impact would be weakened if either were omitted from the third movement. The first paragraph of the final movement, unaccounted for by Barker's explanation of the structure, is thus only less necessary than the apotheosis. It fits not only into a design but also into an emotional pattern; not only into a form but also into a response.

STANLEY EUGENE FISH

'Not so much a teaching as an intangling': Milton's Method in *Paradise Lost*[1] (1967)

I would like to suggest something about *Paradise Lost* that is not new except for the literalness with which the point will be made: (1) the poem's centre of reference is its reader who is also its subject; (2) Milton's purpose is to educate the reader to an awareness of his position and responsibilities as a fallen man, and to a sense of the distance which separates him from the innocence once his; (3) Milton's method is to re-create in the mind of the reader (which is, finally, the poem's scene) the drama of the Fall, to make him fall again exactly as Adam did and with Adam's troubled clarity, that is to say, 'not deceived'. In a limited sense few would deny the truth of my first two statements; Milton's concern with the ethical imperatives of political and social behaviour would hardly allow him to write an epic which did not attempt to give his audience a basis for moral action; but I do not think the third has been accepted in the way that I intend it.

A. J. A. Waldock, one of many sensitive readers who have confronted the poem since 1940, writes: '*Paradise Lost* is an epic poem of singularly hard and definite outline, expressing itself (or so at least would be our first impressions) with unmistakable clarity and point'.[2] In the course of his book, Waldock expands the reservation indicated by his parentheses into a reading which predicates a disparity between Milton's intention and his performance:

> In a sense Milton's central theme denied him the full expression of his deepest interests. It was likely, then, that as his really deep interests could not find outlet in his poem in the right way they might find outlet in the wrong way. And to a certain extent they do; they find vents and safety-valves often in inopportune places. Adam cannot give Milton much scope to express what he really feels about life: but Satan is there, Satan gives him

scope. And the result is that the balance is somewhat disturbed; pressures are set up that are at times disquieting, that seem to threaten more than once, indeed, the equilibrium of the poem.[3]

The 'unconscious meaning' portion of Waldock's thesis is, I think, as wrong as his description of the reading experience as 'disquieting' is right. If we transfer the emphasis from Milton's interests and intentions which are available to us only from a distance, to our responses which are available directly, the disparity between intention and execution becomes a disparity between reader expectation and reading experience; and the resulting 'pressures' can be seen as part of an intelligible pattern. In this way we are led to consider our own experience as a part of the poem's subject.

By 'hard and definite outline' I take Waldock to mean the sense of continuity and direction evoked by the simultaneous introduction of the epic tradition and Christian myth. The 'definiteness' of a genre classification leads the reader to expect a series of formal stimuli – martial encounters, complex similes, an epic voice – to which his response is more or less automatic; the hardness of the Christian myth predetermines his sympathies; the union of the two allows the assumption of a comfortable reading experience in which conveniently labelled protagonists act out rather simple roles in a succession of familiar situations. The reader is prepared to hiss the devil off the stage and applaud the pronouncements of a partisan and somewhat human deity who is not unlike Tasso's 'il Padre eterno'. But of course this is not the case; no sensitive reading of *Paradise Lost* tallies with these expectations, and it is my contention that Milton ostentatiously calls them up in order to provide his reader with the shock of their disappointment. This is not to say merely that Milton communicates a part of his meaning by a calculated departure from convention; every poet does that; but that Milton consciously wants to worry his reader, to force him to doubt the correctness of his responses, and to bring him to the realization that his inability to read the poem with any confidence in his own perception is its focus.

Milton's programme of reader harassment begins in the opening lines; the reader, however, may not be aware of it until line 84 when Satan speaks for the first time. The speech is a powerful one, moving smoothly from the *exclamatio* of 'But O how fall'n' (84) to the regret and apparent logic of 'til then who knew/ The force of those dire Arms' (93–4), the determination of 'courage never to submit or yield'

(108) and the grand defiance of 'Irreconcilable to our grand Foe,/ Who now triumphs, and in th' excess of joy/ Sole reigning holds the Tyranny of Heav'n' (122–4). This is our first view of Satan and the impression given, reinforced by a succession of speeches in Book I, is described by Waldock: 'fortitude in adversity, enormous endurance, a certain splendid recklessness, remarkable powers of rising to an occasion, extraordinary qualities of leadership (shown not least in his salutary taunts)'.[4] But in each case Milton follows the voice of Satan with a comment which complicates, and according to some, falsifies, our reaction to it:

> So spake th' Apostate Angel, though in pain,
> Vaunting aloud, but rackt with deep despair. (125–6)

Waldock's indignation at this authorial intrusion is instructive:

> If one observes what is happening one sees that there is hardly a great speech of Satan's that Milton is not at pains to correct, to damp down and neutralize. He will put some glorious thing in Satan's mouth, then anxious about the effect of it, will pull us gently by the sleeve, saying (for this is what it amounts to): 'Do not be carried away by this fellow: he *sounds* splendid, but take my word for it . . .' Has there been much despair in what we have just been listening to? The speech would almost seem to be incompatible with that. To accept Milton's comment here . . . as if it had a validity equal to that of the speech itself is surely very naïve critical procedure . . . in any work of imaginative literature at all it is the demonstration, by the very nature of the case, that has the higher validity; an allegation can possess no comparable authority. Of course they should agree; but if they do not then the demonstration must carry the day. (pp. 77–8)

There are several assumptions here:

(1) There is a disparity between our response to the speech and the epic voice's evaluation of it.
(2) Ideally, there should be no disparity.
(3) Milton's intention is to correct *his* error.
(4) He wants us to discount the effect of the speech through a kind of mathematical cancellation.
(5) The question of relative authority is purely an aesthetic one. That is, the reader is obliged to harken to the most dramatically persuasive of any conflicting voices.

Of these I can assent only to the first. The comment of the epic voice unsettles the reader who sees in it at least a partial challenge to his own assessment of the speech. The implication is that there is more (or less) here than has met the ear; and since the only ear available is the reader's, the further implication is that he has failed in some way to evaluate properly what he has heard. One must begin by admitting with Waldock the impressiveness of the speech, if only as a *performance* that commands attention as would any forensic *tour de force*; and attention on that level involves a corresponding inattention on others. It is not enough to analyse, as Lewis and others have, the speciousness of Satan's rhetoric. It is the nature of sophistry to lull the reasoning process; logic is a safe-guard against a rhetorical effect only after the effect has been noted. The deep distrust, even fear, of verbal manipulation in the seventeenth century is a recognition of the fact that there is no adequate defence against eloquence at the moment of impact. (Thus the insistence in the latter half of the century on the complete absence of rhetoric. The Royal Society, Sprat promises, will 'separate the knowledge of Nature from the colours of Rhetorick, the devices of Fancy, or the delightful deceit of Fables'.[5] In other words one can analyse the process of decep-tion only after it is successful. The reader who is stopped short by Milton's rebuke (for so it is) will, perhaps, retrace his steps and note more carefully the inconsistency of a Tyranny that involves an excess of joy, the perversity of 'study of revenge, immortal hate' (a line that had slipped past him sandwiched respectably between will and courage), the sophistry of the transfer of power from the 'Potent Victor' of 95 to the 'Fate' of line 116, and the irony, in the larger picture, of 'that were *low* indeed' and 'in *foresight* more advanc't'. The fit reader Milton has in mind would go further and recognize in Satan's finest moment – 'And courage never to submit or yield' – an almost literal translation of *Georgic* IV 84, 'usque adeo obnixi non cedere'. Virgil's 'praise' is for his bees whose heroic posturing is presented in terms that are at least ambiguous:

> ipsi per medias acies insignibus alis
> ingentis animos angusto in pectore versant,
> usque adeo obnixi non cedere, dum gravis aut hos
> aut hos versa fuga victor dare terga subegit.
> hi motus animorum atque haec certamina tanta
> pulveris exigui iactu compressa quiescunt. (82–7)[6]

If we apply these verses to Satan, the line in question mocks him and in the unique time-scheme of *Paradise Lost* looks both backward (the Victor has already driven the rebel host to flight) and forward (in terms of the reading experience, the event is yet to come). I believe that all this and more is there, but that the complexities of the passage will be apparent only when the reader has been led to them by the necessity of accounting for the distance between his initial response and the *obiter dictum* of the epic voice. When he is so led, the reader is made aware that Milton is correcting not a mistake of composition, but the weakness all men evince in the face of eloquence. The error is his not Milton's; and when Waldock invokes some unidentified critical principle ('they should agree') he objects to an effect Milton anticipates and desires.

But this is more than a stylistic trick to assure the perception of irony. For, as Waldock points out, this first epic interjection introduces a pattern that is operative throughout. In Books I and II these 'correctives' are particularly numerous and, if the word can be used here, tactless. Waldock falsifies his experience of the poem I think, when he characterizes Milton's countermands as gentle; we are not warned ('Do not be carried away by this fellow'), but accused, taunted by an imperious voice which says with no consideration of our feelings, 'I know that you *have been* carried away by what you have just heard; you should not have been; you have made a mistake, just as I knew you would'; and we resent this rebuke, not, as Waldock suggests, because our aesthetic sense balks at a clumsy attempt to neutralize an unintentional effect, but because a failing has been exposed in a context that forces us to acknowledge it. We are angry at the epic voice, not for fudging, but for being right, for insisting that we become our own critics. There is little in the human situation more humiliating in both senses of the word, than the public acceptance of a deserved rebuke.

Not that the reader falls and becomes one of Satan's party. His involvement in the speech does not *directly* compromise his position in a god-centred universe, since his response (somewhat unconscious) is to a performance rather than to a point of view that he might be led to adopt as his own. As Michael Krouse notes, 'the readers for whom Milton wrote . . . were prepared for a Devil equipped with what appears on the surface to be the best of arguments' (*Milton's Samson and the Christian Tradition* (1949) p. 102). As a Christian, who has been taught every day to steel himself against diabolical wiles, the reader is more than prepared to admit the justness of the epic voice's *judgment* on Satan. It is the phrase 'vaunting aloud' that troubles, since it seems to deny even the academic admiration one might have for Satan's art as apart from his morality and to suggest that such admiration can never really be

detached from the possibility of involvement (if only passive) in that
morality. (The sneer in 'vaunting' is aimed equally at the performance
and anyone who lingers to appreciate it; Satan himself delivers the final
judgment on this and on all his speeches at IV 83: 'Whom I seduc'd/
With other promises and other *vaunts*'.) The danger is not so much that
Satan's argument will persuade (one does not accord the father of lies
an impartial hearing), but that its intricacy will engage the reader's
attention and lead him into an error of omission. That is to say, in the
attempt to follow and analyse Satan's soliloquy, the larger contexts in
which it exists will be forgotten. The immediate experience of the
poetry will not be qualified by the perspective of the poem's doctrinal
assumptions. Arnold Stein writes, 'the formal perspective does not
force itself upon Satan's speech, does not label and editorialize the
impressive willfulness out of existence; but rather sets up a dramatic
conflict between the local context of the immediate utterance and the
larger context of which the formal perspective is expression. This
conflict marks . . . the tormented relationship between the external
boast and the internal despair.'[7] Stein's comment is valuable, but it
ignores the way the reader is drawn into the poem not as an observer
who coolly notes the interaction of patterns (this is the mode of
Jonsonian comedy and masque), but as a participant whose mind is the
locus of that interaction. Milton insists on this since his concern with the
reader is necessarily more direct than it might be in any other poem;
and to grant the reader the status of the slightly arrogant perceiver-
of-ironies Stein invents would be to deny him the full *benefit* (I use
the word deliberately, confident that Milton would approve) of the
reading experience. Stein's 'dramatic conflict' is there, as are his various
perspectives, but they are actualized, that is, translated into felt meaning,
only through the more pervasive drama (between reader and poem) I
hope to describe.

A Christian failure need not be dramatic; if the reader loses himself in
the workings of the speech even for a moment, he places himself in a
compromising position. He has taken his eye from its proper object –
the glory of God, and the state of his own soul – and is at least in danger.
Sin is a matter of degrees. To think 'how fine this all sounds, even
though it is Satan's', is to be but a few steps from thinking, 'how fine
this all sounds' – and no conscious qualification. One begins by simultaneously admitting the effectiveness of Satan's rhetoric and discounting
it because it *is* Satan's, but at some point a reader trained to analyse as he

reads will allow admiration for a technical skill to push aside the imperative of Christian watchfulness. To be sure, this is not sin. But from a disinterested appreciation of technique one moves easily to a grudging admiration for the technician and then to a guarded sympathy and finally, perhaps, to assent. In this case, the failure (if we can call it that) involves the momentary relaxation of a vigilance that must indeed be eternal. Richard Baxter (*The Saints Everlasting Rest*, c. 1650) warns: 'Not only the open profane, the swearer, the drunkard, and the enemies of godliness, will prove hurtful companions to us, though these indeed are chiefly to be avoided: but too frequent society with persons merely civil and moral, whose conversation is empty and unedifying, may much divert our thoughts from heaven.' In Book IX, Eve is 'yet sinless' when she talks with Satan and follows him to the forbidden tree; but Milton indicates the danger and its vehicle at line 550:

> Into the heart of Eve his words made way,
> Though at the voice much marvelling.

Eve (innocently) surrenders her mind to wonderment ('much marvelling') at the technical problem of the seeming-serpent's voice ('What may this mean? Language of man pronounc't/ By Tongue of Brute') and forgets Adam's injunction to 'strictest watch' (363). There is at least one assertion of Satan's that Eve should challenge, since it contradicts something she herself has said earlier. The proper response to Satan's salutatory 'Fairest resemblance of thy Maker fair' (538) has been given, in effect, by Eve when she recognizes Adam's superior 'fairness' at IV 490 ('I . . . see/ How beauty is excell'd by manly grace/ And wisdom, which alone is truly fair'). Her failure to give that response again is hardly fatal, but it does involve a deviation (innocent but dangerous) from the strictness of her watch. Of course to rebuke the serpent for an excess in courtesy might seem rude; tact, however, is a social virtue and one which Milton's heroes are rarely guilty of. Eve is correct when she declares that the talking serpent's voice 'claims attention due' (566), but attention *due* should not mean *complete* attention. Satan is the arch-conjurer here, calling his audience's attention to one hand (the mehanics of his articulation), doing his real work with the other ('Into the heart of Eve his words made way'). In Book I, Milton is the conjurer: by naming Satan he disarms us, and allows us to feel secure in the identification of an enemy who traditionally succeeds through disguise (serpent, cherub). But as William Haller notes in *The Rise of Puritanism*, nothing is more indicative of a graceless state than a sense of security: 'Thus we live in danger, our greatest danger being that we should feel no danger, and our safety lying in the very dread of feeling safe' (p. 156). Protected from one error (the possibility of listening sympathetically to a disguised enemy) we fall easily into another (spiritual inattentiveness) and fail to read Satan's speech with the critical acumen it demands. In the opening lines of Book x, Milton comments brusquely on Adam's and Eve's fall:

> For still they knew, and ought to have still remember'd. (12)

Paradise Lost is full of little moments of forgetfulness – for Satan, for Adam and Eve, and, most important, for the reader. At I 125–6, the epic voice enters to point out to us the first of these moments and to say in effect, 'For still you knew and ought to have still remembered', remembered who you are (Paradise has already been lost), where you are ('So spake th'Apostate Angel'), and what the issues are (salvation, justification). In this poem the isolation of an immediate poetic effect involves a surrender to that effect, and is a prelude to error, and possibly to sin. Milton challenges his reader in order to protect him from a mistake he must make before the challenge can be discerned. If this seems circular and even unfair, it is also, as I shall argue later, necessary and inevitable.

The result of such encounters is the adoption of a new way of reading. After I 125–6 the reader proceeds determined not to be caught out again; but invariably he is. If Satanic pronouncements are now met with a certain caution, if there is a new willingness to search for complexities and ironies beneath simple surfaces, this mental armour is never quite strong enough to resist the insidious attack of verbal power; and always the irritatingly omniscient epic voice is there to point out a deception even as it succeeds. As the poem proceeds and this little drama is repeated, the reader's only gain is an awareness of what is happening to him; he understands that his responses are being controlled and mocked by the same authority, and realizes that while his efforts to free himself from this rhetorical bind are futile, that very futility becomes a way to self-knowledge. Control is the important concept here, for my claim is not merely that this pattern is in the poem (it would be difficult to find one that is not), but that Milton (a) consciously put it there and (b) expected his reader to notice it. Belial's speech in Book II is a case in point. It is the only speech that merits an introductory warning:

On th'other side up rose
Belial, in act more graceful and humane;
A fairer person lost not Heav'n; he seem'd
For dignity compos'd and high exploit:
But all was false and hollow; though his Tongue
Dropt Manna, and could make the worse appear
The better reason to perplex and dash
Maturest Counsels: for his thoughts were low;
To vice industrious, but to Nobler deeds
Timorous and slothful: yet he pleas'd the ear,
And with persuasive accent thus began. (II 108–18)

The intensity of the warning indicates the extent of the danger: Belial's apparent solidity, which is visible, must be contrasted to his hollowness, which is not, the manna of his tongue to the lowness of mind it obscures; and the 'yet' in 'yet he Pleas'd the ear', more than a final admonition before the reader is to be left to his own resources, is an admission of wonder by the epic voice itself (*yet*, he pleased . . .) and one of the early cracks in its façade of omniscience. Belial's appeal is a skilful union of logical machinery ('*First*, what Revenge?') and rhetorical insinuation. The easy roll of his periods literally cuts through the contortions of Moloch's bluster, and the series of *traductio*s around the word 'worse' are an indirect comment on the 'what can be worse' of the 'Sceptr'd King's' desperation. The ploys are effective, and since in the attempt to measure the relative merits of the two devils we forget that their entire counsel is baseless, the return of the epic voice yields one more slight shock at this new evidence of our susceptibility. Again we are led to forget what we know; again we take our eye from the object (the centrality of God); again we are returned to it with an abruptness that is (designedly) disconcerting:

Thus *Belial* with words cloth'd in reason's garb
Counsell'd ignoble ease, and peaceful sloth,
Not Peace: (226–8)

Waldock complains, 'Belial's words are not only "cloath'd in reason's garb": they *are* reasonable.'[8] Belial's words are *not* reasonable, although a single uncritical reading will yield the appearance of reason rather than the reality of his ignoble ease. Again the flaw in the speech is to be located precisely at its strongest point. Belial cries at line 146: 'for who would lose,/ Though full of pain, this intellectual being,/ Those thoughts that wander through Eternity,/ To perish rather, swallow'd up and lost/ In the wide womb of uncreated night.' In other words, do we wish to give up our nature, our sense of identity? The rhetorical question evokes an emphatic 'no' from the assembled devils and the reader. Yet at line 215 Belial offers his final argument, the possibility of adapting to their now noxious environment: 'Our purer essence then will overcome/ Thir noxious vapor, or enur'd not feel,/ Or chang'd at length, and to the place conform'd/ In temper and in nature, will receive/ Familiar the fierce heat, and void of pain.' If this is less spectacular than the question posed at 146, it is still a direct answer to that question, Belial *is* willing to lose 'this intellectual being'. The choice is not, as he suggests, between annihilation and continued existence, but between different kinds of annihilation – Moloch's suicidal thrust at the Almighty or his own gradual surrender of identity, no less suicidal, much less honest. This will be obvious on a second reading. My intention is not to refute Waldock, but to suggest that while his reaction to the epic voice ('they *are* reasonable') is the correct one, Milton expects his reader to go beyond it, to see in the explicitness of the before and after warnings a comment on his own evaluation of the speech.

Satan and his host need not speak in order to betray us to ourselves. When Satan and Beelzebub move from the lake of fire to dry land, 'if it were Land that ever burn'd', their actions become their rhetoric. Milton's introductory stage-direction (or is it a marginal note) 'nor ever thence/ Had ris'n or heav'd his head, but that the will/ And high permission of all-ruling Heaven' (210-12) parallels the warning against Belial; and again the experience of the verse leads us (literally) to lose sight of the warning. If Belial's words seem reasonable, Satan's act certainly seems autonomous. He *rears* himself 'from off the Pool', and the sense of direct force communicated by the verb is channelled into an image that suggests the rocket thrust of modern propellents: 'on each hand the flames/ Driv'n backward slope their pointing spires'. Do the flames move upward ('pointing') or downward ('backward')? The answer is both; and the impression is one of great movement, Satan's movement. He steers 'incumbent' and while his cumbrousness is introduced to impress us with the strain his unusual weight places on 'the dusky air', we are finally impressed by his ability to manage that weight; Satan rather than the air is the hero of these lines. The 'force' that 'transports a Hill/ Torn from *Pelorus*' is not identified, but since the 'Archfiend' is the nearest available agent, it is attached to him, as is the

entire image. Carried forward by the sequence that began at 'Forthwith
upright he rears' (a second reading will emphasize the irony in 'upright'),
the reader accepts 'Both glorying to have scrap't the *Stygian* flood' (239)
as an accurate summary of the scene presented to him. Not that Satan
and Beelzebub are consciously granted the status of self-sufficient
agents; rather, the question of self-sufficiency does not seem at this
point to be relevant to the reading experience. But of course it is the
central question, or at least it was at 210 when the epic voice introduced
the action; and is again as that same voice returns us to it – in stages:
'Both glorying to have scrap't the *Stygian* flood/ As Gods, and by their
own recover'd strength,/ Not by the sufferance of Supernal Power'
(239–41). First, the words 'As Gods' recall 'the high permission of all-
ruling Heaven' and indicate the blasphemy of 'glorifying'. To the
reader, 'As Gods' is less a continuation of line 239 than a qualification of
the line's literal assertion that protects him (a half-second too late)
against accepting it as true. 'By thir own recover'd strength' changes as
we read it, from an extension of the momentarily neutral 'scrap't the
Stygian flood' to the ironic complement of 'nor ever thence/ Had
ris'n . . .'. 'Not by the sufferance of Supernal Power' is a flat statement
that disdains irony for the simple declarative of truth; the passage is
suddenly and firmly placed in the larger perspective which the reader
again enjoys after a defection to Satan's. Milton's point here is one he
will make again and again; all acts are performed in God's service;
what is left to any agent is a choice between service freely rendered and
service exacted against his will. Satan continually deludes himself by
supposing that he can act apart from God, and in this passage we come
to understand that delusion by (momentarily) sharing it. . . .

   These are almost laboratory experiments, tests insulated by rigid
controls, obviously didactic. The pattern that unites them is reminiscent
of Spenser's technique in the *Faerie Queene*, i 9. There the approach to
Despair's cave is pointedly detailed and the detail is calculated to repel;
the man himself is more terrible than the Blatant Beast or the dragon of
i 12, for his ugliness is something we recognize. Spenser's test of his
reader is less stringent than Milton's; he makes his warning the
experience of this description rather than an abstract statement of disapproval. It is, of course, not enough. Despair's adaptation of Christian
rhetoric (guilt, grace) is masterful and the Redcross Knight (along with
the reader) allows the impression of one set of appearances (the old
man's ugliness) to be effaced by another (the Circean lure of his

rhetoric): 'Sleepe after toyle, port after stormie sea,/ Ease after warre, death after life does greatly please' (40). Spenser eases us along by making it impossible to assign stanza 42 to either the knight or Despair. At that point the syntactical ambiguity is telling; the dialogue is over, and we have joined them both in a three part unanimity that leads inexorably to the decision of 51:

> At last, resolv'd to worke his finall smart
> He lifted up his hand that backe again did start.

Una's exhortation and accusation – 'Come, come away, fraile, feeble, fleshly wight' – is for us as well as her St George, and we need the reminder that she brings to us from a context *outside* the experience of the poem: 'In heavenly mercies has thou not a part?' Without this *deus ex machina* we could not escape; without Milton's 'snubs' we could not be jolted out of a perspective that is after all *ours*. The lesson in both poems is that the only defense against verbal manipulation (or appearances) is a commitment that stands above the evidence of things that are seen, and the method of both poems is to lead us beyond our perspective by making us feel its inadequacies and the necessity of accepting something which baldly contradicts it. The result is instruction, and instruction is possible only because the reader is asked to observe, analyse, and *place* his experience, that is, to think about it.

In the divorce tracts Milton reveals the source of this poetic technique when he analyses the teaching of Christ, 'not so much a teaching as an intangling'.[9] Christ is found 'not so much interpreting the Law with his words, as referring his owne words to be interpreted by the Law'.[10] Those who would understand him must themselves decipher the obscurities of his sayings, 'for Christ gives no full comments or continu'd discourses ... scattering the heavenly grain of his doctrin like pearle heer and there, which requires a skilfull and laborious gatherer'.[11] In order better to instruct his disciples, who 'yet retain'd the infection of loving old licentious customs', he does not scruple to mislead them, temporarily: 'But why did not Christ seeing their error informe them? for good cause; it was his profest method not to teach them all things at all times, but each thing in due place and season ... the Disciples took it [one of his gnomic utterances] in a manifest wrong sense, yet our Saviour did not there informe them better. ... Yet did he not omitt to sow within them the seeds of sufficient determining, agen the time that his promis'd spirit should bring all things to their memory.'[12] 'Due

season' means when they are ready for it, and they will be ready for it
when the seeds he has sown obliquely have brought them to the point
where a more direct revelation of the truth will be efficacious; until
then they are allowed to linger in error or at least in partial ignorance.
Recently H. R. MacCallum has shown how Michael uses a strategy of
indirection and misdirection to lead Adam from the sickness of despair
to faith and spiritual health.[13] Michael's strategy in Book XI is Milton's
strategy in the entire poem, whereby his reader becomes his pupil,
taught according to his present capacities in the hope that he can be
educated, in tract of time, to enlarge them.

II

The wariness these encounters with demonic attraction make us feel is
part of a larger pattern in which we are taught the hardest of all lessons,
distrust of our own abilities and perceptions. This distrust extends to all
the conventional ways of knowing that might enable a reader to locate
himself in the world of any poem. The questions we ask of our reading
experience are in large part the questions we ask of our day-to-day
experience. Where are we, what are the physical components of our
surroundings, what time is it? And while the hard and clear outline of
Paradise Lost suggests that the answers to these questions are readily
available to us, immediate contexts repeatedly tell us that they are not.
Consider, for example, the case of Satan's spear. I have seen responsible
critics affirm, casually, that Satan's spear is as large as the mast of a ship;
the poem of course affirms nothing of the kind, but more important, it
deliberately encourages such an affirmation, at least temporarily:

> His spear, to equal which the tallest Pine
> Hewn on *Norwegian* Hills to be the Mast
> Of some great Ammiral, were but a wand. (I 292–4)

Throughout *Paradise Lost*, Milton relies on the operation of three truths
so obvious that many critics fail to take them into account: (1) the
reading experience takes place in time, that is, we necessarily read one
word after another; (2) the childish habit of moving the eyes along a
page and back again is never really abandoned although in maturity the
movement is more mental than physical, and defies measurement;
therefore the line as a unit is a resting-place even when rhyme is absent;
(3) a mind asked to order a succession of rapidly given bits of detail

(mental or physical) seizes on the simplest scheme of organization which offers itself. In this simile, the first line supplies that scheme in the overt comparison between the spear and the tallest pine, and the impression given is one of equality. This is not necessarily so, since logically the following lines could assert any number of things about the relationship between the two objects; but because they are objects, offering the mind the convenience of focal points that are concrete, and because they are linked in the reading sequence by an abstract term of relationship (equal), the reader is encouraged to take from the line an image, however faint and wavering, of the two side by side. As he proceeds that image will be reinforced, since Milton demands that he attach to it the information given in 293 and the first half of 294; that is, in order to maintain the control over the text that a long syntactical unit tends to diminish, the reader will accept 'hewn on Norwegian hills' as an adjunct of the tallest pine in a very real way. By providing a scene or background (*memoria*) the phrase allows him to strengthen his hold on what now promises to be an increasingly complex statement of relationships. And in the construction of that background the pine frees itself from the hypothetical blur of the first line; it is now real, and through an unavoidable process of association the spear which stood in an undefined relationship to an undefined pine is seen (and I mean the word literally) in a kind of apposition to a conveniently visual pine. (This all happens very quickly in the mind of the reader who does not have time to analyse the cerebral adjustments forced upon him by the simile.) In short the equation (in size) of the two objects, in 292 only a possibility, is posited by the reader in 292–4 because it simplifies his task; and this movement towards simplification will be encouraged, for Milton's fit reader, by the obvious reference in 'to be the Mast/ Of some Great Ammiral' to the staff of the Cyclops Polyphemus, identified in the *Aeneid* as a lopped pine[14] and likened in the *Odyssey* to 'the mast of some black ship of twenty oars.'[15]

The construction of the image and the formulation of the relationship between its components are blocked by the second half of line 294, 'were but a wand'. This does several things, and I must resort to the mechanical aid of enumeration: (1) in the confusion that follows this rupture of the reading sequence, the reader loses his hold on the visual focal points, and is unable to associate firmly the wand with either of them. The result is the momentary diminution of Satan's spear as well as the pine, although a second, and more wary, reading will correct this; but corrected, the impression remains (in line 295 a miniature Satan supports himself on a wand-like spear) and in the larger perspective, this aspect of the simile is one of many instances in the poem where Milton's praise of Satan is qualified even as it is bestowed.

(2) The simile illustrates Milton's solution of an apparently insoluble problem. How does a poet provide for his audience a perspective that is beyond the field of its perception? To put the case in terms of *Paradise Lost*, the simile as it functions in other poems will not do here. . . . A man exists and a wolf exists and if categories are enlarged sufficiently it can be said without distortion that they exist on a comparable level; a man exists and Satan (or God) exists, but any statement that considers their respective existences from a human perspective, however inclusive, is necessarily reductive, and is liable to falsify rather than clarify; and of course the human perspective is the only one available. Had Milton asserted the identity of Satan's spear and the tallest pine, he would not only have sacrificed the awe that attends incomprehensibility; he would also have lied, since clearly the *personae* of his extra-terrestrial drama are not confined within the limitations of our time and space. On the other hand, had he said that the spear is larger than one can imagine, he would have sacrificed the concreteness so necessary to the formulation of an effective image. What he does instead is grant the reader the convenience of concreteness (indeed fill his mind with it) and then tell him that what he sees is not what is there ('there' is never located). The result is almost a feat of prestidigitation: for the rhetorical negation of the scene so painstakingly constructed does not erase it; we are relieved of the necessity of believing the image true, but permitted to retain the solidity it offers our straining imaginations. Paradoxically, our awareness of the inadequacy of what is described and what we can apprehend provides, if only negatively, a sense of what cannot be described and what we cannot apprehend. Thus Milton is able to suggest a reality beyond this one by forcing us to feel, dramatically, its unavailability.

(3) Finally, the experience of reading the simile tells us a great deal about ourselves. How large is Satan's spear? The answer is, we don't know, although it is important that for a moment we think we do. Of course, one can construct, as James Whaler does, a statement of relative magnitudes (spear is to pine as pine is to wand)[20] but while this may be logical, it is not encouraged by the logic of the reading experience which says to us: If one were to compare Satan's spear with the tallest pine the comparison would be inadequate. I submit that any attempt either to

search out masts of Norwegian ships or determine the mean length of wands is irrelevant, however attractive the prospect to a certain kind of mind.

Another instance may make the case clearer. In Book III, Satan lands on the Sun:

> There lands the Fiend, a spot like which perhaps
> Astronomer in the Sun's lucent Orb
> Through his glaz'd optic Tube yet never saw. (588–90)

Again in the first line two focal points (spot and fiend) are offered the reader who sets them side by side in his mind; again the detail of the next one and one half lines is attached to the image, and a scene is formed, strengthening the implied equality of spot and fiend; indeed the physicality of the impression is so persuasive that the reader is led to join the astronomer and looks with him through a reassuringly specific telescope ('glaz'd optic Tube') to see – nothing at all ('yet never saw'). In both similes the reader is encouraged to assume that his perceptions extend to the object the poet would present, only to be informed that he is in error; and both similes are constructed in such a way that the error must be made before it can be acknowledged by a surprised reader. (The parallel to the rhetorical drama between demonic attraction and authorial rebuke should be obvious.) For, however many times the simile is reread, the 'yet never saw' is unexpected. The mind can not perform two operations at the same time, and one can either cling to the imminence of the disclaimer and repeat, silently, '"yet never saw" is coming, "yet never saw" is coming', or yield to the demands of the image and attend to its construction; and since the choice is really no choice at all – after each reading the negative is only a memory and cannot compete with the immediacy of the sensory evocation – the tail-like half-line always surprises.

Of course Milton wants the reader to pull himself up and reread, for this provides a controlled framework within which he is able to realize the extent and implication of his difficulty, much like the framework provided by the before and after warnings surrounding Belial's speech. The implication is personal; the similes and many other effects say to the reader: 'I know that you rely upon your senses for your apprehension of reality, but they are unreliable and hopelessly limited.' Significantly, Galileo is introduced in both similes; the Tuscan artist's glass represents the furthest extension of human perception, and that is not enough. The entire pattern, of which the instances I analyse here are the smallest part, is, among other things, a preparation for the moment in Book VIII when Adam responds to Raphael's astronomical dissertation: 'To whom thus Adam clear'd of doubt.' Reader reaction is involuntary: cleared of doubt? by that impossibly tortuous and equivocal description of two all too probable universes?[17] By this point, however, we are able to place our reaction, since Adam's experience here parallels ours in so many places (and a large part of the poem's meaning is communicated by our awareness of the relationship between Adam and ourselves). He *is* cleared of doubt, not because he now knows how the universe is constructed, but because he knows that he can not know; what clears him of doubt is the certainty of self-doubt, and as with us this certainty is the result of a superior's willingness to grant him, momentarily, the security of his perspective. Milton's lesson is one that twentieth-century science is just now beginning to learn:

> Finally, I come to what it seems to me may well be from the long range point of view the most revolutionary of the insights to be derived from our recent experiences in physics, more revolutionary than the insights afforded by the discoveries of Galileo and Newton, or of Darwin. This is the insight that it is impossible to transcend the human reference point. . . . The new insight comes from a realization that the structure of nature may eventually be such that our processes of thought do not correspond to it sufficiently to permit us to think about it at all.[18]

In *Paradise Lost*, our sense of time proves as illusory as our sense of space and physicality. Jackson Cope quotes with approval Sigfried Giedion and Joseph Frank who find in modern literature a new way of thinking about time:

> The flow of time which has its literary reflection in the Aristotelian development of an action having beginning, middle and end is . . . frozen into the labyrinthine planes of a spatial block which . . . can only be perceived by travelling both temporally and physically from point to point, but whose form has neither beginning, middle, end nor center, and must be effectively conceived as a simultaneity of multiple views.[19]

And Mrs Isabel MacCaffrey identifies the 'simultaneity of multiple views' with the eternal moment of God, a moment she argues that Milton makes ours:

> The long view of time as illusory, telescoped into a single vision, had been adopted in fancy by Christian writers. . . . Writing of Heaven and the little heaven of Paradise, Milton by a powerful releasing act of the imagination

transposed the intuitive single glance of God into the poem's mythical structure. Our vision of history becomes for the time being that of the Creator 'whose eye Views all things at one view' (II 189–90); like him, we are stationed on a 'prospect high Wherin past, present, future he beholds' (III 77–8).[20]

The experience of every reader, I think, affirms the truth of these statements; Milton does convince us that the world of his poem is a static one which 'slights chronology in favor of a folded structure which continually returns upon itself, or a spiral that circles about a single center'.[21] The question I would ask is how does he so convince us? His insistence on simultaneity is easily documented. How many times do we see Christ ascend, after the war in Heaven, after the passion, after Harrowing Hell, after giving Satan his death wound, after the creation, after the final conflagration, at the day of final judgment? How many times do our first parents fall, and how many times are they accorded grace? The answer to all these questions is, 'many times' or is it all the time (at each point of time) or perhaps at one, and the same, time. My difficulty with the preceding sentence is a part of my point: I cannot let go of the word 'time' and the idea of sequence; timelessness (I am forced to resort to a question-begging negative) is an interesting concept, but we are all of us trapped in the necessity of experiencing in time, and the attempt even to conceive of a state where words like day and evening measure space rather than duration is a difficult one; Chaucer's Troilus, among others, is defeated by it. Mrs MacCaffrey asserts that 'spatial imagining' is part of Milton's 'mental climate' and the researches of Walter Ong, among others, support her; but if Milton has implanted the eternal moment 'into the poem's mythical structure', how does the reader, who, in Cope's words, must travel 'temporally and physically from point to point', root it out? Obviously many readers do not; witness the critics who are troubled by contradictory or 'impossible' sequences and inartistic repetitions. Again the reactions of these anti-Miltonists are the surest guide to the poet's method; for it is only by encouraging and then 'breaking' conventional responses and expectations that Milton can point his reader beyond them. To return to Waldock, part of the poem's apparently 'hard and definite' outline is the easy chronology it seems to offer; but the pressures of innumerable local contexts demand adjustments that give the lie to the illusion of sequence and reveal in still another way the inability of the reader to consider this poem as he would any other.

In the opening lines of Book 1, chronology and sequence are suggested at once in what is almost a plot line: man disobeys, eats fruit, suffers woe and awaits rescue. It is a very old and simple story, one that promises a comfortable correlation of plot station and emotional response: horror and fear at the act, sorrow at the result, joy at the happy ending, the whole bound up in the certain knowledge of cause and effect. As Milton crowds more history into his invocation the reader, who likes to know what time it is, will attempt to locate each detail on the continuum of his story line. The inspiration of the shepherd, Moses, is easily placed between the fall and the restoration; at this point many readers will feel the first twinge of complication, for Moses is a type of Christ who as the second Adam restores the first by persevering when he could not; as one begins to construct statements of relationship between the three, the clarity of lines 1–3 fade. Of course there is nothing to force the construction of such statements, and Milton thoughtfully provides in the very next line the sequence-establishing phrase, 'In the Beginning'. Reassured both by the ordering power of 'beginning' and by the allusion to Genesis (which is, after all, the original of all once-upon-a-times), the reader proceeds with the invocation, noting, no doubt, all the riches unearthed by generations of critical exegesis, but still firmly in control of chronology; and that sense of control is reinforced by the two-word introduction to the story proper: 'Say first', for with the first we automatically posit a second and then a third, and in sum, a neat row of causal statements leading all the way to an end already known.

The security of sequence, however, is soon taken away. I have for some time conducted a private poll with a single question. 'What is your reaction when the second half of line 54 – "for *now* the thought" – tells you that you are *now* with Satan, in Hell?' The unanimous reply is, 'surprise', and an involuntary question: How did I come to be here? Upon rereading, the descent to Hell is again easy and again unchartable. At line 26 the time-scheme is still manageable: there is (a) poet time, the *now* in which the reader sits in his chair and listens, with Milton, to the muse, and (b) the named point in the past when the story ('our Grand Parents . . . so highly to fall off') and our understanding of it ('say first what cause') is assumed to begin. At 33, the 'first' is set back to the act of Satan, now suggested but not firmly identified as the cause of 27, and a third time (c) is introduced, further from (a) than (b), yet still manageable; but Satan's act also has its antecedent: 'what time his

Pride/ Had cast him out from Heav'n' (36–7); by this point, 'what time' is both an assertion and a question as the reader struggles to maintain an awkward, backward-moving perspective. There is now a time (*d*) and after (that is, before) that an (*e*) 'aspiring . . . He trusted to have equalled the most High' (38, 40). Time (*f*) breaks the pattern, returning to (*d*) and providing, in the extended description of 44–53, a respite from sudden shifts. To summarize: the reader has been asked repeatedly to readjust his idea of 'in the beginning' while holding in suspension two plot lines (Adam and Eve's, and Satan's) that are eventually, he knows, to be connected. The effort strains the mind to its capacity, and the relief offered by the vivid and easy picture of Satan falling is more than welcome.[22] It is at this time, when the reader's attention has relaxed, that Milton slips by him the 'now' of 54 and the present tense of 'torments', the first present in the passage. The effect is to alert the reader both to his location (Hell) and to his inability to retrace the journey that brought him there. Rereading leads him only to repeat the mental occupations the passage demands, and while the arrival in Hell is anticipated, it is always a surprise. The technique is of course the technique of the spot and spear similes, and of the clash between involuntary response and authorial rebuke, and again Milton's intention is to strip from us another of the natural aids we bring to the task of reading. The passage itself tells us this in lines 50–1, although the message may pass unnoted at first: 'Nine times the Space that measures Day and Night.' Does space measure day and night? Are day and night space? The line raises these questions, and the half-line that follows answers them, not 'to mortal men' who think in terms of duration and sequence, not to us. In this poem we must, we will, learn a new time.

The learning process is slow at first; the reader does not necessarily draw the inferences I do from this early passage; but again it is the frequency of such instances, that makes my case. In Book II, when the fallen Angels disperse, some of them explore 'on bold adventure' their new home. One of the landmarks they pass is 'Lethe the River of Oblivion', and Milton pauses to describe its part in God's future plans: 'At certain revolutions all the damn'd/ . . . They ferry over this *Lethean* Sound/ Both to and fro, their sorrow to augment,/ And wish and struggle, as they pass to reach/ The tempting stream, with one small drop to lose/ In sweet forgetfulness all pain and woe,/ All in one moment and so near the brink;/ But Fate withstands' (597–8, 604–10). At 614 the poet continues with 'Thus roving on/ In confused march forlorn', and only the phrase 'adventurous bands' in 615 tells the reader that the poet has returned to the fallen angels. The mistake is a natural one: 'forlorn' describes perfectly the state of the damned, as does 'Confused march' their movements 'to and fro': indeed a second reflection suggests no mistake at all; the fallen angels *are* the damned, and one drop of Lethe would allow them to lose their woe in the oblivion Moloch would welcome. Fate *does* withstand. What Milton has done by allowing this momentary confusion is point to the identity of these damned and all damned. As they fly past Lethe the fallen angels are all those who will become them; they do not stand for their successors (the word defeats me), they *state* them. In *Paradise Lost*, history and the historical sense are denied and the reader is forced to see events he necessarily perceives in sequence as time-identities. Milton cannot re-create the eternal moment, but by encouraging and then blocking the construction of sequential relationships he can lead the reader to accept the necessity of, and perhaps even apprehend, negatively, a time that is ultimately unavailable to him because of his limitations.

This translation of felt ambiguities, confusions and tautologies into a conviction of timelessness in the narrative is assured partially by the uniqueness of Milton's 'fable'. 'For the Renaissance', notes Mrs MacCaffrey, 'all myths are reflections, distorted or mutilated though they may be, of the one true myth.'[23] For Milton all history is a replay of the history he is telling, all rebellions, one rebellion, all falls, one fall, all heroism the heroism of Christ. And his readers who share this Christian view of history will be prepared to make the connection that exists potentially in the detail of the narrative. The similes are particularly relevant here. The first of these compares Satan to Leviathan, but the comparison, to the informed reader, is a tautology; Satan *is* Leviathan and the simile presents two aspects of one, rather than the juxtaposition of two, components. This implies that Satan is, at the moment of the simile, already deceiving 'The Pilot of some small night-founder'd Skiff'; and if the reader has attended to the lesson of his recent encounter with the epic voice he recognizes himself as that pilot, moored during the speech of I 84–126 by the side of Leviathan. The contests between Satan and Adam, Leviathan and the pilot, rhetoric and the reader – the simile compresses them, and all deceptions, into a single instant, forever recurring. The celebrated falling-leaves simile moves from angel form to leaves to sedge to Busiris and his Memphian Chivalry, or in typological terms (Pharaoh and Herod are the most common types of Satan) from fallen angels to fallen angels. The compression here is so complex that it defies analysis: the fallen angels as they *lie* on the burning lake (the Red Sea) are already *pursuing* the Sojourners of Goshen (Adam and Eve, the Israelites, the reader) who are for the moment on the safe shore (Paradise, the reader's chair). In Book XII 191, Pharaoh becomes the River-dragon or Leviathan (Isaiah xxvi 1), pointing to the ultimate unity of the Leviathan and falling-leaves similes themselves. As similes they are uninformative; how numberless are the fallen angels? they are as numberless as Pharaoh's host, that is, as fallen angels, and Pharaoh's host encompasses all the damned who have been, are, and will be, all the damned who will fly longingly above Lethe. As vehicles of perception they tell us a great deal, about the cosmos as it is in a reality we necessarily distort, about the ultimate subjectivity of sequential time, about ourselves.

There are many such instances in the early books and together they create a sensitivity to the difficulties of writing and reading this particular poem. When Milton's epic voice remarks that pagan fablers err relating the story of Mulciber's ejection from Heaven (I 747), he does not mean to say that the story is not true, but that it is a distorted version of the story he is telling, and that any attempt to apprehend the nature of the angels' fall by comparing it to the fall of Mulciber or of Hesiod's giants involves another distortion that can not be allowed if *Paradise Lost* is to be read correctly. On the other hand the attempt is hazarded (the reader cannot help it), the distortion is acknowledged along with the unavailability of the correct reading, and Milton's point is made despite, or rather because of, the intractability of his material. When Satan's flight from the judgment of God's scales (IV 1015) is presented in a line that paraphrases the last line of the *Aeneid*, the first impulse is to translate the allusion into a comparison that might begin, 'Satan is like Turnus in that . . .'; but of course, the relationship as it exists in a reality beyond that formed by our sense of literary history, is quite the opposite. Turnus's defiance of the fates and his inevitable defeat are significant and comprehensible only in the light of what Satan did in a past that our time signatures can not name and is about to do in a present (poem time) that is increasingly difficult to identify. Whatever the allusion adds to the richness of the poem's texture or to Milton's case for superiority in the epic genre, it is also one more assault on the confidence of a reader who is met at every turn with demands his intellect cannot even consider.

III

Most poets write for an audience assumed fit. Why is the fitness of Milton's audience a concern of the poem itself? One answer to this question has been given in the preceding pages: only by forcing upon his reader an awareness of his limited perspective can Milton provide even a negative intuition of what another would be like; it is a brilliant solution to the impossible demands of his subject, enabling him to avoid the falsification of anthropomorphism and the ineffectiveness of abstraction. Another answer follows from this one: the reader who fails repeatedly before the pressures of the poem soon realizes that his difficulty proves its major assertions – the fact of the fall, and his own (that is Adam's) responsibility for it, and the subsequent woes of the human situation. The reasoning is circular, but the circularity is appropriate to the uniqueness of the poem's subject matter; for while in most poems effects are achieved through the manipulation of reader response, this poet is telling the story that *created* and still creates the responses of its reader and of all readers. The reader who falls before the lures of Satanic rhetoric displays again the weakness of Adam, and his inability to avoid repeating that fall throughout indicates the extent to which Adam's lapse has made the reassertion of right reason impossible. St Paul articulates the dilemma of fallen man when he cries, 'For the good that I would I do not: but the evil which I would not, that I do' (Romans vii 19). The true horror of the Fall is to be found here, in the loss of that happy state in which man's faculties worked in perfect harmony, allowing him accurately to assess his responsibilities and to meet them. Fallen man is hopelessly corrupt and his corruption resists even the grace freely offered to him through the intercession of Jesus Christ. Man's soul becomes the scene of a battle between the carnality of the first Adam (the old, unregenerate, man) and the righteousness of the second (the new, regenerate, man); and in the seventeenth century the image of an intestine warfare that is simultaneously the sign of the fall and an indication of Christ's entry into the soul is to be seen everywhere:

There is in Man, by reason of his general *Corruption*, such a distemper wrought, as that there is not onely *crookednesse* in, but dissension also, and fighting betweene his parts: And, though the Light of our *Reason* be by Man's Fall much dimmed and decayed; yet the remainders thereof are so adverse to our unruly *Appetite*, as that it laboureth against us. (Edward Reynolds, *A Treatise of the Passions and Faculties of the Soul of Man*, 1640)

Reason therefore may rightly discern the thing which is good, and yet the will of man not incline itself thereunto, as often the prejudice of sensible experience doth oversway. (Hooker, *Ecclesiastical Polity*, I vii 6)

Our erected wit maketh us know what perfection is, and yet our infected will keepeth us from reaching unto it. (Sidney, *Apologie for Poetrie*, 1595)

Milton transforms this commonplace into a poetic technique; he leads us to feel again and again the conflict between the poem's assumed morality and our responses, and to locate the seat of that conflict in our fallen nature and not in any failure in composition. In short, the reader's difficulty is the result of the act that is the poem's subject. The reading experience becomes the felt measure of man's loss and since Milton always supplies a corrective to the reader's errors and distortions, what other critics have seen as the 'disquieting' aspect of that experience can be placed in a context that makes sense of it. Through the process of trial and error we become better able to understand our limitations and ultimately, perhaps to transcend them. Not that we drive the Old Adam out of our hearts: this will be Christ's final victory – 'Not by destroying Satan, but his works/ In thee' (XII 394–5). What we can do is prepare ourselves to accept him and Milton aids us by delivering us to our errors – but only for an instant. It is important that we recognize and correct our mistakes immediately, lest they become a permanent part of our attitudes toward the poem's issues and distort our reading. 'Correct' of course is misleading. The mistakes have been made, and cannot be discounted. Indeed they are necessary if the poem is to bring us to that self-awareness Milton desires for us. Like his God, Milton is an affectionate but firm taskmaster who protects us from our weaknesses by making us know them. When, in the second part of *Pilgrim's Progress*, Christiana wonders why she and her companion were not forwarned of the danger lurking 'so near the Kings Palace' or, better still, provided with a 'Conductor', Reliever answers: 'Had my Lord granted you a Conductor, you would not neither, so have bewailed that oversight of yours in not asking for one, as now you have occasion to do. So all things work for good, and tend to make you more wary';[24] and Mercy adds, 'by this neglect, we have an occasion ministered unto us to behold our own imperfections'.[25] With the same compassionate and deliberate neglect, Milton makes the whole of

Paradise Lost just such an occasion, the poet's version of what the theologian calls a 'good temptation':

> A good temptation is that whereby God tempts even the righteous for the purpose of proving them, not as though he were ignorant of the disposition of their hearts, but for the purpose of exercising or manifesting their faith or patience ... or of lessening their self confidence, and reproving their weakness, that ... they themselves may become wiser by experience.[26]

The long-range result of this technique is the creation of a 'split reader', one who is continually responding to two distinct sets of stimuli – the experience of individual poetic moments and the ever-present pressure of the poem's official doctrine – and who attaches these responses to warring forces within him, and is thus simultaneously the location and the observer of their struggle. This division in the reader is nowhere more apparent or more central to Milton's intention than in Book IX when Adam chooses to disobey. Waldock raised a very real question (which he then answered too quickly) when he argued that at its most crucial point, 'the poem asks from us, at one and the same time, two incompatible responses ... that Adam did right, and ... that he did wrong. The dilemma is as critical as that, and there is no way of escape.'[27] Almost immediately Paul Turner replied by pointing out that the poet does not want us to escape: 'What would happen if ... the reader did *not* feel inside himself a strong, almost overwhelming impulse to do what Adam did. What sort of significance ... would remain?'[28] The ambivalence of the response is meaningful because the reader is able to identify its components with different parts of his being: one part, faithful to what he has been taught to believe (his 'erected wit') and responsive to the unmistakable sentiments of the poem's official voice, recoils in the presence of what he *knows* to be wrong; but another part, subversive and unbidden (his 'infected will') surprises and overcomes him and Adam is secretly applauded. It would be a mistake to deny either of these impulses; they must be accepted and noted because the self must be accepted before it can be transformed. The value of the experience depends on the reader's willingness to participate in it fully while at the same time standing apart from it: he must pass judgement on it, at least on that portion of it which is a reflection of his weakness. So that if we retain Waldock's formula, a description of the total response would be, Adam is wrong, no, he's right, but, then, of course he is wrong, and so am I. This last is not so much a product of the scene itself as of the moral conditioning the poem has exposed us to and of the self-consciousness it encourages. In effect the reader imposes this final certainty on the ambiguity of the poetic moment (this is the way of escape), but, in doing so, he does not deny its richness; indeed he adds to it by *ordering* it, by providing another perspective which gives the ambiguity meaning and renders it edifying; moreover, the uneasiness he feels at his own reaction to the fact of sin is a sign that he is not yet lost: 'If in the act of being surprised and overcome by sin, his heart nevertheless rises against it . . . then it is only the old Adam and not his true spiritual self that has offended.'[29]

One might ask at this point, why read a poem that treats its reader so badly? Why continue to suffer an experience that is unpleasant? The answer is simply that for the seventeenth-century Puritan and indeed for any Christian in what we might call the Augustinian tradition, the kind of discomfort I have been describing would be paradoxically a source of comfort and the unpleasantness a source of pleasure. Milton did not write for the atheist, but for the 'cold' Christian (neither saint nor apostate) who can not help but allow the press of ordinary life to 'divert his thoughts from Heav'n'. In the same way, the sense of sin so necessary to a properly disposed Christian soul, is blunted rather than reinforced by the familiar recitation of scriptural commonplaces in sermons. One may hear every day of the depravity of natural man and of the inefficacy of unaided human efforts, but, inevitably, the incantational repetition of a truth lessens its immediate and personal force, and the sinner becomes complacent in a verbal and abstract contrition. *Paradise Lost* is immediate and forceful in the communication of these unflattering truths, again following the example of Christ who administers to the Pharisees 'not by the middling temper . . . but by the other extreme of *antidote* . . . a sharp & corrosive sentence against a foul and putrid licence; not to eate into the flesh, but into the sore'.[30] In the manner of the Old Law, the poem is designed to 'call forth and develope our natural depravity . . . that it might impress us with a slavish fear . . . that it might be a schoolmaster to bring us to the righteousness of Christ'.[31] And since perpetual vexation and self doubt are signs that the spirit of the Lord is at work, Milton's reader welcomes an experience he knows to be salutary to his spiritual health; a 'good temptation' he points out 'is therefore rather to be desired'.[32] Of course the reader never learns anything he did not know before he entered the poem; but the knowledge that comes from the *forced* and *conscious* rediscovery of old truths is particularly valuable, and, in an important sense, new. It should be noted, in addition, that the reading offered here is a partial one. I have isolated this pattern in order to make a precise and rather narrow point about the way the poem works on one level. In Milton's larger scheme the conviction that man can do nothing is accompanied by the conviction that Christ has taken it upon himself to do it all. As Joseph Summers writes, in another context, 'The essential "act" is that the individual should abandon the pretence that he *can* act in any way pertaining to salvation: he must experience the full realiza-tion that salvation belongs to God, that nothing he can do either by faith or works can help. The doctrine is moreover, "comforting", for "all things" are "more ours by being his"' (*George Herbert* (1954) p. 61). We are told this at the first – 'till one greater Man/ Restore us and regain the blissfull seat' – but in the course of our struggles with Books I and II, we *forget*, as Milton intends us to, so that we can be reminded dramati-cally by the glorious sacrifice of Book III. Milton impresses us with the negativity and despair of one aspect of Christian doctrine so that he can send us joyfully to the promise of another.

We shall learn Milton's lessons only if we enter the poem on his terms. The fifth inference I drew from Waldock's criticism of the intrusive epic voice was that for him the question of relative authority is a purely aesthetic one. 'Milton's allegations clash with his demonstra-tions . . . in any work of imaginative literature at all it is the demonstra-tion . . . that has the higher validity: an allegation can possess no comparable authority.' In his brilliantly perverse *Milton's God* William Empson asserts 'all the characters are on trial in any civilized narrative'[33] and Waldock would, I think, include the epic voice in this statement. The insistence on the superiority of showing as opposed to telling is, as Wayne Booth has shown, a modern one, and particularly unfortunate in this case since it ignores the historical reality of the genre.[34] When Homer names Achilles wrathful, do we search the narrative for proof he is not; is Odysseus's craft on trial or do we accept it because we accept the authority of the epic voice? Do we attempt to make a case for Aeneas's *im*piety? There is an obvious retort to all this: the authority of epic voices in other epics is accepted because their comments either confirm or anticipate the reading experience; Milton invites us to put his epic voice on trial by allowing the reading experience to contradict it. (Waldock: 'Of course they should agree.') I agree that the reader can not help but notice the clash of authorities; his familiarity with the

genre would lead him to look to the epic voice for guidance and
clarification. But I do not think that any fit reader would resolve the
problem, as Waldock does, and decide immediately and happily for the
poem (and for himself) and against the prescience of its narrator. Milton
assumes a predisposition in favour of the epic voice rather than a
modern eagerness to put that voice on trial; he expects his reader to
worry about the clash, to place it in a context that would resolve a
troublesome contradiction and allow him to reunite with an authority
who is a natural ally against the difficulties of the poem. There is at
least a Virgilian precedent: in the fourth book of the *Aeneid*, a great deal
of Virgil's meaning is communicated through the felt contrast between
the persuasiveness of Dido's appeal to Aeneas and the quiet firmness of
his rejection of her. So successful is the poet that at least one of his
editors becomes angry with him: 'To an appeal which would move a
stone Aeneas replies with the cold and formal rhetoric of an attorney . . .
Aeneas is left "stammering and preparing to say many things" – a hero
who had, one would think, lost his character for ever. But Virgil seems
unmoved by his own genius, and begins the next paragraph quite
placidly *at pius Aeneas* . . . ! How the man who wrote the lines placed
in Dido's mouth could immediately afterwards speak of "the good
Aeneas etc." is one of the puzzles of literature.'[35] Not so puzzling when
one realizes that the scene is designed to dramatize for the reader
exactly what the adjective *pius* means. The reader is allowed to feel the
pull Dido exerts on him and then to hear the reply of Aeneas, *Iovis
monitis immota* (331). With Page, many readers will for a moment
hesitate to accept this action as a truly virtuous one, until the narrator
steps in authoritatively with his 'placid' *at pius Aeneas*. In the following
lines the reality of Dido's claim on our attention is acknowledged, but
subordinated to a higher claim:

> At pius Aeneas, quamquam linire dolentem
> solando cupit et dictis avertere curas,
> multa gemens magnoque animum labefactus amore
> iussa tamen divum exsequitur classemque revisit. (393–6)

The dramatic and moral tensions of the moment are exhibited in the
syntax; the main clause is a simple declarative, cold, absolute and, one
could say, insensitive to complexity, 'the good Aeneas follows the
orders of the Gods and returns to the fleet'; but contained within the
main clause and literally surrounded by it are all the considerations

Aeneas must reject along with Dido, her sorrow, his own inclinations,
the fact of love: 'although he desires to assuage her sorrows and turn
aside her grief with his words, sighing much, his soul shaken by his
mighty love'. The firmness and precision of the narrator's comment
guides the reader and leads him to a clearer conception of Aeneas's
heroism which is here measured by the effort of will it requires to leave
Dido.[36] Indeed, the experience of the scene redefines heroism completely as does our experience of Satan. Satan's initial attractiveness
owes as much to a traditional idea of what is heroic as it does to our
weakness before the rhetorical lure. He exemplifies a form of heroism
most of us find easy to admire because it is visible and flamboyant (the
epic voice also admires: the 'though in pain' of 'So spake th' Apostate
Angel, though in pain' is a recognition of the steadfastness that can
belong even to perversity; the devil is always given his due).[37] Because
his courage is never denied (instead Milton insists on it) while his virtue
and goodness are (in the 'allegations' of the epic voice), the reader is led
to revise his idea of what a true hero is. If this poem does anything to its
readers, it forces them to make finer and finer discriminations. Perhaps
the most important aspect of the process I have been describing – the
creation of a reader who is fit because he knows and understands his
limitations – begins here at I 125 when Milton's authorial corrective
casts the first stone at the ideal of martial valor and points us toward the
meaningful acceptance of something better.[38]

NOTES

1. This article incorporates, with some additions, two articles published in the summer
and autumn issues of *Critical Quarterly* (1965). In its present form it is the first chapter of
my book, *Surprised by Sin: the Reader in Paradise Lost* (1967).

2. *Paradise Lost and its Critics* (1947) p. 15. I consider Waldock's book to be the most
forthright statement of an anti-Miltonism that can be found in the criticism of Leavis and
Eliot, and, more recently, of Empson, R. J. Zwi Werblowsky, H. R. Swardson and John
Peter. Bernard Bergonzi concludes his analysis of Waldock by saying, 'no attempt has
been made to defend the poem in the same detailed and specific manner in which it has
been attacked' – *The Living Milton*, ed. Frank Kermode (1960) p. 171. This essay is such an
attempt. Bergonzi goes on to assert that 'a successful answer to Waldock would have to
show that the narrative structure of *Paradise Lost does* possess the kind of coherence and
psychological plausibility that we have come to expect from the novel. Again there can be
no doubt that it does not' (p. 174). I shall argue that the coherence and psychological
plausibility of the poem are to be found in the relationship between its effects and the mind
of its reader. To some extent my reading has been anticipated by Joseph Summers in his
brilliant study, *The Muse's Method* (Harvard, 1962). See especially pp. 30–1: 'Milton
anticipated ... the technique of the "guilty reader" .... The readers as well as the charac-

ters have been involved in the evil and have been forced to recognize and judge their involvement.' See also Ann Ferry's *Milton's Epic Voice: the Narrator in Paradise Lost* (Harvard, 1963) pp. 44–66: 'We are meant to remember that the events of the poem have already occurred . . . and that it is because of what happens in the poem, because we and all men were corrupted by the Fall, that we stand in need of a guide to correct our reading of it. The narrative voice is our guide' (p. 47).

3. *Paradise Lost and its Critics*, p. 24.

4. Ibid. p. 77.

5. Quoted by Basil Willey in *The Seventeenth-century Background* (New York, 1955) p. 211.

6. As Davis Harding points out – *The Club of Hercules* (Urbana, 1962) pp. 103–8 – this passage is also the basis of the bee simile at line 768. The reader who catches the allusion here at line 108 will carry it with him to the end of the book and to the simile. One should also note the parallel between the epic voice's comment at 126 and Virgil's comment on Aeneas's first speech (as Milton's early editors noted it): 'Talia voce refert, curisque ingentibus aeger/ spem voltu simulat, premit altum corde dolorem.' But as is always the case in such comparisons, Satan suffers by it, since his deception is self-deception and involves an attempt to deny (to himself) the reality of an authority greater than his, while Aeneas's deception is, in context, an evidence of his faith in the promise of a higher authority. The hope he feigns is only partially a pretence; if it were all pretence, he would not bother.

7. *Answerable Style: Essays on Paradise Lost* (Minneapolis, 1953) p. 124.

8. *Paradise Lost and its Critics*, p. 79. Cf. John Peter, *A Critique of Paradise Lost* (1960) p. 44: 'the comments [of the epic voice] seem simply biased . . . His premises are correct and he deduces from them a perfectly feasible plan.'

9. *Complete Prose Works of John Milton*, ed. Ernest Sirluck (New Haven, Conn., 1959) II 642.

10. Ibid. p. 301.

11. Ibid. p. 338.

12. Ibid. pp. 678–9.

13. 'Milton and Sacred History: Books XI and XII of *Paradise Lost*', in *Essays in English Literature from the Renaissance to the Victorian Age, Presented to A. S. P. Woodhouse*, ed. Millar MacLure and F. W. Watt (Toronto, 1964) pp. 149–68.

14. III 659. Harding insists that 'if this passage does not conjure up a mental picture of Polyphemus on the mountaintop, steadying his footsteps with a lopped pine . . . it has not communicated its full meaning to us' (*The Club of Hercules*, p. 63). In my reading a 'full reading' of the passage involves the recognition of the inadequacy of the mental picture so conjured up.

15. The translation is E. V. Rieu's in the Penguin Classic edition (Baltimore, 1946) p. 148.

16. 'The Miltonic Simile', in *Publications of the Modern Language Association of America*, XLVI (1931) 1064.

17. Milton clearly anticipates this reaction when he describes the dialogue in the 'argument'; 'Adam inquires concerning celestial Motions, is *doubtfully* answer'd' (emphasis mine). See also V 261–6: 'As when by night the Glass of *Galileo*, less assur'd, observes/ Imagin'd Lands and Regions in the Moon:/ Or Pilot from amidst the *Cyclades/ Delos* or *Samos* first appearing kens/ A cloudy spot.' It should be noted that in all these passages certain details form a consistent pattern: Galileo, the moon, spots (representing an unclear vision) etc. The pattern is fulfilled in Raphael's disquisition on the possible arrangement of the heavens. See Thomas Greene's excellent reading of Raphael's descent (*The Descent from Heaven: a Study in Epic Continuity* (New Haven, Conn., 1963) p. 387): 'The fallen reader's imperfect reason must strain to make out relations as the pilot strains with his physical eyes, as Galileo strains with his telescope, as the fowls gaze with mistaken recognition on the angel, as Adam and Eve will fail to strain and so blur our vision.'

18. Percy Bridgman, in *The Limits of Language*, ed. Walker Gibson (New York, 1962), p. 21.

19. *The Metaphoric Structure of Paradise Lost* (Baltimore, 1962) pp. 14–15.

20. *Paradise Lost as Myth* (Cambridge, Mass., 1959) p. 53.

21. Ibid. p. 45.

22. The technique is reminiscent of Virgil's 'historical present', which is used to bring the action of the epic before the reader's eyes. Recently Helen Gardner has reached conclusions similar to those offered here concerning the operation of time and space in the poem: See her *A Reading of Paradise Lost* (1965) pp. 39–51: 'Milton's poem must move in time, yet he continually suggests that the time of his poem is an illusion' (p. 39); 'Milton, as he plays us into his poem, is using our human measurement to convey vastness sensuously' (p. 40); 'He continually satisfies and then defeats our powers of visualization' (p. 41).

23. *Paradise Lost as Myth*, p. 14.

24. *The Pilgrim's Progress*, ed. J. B. Wharey, rev. R. Sharrock (1960) p. 196.

25. Loc. cit.

26. *The Works of John Milton*, ed. F. A. Patterson *et al.* (New York, 1933) xv 87–9. Cf. Bunyan's Apology for his Book where he defends a method similar to Milton's and for similar reasons: 'You see the ways the Fisher-man doth take/ To catch the Fish; what Engins doth he make?/ . . . Yet Fish there be, that neither Hook, nor Line,/ Nor Snare/ nor Net, nor Engine can make thine;/ They must be grop'd for, and be tickled too,/ Or they will not be catcht, what e're you do' (p. 3); 'This Book will make a Travailer of thee,/ If by its Counsel thou wilt ruled be;/ It will direct thee to the Holy Land,/ If thou wilt its Directions understand;/ Yea, it will make the sloathful active be;/ The Blind also, delightful things to see' (op. cit. pp. 6–7).

27. *Paradise Lost and Its Critics*, p. 56. See also Peter, *Critique*, pp. 130–1.

28. 'Woman and the Fall of Man', in *English Studies*, XXIX (1948) 16.

29. A paraphrase by William Haller, in *The Rise of Puritanism* (New York, 1938) p. 157, of a point made in the *Garden of Spirituall Flowers*.

30. *Complete Prose Works*, II 668.

31. *The Works of John Milton*, XVI 131.

32. See note 26.

33. *Milton's God* (Norfolk, 1961) p. 94.

34. *The Rhetoric of Fiction* (Chicago, 1961) p. 4: '. . . even Homer writes scarcely a page without some kind of direct clarification of motives, of expectations, and of the relative importance of events. And though the gods themselves are often unreliable, Homer – the Homer we know – is not. What he tells us usually goes deeper and is more accurate than anything we are likely to learn about real people and events.'

35. From the introduction of T. E. Page's edition of the *Aeneid*, 2 vols (1909) I xviii–xix.

36. Again there is a Christian analogue in *The Pilgrim's Progress* when Christian stops his ears against the cries of his family 'and ran on crying, Life, Life, Eternal Life'. See edition quoted above, p. 10.

37. Patrick Hume in his notes to the poem (1795) suggests still another possible reading for this couplet: 'Though in torment, making vain boastings' (p. 10). That is, even while he is racked with pain, Satan cannot resist an occasion for hearing his own voice. Presumably, he would find something better to do.

38. An obvious objection to this way of resolving the contradictions so many have seen in *Paradise Lost* is the excessively self-conscious reader it posits, a reader who continually makes discriminations of incredible delicacy, a reader who is able to accept, even use, reproof and confusion, a reader who is, in sum, the detachedly involved observer of his own mental processes. Could Milton have assumed such a reader? I believe that he could have and did, and that my reading is true not only to the poem, but to its historical context,

although the remarks that follow are intended to be the barest outline of an argument presented in my *Surprised by Sin*. My argument is based on the opposition of rhetoric, the art of appearances, to dialectic, the pursuit of a scientific–mathematical truth. Aristotle locates the power of rhetoric in the 'defects of our hearers' (*Rhetoric*, III 1); the pressures of Christianity transforms the vagueness of the 'defects of our hearers' into the precision of 'original sin'. Each text presents a problem for the Christian reader who must learn to resist the impulse to dwell on the niceties of rhetoric and attend only to the moral doctrine contained therein. Of course a rhetorical stimulus can be resisted if it is first recognized, that is, felt. The crucial moment, in the reading experience, then, is the moment between the first response to the lure and its rejection or acceptance. That moment is analogous to the crucial stage in the progress of sin, that moment between the consideration of sin and assent or rejection. The three stages of sin – suggestion–delectation–consent – find their analogies in the reading experience – response to the pull of the rhetorical, the moment of decision (whether or not to surrender to it), the abandonment of one's intellectual awareness to it. In practical terms this results in a programme of Christian reading, one that involves referring all appeals to the repository of Christian morality a reader must bring to a poem if it is to be read 'properly'. Boccaccio writes: 'But I repeat my advice to those who would appreciate poetry, and unwind its difficult involutions. You must read, you must persevere, you must sit up nights; you must inquire, and exert the utmost power of your mind' (*Boccaccio on Poetry*, ed. C. G. Osgood (Princeton, 1930) p. 62). In Milton's poem the epic voice acts as surrogate for the 'power of mind' that has defected to the lures the poem offers. What Milton does, then, is translate a philosophical–religious commonplace into a method of procedure. The method is possible and successful because the reader is taught by his theology to see in its operation the evidence of his own weakness or sin. In other words, rhetoric becomes the object attacked, and since rhetoric is firmly attached in the poem to the psychology of fallen man, the attack is finally on the reader who is forced by an inspired epic voice to acknowledge its success. The entire pattern is framed in the seventeenth century by an epistomology that stresses analysis and precision, and preaches a distrust of the rhetorical and emotional, and by an aesthetic that regards a poem as a potential instrument of conversion.

ARNOLD WILLIAMS

The Motivation of Satan's Rebellion in *Paradise Lost* (1945)

THOUGH, until very recently, critics have paid scant attention to the motivation of Satan's rebellion, it must be clear that this motivation is of cardinal importance to *Paradise Lost*. Without Satan's rebellion, man would possibly not have been created and would certainly not have fallen, and no justification of the ways of God to man would have been necessary or possible.[1] A proper understanding of the rebellion of Satan is likewise essential to the whole philosophic meaning of the epic. When Satan summons his followers to council in the North, evil enters the cosmos. Satan's action initiates the whole sequence of the expulsion of the rebel angels, the creation of man to take their place, the temptation and fall of man, and finally his regeneration by grace. So much hinges on the motivation of Satan's rebellion that an organized inquiry should be conducted into the methods by which Milton motivates Satan's rebellion, the exact meaning of Satan's actions, the sources on which Milton drew, and the dramatic validity of the account in *Paradise Lost* of the fall of the angels. This study attempts to sketch such an inquiry.[2]

When Milton approached the problem of how to motivate Satan's rebellion, he had, as for almost every other incident in *Paradise Lost*, a tradition behind him. Unfortunately, the tradition was more meager and confused on this one point than on nearly any other. Apparently Satan made his entry into the story of the Fall much later than the other characters: Adam, Eve, the Serpent (unidentified with Satan), and even Lilith, Adam's putative first wife, of whom Milton makes no use. So it happened that Milton could get from the Fathers, from rabbinical literature, and above all from the commentaries on Genesis rather consistent and detailed accounts of a great many matters of small import to his epic, but precious little usable material explaining why and how Satan rebelled against God in the first place.

In fact, in the whole traditional story of the creation and fall of man, the original motivation of Satan is the weakest link. Satan seems an imperfectly digested addition to the story, apparently the result partially of Persian influence and partially of a desire to cover up the crude animism of the original myth.[3] It was not, indeed, until relatively late that the serpent was understood as merely an agent or a disguise for Satan. The Book of Enoch, a pseudepigraph written by several hands between 170 and 64 B.C., is probably the first documentary evidence of a belief that the temptation of man was the work of a fallen angel.[4] In Enoch we find the notion that Gâdreêl, one of the 'satans', was the one who 'led astray Eve'.[5]

Even later in development is any satisfactory explanation of how the angels fell, how Satan became the adversary. There are three such explanations, all dating from the period of the two or three centuries immediately before and after the beginning of the Christian Era. Enoch supplies the first of these, actually an exegesis of Genesis 6: 1–5, which tells how the 'sons of God' took wives of the 'daughters of men'. According to Enoch, certain angels sent to guard mankind were lured by women and sinned carnally with them (Enoch vi 1–8). Since this explanation places the fall of the angels long after the temptation and fall of man, it is quite inconsistent with the notion that one of the fallen angels tempted Eve. Nevertheless, it was widely accepted and is echoed by many of the early Christian Fathers. It is one of the motivations that Milton might have used for his Satan. He alludes to it, but it obviously could not serve his purpose.[7]

Another possible motivation for Satan is found in the Adam and Eve books, which in various versions were popular over Europe in the Middle Ages. According to one of these, the Latin *Vita Adae et Evae*, when man was created God commanded the angels to worship him. The account is that of Satan, who after the Fall, tells Adam:

> When God blew into thee the breath of life and thy face and likeness was made in the image of God, and Michael also brought thee and made [us] worship thee in the sight of God. . . .

Michael worshipped first, but when Satan's time came he refused:

> I will not worship an inferior and younger being [than I]. I am his senior in the Creation, before he was made was I already made.[8]

This motivation of Satan's fall without doubt contributed a great deal to later Christian explanations of Satan's rebellion. The worship of man was more spiritually construed as the worship of God as man, that is, of

Christ. Hence Satan's sin was the refusal to accept the incarnation of God as man, an act by which man outranked the angels in the order of beings. Such a motivation would, if Milton knew it, be suited to the purpose of *Paradise Lost*.

For some reason hard to ascertain, however, this explanation failed to become the commonest one. It even enjoys scriptural authority of a sort. Hebrews 1: 6, 'And again when he bringeth in the first begotten into the world, he saith, And let all the angels of God worship him', seems to suggest the notion of commanded worship. Nevertheless, it is overshadowed in both theology and literature by the well-known account of the rebellion of Lucifer based on Isaiah 14: 12–15. Isaiah is clearly addressing himself to some prince of Babylon when he writes, 'How art thou fallen, O Lucifer.' However, generations of exegetes, from before the time of Augustine, understood the passage as either a figurative or a literal account of the rebellion and fall of Satan and the lost angels. The common explanation of Satan's fall is, then, that puffed up with pride and ambition, he sought to equal or surpass the Almighty, and for this offense was cast out of heaven into hell.

Like the other two explanations, this one also took form in the pseudepigrapha. *The Book of the Secrets of Enoch*, written between 30 B.C. and A.D. 70, has the following account:

> And one from out the order of angels, having turned away with the order that was under him, conceived an impossible thought, to place his throne higher than the clouds above the earth, that he might become equal in rank to my [God's] power.
> And I threw him out from the height with his angels, and he was flying in the air continuously above the bottomless.[9]

This angel is later identified with Satanail, and Secrets gives the further information that it was he who seduced Eve.[10]

This is substantially the account generally found in both theology and literature. The authority of Augustine, who strenuously opposed the motivation of Satan's fall from carnality[11] and regarded the prince of Babylon whose doom is told in Isaiah as a type of Satan, sufficed to ensure the dominance in theology of the motivation from pride. On the basis of John 8: 44, which says that Satan 'was a murderer from the beginning and abode not in the truth', Augustine writes that Satan's sin was refusal to subject himself piously to the Almighty. He proudly refused from the very first moment of his existence to render obedience.[12]

The motivation from envy survived in the Middle Ages in the *Vita* and accounts based on it, but except for these, the account of Satan's fall derived from Isaiah and sanctioned by Augustine remained standard for more than a thousand years. One finds it in scholastic theology.[13] It is common in the accounts of poets and dramatists. The Old English *Genesis B*, sometimes offered as a source for *Paradise Lost*, presents Satan, next in power to God, as thinking how he can set himself up a throne stronger than God's. 'Why am I to toil?' he asks himself. Relying on his strong comrades, he resolves to be God and works northwards and westwards to set up his throne. For this presumption he is cast out of heaven.[14]

The *Cursor Mundi* and the craft plays continue the same tradition. In the former Lucifer decides to set his seat against that of God:

> . . . mi sete i sal
> Gain him þat heist es of all;
> In þe north side it sal be sette
> O me seruis sal he non gette
> Qui suld I him seruis yeild?
> Al sal be at myn auen weild.[15]

The craft plays use the same motivation, adding a bit to the external action. In the four great cycles the account is that God left his throne vacant for a while to go to look over creation. Satan became ambitious, sat in the empty throne, proceeded to exact homage as God, was discovered by God when He returned, and was cast into Hell together with those angels who had done him reverence.[16]

In the Renaissance, too, pride and ambition are frequently given as the reasons for Satan's rebellion. Hugo Grotius makes pride the main motivation of Satan: he

> refused to call his God
> More than his equal.[17]

Quantities of allusions to Satan's ambition or pride could be gathered, of which one from Shakespeare and one from Bacon suffice. In *Henry VIII* Wolsey urges Cromwell to

> fling away ambition:
> By that sin fell the angels. (III ii 440-1)

Bacon writes that 'the desire of power in excess caused the angels to fall'.[18]

This survey of the traditional treatments of Satan's rebellion indicates the problem Milton faced in making Satan a principal character in *Paradise Lost*. On the figure of Satan the whole epic hinges. He must be of heroic proportions, for a weak or trivial Satan, like Marlowe's Mephistophilis, would have failed to provide the antagonism necessary in a poem of epic proportions. Cardinal to the delineation of a Satan of heroic proportions is the problem of motivating his rebellion. A weak motivation or none at all would have impaired the probability and wrecked the dramatic conflict of the epic.

Yet Milton has little to work with if he takes the standard motivation from pride. He has only the abstract vices of pride and lust for power. Like an Adam without free will, a Satan motivated only by pride in the abstract is a mere Satan 'of the motions'. Milton could not, like the authors of the craft plays, have Satan suddenly announce that he had decided to set his throne higher than God's. Nor could he accept Augustine's dictum that Satan was evil from the beginning of his existence. The trouble with the motivation from pride is that it answers one question by asking another. As the medieval theologian, Rupertus Tuitensis, writes, 'Quae causae fuerint superbiendi?' It starts with the premise that Satan is evil, that he needs no motivation and hardly any occasion. But even an Iago needs an opportunity to translate his innate moral perversion into overt act. And what was Satan's opportunity?

Milton must have wrestled with this problem. The third draft of the planned drama on the subject of the fall, preserved in the Cambridge Manuscript, shows that already Milton had assigned the narrative of Satan's rebellion and fall an important place in the play. Here the chorus has the part of telling 'Lucifers rebellion and fall' in act three. The fourth act includes a narrative by the chorus of 'the battle and victory in Heaven against him and his accomplices'. Already in the late thirties or early forties Milton realized how important was the motivation of Satan. Sometime in the succeeding years, when the drama gave way to the epic, he perceived his advantages.

One of these comes from the substitution of the epic for the dramatic form. Writing an epic, he can begin *in medias res* with a little more grace than if he were writing a play. The epic method of development thus gave him time to build up the character of Satan into an artistically convincing portrait of pride, ambition, and envy before he had to supply the motivation for Satan's rebellion. The characterization of Satan is chiefly contained in Books I and II and flows over into Book IV, all of which deal with events after his rebellion, which is told in Book v. The reader then comes to the account of the rebellion with a characterization of the fallen Satan in his mind and is inclined to read into the unfallen Satan the vices of the fallen Satan.

Moreover, the motivation from pride receives full expression in the first two books. Satan is the tempter 'Stird up with Envy and Revenge'. His 'Pride/ Had cast him out of Heav'n'. He 'trusted to have equal'd the Most High'. He calls himself 'The proud possessor' of hell and boasts that God shall never extort obedience or servitude from him. What Augustine and the later Fathers had established as the standard motivation of Satan, what the writers of the craft plays had clumsily tried to externalize in the business of the throne, here attains such artistic perfection that Milton's Satan has become the concrete artistic expression of pride. Had Milton stopped here, perhaps his motivation of Satan would have been convincing to any but the most critical readers, for most of us would doubtless not have noticed that the motivation was thoroughly *ex post facto*. Yet this could have been but a brilliant *tour de force*; it would have failed to trace the steps by which 'one of the first, if not the first' of the sons of light became the proud adversary, external champion of evil.

That Milton realized the weakness of the motivation from pride, even while he was using it, appears from various little hints found here and there in the first four books. For instance Satan is 'Stird up with Envy', not pride or ambition. And there is another interesting hint in Book II which we shall notice presently. At any rate, when the time comes to supply the full narrative of Satan's rebellion, Milton makes only supplementary use of the motivation from pride. Instead, he places main emphasis on the motivation from envy.

The account of Satan's rebellion, which is chronologically the beginning of *Paradise Lost*, begins towards the middle of Book v. On a day in Heaven's Great Year, Raphael tells Adam, the Father made an announcement to the assembled host of heaven:

> This day I have begot whom I declare
> My onely Son, and on this holy Hill
> Him have anointed, whom ye now behold
> At my right hand; your Head I him appoint;
> And by my self have sworn to him shall bow
> All knees in Heav'n, and shall confess him Lord:
> Under his great Vice-gerent Reign abide

> United as one individual Soule
> For ever happie: him who disobeyes
> Mee disobeyes, breaks union, and that day
> Cast out from God and blessed vision, falls
> Into utter darkness, deep ingulft, his place
> Ordaind without redemption, without end. (v 603–15)

Few passages in *Paradise Lost* have aroused more controversy, and we must, before analyzing the motivation of Satan, be sure what these lines actually mean. Some, of whom Raleigh and Saurat are the chief, have taken 'begot' literally and have held that Milton was making God say that He had actually generated the Son at a specific point of time after the angels had already been created.[19] More numerous are those that take 'begot' in other than a literal sense. Masson, Fletcher, Grierson, and, more recently, Kelley and Gilbert offer various explanations, the common element of which is that 'begot' is to be taken figuratively to mean something like 'exalted'.[20]

Gilbert, the most recent scholar to consider the problem, has gone far to clear up the theological meaning of the passage and to refute those who take 'begot' in a literal sense. The key scriptural text for the understanding of the passage, as Gilbert shows and as Newton long ago hinted,[21] is the second psalm, particularly verses 6 and 7:

> Yet have I set my kin upon the holy hill of Zion. I will declare the decree: the Lord hath said unto me, Thou art my Son; this day have I begotten thee.

This action is precisely what Milton is describing in the passage under consideration. The parallelism is complete. Moreover, Gilbert further shows, Milton in referring the psalm to the exaltation of the Son and his victory over the enemies of God is in thorough accord with the commentators of the sixteenth and seventeenth centuries, both Protestant and Catholic, as represented by Ames, Calvin, and Bellarmine.

In understanding the enemies of the Father and the Son as Satan and his followers Milton has 'done something not contemplated by any of the expositors of the second psalm I have encountered, though naturally enough developed from their explanations'.[22] Just how much development Milton must be credited with is hard to determine, but it is certainly not great.

There is, then, little doubt that what the Father announced was not the generation, but the exaltation of the Son. This announcement sets off Satan's rebellion. Immediately Satan construes the new honor conferred on the Son as derogatory to his own glory. He begins plotting a sort of counter-revolution.[23] As the angelic host sleeps that night, Satan arouses his legions and calls them to council in the 'quarters of the North'. There, under guise of rendering allegiance to the Son, they plot rebellion. Milton carefully underlines Satan's motivation:

> . . . yet fraught
> With envie against the Son of God, that day
> Hounourd by his great Father, and proclaimd
> *Messiah* King anointed, could not beare
> Through pride that sight. . . . (v 661-5)

The complete motivation of Satan, as Milton here explains it, is compounded of several elements. We recognize the tradition stemming from Isaiah in the pride and haughtiness of Satan ('could not beare/ Through pride') as well as in the fact that Satan calls his council in the 'quarters of the North'. But besides the general conception of Satan as proud and haughty there is the specific incident of the announcement. Here the dominant motif is envy ('yet fraught/ With envie'). This motivation clearly stems from the second of the motivations of Satan presented above, the one contained in the *Vita*. In both the *Vita* and *Paradise Lost* God makes an announcement and commands an act of obedience by the angels. In both documents Satan refuses to perform the act of obedience.

That some account stemming from the *Vita* was in Milton's mind is shown by a passage in Book II of *Paradise Lost*. Here Beelzebub clearly states that God announced to the angels before Satan's rebellion an intention to create man:

> There is a place
> (If ancient and prophetic fame in Heav'n
> Err not) another World, the happy seat
> Of som new Race call'd *Man*, about this time
> To be created like to us, though less
> In power and excellence, but favour'd more
> Of him who rules above; so was his will
> Pronounc'd among the Gods, and by an Oath
> That shook Heav'ns whol circumference, confirm'd. (II 345-53)

This sounds very much like the announcement of the creation of man which figures so prominently in the *Vita* and accounts derived from it. But what God actually does announce in Book V is not the creation of man but the exaltation of the Son. And what the angels are commanded to do is not, as in the *Vita*, to worship man, but to render obedience to the Son as vice-gerent. What then appears to have happened is that at some stage of *Paradise Lost* Milton planned to use the *Vita* motivation or something pretty close to it, possibly the Christianized version. For reasons which we shall see he gave this up. Whether he had already written Beelzebub's speech or whether this speech is an unconscious throwback to an earlier stage in the evolution of the epic we cannot know.

To understand exactly what Milton has done we must look at some contemporary accounts of the rebellion of Satan. Speculation about whether the incarnation of the Son was revealed to the angels is found in many medieval theologians.[24] In the Renaissance at least one theologian and several dramatists and poets used an account of the rebellion of Satan which assumed that the incarnation was revealed to the angels and that Satan rebelled because he would not accept the incarnation. By choosing man as the form which the Son was to take, God degraded the angels below the dignity of man.

Zanchius, a Protestant theologian of the late sixteenth century, has a complete account of the rebellion of Satan using precisely this motivation. Though the mystery of Christ, he writes, was not revealed as a whole until long afterwards, God decreed it from the very beginning. John 8:44 says that Satan 'abode not in the truth'. What was this truth? It was the truth that God would assume, not the form of the angels, but that of the seed of Abraham. He would be made man; he would become the head of the angels. Thus, human nature would be exalted over angelic, for no one, angel or man, would be saved except through the grace of Christ.

This summary of the incarnation, though not the whole of the mystery, Zanchius continues, God revealed or proposed for belief to the angels from the beginning. This is proved by the fact that the one truth which has been rejected by all the foes of Christ, and particularly by Satan, is the incarnation. Satan has always sought to persuade mankind that Christ is either not God or not man. Hence, even from the beginning of the world Satan and his followers have hated this truth. In the beginning, though God proposed it to them as necessary for salvation, they would not accept it. The first and principal sin of the angels, then, was that, puffed up with the excellence of their own nature, they rejected the mystery of the incarnation when it was proposed to them. They would not believe that human nature was to be exalted above angelic.[25]

Several of the seventeenth-century epic and dramatic treatments of the fall of the angels use or suggest this motivation of Satan's rebellion.[26] Bishop Newton long ago noted that one Odoricus Valmorana had written a long epic titled *Demonomachiae, sive De Bello Intellegentiarum super Divini Verbi Incarnatione* (1623). The subtitle 'war of the intelligences over the incarnation of the divine word' sufficiently indicates the motivation of Satan. Newton found the poem 'very like *Paradise Lost*. It opens with the exaltation of the Son of God; and thereupon Lucifer revolts and draws a third part of the Angels after him into the *quarters of the North*.'[27]

Andreini's *L'Adamo* (1613) also alludes to the announcement of the incarnation as a motivation of Satan's rebellion. One of the lesser devils, named Lucifer, says that the chief source of grief of the fallen angels is the knowledge that man is to take their place in heaven. To this, Satan replies that even worse is the knowledge that by the incarnation a man shall be exalted. And Lucifer then asks if angels must bend their knees to man:

> Dovrà l'Angelo adunque inchinar l'Uomo?[28]

Joseph Beaumont's *Psyche* (1648) has almost precisely the same account as the *Vita*. Satan demands whether it was not enough that against the law of promogeniture angels should be subordinated to men without adding the crowning insult of their taking the place of the fallen angels in heaven?[29] Thomas Heywood's *The Hierarchie of the Blessed Angels* (1635) contains a clear statement that the revelation of the incarnation was the immediate cause of Satan's rebellion:

> To them [the angels] iust in the end of the Creation
> He did reueale his blest Sonnes Incarnation:
> But with strict commandment, that they
> Should (with all Creatures) God and man obey.
> Hence grew the great dissention that befell
> 'Twixt *Lucifer* and Prince *Michael*.[30]

Perhaps the best literary work before *Paradise Lost* to use the motivation from envy is the *Lucifer* of the Dutch poet and dramatist, Joost van Vondel. As *Lucifer* opens, Appolyon is returning to report to Lucifer the creation of the world. Gabriel then announces the divine decree

conferring supremacy on the human race. On this decree the whole
action of the play turns. Part of the angelic host resent the position of
inferiority assigned to them.[31] Especially notable in Gabriel's speech is
the prophecy, which also serves as the reason for the exaltation of men
over angels, that the 'Eternal Word, clothed in bone and flesh' shall be
'anointed King and Lord and Judge'. In the second act we see the effect
of this announcement on Lucifer and his followers. Beelzebub complains
that 'an earthworm, made out of a clump of clay' has the door of heaven
open to him and asks why God should exalt a 'younger son of Adam's
loins' over Lucifer.[32]

From these passages it is clear that the motivation from envy enjoyed
some popularity among literary men of the seventeenth century. It
must certainly have been known to Milton, and it came to him well-
recommended. The account of Satan's rebellion which makes its cause
an announcement of the incarnation supplies a dramatic enough
motivation for Milton's epic. Nevertheless, it is apparent that Milton's
motivation differs somewhat from those we have seen and from that
given by Zanchius. Though an announcement plays an important part
in Milton's account, what God announces is not the incarnation but
merely the begetting of the Son. Why this change?

One reason is that Milton's chronology of the creation differs from
that of Zanchius and the rest. They all accept the conventional theory
that the creation of the angels took place within the six days. Hence,
since the creation of the angels preceded that of man by but a few days,
there is no inconsistency in having the announcement of the creation of
man plus the revelation of the incarnation, the rebellion of the angels,
and the temptation of man take place in a very short period of time –
even in one day, if the dramatist is intent on preserving the Aristotelean
unity of time. But Milton has the creation of the angels precede
the creation of the world. In fact, he strongly suggests that the fall of the
angels is, if not the cause, at least the incident that precipitates
the creation of the world and man. Hence, had he used without change the
motivation found in Zanchius and the rest, he would have involved
himself in dramatic difficulties, to say the least.

There is another reason that must have deterred Milton from
accepting the common motivation from envy. It is theologically
inconsistent also. The announcement of the incarnation preceded the
necessity of the incarnation. The Son took human form to save fallen
man. But man had not fallen when the incarnation was announced to

the angels. In fact, the announcement of the incarnation provided the occasion for man's fall, since it caused Satan's defection and thus provided the tempter. Certain theologians, Calvin most notably, were not loath to point out the curious position into which such an announcement of the incarnation put God and the logical entanglements it involved. Calvin calls the notion 'a frivuolous speculation'.[33] This must have been an important deterrent for Milton, who could not be satisfied with poetic plausibility and dramatic truth alone. His 'fit audience' would demand theological correctness, and, anyway, Milton was not a man who could put poetry ahead of truth.

So Milton's task is to salvage from the undoubtedly dramatic account of Satan's rebellion what is most useful for his purpose, while freeing it from logical and theological contradiction and inconsistency. This is the development of the motivation from envy with which Milton can be credited. And it is entirely negative. Milton preserves the announcement, but subtracts the features which Calvin and others had objected to. What God announces in *Paradise Lost* is that He has begotten the Son. Beyond the undoubted fact that some species of exaltation is meant, it is difficult to say specifically what this begetting really is. Milton has left the exact nature of the exaltation purposefully vague. At the same time, he retains the motivation from envy.

Thus, *Paradise Lost* exhibits in the handling of Satan's rebellion a perfect sample of creative fusion and harmony. In a psychological sense, Satan's sin is pride. All sin is, in essence, the separation of the creature from God, and this separation occurs when the creature, through pride and ambition, sets himself and his desires above the will of the Creator. Hence the motivation from pride is basic, as Milton recognizes in repeated characterizations of Satan. But the manifestation of this pride takes the specific form of envy of the Son. Ambition to be first also enters into the complex of evil. So perfectly fused are these elements that few readers of Milton unaware of the theological background I have sketched are conscious that there are various motivations for Satan's rebellion or that Milton blended them.[34]

The result is a real triumph of artistic handling, though it can hardly be called invention, unless subtraction rather than addition is the main quality of invention. At any rate, all the dramatic intensity which results from the envy of Satan is present in *Paradise Lost*. The language is largely scriptural, and so it can offend no one, whether orthodox or heterodox. Nor has Milton denied himself any advantage that might come from the alternate motivation from pride. Both are represented in *Paradise Lost*. Without sacrificing the characterization of Satan as a proud rebel, without having to invent where invention is hazardous, Milton still avoids all contradictions and inconsistencies, both of narrative and religious beliefs, and achieves a solid and convincing motivation of the great antagonist.

NOTES

1. It is Satan's belief that he had 'dispeopl'd Heav'n' (VII 150-61) that God offers as reason for the creation of another world and another race to take the place of the fallen angels.

2. Throughout this article I am under exceeding obligation to Grant McColley, *Paradise Lost* (Chicago, 1941), to Maurice Kelley, *This Great Argument* (Princeton, 1941), and to Allan H. Gilbert, 'The Theological Basis of Satan's Rebellion and the Function of Abdiel in *Paradise Lost*', in *Modern Philology*, XL (1942) 19-42.

3. Rabbi Jung, who has gone into the accounts of the fall of the angels probably more deeply than anyone else, finds in authentic Hebrew tradition no trace of the concept of Satan as an originally good angel, now fallen and become the unalterable enemy of God: *Fallen Angels in Jewish, Christian and Mohammedan Literature* (Philadelphia, 1926). It should be noted, however, that Rabbi Jung's definition of 'authentic Hebrew traditions' is rather narrow. He includes only what may be called official Judaism, the Mishna in particular. The unofficial and heterodox tendencies preserved in the pseudepigrapha he does not consider as authentic. It is precisely in the pseudepigrapha that one finds the nearest approach to the New Testament character of Satan.

4. *The Apocrypha and Pseudepigrapha of the Old Testament*, ed. R. H. Charles (Oxford, 1913) II 163.

5. Enoch lxix 6. I use 'Enoch' to mean *The Book of Enoch. The Book of the Secrets of Enoch* I shall call 'Secrets'. Scholars often use 'I Enoch' and 'II Enoch' to denote these books, a practice which may cause the unfamiliar to think of the two books as composing a unity like 1 and 2 Kings. They do not.

6. Enoch vi 1-8.

7. Denis Saurat, *Milton Man and Thinker* (New York, 1925) pp. 257-8.

8. *Vita Adae et Evae*, xii-xvii, ed. L. S. A. Wells, in *Apocrypha and Pseudepigrapha*, ed. Charles. According to Wells, there are numerous manuscripts of the *Vita* dating from the Middle Ages (pp. 124-4). Two Middle English versions are given by Carl Horstmann, *Sammlung Altenglischer Legenden* (Heilbronn, 1878). Ancient versions of the *Vita* are found in Armenian, Syriac, Syriac and Arabic, and Ethiopic. All these go back, thinks Wells, probably to a Hellenistic Jew who wrote between A.D. 60 and 300. The legends are even more ancient and are represented elsewhere in Jewish literature: Louis Ginzburg, *The Legends of the Jews*, trans. Henrietta Szold (Philadelphia, 1913) I 62-4. Jung, *Fallen Angels*, pp. 56-6, in keeping with his theory, does not take these legends as authentic Jewish tradition.

9. Secrets, xxv 4-5. This took place between the second and third days of creation.

10. Secrets, xxxi 4-5.

11. *De Civitate Dei*, ed. J. E. C. Weldon (1924), xv, ch. 23 (II 172-7). This does not mean that the Enoch tradition disappeared or the motivation from lust. The writings of the early Fathers kept both alive, as did also the very condemnation of Augustine. Many of the

sixteenth- and seventeenth-century commentaries repeat the story, e.g. Pareus, *In Genesin*, in *Opera Theologica* (Venice, 1628) p. 161. Pareus gives a late medieval source, Lyra's *Postilliae*.

12. *De Civitate Dei*, XI 13 (I 481).

13. For instance, Petrus Lombardus, *Sentenarium libri quatuor*, in J. P. Migne, *Patrologiae Cursus Completus*, Series secunda, tom. I (1845), lib. II, dist. vi, q. 2 (col. 154).

14. *The Junius Manuscript*, ed. G. P. Krapp (New York, 1931), 'Genesis', lines 247–90.

15. *Cursor Mundi*, ed. Richard Morris, EETS OS 57, 'Cotton Version', lines 457–62.

16. *Chester Plays*, ed. Hermann Diemling, EETS ES 62, lines 89–208; *Ludus Coventriae*, ed. K. S. Black, EETS ES 120, 'Creation of Heaven and the Angels'; *Townley Plays*, ed. George England, EETS ES 71, 'The Creation', lines 61–131; *York Plays*, ed. Lucy T. Smith, I i and ii 32–120.

17. *The Adamus Exul of Grotius*, trans. Francis Barham (1839) p. 15.

18. 'Of Goodness and Goodness of Nature', in *Works*, ed. J. Spedding, R. L. Ellis, and D. D. Heath (Boston, n.d.) II 118.

19. Sir Walter Raleigh, *Milton* (1909) p. 86. Raleigh writes that Milton 'flies in the face of the Anasthasian Creed by representing the generation of the Son as an event occurring in time'. Saurat in a review of H. J. C. Grierson's *Milton and Wordsworth*, in *Review of English Studies*, XIV (1938) 225–8, writes that Milton 'means the reader to take this quite literally, since otherwise there can be no drama'. To those who point out the inconsistency between this understanding of 'begot' and the numerous passages in both *Paradise Lost* and *De Doctrina* which speak of the Son as generated from the beginning, Saurat replies that Milton is writing poetry, not theology. This seems to me a false opposition of the two forms Milton was seeking to combine: he was writing theology in poetic form.

20. David Masson, *Poetical Works of John Milton* (1890) III 473; H. F. Fletcher, *Milton's Rabbinical Readings* (Urbana, 1930) pp. 150–6; H. J. C. Grierson, *Milton and Wordsworth* (New York, 1937) pp. 98–9. Masson distinguishes between the Son existing eternally as the divine Logos and the Son begotten as the Son in point of time. Fletcher thinks the passage reflects the rabbinical notion that all things were created at one time but revealed only at their appointed times. Grierson quotes a passage from *De Doctrina* (I 5) which distinguishes between two senses of 'begot', the one literal and the other metaphorical, referring to the exaltation of the Son. Grierson takes the 'begot' of v 603 as the metaphorical begetting. Kelley, *This Great Argument*, pp. 94–101 attempts to harmonize Grierson and Saurat by taking 'begot' as metaphorical, but at the same time conceding that, since *Paradise Lost* is poetry, not theology, it contains inventions that go beyond the doctrinal statement of *De Doctrina*. Below I shall show that Milton's motivation of Satan contains relatively little invention and does not go far beyond other seventeenth-century treatments of the same theme.

21. *Poetical Works of Milton*, ed. H. J. Todd (1801), comment on *Paradise Lost*, v 603.

22. Op. cit. p. 26.

23. That is, Satan represents the elevation of the Son as a revolution in the government of heaven (v 772–802). His revolt then is a sort of counter-revolution.

24. For instance, St Thomas Aquinas, *Summa Theologica*, I 57 5.

25. *De Operibus Dei*, in *Operum Theologicorum* (Geneva, 1613) III, cols. 170–2. Concerning Milton's knowledge of Zanchius, see my 'Milton and the Renaissance Commentaries on Genesis', in *Modern Philology*, XXVII (1940) 270–1.

26. I have added nothing to the list of literary treatments cited by Grant McColley in 'Paradise Lost', in *Harvard Theological Review*, XXXIII (1939) 185–6, and repeated in his book, *Paradise Lost*, pp. 32–4. I have checked all his citations except that to Valmorana, which I have been unable to procure.

27. *Works*, ed. Todd, comment on *Paradise Lost*, v 689.

28. *L'Adamo*, ed. Ettore Allodoli (Lanciano, 1913) I i 436–53.

29. Canto i, stanza 31, in *Chertsey Worthies' Library*, ed. Grosart (1880) vol. I.
30. 'The Powers', bk IV (p. 342).
31. Cf. George Edmondson, *Milton and Vondel* (1885) p. 49. Since Edmondson's use of Vondel has sometimes been questioned I append Vondel's lines:

> Ae schijnt het Geestendom alle andere t'overtreffen.
> God sloot van eeuwigheid het menschdom te verheffen,
> Ook boven't Engelsdom, en op voeren tot
> Een klaaheid en een licht, dat niet verschilt van God
> Gij zult het eeuwig Woord, be kleed met been en aren
> Gezalft tot Heer en Hooft en Rechter, al de schaven
> Der Geesten, Engln en menschen te gelijk,
> Zien rechten, uit zijn troon en interschaduwd Rijk.

Lucifer, Act I, lines 217–24.

32.
> De poort des Hemels staet voor Adams afkomst open
> Een aerdtworm, uit een' klomp van aerde en klay gekropen
> Braveert uw morgentheit.
> Zou God een jonger zoon, geteeld uit Adams lenden,
> Verheffen boven hem?

Act II, lines 418–22.

33. *A Commentarie of John Caluine vpon . . . Genesis*, trans. Thomas Tymme (1587) p. 87.
34. I am indebted to Professor Louis I. Bredvold for the main ideas expressed in this paragraph.

MURRAY W. BUNDY

Milton's Prelapsarian Adam (1945)

WHEN in 1674 Milton created Book VIII of *Paradise Lost* by the division of Book VII at line 640, he more clearly defined his epic structure by assigning to a single book materials which constitute an artistic unit. Thitherto they had seemed primarily parts of the creation story. The formation of a new book beginning with Adam's doubts concerning God's cosmic economy and ending with the rebuke of his uxoriousness focused the attention, immediately before the temptation, upon the *ethos* and the *dianoia* of the protagonist. We may study 'original righteousness' before the Fall.

This is not to assert that the plan of an epic of ten books was artistically faulty. The discussion of astronomy, Adam's account of his first consciousness, his translation to the garden, his talk with God, and the creation of Eve, and the lover's ecstasy which brought the angelic rebuke – all of these are parts of the creation theme. The seeming digression concerning astronomy, for example, may be read as a kind of critical retrospect, after the elaboration of Genesis i, before the development of the central theme in terms of the two human actors; and Adam's story, culminating in the creation of Eve, had been for Milton, since the time of the plans in the Cambridge MS,[1] essentially a part of the narrative of creation. Those dramatic plans, indeed, seem to point to the difficulty of finding the right place in a tragedy for 'the creation of Eve, with their love and marriage'.[2] There is no question, then, of the poet's original intention in having included all of these materials in a book of nearly thirteen hundred lines. It is more important to determine why he divided the book. We may, of course, assume with Verity that, in making an epic of twelve books, the poet arrived 'at a more Virgilian number'.[3] This, however, is to attribute to Milton an anxiety about formal pattern which he reveals nowhere in his other poems, save, perhaps, in the sonnets; and, in stressing the Virgilian model, it ignores the poet's professed intention of vying with Tasso, who had written an epic of twenty books.[4]

If the reader is reluctant to believe that Milton was eager to have the right number of books, he may be attracted to another possible explanation: that the artist was conscious of the disproportionate length of two of the original books (vii with 1293 lines and x with 1550 lines). To appeal to a consideration of mechanical symmetry and proportion is, again, to ignore the evidence of the other poems. Only in the immortal pair of lyrics of the college days can one find such formal symmetry; and *Paradise Regained* is evidence of the poet's comparative indifference, in his mature genius, to this consideration. If he had thought in 1674 that two books were too long, it is probable that he would have considered three books (vii, 640 lines, viii, 653 lines, and xii, 649 lines) resulting from the division too short; and one of the original books (ix, 1189 lines) too long.

One is more likely to find the explanation of the change in Milton's desire to clarify his intention. By beginning a new book with Adam's criticism of God's cosmic plan and ending, as we shall see, with a comparable criticism of the creation of Eve, the poet shifted the attention from the creation as such, God's plan, to man's capacity to understand and willingness to accept that plan. In this greatest of all tragedies, the chief actor could not be presented as a passive agent in a conflict of supernatural forces, the mere dupe of a skillful antagonist and the victim of feminine charm. Here, just before the temptation, an entire book is devoted to a study of Adam's intellectual and moral nature, his rationality as one made in the image of his Maker, and his 'liability to fall'[5] with which man was created. To bring together materials supporting this generalization is the purpose of this study.

We may understand this intention more clearly by sensing the balance which the poet achieved by thus segregating and focusing this material at this point. In Book iv, just before the dream-temptation of Eve – and just before the poem reaches the first of two great moments of dramatic conflict on earth – the attention is concentrated upon Eve's intellectual and moral nature.[6] Here, in Book viii, just before the actual sin, to which the dream-temptation had been the prelude, and at a comparable point in the second half of the poem, the reader is invited to study Adam *alone*.

The reader must remember that, immediately after Adam had introduced his doubts concerning celestial motions, Eve suddenly left, ostensibly because she preferred to have her astronomy at second hand, counting on her spouse to 'intermix Grateful digressions and solve high dispute with conjugal caresses' (*PL*, VIII 50–7). Milton is at pains to assure us that she was not bored and that she was capable of listening to high discourse (*PL*, VIII 48–50). All of this strikes one as curious, especially when it is recalled that in Book IV Eve, star-gazing, had been similarly perplexed by this question of cosmic economy:

> But wherefore all night long shine these, for whom
> This glorious sight, when sleep hath shut all eyes? (*PL*, IV 657–8)

Adam at the time had suggested an explanation, even before Raphael had told his story, as succinct as the teacher could have given (*PL*, IV 661–88). It is clear, then, that Adam and Eve had already shown great interest in the kind of doubt with which Book VIII begins. Why, then, is she unwilling to remain to hear the answer of an expert?

There are two explanations, both of which point to the poet's conscious art. By representing Eve as reluctant to undertake again this matter of 'high dispute' without the antidotes of 'grateful digressions' and 'conjugal caresses', the poet reminds the reader that this is a subject which has already been considered in the earlier analysis of Eve's mental state. By causing her to withdraw, he invites our entire attention to Adam as he opens the new book with his variant of a question first proposed by Eve.

II

We come now to an analysis of Book VIII as primarily a study of the protagonist on the eve of temptation.

To understand the first theme, the inquiry concerning celestial motions, the reader must keep in mind the dominant impressions which Raphael had sought to create in his account of creation. This is not primarily a poetic elaboration of a few verses in Genesis or an attempt to vie with Tasso, Du Bartas, and others in the handling of the creation theme as part of the Christian epic. It is part of a story in which a heavenly teacher has been sent to warn man and, as part of his commission, to impart such knowledge as would enable him to withstand temptation (*PL*, V 229–45). The emphasis today upon a search for Milton's sources in hexameral literature and the like distracts the

attention from the central theme of Book VII, the instruction by an
angelic teacher of Adam and Eve on the eve of temptation.

Although Adam at the outset affected a healthy curiosity (*PL*, VII
61–2), he was at the same time perplexed to know

> what cause
> Mov'd the Creator in his holy Rest
> Through all Eternity so late to build
> In Chaos. (VII 90–3)

He already entertains, one observes, a theology (orthodox, indeed) of a
self-sufficient Deity; and this is at odds with his conception of divine
creative activity. Raphael's reply in his narrative keeps in mind the
mental state of the inquiring pupil. God is represented as saying:

> I can repair
> That detriment, if such it be to lose
> Self-lost, and in a moment will create
> Another World, out of one man a Race
> Of men innumerable, there to dwell,
> Not here, till by degrees of merit rais'd
> They open to themselves at length the way
> Up hither, under long obedience tri'd,
> And Earth be chang'd to Heav'n, and Heav'n to Earth,
> One Kingdom, Joy and Union without end. (VII 152–61)

This is the theme emphasized in the account of the creation story: it is
in part compensation for a loss, but it is much more. Raphael's prologue
to his narrative of creation is God's proclamation of a new world, the
apex of which is man; and man is called upon both to understand
the plan and to subordinate his will to the realization of that plan, the
inauguration of a new Heaven on earth. He is called upon to assume his
creative role in the exercise of both his understanding and his will.

The narrative, then, is primarily didactic: instruction in God's ways
as the necessary condition for obedience. Man must learn, for example,
that the apparently great may exist for the sake of the apparently small.
Light comes first as the condition of subsequent acts of creation, and the
first day is the 'Birthday of Heav'n and Earth' (*PL*, VII 256). The
separation of Heaven and Earth becomes, in turn, the condition of life
on earth, and the specific creation of two great lights makes possible
both the distinction of 'Glad Evening and glad Morn' (*PL*, VII 386) and

the whole process of biological generation, the acme of which, 'the end of all yet done', is to be Man:

> a Creature who not prone
> And Brute as other Creatures, but endu'd
> With Sanctity of Reason, might erect
> His Stature, and upright with Front serene
> Govern the rest, self-knowing, and from thence
> Magnanimous to correspond with Heav'n,
> But grateful to acknowledge whence his good
> Descends, thither with heart and voice and eyes
> Directed in Devotion, to adore
> And worship God Supreme, who made him chief
> Of all his works. (VII 506–16)

Raphael's narrative from beginning to end emphasizes the dignity of Man and insists that that dignity can be achieved only through an understanding of a Divine plan and willing obedience. Man, 'endu'd with Sanctity of Reason', must understand this cosmic law of the subordination of means, however dazzling, to the prime end, 'the Master work' capable of governing the rest since he is 'self-knowing', and, in consequence, 'Magnanimous to correspond with Heav'n'.[7] He will then be able to recognize God's purpose in having created a vast universe for the sake of its human habitant. This magnanimity is to be revealed in obedience immediately apparent in adoration and worship of the creator.

All of this must be kept in mind as one comes to Adam's inquiry, with which Book VIII opens. Here is instantly revealed a dangerous inability or unwillingness to accept the angel's philosophy of creation:

> When I behold this goodly Frame, this World,
> Of Heav'n and Earth consisting, and compute
> Thir magnitudes, this Earth a spot, a grain,
> An Atom, with the Firmament compar'd
> And all her number'd stars, that seem to roll
> Spaces incomprehensible . . .
>   merely to officiate light
> Round this opacous Earth, this punctual spot,
> One day and night; in all thir vast survey
> Useless besides, reasoning I oft admire
> How Nature wise and frugal could commit
> Such disproportions, with superfluous hand
> So many nobler Bodies to create . . . (VIII 15–28)

This is something more than a criticism of a geocentric universe: it is a
censure of the whole cosmic economy which Raphael had painstakingly
elaborated. It shows a state of mind reluctant to accept the emphasis
upon subordination of means to ultimate ends and therefore unwilling
to accept the law of obedience.

This critical Adam, as we shall see, is far different from the Adam of
the central portion of the book, who assures Raphael that his first
impulses upon his creation had been to find a Maker to adore:

> Tell me, how may I know him, how adore,
> From whom I have that thus I move and live,
> And feel that I am happier than I know. (VIII 280–3)

Since that day experience had prompted speculation and doubt,
perhaps induced by the talk with Eve.

In recent years Raphael's reply has been a subject of investigation
which has, on the whole, distracted the attention from its purpose and
importance. We are, indeed, in a better position today to determine
what contemporary materials entered into the shaping of three hundred
lines;[8] but as a result we are in danger of reading the passage as primarily
a reflection of Milton's interest in the science of his time, forgetting
meanwhile that a teacher is dealing with a pupil on the eve of temptation. Because we forget the epic setting we are shocked when we read
Raphael's reply with its apparent obscurantism:

> Solicit not thy thoughts with matters hid,
> Leave them to God above. (VIII 167–8)

We must remember that he is carrying out his instructions. Adam had
assumed a geocentric universe as the result of his superficial observations, and he had presumed, again superficially, to question the wisdom
of a Creator in having contrived a universe in which the greater and
brighter planets serve the smaller and less bright. In his answer to his
wife's perplexity propounded in Book IV, he had already shown a
capacity for arriving at the right explanation; but at this moment,
perhaps as a result of the colloquy with Eve, he is prone to question a
cosmic plan which demands the recognition of his primacy among
creatures as the necessary condition of obedience.

Patiently, in more direct terms, the Raphael of Book VIII reiterates
the general truths which he had presented in the narrative: 'that Great
or Bright infers not Excellence' (PL, VIII 90–1), that the Earth, although

apparently much smaller than the Sun, may contain more solid good, that the Sun has no effect upon itself, but upon the Earth, where its beams, 'unactive else, thir vigor find' (*PL*, VIII 91–7). Once again he stresses the main theme:

> Yet not to Earth are those bright Luminaries
> Officious, but to thee Earth's habitant. (VIII 98–9)

Patient repetition, with new emphasis, is part of the skill of the angelic teacher.

Soon thereafter Raphael introduces the well-known reference to the Copernican hypothesis:

> What if the Sun
> Be centre to the World, and other Stars
> By his attractive vertue, and their own
> Incited, dance about him various rounds? (VIII 122–5)

This has been repeatedly discussed as primarily indicative of the poet's interest in the new astronomy as an alternative to the Ptolemaic system and a more adequate explanation of cosmic phenomena.[9] Properly viewed as a part of the teacher's answer to his pupil, it is neither an alternative nor an explanation. It is hypothesis for the sake of argument, as a reply to Adam's superficial reasoning. Let us assume, says the teacher, that the sun is saved his labor, about which you have complained, and that the 'Earth industrious of herself fetched day' (*PL*, VIII 137). In such a heliocentric universe, in which suns and moons, communicating male and female light, animate the world, you are faced with a similar difficulty in explaining God's plan in terms of a human conception of cosmic economy. You must contemplate either 'such vast room in Nature unpossesst', or, as the necessary alternative, other inhabited globes (*PL*, VIII 140–58). In thus deliberately creating a logical dilemma, Raphael is not concerned with the correctness or incorrectness of the heliocentric theory, but with a pragmatic consideration, the preparation of Adam to undergo a test which will involve both intellectual and moral qualities. He must first make his pupil conscious of his faulty logic: to assume, for the sake of argument, that the sun is the center and that it does not merely officiate light involves difficulties as grave as those involved in the acceptance of Raphael's account. At the particular moment the attention must be fixed on the central theme, the dignity of man guaranteed by the purpose of the plan, his creation as its apex. Obedience, in turn, the condition of happiness for that creature, is contingent upon his admiration of the wisdom of the Maker. When Raphael warns, 'Think only what concernes thee and thy being', he is not decrying scientific investigation. He is attacking only an idle and superficial speculation which leaves the pupil in a state of perplexity and doubt when the enemy is at the door.

Adam, we are told, was 'cleer'd of doubt'. Although his reply gives no hint of dissatisfaction, and is, in fact, an admirable summary of the lesson by an apt pupil, it may be regarded, along with Eve's reply in the comparable situation in Book IV, as graceful acquiescence.[10] One must not overlook the self-justification which immediately follows:

> But apt the Mind or Fancy is to rove
> Uncheckt, and of her roving is no end;
> Till warn'd or by experience taught, she learn . . . (VIII 188–90)

In terms of seventeenth-century psychology the pupil is represented as defending himself on what for Milton were familiar grounds: it is only natural that a man's fancy, that unstable part of the soul, should have led him to idle speculation. There are two faults here: he has blamed the aberrations of fancy, when he should have blamed his faulty reasoning, and he has attempted to excuse himself on the ground that it is natural to give play to the fancy, a justification which would have been tolerated by no reputable seventeenth-century moralist.[11] There follows that curious 'till warn'd or by experience taught. . . .' He has been warned. Why, then, does he add 'by experience taught' since the anticipation of experience involves a curious anachronism? Perhaps at this point the poet is speaking and pointing to an indisputable fact about human nature: that man – as typified by Adam even before the fact of original sin – is incapable of accepting instruction without its complement, experience, the process to be described at length in Books IX and X. This introduction of an alternative to instruction, experience, significantly unchallenged by Raphael, must, indeed, be taken into account in any complete record of Milton's conception of man's 'original righteousness'. There is also a note of danger as Adam turns with too great alacrity from 'this high pitch' and proposes a less strenuous subject, his own story.

III

We proceed now from this initial consideration of 'sinless' Adam contemplating God's creation of a macrocosm, to the central theme of the book, his account of his own creation. This involves his first consciousness (253–87), the dream during which he is conveyed to the garden (288–311), and his talk with God (311–452) involving the dialogue concerning solitude. It is separated from the last third of the book by a trance during which Eve is created (452–80).

At the outset, after the angel's gracious excuse for listening, his absence from Heaven on the sixth day, Adam describes a setting which invites comparison with the corresponding portion of Book IV:

> As new wak't from soundest sleep
> Soft on the flow'ry herb I found me laid
> In Balmy Sweat. . . . (VIII 253–5)

The reader will recall Eve's account to Adam of her first consciousness:

> That day I oft remember, when from sleep
> I first awak't, and found myself repos'd
> Under a shade on flow'rs. . . . (IV 449–51)

The artistic intent is unmistakable: the poet wishes the reader to compare the states of mind of these two human agents in the drama of the Garden as each starts into consciousness on a bed of flowers.

In the earlier account, Eve is represented as only for a fleeting moment

> much wond'ring where
> And what [she] was, whence thither brought, and how. (IV 451–2)

Quickly attracted by the sound of running water, she makes her way to a pool and lies down on a green bank. There, pleased by her own reflection in the clear, smooth lake, she is in danger of pining in vain desire for her own image; but a voice warns her that she is falling in love with a shadow. Her guide forthwith takes her to Adam, who at first glance, compared with the 'smooth wat'ry image', is to Eve 'less fair, less winning soft, less amiably mild' (*PL*, IV 479–80). This is the substance of Eve's reminiscence in Book IV.

Adam tells Raphael that his first impulse was to gaze toward heaven:

> Straight toward Heav'n my wondering Eyes I turn'd,
> And gaz'd a while the ample Sky, till rais'd

By quick instinctive motion up I sprung,
As thitherward endeavouring, and upright
Stood on my feet. (VIII 257–61)

Looking around him, he immediately takes in his environment. Then
comes self-consciousness, first expressed in lively physical activity, and
quickly issuing in the behavior of a rational being; he speaks, and gives
names to objects,[12] beginning with the Sun, 'faire Light', and then
proceeds – this is significant – in these first sentient moments to infer
from these evidences of creation an omnipotent Creator:

Tell, if ye saw, how came I thus, how here?
Not of myself: by some great Maker then,
In goodness and in power praeëminent. (VIII 277–9)

He would know this Maker that he may adore Him; and when the
desire is not immediately satisfied, again he sits upon a bank of flowers,
where sleep and a dream follow, involving the translation to the
garden.

Eve, on the contrary, never arrives in her first experience at complete
self-consciousness, a sense of herself as thinking subject in relation to
objects to be apprehended. She is seemingly incapable of entering upon
the train of thought which would infer a Creator to be adored. We
would call her today an extreme introvert, in danger of Narcissism,
from which she is saved by a warning voice and the sight of Adam.

Adam, on the other hand, is a healthy extrovert, aware of his
environment, bringing into play his whole sentient being, and from the
outset enjoying the exercise of his Divine prerogative, Reason. Man –
specifically Man – was made in the image of his Maker.[13]

The next portion of this central third of the Book is enclosed within a
dream involving Adam's translation to the Garden and a trance during
which Eve is created. At first glance, this dream seems to be primarily a
means of enabling the poet to incorporate into Adam's narrative part of
the account in Genesis i: 'And the Lord God planted a garden eastward
in Eden; and there he put the man whom he had formed'.

It is an example of the skillful use of an epic device; but its primary
importance is in suggesting again comparable materials in Eve's
experience recorded in Book IV. There Satan had been presented as

Squat like a Toad, close to the ear of Eve:
Assaying by his Devilish art to reach

> The Organs of her Fancy, and with them forge
> Illusions as he list, Phantasms and Dreams. . . . (IV 800–3)

This is a devil-inspired dream, the details of which are recorded at the beginning of Book V. Adam's experience, recounted here in Book VIII, is a God-given dream.[14] Eve's dream, coming after several days in the garden, is composed of the materials of her experience, including her thwarted impulses and her recent talk with Adam.[15] Adam's dream, in contrast, can have no source in experience, but is an immediate response to his demand for a Maker to adore. God calls upon his creature to rise, takes him by the hand, and, carrying him 'over fields and waters, as in Aire', leads him to the Garden. There, when he sees 'each tree loadn with fairest fruit, that hung tempting', sudden appetite is stirred in him 'to pluck and eate'. Thereupon he wakes to find his dream a reality; and God, revealing Himself as 'author of all this thou seest', makes the bequest of the Garden, prohibits the fruit of the one tree, and gives him lordship of all other creatures (*PL*, VIII 311–48).

This divine dream is at each point contrasted with Eve's experience. Her dream, unlike Adam's, is a dream of night. She is also called by a Voice (which she mistakes for Adam's) to walk by night to appreciate the stars, shining 'in vain, if none regard'. Adam, on the contrary, whose first impulse had been to look up at the sun and then to seek the source of light and his own being, is led in his dream to contemplate the glory of his Creator through his gifts. Eve, whose first impulse was to admire herself, is tempted in a dream to present herself to nature as an object of adoration. Like Adam, she is led by her guide to a tree – here the tree of interdicted knowledge – and, like him, is tempted to pluck and eat. Adam finds his dream translated into reality, and the appearance of his guide forestalls wandering, presents an object of religious adoration, and introduces a prohibition which is to be the test of obedience. Eve's guide – present only in her dream – offers only forbidden fruit and incites to disobedience. In response to impulses already apparent in her talk with Adam, she is promised, not a God to adore, but an idolatry of which she will be the object:

> be henceforth among the Gods
> Thyself a Goddess. (V 77–8)

Unlike Adam, Eve 'could not but taste', whereupon she was led up into the clouds, to wake, finding no guide, and happy only to find that this was only a dream.

Why this studied contrast involving voices, guides, trees, and their fruits, and adoration, religious and idolatrous? In the light of the fact that Eve's dream is woven out of the materials of experience and Adam's is in response to his first impulse as a sentient being, the conclusion is unmistakable: Milton thus points out that Adam at the moment of his creation was not susceptible to the kind of temptation to which Eve's dream showed that she was susceptible.[16]

The next portion of this central section of the book, still concerned with Man before the creation of woman, may be called, in Milton's language, a good temptation, a trial by the Creator of his creature to see whether he is good. Now it is true that the poet, following the Biblical formula in Genesis i, introduces the Divine benediction after the account of each day, 'He saw that it was good', and the comprehensive 'Behold all was entirely good' at the end of the sixth day must therefore include 'man both male and female'. When, however, in Book VIII he turns to Genesis ii, with its account of separate acts of creation of man and woman, he seemingly ignores the implication of Genesis i 27 and represents God as trying Adam specifically (before the Creation of Eve) to see whether *he* is good.

We have said that this is a good temptation. In harmony with Protestant thought in his day, Milton later wrote in *Christian Doctrine*:

> A good temptation is that whereby God tempts even the righteous for the purpose of proving them, not as though he were ignorant of the disposition of their hearts, but for the purpose of manifesting their faith or patience.... [17]

Both faith and patience, as well as rational capacity, are tested in this first colloquy with God in the garden; and at its end God tells Adam:

> Thus far to try thee, Adam, I was pleas'd,
> And find thee knowing not of Beasts alone,
> Which thou hast rightly nam'd, but of thyself,
> Expressing well the spirit within thee free,
> My Image.... (VIII 437-41)

A moment later this is called a 'trial':

> To see how thou couldst judge of fit and meet.

We must, then, read the entire passage (357-452), not primarily as a study of Milton's use of Biblical materials, but as a trial by God – and Milton – of the original goodness of man.

Adam, having sought to name a creator of all good gifts, suddenly expresses his anxiety that there is no one to partake of all this bounty with him:

> In solitude
> What happiness, who can enjoy alone,
> Or all enjoying, what contentment find? (VIII 364-6)

For Milton, social consciousness came early in Paradise. When God reminds Adam that his realm is large, that he knows the languages and ways of inferior creatures, and that they 'also know and reason not contemptibly', man, in spite of the peremptory tone, persists:

> Among unequals what society
> Can sort, what harmony or true delight? (VIII 383-4)

Adam asks for a fellowship

> fit to participate
> All rational delight, wherein the brute
> Cannot be human consort. (VIII 390-2)

In the reply, Milton comes dangerously close to sentiments not in keeping with Divine attributes: almost in sarcasm God accuses Adam of 'a nice and suttle happiness' in proposing to taste 'no pleasure, though in pleasure solitarie'; and He asks whether He can, then, be called happy, since 'alone from all Eternitie' He can hold converse only with creatures who to him are inferior:

> infinite descents
> Beneath what other Creatures are to thee? (VIII 410-11)

It is a dilemma calculated to confound any disputant incapable of right reason. Adam has a ready reply: since there is no deficiency in God, there is no need for Him to repair a deficiency:

> No need that thou
> Shouldst propagate, already infinite
> And through all numbers absolute, though One. (VIII 419-21)

With man it is quite different:

> But Man by number is to manifest
> His single imperfection, and beget
> Like of his like, his Image multipli'd
> In unity defective, which requires
> Collateral love, and dearest amity. (VIII 422-6)

As evidence of Adam's goodness, his creation in the image of his Maker, and hence his capacity for self-knowledge, Milton has given to this newly created man the poet's own philosophy of marriage.[18] Adam also reminds God that, under no necessity of seeking social communication, He can, if He will, raise His creature to the necessary plane for communication, whereas Man cannot. To this there is hardly an answer save the alternatives of deifying man or acceding to man's request. Thereupon God acknowledges that all of this was only to try him.

Milton's intention becomes apparent when one observes the liberty which has been taken at this point with the Biblical narrative. In Genesis ii 18 God recognizes that 'it is not good that Man should be alone'.[19] The poet does much more than elaborate the passage. He makes the recognition of this truth by Adam and his ability to justify it on logical grounds the test of man's goodness. It is true that here at the end of the dialogue God tells Adam that He knew all of this and that He intended for him 'no such company as then thou sawst'; but the dialogue strongly implies that God can grant only as man, made in His image, can through his rational nature frame and defend his petition. Since he has been found 'knowing not of Beasts alone . . . but of thyself', since he can 'judge of fit and meet', Man, found good, will be given – Eve. Here at the heart of Book VIII is Milton's great paradox: The test of man's goodness is his ability to anticipate the Divine verdict that 'it is not good for Man to be alone' by inferring that Man requires society, that society involves propagation, and therefore a companion. Adam's theoretically desirable woman is a construction of his rational faculty. The fulfillment will be something quite different: not a conception to be comprehended by the reason, but a creature to be apprehended by another, and, for the seventeenth century, a 'lower' nature in which appetite, fancy, and passion for the first time came fully into play. This paradox, which can be wrought by God's gift, becomes the subject of the last third of the book.

IV

The colloquy with God, the central theme of the book, had been preceded by a dream. It ends with a trance; or, perhaps better, the third and final portion of this study of Adam begins with a trance. Again, there is deliberate artistic intention. Although in the seventeenth

century dreams and trances were sometimes distinguished (cf. *PL*, VIII
292–4), they were similar in emphasizing the role of fancy (or imagination) in man's behavior.

> Mine eyes he clos'd, but op'n left the Cell
> Of Fancy my internal sight, by which
> Abstract as in a trance methought I saw . . . (VIII 460–2)

When Adam in his dream sees trees and fruit and is impelled to pluck
and eat, and when, in turn, in his trance he sees a creature taking shape
'so lovely fair'

> That what seem'd fair, in all the World, seem'd now
> Mean, or in her summ'd up, in her contain'd . . .

the poet is reminding the reader that man's behavior as distinguished
from his thought is impelled by fancy directing concupiscence or concupiscible appetite: the Divine dream resulted in no act, since, after the
stirring of sudden appetite, reality interrupted the normal response.[20]

Adam's trance had results quite different from those of his dream.
The trance was, of course, God-given and therefore could not intend
wrong conduct; but we must remember that, in leaving open the cell of
fancy, God permitted a first sight of a creature

> Manlike but different sex, so lovely fair
> That what seemd fair in all the world seemd now
> Mean or in her summed up. . . .

This is quite different from the abstract notion of a companion contemplated in the discourse with God. Reason presented to Adam the idea of
a woman capable of companionship and propagation. She had no
significance for his fancy or his emotions. In his trance, however, the
Fancy presented a creature who so powerfully engaged his fancy that
any reminiscence of the event prompted extravagant, irrational com-
mendation. Even after one has allowed for the work of the memory
during the intervening days (and memory was an aspect of fancy), the
fact remains that from the moment that Adam saw Eve in his trance,
Fancy entered upon her dangerous work. A rational Adam had sought
a reality corresponding to his idea. The very moment of the fulfillment
of his desire involved, not the satisfaction of his reason, but the stimulation of fancy, appetite, and passion, and, in this psychological dualism, a
commonplace of the seventeenth century, the struggle of these two
natures, higher and lower, to dominate the will.

This first sight of seductive Eve in the trance invites comparison with the erotic dream of contemporary poetry: Adam talks like a Cavalier poet, when he exclaims:

> Shee disappear'd, and left me dark, I wak'd
> To find her, or for ever to deplore
> Her loss, and other pleasures all abjure. (VIII 478–80)

But he had just told Raphael that his first satisfaction in contemplating creation had led him to seek an adequate name for God, and, when he sought a fellowship, it was to share all of these pleasures with one 'fit to participate all rational delight'.

Unlike the Cavalier dream, however, Adam's lovely apparition became a reality:

> Such as I saw her in my dream, adorned
> With what all Earth or Heaven could bestow
> To make her amiable. (VIII 482–4)

In the exaggerated language of an ecstatic lover, he exclaims:

> Grace was in all her steps, Heav'n in her Eye,
> In every gesture dignity and love. (VIII 488–9)

When he turns to thank his Creator, 'giver of all things fair', he characterizes her as 'fairest . . . of all his gifts'. He adds: '. . . nor enviest'. This is to imply that God in giving man the fairest of gifts did not envy man his possession. One may ask what Adam knew about envy. To say this is to think of God as capable of envy. When one turns back to Adam's account of his talk with God, one concludes that this sight of Eve, for the first time engaging the faculties of the lower soul, was playing havoc with his rational nature.

This brings us to another important phase of Milton's analysis of man's 'liability to fall': the effect of beauty upon the fancy and hence upon concupiscible appetite and passion. The last, as Saurat has pointed out,[21] is an important element in the Miltonic psychology of temptation and sin; but the dualism which sets passion over against reason is historically too simple an explanation. Passion is an ultimate effect. The cause in Adam's case is to be found in the alliance of Beauty with fancy, and the appetites. Nowhere is the poet more typically Puritan than in this distrust of the effects of Beauty upon the concupiscible appetite and the consequent disturbance of the life of reason.

It is a theme first developed in the discourse of Comus with the Lady (lines 737–51), emphasized in the account of Eve's dream in Book IV of *Paradise Lost*,[22] touched upon again in Belial's proposal to tempt Christ by setting women in his eye (*PL*, II 153–4), 'Among daughters of men the fairest found', and given pointed exposition in *Samson Agonistes*:

> Yet beauty, though injurious, hath strange power
> After offence returning to regain
> Love once possessed, . . . (1003–5)

There is, perhaps, an autobiographical note as the poet, recalling his early susceptibility to beauty, contemplated the effect upon his life of the attempted realization of his ideal of marriage. We may be hearing Milton as Adam tells the angel:

> here passion first I felt,
> Commotion strange, in all enjoyments else
> Superior and unmov'd, here only weak
> Against the charm of Beauty's powerful glance. (VIII 530–3)

Specifically, the element disturbing the life of reason in the erotic life is 'Beauty's powerful glance'. It is beauty again which Adam names, immediately after the sin, as inflaming his sense

> With ardor to enjoy thee, fairer now
> Then ever, bountie of this vertuous Tree. (IX 1032–3)

Having made this confession to the angel, Adam offers three possible explanations:

> Or Nature fail'd in mee, and left some part
> Not proof enough such Object to sustain,
> Or from my side subducting, took perhaps
> More than enough; at least on her bestow'd
> Too much of Ornament. (VIII 534–8)

He is asserting that either he was created deficient, or the creation of Eve made him deficient, or Eve was too beautiful! All three not only evade the issue of man's moral responsibility, but, like Adam's questioning of celestial motions, they constitute criticisms of God's creative acts. Immediately, however, he adds that he knows that she is the inferior both 'in the mind and inward faculties' and in outward qualities as 'resembling less His image who made both'. This might for the moment have forestalled Raphael's rebuke; but with the image of the beloved

fair dominant in his fancy, he utters extravagances comparable to the
erotic poetry of Milton's day:

> yet when I approach
> Her loveliness, so absolute she seems
> And in her self compleat, so well to know
> Her own, that what she wills to do or say,
> Seems wisest, virtuousest, discreetest, best. (VIII 546–50)

After Raphael's efforts to impress upon Man his true nature, subordinate
to his Maker, but superior to all other creatures, this is the result: Eve
not only seems 'absolute' and 'self-compleat', but, according to the
superlatives of this harshest succession of sibilants in English verse, her
will rather than God's is the *summum bonum*. What follows is even more
serious:

> All higher knowledge in her presence falls
> Degraded, Wisdom in discourse with her
> Loses discount'nanc't, and like folly shows;
> Authority and Reason on her wait,
> As one intended first, not after made
> Occasionally; and to consummate all,
> Greatness of mind and nobleness thir seat
> Build in her loveliest, . . . (VIII 551–8)

This is something much more dangerous than the glorification of Love
and Beauty reminiscent of the Cavalier lyric: it is not only a denial of
God's purpose in the order of the two human creations, but it is a
repudiation of the order, in that plan, of Wisdom and Beauty, an order
which Eve had already acknowledged in her acquiescence to the
superiority of Adam:

> How beauty is excell'd by manly grace
> And wisdom, which alone is truly fair. (IV 490–1)

The tragic seriousness in all of this lies in the complete degradation of
Wisdom, the personification of higher reason associated in the poet's
mind with Urania:

> Descend from Heav'n Urania, . . .
> Thou with Eternal Wisdom didst converse,
> Wisdom thy Sister, and with her didst play
> In presence of th' Almighty Father, . . . (VII 1 and 9–11)

Here Adam is asserting that, in discourse with Eve, Wisdom, sister of Urania, would not only lose but look ridiculous. Eve was so emphatically the prime creation, the acme of all creation, that Authority and Reason would seem to be only the handmaids of this goddess. She is the consummation of all creation in alone possessing that very magnanimity which Raphael had already, in his account of the creation of man, named as the chief virtue of Man, the effect of rational self-knowledge.

Raphael's stern rebuke is first directed at this gratuitous degradation of Wisdom:

> Accuse not Nature, she hath done her part;
> Do thou but thine, and be not diffident
> Of Wisdom, she deserts thee not if thou
> Dismiss not her, when most thou need'st her nigh,
> By attributing overmuch to things
> Less excellent, as thou thyself perceiv'st. (VIII 561-6)

The head of Adam's offence lies, then, not alone in his preference for Beauty, but in his diffidence or, literally, lack of faith in wisdom. Here Milton reveals his familiarity with Protestant discussions of temptation, and specifically with one of the temptations of Christ, lack of faith (*apisteia*) in the source of all strength.[23] Christ preserves his faith in the first temptation through self-knowledge, i.e. the consciousness that he is the Son of God. This is His 'greatness of mind and nobleness', His magnanimity. The second Adam will triumph, through faith, over the temptation to which the first Adam succumbs. Book VIII prepares the reader for the tragedy of Book IX by presenting a protagonist whose *hamartia* is in part *apisteia*, a lack of faith in his own nature and in that wisdom to which he might have turned in his hour of trial. Having confused, in his uxoriousness, the roles of Beauty and Wisdom, preferring the judgment of fancy and concupiscence to that of reason, he was no longer able to recognize wisdom as Man's prerogative. The first sight of Eve and the stimulation of the 'lower nature' bring the fatal preference for beauty; and in Book IX, as the result, all higher knowledge falls degraded, Wisdom in discourse with her loses discountenanced, and Authority (God's command) and Reason (Man's prerogative) are reduced to ancillary roles. In this distortion of values they become Eve's handmaids.

Eve, however, never makes this mistake of reversing the right order of Wisdom and Beauty. Conscious of inferiority, she knows that

Wisdom is higher, and deceived by the sophistry of Satan, she accepts forbidden fruit as having virtue to make wise, and, after the sin, she worships the tree as the wisdom-giving plant. She seeks deliberately to disturb the Divine plan by which

> beauty is excell'd by manly grace
> And wisdom which alone is truly fair.

Adam, on the other hand, 'against his better reason' was 'fondly overcome by female charm'.

V

Thus Book VIII, truncated in 1674 from the creation story, to which it had apparently been only a long appendage, can be seen in its proper relation to the catastrophe of Book IX. It is primarily a study of Adam's *ethos* before the Fall. Like the Eve of Books III and IV, he had his 'liability to fall'. First, in the questioning of the astronomy there was a tendency to superficial judgment based upon the evidences of the senses, a preference for the less excellent because it was bright, and the consequent criticism of God's plan, which had demanded recognition of man's primacy.

Finally, there was fatal concupiscence, involving the preference of Beauty to Wisdom, and, again, a repudiation of the divine plan through his lack of faith in this primacy. These two criticisms, the one at the beginning of the cosmic creation with its principle of order and subordination, the other at the end of the human creations, with their comparable principles of subordination, motivate the disobedience of Book IX.

Between these two presentations of a potentially sinful Adam, we find artistically set off by a dream and a trance (preludes to the full play of fancy) an Adam at the moment of creation, endowed with sanctity of Reason, in talk with his Maker, proving his goodness by inferring the need of a companion. God gave him Eve, and, with her advent, the occasion for the activity of the whole sentient being – fancy, concupiscence, the affections – and the inevitable conflict in this psychological dualism with his rational nature. This was the necessary price of sweet society. Thus, in the book which precedes the account of the fall, Milton presents his great paradox.

NOTES

1. See the third and fourth drafts conveniently reproduced in J. H. Hanford, *A Milton Handbook*, 3rd ed. (New York, 1941) pp. 183–6.

2. Cf. Act II of the third draft, 'Chorus sing the marriage song and describe Paradise', the only action of this act, with a passage of what is apparently the first act of the fourth draft, wherein Paradise is described and the Angel Gabriel related 'what he knew of Man, as the creation of Eve, with their love and marriage'. Having determined that 'the battle and victory in Heaven' must be the theme of the second act, Milton is trying to find a place for congenial, but essentially undramatic, materials.

3. Milton's *Paradise Lost*, ed. A. W. Verity (1910), Introduction, p. xlvi.

4. *Reason of Church Government*, bk II, Preface, in *Prose Works*, ed. J. A. St John (1868–72) II 478.

5. *Christian Doctrine*, ch. 11, in *Prose Works*, IV 253: 'This sin originated, first in the instigation of the devil . . . Secondly, in the liability to fall with which man was created'.

6. See Murray W. Bundy, 'Eve's Dream and the Temptation in *Paradise Lost*', in *Research Studies of the State College of Washington*, x (Dec. 1942) 273–91.

7. Milton has in mind the magnanimous man of Aristotle's *Nichomachean Ethics*, IV vii; cf. *Samson Agonistes*, 522–5:

> when in strength
> All mortals I excell'd, and great in hopes
> With youthful courage and magnanimous thoughts
> Of birth from Heav'n foretold . . .

8. See Grant McColley, *Paradise Lost* (Chicago, 1940) pp. 86–97.

9. See McColley, *Paradise Lost*.

10. See Bundy, in *Research Studies*, x (Dec. 1942) 284.

11. Cf. John Flavel, *A Treatise on Keeping the Heart* (New York, n.d.) p. 67: 'And amongst all the faculties of the soule most of the disquiet and unnecessary trouble of our lives arises from the vanity and ill government of that power of the soule which we call imagination and opinion, bordering between the senses and our understanding; which is nothing else but a hollow apprehension of good or evil taken from the senses. Now because outward good or evil things agree or disagree to the senses, and the life of sense is in us before the use of reason, and the delights of sense are present, and pleasing, and suitable to our natures: Thereupon the imagination setteth a great price upon sensible good things.' See also R. Sibbs, *The Soules Conflict with Itselfe*, 4th ed. (1651) p. 157: 'Beg of God a mortified fancy. A working fancy (Saith one) how much sooner it be extolled among men, is a great snare to the soul, except it work in fellowship with right reason and a sanctified heart. The fancy is the power of the soul, placed between the senses and the understanding; it is that which first stirs itself in the soul, and by its motions the other powers of the soul are brought into exercise: it is that in which they are first formed, and as that is, so are they. If imaginations be not first cast down, it is impossible that every thought of the heart should be brought into obedience to Christ. The fancy is naturally the wildest and most untameable power of the soul.'

12. Cf. *Christian Doctrine*, ch. 7, in *Prose Works*, IV 195: 'Man being formed after the image of God, it followed as a necessary consequence that he should be endued with natural wisdom, holiness, and righteousness. . . . Certainly without extraordinary wisdom he could not have given names to the whole animal creation with such sudden intelligence.'

13. Cf. *Tetrachordon*, in *Prose Works*, III 324–5: 'It might be doubted why he saith, "In the image of God created he him," not them, as well as "male and female" them . . . But St Paul ends the controversy, by explaining, that the woman is not primarily and immediately the image of God, but in reference to the man: "The head of the woman," said he,

1 Cor. xi, "is he the man;" "he the image and glory of God, she the glory of the man;" he not for her, but she for him.'

14. For the distinction of supernatural dreams, see Moses Amyraut, *Discours sur les songs divins* (Saumur, 1656) trans. by James Lowde, *A Discourse concerning the Divine Dreams* (1676); see also Bundy, in *Research Studies*, x (Dec. 1942) 277 and *passim*.

15. Ibid. pp. 280 ff.

16. Of course, we must remember that we are invited to compare Adam, newly created, with Eve after experience had intervened. The same kind of consideration, however, leads one to observe that we are also invited to compare this account of Adam on the day of the creation with an Adam who, as we have seen, after experience was capable of questioning God's cosmic plan, and who is about to reveal an even more dangerous state of mind in his talk about the creation of Eve.

17. *Prose Works*, III 209.

18. See *Doctrine and Discipline of Divorce*, ch. XI.

19. *Prose Works*, III 329–30: '"It is not good" God here presents himself like to a man deliberating; both to show us that the matter is of high consequence, and that he intended to found it according to natural reason, not impulsive command. . . . "Not good" was as much to Adam before his fall, as not pleasing, not expedient.' Cf. *Doctrine and Discipline of Divorce*, in *Prose Works*, III 191.

20. We may add that Eve's devil-inspired dream, in which she was impelled to pluck and eat, also had no immediate consequence since she recognized it as a dream; but, unlike Adam's, the effect upon fancy and appetite prepared the way for the temptation.

21. Denis Saurat, *Milton: Man and Thinker* (New York, 1925) pp. 56–8.

22. *PL*, v 35–63; cf. Bundy, in *Research Studies*, x (Dec. 1942).

23. See A. H. Gilbert, 'The Temptation in *Paradise Regained*', in *Journal of English and Germanic Philology*, xv (1916) 599–611.

CLEANTH BROOKS
Eve's Awakening (1954)

PERHAPS more than any other poet Milton has suffered from mis-applied biographical interest and misapplied interest in his ideas. A great deal of the distaste for Milton's poetry in the last seventy-five years has sprung from a dislike of Milton the man – as I heard Professor Douglas Bush ruefully remark a few years ago. And though Milton's ideas are important – *Paradise Lost* is not just a superb organ music throbbing in an intellectual void – still, our concern for this theological and philosophical consistency can push us into ruinous distortions of his poetry.

There is, of course, no patented way to read Milton, indeed, and if there were such a way, I, least of all, would lay any claim to possessing it. But I do think that a consideration of the structure of the poem, of the interplay of part with part, of image with image, and an emphasis upon the way in which ideas are bodied forth and thus qualified as well as defined by the images might furnish a partial corrective to over-weening biographical and ideological emphases. I shall lean very hard upon the Milton scholarship of the last twenty years, and I do not promise that I shall write anything that is fresh and new about Milton's ideas as such. The point that I should like to make in this essay is a highly important point: that Milton's great poem shows the thinking through images which must characterize any genuine poem.

For example, the passages with which I am concerned in this paper bear heavily upon the relationship of man to woman, and thus we run at once into a problem that sets the modern reader's teeth on edge. Does Milton really think that man is superior to woman – that a wife should be subject to her husband? So many of us are made furious by what we are told was Milton's treatment of his first wife, Mary Powell, and by what we take to be his stiff-necked Puritan opinions, that we are quite unable to read his great poem. We stop reading the poem to quarrel with Milton the defective sociologist. I could wish that Professor W. R. Parker would be able to prove that the sonnet beginning 'Me thought I saw my late espoused saint' was actually written to commemorate Mary Powell rather than Katherine Woodcock, his second wife. Perhaps it cannot be proved. And surely truth and rigidly honest scholarship have first place. But if it could be proved convincingly, that proof would do more, I am satisfied, to commend Milton to the modern reader than anything else that I can think of. Be that as it may, Milton is on record in one of his divorce pamphlets to the effect that a woman may have more intelligence than her husband, and that wisdom, not the mere fact of maleness, should govern the family decisions. But whatever may be said in extenuation of Milton's ideas on the subject, in his poetry Milton, as a matter of course, makes use of the traditional concept of woman. And if that in itself be irritating, then we must be prepared to be irritated with such moderns as William Butler Yeats, D. H. Lawrence, and William Faulkner, where, unless I utterly mistake myself, the traditional view of woman is also dominant.

One of the most charming passages in the poem occurs in Book IV when Eve gives her account of her first moments of consciousness and of her first meeting with Adam. It is worth pondering for its own sake, but we shall find it is also a nice example of the careful articulation of Milton's poem.

Eve tells how she waked, and immediately began to wonder, as she says, 'where/ And what I was, whence thither brought, and how'. Eve is no infant for whom the world is a confused blooming buzz. She has been created mature, and moreover she represents unfallen humanity with its keen preceptions and its vigorous and powerful intellect. These she proceeds to apply at once to the situation in which she finds herself. René Descartes could do no better: she says not *Cogito, ergo sum,* but *Admiror, ergo sum* – I wonder, therefore I am. She is a conscious being: she immediately speculates on what kind of being, and she infers at once that some power has brought her here from some place and by some means. But she is charmingly feminine withal. She is quickly attracted by the murmur of running water to the banks of a little lake, a lake that mirrors the sky and that seems to be another sky. Peering into it she sees an image with 'answering looks/ Of sympathie and love':

> I started back,
> It started back, but pleased I soon returned,
> Pleas'd it returned as soon. . . .

From this Narcissistic indulgence, Eve is called away by the voice of

God. He is invisible but by addressing her as 'Fair creature', He takes cognizance of her love of beauty, and by telling her that what she sees is an image of herself, he takes account of her bewilderment and her need for companionship. He promises her

> I will bring thee where no shadow staies
> Thy coming, and thy soft imbraces, hee
> Whose image thou art, him thou shall enjoy
> Inseparable thine . . .

Adam has been made in God's image; Eve has been made of Adam's substance, and as the invisible Voice here tells her, she has been made in Adam's image as well, and she is to bear to him, 'Multitudes like thy self' — that is, beings made in his image and hers.

Milton's scheme of hierarchy is thus set forth concretely and succinctly. The sense in which Man is made in God's image — and the sense in which Eve is made in Adam's image — will come in for more attention in Book VIII: it is that quality which distinguishes man from the brute creation, the possession of reason, already exemplified in Eve's first conscious response to the world in which she finds herself. More of that anon.

For the moment I want to point out that Milton has also in this brief passage touched on what will be Eve's difficulty and what will constitute later the devil's prime means for tempting her. She is sensitive to beauty, and she finds it easier to love the image of herself as mirrored in the forest pool than the image of herself as mirrored less obviously in Adam. For when she is led into Adam's presence, as she confesses to him later,

> Yet [thee] methought less faire,
> Less winning soft, less amiably milde,
> Then that smooth watry image . . .

and so she retreats from him. Later at the climax of the poem, Adam too will have to choose between images: his image mirrored in Eve and God whose image he himself mirrors. He will choose the more obviously enchanting image, that reflected in Eve. The act will be a kind of Narcissism, a kind of self-love. It will cut him off from the primal source of life and power, and throw him back upon himself, though of course he is not capable of sustaining himself.

I must apologize for being drawn away from our chosen passage again and again to follow up implications. But the passage is rich, and this very process of deserting it to point its ties with other sections of the book may become a virtue if it shows us how tightly Milton has articulated his great poem.

But to recur to the narrative. For Eve it is not a matter of love at first sight; but for Adam, it is, and his plea to Eve constitutes one of the most moving passages in the poem;

> Return fair Eve,
> Whom fli'st thou? whom thou fli'st, of him thou art,
> His flesh, his bone; to give thee being I lent
> Out of my side to thee, neerest my heart
> Substantial Life, to have thee by my side
> Henceforth an individual solace dear;
> Part of my Soul I seek thee, and thee claim
> My other half. . . .

Adam, who seems to the modern reader so often priggish and pedantic, will not seem so here. It is a love speech, and it moves Eve. She speedily comes to see Adam as more amiable than 'that smooth watry image' – sees, as she later puts it,

> How beauty is excelld by manly grace
> And wisdom, which alone is truly fair.

Milton's doctrine that wisdom is superior to sensuous beauty is present here, but for once Milton almost gets by with his presentation of it. By dramatizing the doctrine, and by putting it not into Adam's mouth but into the mouth of Eve Milton renders the doctrine inoffensive to any but the most belligerent modern reader.

The psychology of Eve is sound and convincing. To the student of Freud it may seem even preternaturally so; for Milton has made Eve recapitulate the whole process of the child's growing up and transferring the affections to the other sex. According to Freud, the child must transcend the mother image with which it has first associated warmth, nourishment, and affection, and center its affections elsewhere. In the case of the female child the task is more difficult, for it must transcend an image of its *own* sex. But neatly as the symbolism fits into the Freudian system, it is not part of my purpose to place any stress on this.

What I want to emphasize is the power of the passage as an integral part of the poem. We need not fear that we are over-reading it. Milton has been careful to give not only the first conscious thoughts of Eve, but also the first conscious thoughts of Adam, of Lucifer, and of Sin and

Death. He has built to, and away from, our passage most cunningly. For instance, Sin is born from Lucifer as Eve is born of Adam. Like Athena, Sin bursts full armed from Lucifer's head. But with Lucifer it is not love at first sight. *He* recoils from her, and only later she comes to please him – only later that he finds himself as Sin says, 'full oft/ Thyself in me thy perfect image viewing. . . .' But the Narcissism of Lucifer soon leads to incest, and of this union Death is born.

Milton then doubles the theme once more; for Sin tells that when she had borne Death, she fled from him, but that Death immediately pursued her and raped her, begetting the horde of yelling monsters that now surrounded her and feed upon her. These passages prepare for, and insist upon, a parallelism between Eve's relation to Adam and Sin's to Lucifer. If we still have any doubt of this, listen to Sin's speech to Lucifer:

> Thou art my Father, thou my Author, thou
> My being gav'st me; whom should I obey
> But thee, whom follow?

And compare it with Eve's speech to Adam in Book IV:

> My author and Disposer, what thou bidst
> Unargu'd I obey. . . .

So much for the relation of the female characters to the male. But I want to return to the larger theme – in this case, to Adam's first thoughts as a conscious being. Like Eve, Adam first contemplates the sky, but not the sky reflected in a pool. He looks up 'Strait toward Heav'n', he says. Next he observes the created world, and infers at once that the creation including himself as creature implies a creator. He addresses the 'Fair Creatures', which he sees about him, entreating them to

> Tell me, how may I know him, how adore,
> From whom I have that thus I move and live,
> And feel that I am happier than I know.

But the creation – though its very presence testifies to a great Maker – is dumb; it cannot name Him, and it is necessary that the Divine Being himself appear to tell Adam that He is the Author of 'all this thou seest' and to offer him life in the Garden with the sole prohibition of the fruit of one tree. Adam then gives names to the fish, birds, and beasts, over whom he has been given dominion. But whereas Eve soon discovers

her own image and longs for union with it, Adam from the first looks
about to find his own image and cannot find it. He does not find it in
the beasts about him and he asks of his Maker

> In solitude
> What happiness, who can enjoy alone,
> Or all enjoying, what contentment find?

In the colloquy that follows between Adam and God, Milton has been
daring enough to imply in God a sense of humor – the merest trace of
good-humored teasing. I think that Milton's maneuver is successful, or
almost so. But that is not my point here: I call attention to the fact
because most of us are so convinced that Milton is unbendingly
solemn, that we ourselves become rigidly solemn readers – to the
detriment of the poem.

To summarize the argument briefly: God asks why Adam, in view
of the plentitude of the creatures, should worry about solitude. And
He forestalls Adam's easiest reply by pointing out that reason is not the
sole and absolute prerogative of man, for God is made to say that the
beasts have 'Thir language and their wayes, they also know/ And reason
not contemptibly.' To this Adam replies by urging the fact that there
can be no true fellowship among unequals: and it is fellowship that
he seeks, fellowship 'fit to participate/ All rational delight'. I would
emphasize the word *delight* quite as much as the word *rational*. Adam's
point is evidently that reason as a mere instrument of the will – for
example, reason as exemplified in the white rat that has learned to run a
maze for food or in the ape that has been taught to put one box on
another to reach a banana – reason as pure means is not enough. There
must be the ability to share in rational pleasures.

This view of reason is out of fashion in our times. Milton reborn
today might easily come to feel that our ideal was to produce highly
skilled technicians who should relax from their technical labors by
amusing themselves with the trash of Hollywood and television. But
the meaning of 'rational delight' is crucial if we are to understand this
poem.

When God, still apparently refusing to concede Adam's point, calls
attention to His own solitude, Adam correctly puts the distinction
between God and His creatures: God is perfect; man is not; man's only
recourse to remedy his defect is to 'beget/ Like of his like, his Image
multiplied'. Man, that is to say, can solace himself only in a human

community. With 'his Image multiplied' we are back to our word *Image* once more. Man needs to see himself in the creation and he cannot find himself mirrored in the creation of fish, birds, and beasts.

This is the answer that God is waiting for. And he picks up this term *image* in his next speech to Adam, congratulating him on 'Expressing well the spirit within thee free,/ My image not imparted to the Brute.' His questions to Adam have been but a test. He has known all along that it was 'not good for Man to be alone', and he promises to create forthwith

> Thy likeness, thy fit help, thy other self.

It is now time to turn to Lucifer's account of what he felt at his creation. The relevant passage is that in which Lucifer is replying to Abdiel's charge that Lucifer is the creature of God, made by God, and now rebelling against his Maker. Lucifer haughtily replies as follows:

> That we were formd then saist thou . . .
> . . . strange point and new!
> Doctrin which we would know thence learnt: who saw
> When this creation was? rememberst thou
> Thy making, while the Maker gave thee being?
> We know no time when we were not as now;
> Know none before us, self-begot, self-rais'd
> By our own quick'ning power, when fatal course
> Had circl'd his full Orbe, the birth mature
> Of this our native Heav'n, Ethereal Sons.
> Our puissance is our own. . . .

Now Satan is very clever here, and I am not sure that C. S. Lewis's admirable commentary quite does him full justice. Lucifer, like a good scientist, demands evidence of the senses. 'We know no time when we were not as now.' Of course not; one cannot as a conscious being have experience of a period in which he was not a conscious being. (How quickly Eve can master this devil's logic we shall see in Book IX.) Lucifer rejects all hypotheses of creation. The mirror is here demanding equality with the source of light which it reflects: that is, the mirror is saying: 'I am no mere reflector of light; I am a source of light.'

It is true that Lucifer, in his debate with Abdiel, does not use the word *image* nor does he make use of the light–mirror configuration. But that basic symbolism runs through the poem. One remembers that Lucifer in Book I is compared to the sun, the wintry sun peering

through the mists, or a sun in dim eclipse, shedding disastrous twilight.
And one remembers his address to the sun in Book IV in which he
expresses his hatred of its beams. And one remembers most of all the
great parable of just hierarchy as represented in the starry heavens:

> Of light by farr the greater part God took,
>   . . . and plac'd
> In the Suns Orb, made porous to receive
> And drink the liquid Light, firme to retaine
> Her gather'd beams, great Palace now of Light,
> Hither as to thir Fountain other Starrs
> Repairing, in thir gold'n Urns draw Light,
> And hence the Morning Planet guilds his horns. . . .

Even those stars which have a modicum of their own light, 'Thir small
peculiar', draw upon the great fountain of the sun, 'by tincture or
reflection'. The Morning Planet is of course the morning star, Lucifer,
and Milton could count upon his reader's – though not apparently upon
modern editors' – remembering Isaiah, xiv 12–13: 'How art thou
fallen from heaven, O Lucifer, son of the morning! how art thou cut
down to the ground. . . . And thou saidst in thy heart, I will ascend into
heaven, I will exalt my throne above the stars of God. . . .'

Lucifer has been unwilling to augment his own light – his 'small
peculiar' by reflecting light from the great source of light. He has set
himself up as a source. He puts himself in competition with God. Small
wonder that the fervent angel Abdiel addresses Lucifer as one 'alienate
from God . . . Spirit accurst . . .'

This is the sin into which Adam and Eve are to fall: that of alienation
from God. The mirror will turn away from the light in the vanity of
thinking itself as light-giving. God's image will no longer be reflected in
it because it has tilted itself away from God. When in Book XI, Adam
wonders that God will allow Man made in His image to become
deformed with plague and pestilence, the angel Michael answers him
by saying

> Thir Makers Image . . . then
> Forsook them, when themselves they villified. . . .

The motivation for this act of secession will be pride – both in Lucifer
and in Adam and Eve. God will be regarded no longer as father but as
tyrant; not as loving overlord but as rival; and man, seceding from

God, will attempt to set himself up as a god. When Eve tastes the forbidden fruit, the poet grimly comments 'nor was God-head from her thought'.

Now in summarizing thus, I am of course saying little that is new. The general point is a familiar one, though not an unchallenged one. My justification in proceeding through the account once more is to indicate how carefully Milton has worked it out in certain dominant images and how he has implied the nature of the fall in his account of the creation of Adam and Eve. Eve must not forget what she was once able to infer so clearly: that she is a creature and therefore cannot assume the prerogatives of the Creator; and Eve must not become obsessed with her own lovely image; the superficial reflection of herself in a lower element. As for Adam, he must not become obsessed with that lovely image either – to the point of preferring that image to the image of God.

But I mean to go beyond this summary to some speculations about the kind of knowledge to which Adam and Eve attain by eating the fruit. Here there is no widespread agreement among Milton authorities. Conjectures range from the acquisition of scientific knowledge to no knowledge at all. I have already written on this topic recently, and perhaps my best expedient here is to cite a portion of that paper as published in *Publications of the Modern Language Association of America* (LXVI (1951) 1051–3).

'What knowledge, then, does the Forbidden Fruit confer? I think that an earlier section of Eve's speech can set us on the right track. She has exclaimed:

> For good unknown, sure is not had, or had
> And yet unknown, is as not had at all.

This seems plausible to her, and since we are fallen men, it probably seems plausible to us. How can you have something that you don't know you have? Or if you have it, how does an ignorant possession of it do you any good? For most of us this is not devil's logic; it is just logic. If Milton is to maintain the opposite – and I think that he does – then he will have to present his case through extra-logical devices including paradox.

'The Forbidden Fruit gives Adam knowledge of good and evil as *we* know them. But it gives him such knowledge only at the price of extirpating another kind of knowledge. Milton maintains that the other kind of knowledge was possible – though none of his readers, being mortal men, could have experienced it. God is made to say that Adam would have been happier "to have known/ Good by itself". That state is properly mythical. Has Milton been able to intimate it – to suggest to us what it was like? We must expect to see him play upon the various senses of the word *know* – not as an idle rhetorical gesture but in order to refashion from our various dictionary uses a sense of *know* which will be relevant to the myth that he is presenting.

'The good that Adam possesses, he does not "know" he possesses. He will know that he had it only after he has lost it. Adam states this in so many words after the Fall:

> we know
> Both Good and Evil, Good lost, and Evil got,
> Bad Fruit of Knowledge, if this be to know . . . (IX 1071–3)

But this state of affairs has been implicit in all the earlier action. Earlier, Adam could say: "[I] feel that I am happier than I know." One cannot substitute for this: "[I] know that I am happier than I know." Grammatically this is literal nonsense; theologically it is also nonsense. One can only say: "[I] know that I *was* happier than I *knew*." Earlier the angels have sung:

> thrice happie if they know
> Thir happiness . . . (VII 631–2)

Later God pronounces:

> Happier, had it suffic'd Man to have known
> Good by it self, and Evil not at all. (XI 88–9)

Milton, speaking as chorus in Book IV, and with all the stops of verbal wit pulled out, stresses the paradox:

> Blest pair; and O yet happiest if ye seek
> No happier state, and know to know no more. (774–5)

'The unfallen Adam is really very much like the child described in Wordsworth's Immortality Ode: Wordsworth might indeed be describing Adam in the epithets he bestows upon the child: "Nature's Priest", "best Philosopher, Seer blest", "Thou, over whom thy Immortality/ Broods like the Day, a Master o'er a Slave." Yet the Child cannot impart his philosophy and does not "know" that he possesses it. If he is an "Eye among the blind", he is also "deaf and silent". One cannot even acquaint him with the knowledge that he possesses without destroying his knowledge by making self-conscious and abstract what is concrete and joyful and unself-conscious. The poet was himself once such a child, and having lost the child's knowledge, knows at last what it was that he once possessed. But he cannot "know" it *and* possess it. I am tempted to complete the parallel by saying that Wordsworth at the end of the Ode speaks very much like the fallen but repentant Adam at the end of *Paradise Lost*: both have attained a wisdom out of suffering and "the faith that looks through death".

'One is tempted to go still further and say that for Adam and Eve, their immortality does indeed brood over them like "a Master o'er a Slave"; that Eve, responding to Lucifer's words, throws off her immortality because she is persuaded that she is enslaved; that her assertion of individuality and separateness challenges the complete harmony in which she moves, and finds in death its necessary consequence.'

In the paper from which I have just been quoting, I was concerned primarily with the use of the word *fruit* in *Paradise Lost*, and with the necessity for making use of myth – a necessity which the very nature of his problem had enjoined upon Milton. But I should like to go on to connect this account with the whole matter of God's image as reflected in Adam and Eve. As I have remarked in commenting on the child of Wordsworth's poem: one cannot even 'acquaint him with the knowledge that he possesses without destroying his knowledge by making self-conscious and abstract what is concrete and joyful and unself-conscious'. It is this kind of self-consciousness that constitutes the knowledge that Adam and Eve gain from eating the forbidden fruit.

Dorothy Sayers remarks that St Augustine suggests that the Fall is a lapse into self-consciousness, and though I am not certain that I have located in Augustine the passage or passages to which she refers, it is very true that there are passages in his *City of God* that do point toward self-consciousness as the knowledge conferred by the act of plucking and eating the fatal apple. For example, in bk. XIV, ch. XIII, St Augustine writes:

> This then is the mischief: man liking himself as if he were his own light turned away from the true light, which if he had pleased himself with, he might have been like . . . it is good that the proud should fall into some broad and disgraceful sin, thereby to take a dislike of themselves, who fell by liking themselves too much. . . . Therefore says the Psalmist: 'Fill their faces with shame, that they may seek Thy name, O Lord': that is, that they

may delight in Thee and seek Thy name, who before delighted in themselves, and sought their own.

For anyone who knows how heavily Milton draws on this fourteenth
book of *The City of God* and how closely he follows St Augustine even
in the nuances of interpretation of the Garden story, Augustine's
emphasis on the human pair's preoccupation with self suggests that
such will be Milton's emphasis. But the evidence is in *Paradise Lost*
itself.

The theme of self-consciousness comes out clearly in Satan's opening
words to Eve in the great temptation scene. He begins by flattering Eve,
for to succeed he must draw her attention back to the image of herself
which she first saw in the forest pool. He calls her 'Fairest resemblance
of thy Maker faire . . .'. She it is who most beautifully represents God's
image. All things in the universe that are fair and good are united in her
'Divine/ Semblance'. By calling her 'Sovran of Creatures, universal
Dame', he literally declares her Miss Universe of the year 1. I shall not
go through the Serpent's argument in detail. It is brilliantly plausible.
Suffice it to say that it ends as it begins: in an appeal to Eve, to Eve's
own pride in herself – a pride that will blot out any sense of inferiority
to God and hence of any obligation to him.

Adam's decision to taste the forbidden fruit seems very differently
motivated. He knows at once that Eve is lost and says so at once. But
he means to die with her:

> som cursed fraud
> Of Enemie hath beguil'd thee, yet unknown,
> And mee with thee hath ruind, for with thee
> Certain my resolution is to Die.

Milton furnishes Adam with the noblest motivation to sin, and
properly so. The poem gains thereby. But Adam's sin is ultimately of
the same kind as Eve's: the first words that he addresses to her tell the
story:

> O fairest of Creation, last and best
> Of all Gods Works

he calls her in his agony. And if the words are primarily a testimony to
his genuine love for her, and so have their pathos, they also imply the
choice that he is to state a few lines later. For him, the Creation is
summed up in her, not in the Creator. It is a hard choice, but there is no
hesitancy in his mind if he is to be forced to choose. Adam's choice, to

be sure, seems to be a detached and unselfish choice, but only apparently so. It is a choice between his community and the divine community – between his little empire and the whole realm of God.

Thus far I have, I am sure, seemed to stress not the human pair's self-consciousness – as we usually employ that word – but their consciousness of self. But the consciousness of self with its pride is nearly related to self-consciousness with its sense of shame, and if the motivation to sin springs from too much regard for self, with the Fall comes self-consciousness in the senses that associate it with shame, with isolation and alienation, and with the loss of the innocent rapport with the world about one. This is the only knowledge that the act of eating the apple brings the human pair.

The fact comes out nowhere more plainly than in their changed relation in the sex act. The life of the senses had existed before the Fall, and Milton is as fervent as D. H. Lawrence in emphasizing the purity and holiness of their sexual desires and just as emphatic as Lawrence in recognizing the physical implications. But the sex act now after their rebellion against God's order has a different focus. Adam begins to regard Eve with the eye of a sensual connoisseur; he makes comparisons between the emotion aroused in him now as compared with that on other occasions; he has never known 'true relish' until now that he has tasted the fruit and he anticipates a special relish now in the act of love. Adam and Eve are each preparing to use the other for his own enjoyment. They are 'knowing' and self-conscious about the sexual relations in a way in which they have not been before this.

It is usual to take this passage as a symbolization of the conquest of reason by passion – of the conquest of the lower faculties over the higher faculties. And surely this is a proper and important interpretation. Milton himself has underlined it. But the over-emphasis on the sensual aspect of the relation which now occurs puts an end to the old harmonious relationship in which body, mind, and spirit all had due part. The sleep into which Adam and Eve fall is restless and full of troubled dreams, and when they wake, their eyes, as Adam complains, are opened; but opened only to see that they have been deceived. The Serpent has cheated them with his promises

> since our eyes
> Op'nd we find indeed, and find we know
> Both Good and Evil, Good lost and Evil got,
> Bad Fruit of Knowledge, if this be to know.

Adam's reproaches to Eve bring on a bitter wrangling between the human pair. The breakup in the universal community implies a further breakup in the human community itself. Adam cannot maintain his loyalty to Eve stated so generously when he elected to die with her. And Eve, reproached by Adam, retorts by making a stinging defense of herself as self:

> Love was not in thir looks, either to God
> Or to each other . . .

The Cavalier poet Lovelace has dealt with the essence of the situation in his little poem 'To Lucasta, on Going to the Wars': 'I could not love thee dear so much,/ Loved I not honor more.' Adam cannot love Eve as much as he ought unless he loves God more: unless he loves God more, ultimately he cannot love Eve at all. Doubtless Milton had read the Lovelace poem, though I am not arguing that he remembers it here. But Milton would have understood the Cavalier poet's paradox, and he was prepared to take it seriously.

There remains one curious further passage to deal with in which man's likeness to God – the sense in which he reflects God's image – is the matter at issue. It is the speech which God makes to the angels in Book XI:

> O Sons, like one of us Man is become
> To know both Good and Evil, since his taste
> Of that defended Fruit; but let him boast
> Happier, had it suffic'd him to have known
> Good by it self, and Evil not at all.

The temptation has been to say that Milton here is bound to his source in Genesis and makes the best of an embarrassing business by turning Genesis iii 22 into a sneer upon God's part. But I think that we can do more with it than this. Man is like God in that he has been made in the image of God. God has said so earlier in congratulating Adam upon 'Expressing well the spirit within thee free/ My image not imparted to the brute'. The brutes cannot sin, for their actions are not free – they are instinctive. The great gift imparted to man lies in Adam's capacity to choose – and this implies the capacity to choose wrongly as well as the capacity to obey God's behests not instinctively but freely and consciously.

Yet if the 'knowledge' that Adam gains is only self-consciousness, how can Milton have God say that Adam has now become like 'us' in coming to know both good and evil? Is God, then, self-conscious and not innocent? I am prepared to answer yes, that God is self-conscious, but that self-consciousness as applied to God does not carry the implications that self-consciousness must carry for a limited being. As perfect omniscience – as creator and not creature – as a limitless being endlessly contemplating his own virtues, God is self-conscious indeed. The whole Western tradition from Aristotle onward is behind Milton here; Milton could assume acquaintance with this tradition and assume it not merely for his fit audience though few. And in *Paradise Lost* itself God is constantly referring to the Son as 'My image' and contemplating himself as perfectly reflected in this 'radiant image of his Glory'. But Adam is not prepared to assume this burden of consciousness. God as creator has, in the fall of angels, experienced loss and rebellion and has not been lessened thereby. He is capable of dealing with rebellion and even of bringing good out of that rebellion. But Adam cannot assume the obligations and responsibilities that go with the Creator's self-knowledge. He is a part, not the whole; a creature, not the Creator. If he ventures to know evil, not as a possibility but as an experience, the process is irreversible – irreversible, that is, in so far as his own efforts avail him. The arm that has cut itself loose from the body cannot rejoin it at will: indeed Adam knows Good lost, and Evil got. Happier indeed it would have been for Adam to know good alone – that is, happier would it have been for him to have remained loyal subject and happy child of God rather than to have tried to set up as a god for himself.

Of course had Adam persisted in his innocence he would have invited the same satiric jeer that Satan darts at the loyal angel Gabriel: 'To thee no reason; Who knowest only good,/ But evil has not tried.' And this will almost certainly be a modern reader's attitude toward the unfallen Adam; for the modern reader believes in experience as the only guide, and innocence for him connotes callowness and immaturity. He forgets that Milton's Garden state is not static and not ultimate; that Milton has provided for Adam's growth in grace and knowledge, until at last Adam's body shall turn 'all to spirit'. (See v 497.) Moreover for many readers the issue has been further complicated by the fact that Milton has stressed so powerfully God's plan for making of Adam's very sin the ground and occasion for Christ's redemption of man. But we leap to conclusions if we assume that because the divine plan foresaw Adam's fall and was prepared to turn it to account, Adam's sin was not really sin but 'good' after all. Too many modern critics of Milton have erred in just this fashion. They have argued that Milton as a renaissance humanist couldn't really have believed that Adam could have been happy to continue in paradise, that Adam's moral development required his sowing his wild oats, and that Milton was really on Lucifer's side unconsciously if not consciously. The real remedy for these misconceptions is to read the poem itself. A careful reading is rewarding. It reveals that Milton is not absent-mindedly repeating theological ideas in which he had really ceased to believe. Quite the contrary. Milton's insight into the perennial problem of man is profound. It is our modern inability to deal with myth that is at fault. If it is, Milton can aid us. For his great poem is not only an enlightened critique of the mythical method. It is a brilliant example of that method.

ROSALIE L. COLIE

Time and Eternity: Paradox and Structure in *Paradise Lost* (1960)

I

PART of the difficulty of *Paradise Lost* lies in its enormous scope, which makes it almost impossible for modern critics to apply their analytical tools; part of its difficulty undeniably lies in its reliant reference to two worlds – the classical and the Biblical – now closed to the common reader. But part of its difficulty, and indeed a concealed difficulty, lies in the nature of Christian doctrine. Milton wrote, as he intended, a poem doctrinal to a nation, a poem designed to teach men various lessons – that Christian doctrine is true, that man can and must live by it, that Christian life, though hard, is infinitely worth the effort it demands. Christian belief is not easy, even intellectually: the Christian is regularly required, for instance, to express his belief in a number of essentially paradoxical articles of faith. To begin with an orthodox paradox from which Milton himself conspicuously fell away, the Christian believes in a Trinity which is One and a Unity which is Triune. He believes in an unknowable God and is instructed that his duty is to know that God; he believes in the resurrection of the dead. In fact, every time the Christian affirms his Creed, he formally recapitulates a number of logical or empirical paradoxes. The point of such formulation, of course, is the denial of logic and mundane experience to assert the mystery of faith.[1] Quoting Tertullian, Sir Thomas Browne proclaimed his especial pleasure in believing what was impossible;[2] a whole school of poets contemporary with him and with Milton exploited in rhetorical paradoxes of great brilliance the conventional Christian paradoxes of grace. But Milton was no Donne, no Herbert, no Alabaster: he was not concerned with the verbal pyrotechnics of theological wit so much as with the straight sense of Christian doctrine and Christian history. According to the evidence of his *De Doctrina Christiana* he rejected as much of the paradoxical matter of orthodox Christian belief as he was

able and used a fairly modern logic to substantiate his own hetero-
doxies. Nonetheless, some Christian paradox is inevitable, even for so
rationalist and classical a poet as Milton. In a classic article, 'Milton and
the Paradox of the Fortunate Fall', Professor Lovejoy discussed the
history and demonstrated the function of the doctrinal paradox central
to *Paradise Lost*, without which the poem could not have come into
existence. There are other 'orthodox paradoxes'[3] in *Paradise Lost*: this
essay is not concerned to identify them all or to trace their histories
among the labyrinths of patristic and conciliar writings, but simply to
discuss two related doctrinal paradoxes directly affecting the poem's
structure.

The first of these paradoxes is of major philosophical importance: the
existence at once of foreknowledge on the part of God and of free will
on the part of man. Generations of students have, like Milton's devils,
debated in vain

> Fixt Fate, Free Will, foreknowledge absolute,
> And found no end, in wand'ring mazes lost. (II 559–60)

The devils could never really hope to find an answer, since alone of
God's creatures they were subject to a 'fixt Fate' that ruled their
existence forever, after their first unwise exercise of free will in heaven.
They could never thereafter know good, though they might recognize
it; for them the paradox of foreknowledge and free will can only
remain unresolved.

Not so for Adam and Eve and Milton's Christian readers. The data of
faith are that God foreknows – and since He is perfect, He can foreknow
only what is true[4] – and that man's will is incontrovertibly free to make
his moral choices in his world. Upon the proper understanding of this
paradox Christian salvation may depend; on the mundane plane, to
understand the poem at all, readers of *Paradise Lost* must accept the
paradox and come to some sort of terms with it.

The paradox of foreknowledge and free will relates to another
metaphysical paradox, that of eternity and time. Eternity was one of
God's attributes and a condition of perfection, of which in art and
poetry the circle was commonly the emblem.[5] God has existed from
eternity. He has neither beginning nor end; even in his name, Jehovah,
He contains all imaginable time, the past, the present, and the future.[6]
'God is the *Alpha* and *Omega*, the *beginning* and the *end*', as Ralph
Venning put it in his *Orthodox Paradoxes*; 'God had never a *beginning*

and shall never have *end.*'[7] Even Beelzebub knows this and tells the
devils in hell that

> he, be sure,
> In highth or depth, still first and last will Reign
> Sole King. . . . (II 323–5)

It is in the medium of His eternity that God has foreknowledge:
because He 'is' all things and thus knows all things, God is beyond
time and outside it, as well as in it. All things, including the historical
events that men experience and identify in time, happen at once and
continually in the mind of God.[8] Dionysius the Areopagite dealt with
God's relation to time in *On the Divine Names*: 'And God we must
celebrate as both Eternity and Time, as the Cause of all Time and
Eternity and as the Ancient of Days; as before Time and above Time
and producing all the variety of times and seasons; and again, as
existing before Eternal Ages, in that He is before Eternity and above
Eternity and his Kingdom is the Kingdom of all the Eternal Ages.'[9]
Augustine's explanation in the *Confessions* is classic for the second point:
'Thy yeeres neyther goe nor come; whereas these yeeres of ours, doe
both goe and come, that (in their order) they may all come. Thy yeeres
are in a standing all at once, because they are still at a stay: nor are those
that goe, thrust out by those that *come*, for that they passe not away at
all; but these of ours shall all bee, even when they shall not all be. Thy
yeeres are one day; and thy day, is not *everyday*, but *today*: seeing thy
To day gives not place unto *To morrowe*, nor comes in place of *yesterday*.
Thy *To day* is Eternity. . . .'[10] For his simpler audience, Ralph Venning
paraphrased the same thought: 'God created all things in time, and
yet . . . all which God doth, is done in eternity.'[11]

The paradox of time and eternity is involved in the Creation itself.
In the mind of God, Creation was instantaneous ('Immediate are the
acts of God'; God 'in a moment will create/ Another world'), yet it
took six days to perform or to be revealed. In God's mind all created
time was one, as Browne saw it: 'Thus God beholds all things, who
contemplates as fully his works in their epitome, as in their full volume;
and beheld as amply the whole world in that little compendium of the
sixth day, as in the scattered and dilated pieces of those five before.'[12] In
Paradise Lost God speaks of all created time in one sentence:

> I can repair
> That detriment, if such it be to lose

> Self-lost, and in a moment will create
> Another World, out of one man a Race
> Of men innumerable, there to dwell,
> Not here, till by degrees of merit rais'd
> They open to themselves at length the way
> Up hither, under long obedience tri'd,
> And Earth be chang'd to Heav'n, and Heav'n to Earth,
> One Kingdom, Joy, and Union without end. (VII 152-61)

During the Creation God kept 'an everlasting Sabbath' quite as if He were not simultaneously creating; furthermore, even though His Creation was accomplished on the sixth day, 'creation is continued in providence every day'.[13] Once the Creation was finally accomplished, as Milton reminds his readers again and again, God is at once in the Creation and out of it, at once in time and beyond it. History and materiality at once are and are not in the mind of God, for whom all history is both one instant and eternity.

Such concepts are natural in theology and quite permissible in metaphysics or mathematics, but they are extremely difficult to deal with in a piece of literature subject to its own laws, where the content, if it is to have relevance, must be presented to its audience concretely and precisely. Milton wrote, certainly, *sub specie aeternitatis* both morally and poetically; his 'fit audience' was never allowed to forget the absoluteness of moral and natural law, however particularized the specific situation and character of Adam and Eve. He also wrote, inevitably, as a created human being at a certain recognizable point in history for other human beings of his time and future times – and, most important consideration of all, the narrative art which he practised in *Paradise Lost* is necessarily governed by chronology. There is no other way to tell a tale, even a tale told with continual reference to abstract theological conceptions of eternity and infinity. Milton says so himself:

> Immediate are the Acts of God, more swift
> Than time or motion, but to human ears
> Cannot without process of speech be told,
> So told as earthly notion can receive. (VII 176-9)

In certain ways Milton's material served him well. Although *Paradise Lost* begins according to the orthodox literary doctrine of Horace, *in medias res*, it could not by its nature begin otherwise: the Christian material it presents outdoes the material of Troy or Latium by its appropriateness. For however precise its focus on man, the whole narrative of *Paradise Lost*, from the elevation of Christ in heaven to the vision of the New Heaven and the New Earth, is *in medias res*, since in the chronology of eternity there is neither beginning nor end, and time is, in Browne's phrase, but a parenthesis in eternity. Nonetheless, though the metaphysical sense in which Milton's material was by its nature *in mediis rebus* may help to explain its extraordinary suitability to the epic pattern he inherited from the ancients, the material itself was not by definition thus made tractable to poetic laws. For the purpose of his narrative, Milton had to establish a chronology of motivation in the events prior to the creation of measured time: after the elevation of Christ, Satan knew jealousy, incited the third part of heaven to rebel, fought the great war in heaven, and fell into hell. All this accomplished, Christ acts as God's instrument in the Creation of the World, taking the necessary narrative 'time' to enter His chariot, to depart from heaven, to ride out across chaos, and with His golden compasses to draw, one by one, all the planets and all the worlds.[14]

Only after all this preparation does the central drama of Adam and Eve begin, and even then, the human action of *Paradise Lost* is not limited to the fall of the first pair and their expulsion from Eden. It involves, on the contrary, the total of human history, of what is past and passing and to come. All that is 'historical' – and it goes without saying that for Milton the historicity of Scriptural record went unquestioned – is contained in the epic, both from the human point of vision and under the aspect of eternity.[15]

For example, we learn in Book III that the action of the first two books of *Paradise Lost* has all taken place under God's eye, that God has supervised the action of Satan and his legions in hell, and that He foresees, in a tremendous vista of history, the whole future of created man.[16] On analysis, Milton's descriptive art is even more remarkable than at first glance it seems. Satan's long views, across the chaos and from the sun down upon the little earth, are magnificent perspectives of that 'universe of space' in which Milton lived,[17] but we come to realize that there can be still longer views than Satan's. God's eye, seeing from an infinitely greater distance, always surveys Satan surveying his distant prospects:

> he then survey'd
> Hell and the Gulf between, and *Satan* there
> Coasting the wall of Heav'n on this side Night

> In the dun Air sublime . . .
> Him God beholding from his prospect high,
> Wherein past, present, future he beholds,
> Thus to his only Son foreseeing spoke. (III 69–72, 77–9)

God's point of view always dominates: it is through God's eyes that we first meet Adam and Eve; only later do we see them from Satan's point of disadvantage.[18]

Just as Satan has not God's perspective of space, he has not God's perspective of time. Satan cannot have foreknowledge, and thus his attempts on man are true attempts, in that he cannot know, in spite of his supernatural craft, success or failure. So much more powerful and sophisticated than Adam, Satan knows no more of the future than he.

Indeed, he knows less. For all the grandeur of his superhuman prospects, Satan is not permitted the panoramic revelation of future time vouchsafed to Adam, who is ultimately granted a limited participation in the divine foreknowledge. Such a favour is hard to bear: at the first sight of human experience, Adam asserts the orthodox argument against attempting to know the future:

> O Vision ill foreseen! better had I
> Liv'd ignorant of future, so had borne
> My part of evil only, each day's lot
> Anough to bear: those now, that were dispens't
> The burd'n of many Ages, on me light
> At once, by more foreknowledge gaining Birth
> Abortive, to torment me ere thir being,
> With thought that they must be. (XI 763–70)

But God has prepared Adam to face the glories of his hard lesson. The way Adam learns his lesson, too, in two long narrative and descriptive books at the end of the poem, also demonstrates the difference between the way God knows time and the way Adam must experience it. Compared with the quick speeches of God in Book III where human history is so compressed as to appear almost immediate in God's mind, the length of Books XI and XII makes the long human experience more real, more actual, both to Adam and to the reader. In further contrast to Book III, a book peculiarly of eternity, Books XI and XII express the long, continuing process of history, the succession of event upon event that is the lot of fallen mankind.

The history of the world is of course prophetic to Adam: not until he has learned his lessons from Raphael, from the tree, from Michael, is he permitted to enter upon the long life of his race. In a process of artistic identification, Adam's experience is brought abreast of that of Milton's readers, so that both Adam and the reader share the view or review of Scriptural history and the final revelation of the new Heaven and Earth – the only narrated events in the poem inevitably prophetic to Milton's readers. In our last view of Adam and Eve,

> They hand in hand with wand'ring steps and slow
> Through *Eden* took thir solitary way. (XII 648-9)

The story simply stops, but it does not end. The world lay all before Adam and Eve in double truth, before them in place and before them in time. Their story cannot end so long as place and time are the dimensions of human history, so long as the generation of mankind continues its course in the Creation. The epic ends as it began, *in medias res*, this time in the midst of actual time, seen and experienced from the point of view of man, rather than, as at the beginning, in the midst of an eternity comprehensible only to the Divine Mind. And at the end as at the beginning, we are left doubly in the midst of things, both in historical time and within eternity, to which at the Last Judgement time shall finally be joined forever.

II

We must be so left, because we ourselves share Adam's expectation of the Judgement and because we are at some point farther along the stretch of history into which at the end of the epic Adam first steps. Man must exercise his free will within that history, and except in very general terms he cannot foreknow the world's end and his own. So Milton's contemporary readers must have felt with Adam and Eve at the end of *Paradise Lost*, for their own errors 'sorrowing, yet in peace', able to shed 'some natural tears' with Adam and Eve and to wipe them soon and go on with the active business of life.

Milton succeeded in the course of the epic in shifting the point of view from that of God, dominant in the early books, to that of man; he did so by making Adam enter history understanding it, in so far as man can, from God's point of view. Milton's readers, living at a point in history so far beyond Adam, are recalled by Adam's situation from their purely human occupations to a renewed realization of God's intentions in history. If ever additional proof were needed that it is man, and neither Devil nor Deity, that is the hero of *Paradise Lost*, such proof may be drawn from the reader's acceptance as his own of Adam's predicament, with all the natural worries and rewards attendant upon the human condition. Milton understood such identification well enough and found its ground in another paradox of Christian doctrine, the notion that Adam is and is in every man. Venning's aphorism puts the idea most simply: 'The Christian knows that he was not when *Adam* was, and yet he believes that he sinned when *Adam* did.'[19] The life of Adam was for each Christian the classic paradigm of moral life – and more. Each man's experience recapitulated Adam's and was Adam's experience; from Adam, as Augustine explained, the world's 'two societies' sprang. John Salkeld, modifying Augustine, made clear that Adam's specific sin was in each Christian:

> But if it bee so as *Austine* saith, *that wee were all originally defiled with the sinne of our first father*, if wee had also besides this some other inherent originall sinne, wee should have the two kindes of originall sinnes, the one by imputation, the other by inhesion; the one inherent in *Adam* only, the other in us derived from *Adam*, which is to speak without ground of Scripture, which only maketh mention of one originall sinne, by which all bee truly called sinners, according to that of the Apostle, *Omnes peccaverunt in Adam*; all have sinned in *Adam*, in *Adam* hee saith, not in themselves....[20]

Because Adam's last vision is of the second coming of Christ and the reception of the saints into bliss, the end of the poem is, appropriately, optimistic. At the beginning of history Adam is brought to realize how God's justice operates with His mercy, and Milton's readers could reaffirm that realization with many more examples from history that Adam could not know. The paradox identifying Adam in each Christian is another way of fusing historical times that no man can literally experience at once, another way of bringing to man's attention the immediacy in God's mind of all the moral choices scheduled across the total duration of the human race.

God grants Adam leave to leave Paradise 'not disconsolate'; unlike the despairing couple Masaccio painted, Milton's Adam and Eve go to find a 'paradise within' 'happier far' than the one they left behind them, go with pride in their human callings both to labour and God. Adam and Eve depart in full awareness of the felicity concealed beneath their act of disobedience; as Adam said,

> full of doubt I stand
> Whether I should repent me now of sin
> By mee done and occasion'd, or rejoice
> Much more, that much more good thereof shall spring. . . . (XII 473–6)

The 'second Adam' would come to save mankind, and mankind would recognize Him just because of Adam's experience of sin: the long panorama of future history is not therefore C. S. Lewis's 'undigested lump of futurity'[21] so much as an assurance to Adam and all men that individual salvation remains important, that human life is not summed up in human defect; but that precisely from human defect springs an enhanced sense of moral choice and of the potentialities of salvation. That Milton deliberately aimed at this strongly optimistic lesson modern analysis of *Paradise Lost* makes clear.[22] As Adam is in each Christian, so is Christ; and in Christ lies the Christian's hope and his joy.

III

In his self-appointed task as poet and moralist, the maker of a poem to teach a nation, Milton shared some of the problems of the creative Deity. As poet, the practitioner of a profession to which he felt himself called as surely as any convinced Christian to any activity, Milton recognized his own function as 'maker' and his responsibility in the creation of a poetic and moral world. His renaissance humanism honoured the long Neoplatonic tradition of the poet as creator; his Christianity identified him irrevocably with Adam and thus with all mankind. Milton's preoccupation with the Creation in *Paradise Lost* is quite obvious;[23] from beginning to end the poem refers to creation, creativity, and re-creation. About the Creation he permitted himself the most obviously unambiguous heterodoxy of the poem, the rejection of the orthodox notion of Creation *ex nihilo* and the postulation of a Creation *ex Deo* counter to the corpus of traditional belief.

In writing the poem, Milton shared with God an aspect of foreknowledge. He 'foreknew', both by revelation and by the immutable authority of Scripture, the unchangeable course of the events of his poem. There was no changing the facts of the fall – after all, Milton wrote at a time when the failure of the Rule of Saints demonstrated to everyone the recurrence of human error – and there was no changing the record of human history. Equally, for the believer there was no

changing the ultimate end of the world and of the human race. To these
data Milton's narrative had to conform: even more than in ancient
tragedy, his plot assumed knowledge and foreknowledge on the part of
his audience.

But he could also exercise his free will in the choice of poetic
material, of ornament, of arrangement. Where matters of doctrine
were not irrevocably laid down but were 'indifferent',[24] Milton was
free to vary or to veil, even to invent; he was free to expand or explain
as he chose, particularly about motivations – just why Satan fell,
through what particular weaknesses he was able to seduce Adam and
Eve, for what purposes Raphael and Michael were selected to instruct
mankind. He was free to arrange his universe (ambiguously, as so
many scholars have pointed out) to suit the imaginative needs of his
poem; he could begin and end wherever he chose and could arrange the
order of events in whatever way he considered most significant or
most artful.

In this respect, his efforts to reconcile poetically the paradoxes
involved in the concepts of eternity and time, of foreknowledge and
free will, affected the structure and technique of his poem. Form and
material both called for epic; Milton's brilliant dealings *in mediis rebus*
have already been discussed. The extraordinary balance of the poem, at
beginning and end and at the points of stress throughout, could also
have been achieved only by most strategic use of material. Horace
would have given full marks to Milton's order, with the first six books
beginning and ending upon the same event, so entirely differently
understood at the end of Book VI; with the second half of the poem
beginning in the Creation and ending in continuing re-creation.

The books of Eden (IV, IX, X) fall at points of balance within the two
halves of the epic; the climax of Book IX is both a contrast to the idyll of
Book IV and a fulfilment of the foreknown in Book III. The life of the
devils in Book I and Book II is contrasted and compared to the life of
man in XI and XII; the irony that the Devil's act of destruction is God's
act of re-creation solves, for poetic purposes at the very least, the
problem of evil.

Milton's treatment of Creation may provide one kind of commentary
upon his method of organization. We have seen how he used the act of
Creation to contrast the immediacy of acts performed in eternity with
the duration of acts accomplished in time, and how he connected the
physical and metaphysical aspects of creation with the moral problem

of re-creation. He prepared for the narrative of the Six Days' Work in many ways, in constant reference or metaphor, in narrative, and in structure itself. Before Book VII, the hexaemeral book, we have heard of the Creation five times already – from Beelzebub and from Satan, who had heard earlier rumours of such a creation; from the 'Anarch old' in his address to Satan in chaos; from Uriel, who describes it briefly and beautifully in the adequate language of supernatural beings; and from God, who tells, even more briefly, His Son about the Creation. Structurally, Milton prepared with the utmost care for his full account of the Creation: as far as Satan is concerned, God's ways toward him must be justified in full to Adam (and consequently to the readers) before man can understand the significance of the Creation. Raphael therefore clears away all doubts about the propriety of Satan's behaviour which might have arisen in the first part of the poem. In his narrative in Book V, as well of course as in the whole tale from Book V to Book VII, Raphael unites the past and the future. He forewarns Adam by the example of Satan and forearms him by the example of Abdiel, and he explains to the audience the nature of the action they have already poetically witnessed.

This is not all. We meet created beings in an order that reinforces the ambiguities of a universe at once external and temporal. First we meet Satan and the devils fallen, then God and His Son, then Adam and Eve. The actual narrative of the Creation, broken at so many points, begins with the making of the last creature, Eve, who in Book IV tells Adam of her own sensations at the beginning of her conscious life. Milton is too subtle simply to work backward in the creation from end to beginning; Raphael's story in Book VII gives the order of Genesis, much amplified, and is followed by Adam's polite counter-tale of his creation and his part in persuading God to create Eve.

After the tale of Creation is finished in Book VIII, the story proceeds chronologically. Adam and Eve fall, are sentenced, and are brought to understand the parts they must play in the future of their race. The question of physical creation fuses with that of spiritual re-creation, symbolized particularly in the story of the Flood and confirmed in the revelation of the Messiah. At the poem's end, Adam and Eve learn something more of the relation of Creation to procreation, for Eve learns that she shall ultimately bear the seed flowering in the Messiah.

Milton had other techniques to deal across the barriers of time and eternity. In his use of epic simile, for example, he often joins superhuman

action to human by means of his own and his reader's sense of history.
Galileo, whom he may have known personally, thrice enters the epic,
once when Satan's shield is likened to the moon (I 286 ff), once when
Satan in the sun is likened to a sunspot (III 588–90), once when Raphael's
flight among the heavenly bodies is likened to the mysterious revelations of the telescope (V 261–3). In each case, the supernatural and
almost unimaginable is made actual by so specific an analogy. Old
Testament history is constantly evoked – the bondage of Israel (I 305 ff,
338 ff), the shameful idolatries which shall occur later in human history
than the reference to them:

> Though of thir Names in heav'nly Records now
> Be no memorial, blotted out and ras'd
> By thir Rebellion, from the Books of Life,
> Nor had they yet among the Sons of *Eve*
> Got them new Names. . . . (I 361–5)

Milton describes the Paradise of Fools as Satan passes by it in terms of
what it will become, not of what it then was. The dwellers in Babel,
Empedocles, Cleombrotus, 'Friars/ White, Black and Grey, with all
thir trumpery' which he imagines are not at that moment in existence;
only after the fall shall the Paradise of Fools be

> to few unknown
> Long after, now unpeopl'd, and untrod. (III 496–7)

By likening Satan to the 'Soldan' and his wealth to that of Babylon,
Egypt, Ormus, and India, Milton crosses the barriers of period to
reassert the constancy of the battle between Christendom and paganism.
He uses not only the geographical revelations of European expansion
but the functions of men of that time as well: merchants and sailors
with their specific experiences are called up (II 38 ff; IV 159 ff; X 290 ff)
to remind readers of the reality of the experiences of supernatural
beings. After the fall, Adam and Eve cover their newly-recognized
nakedness, appearing as

> of late
> *Columbus* found *th' American* so girt
> With feather'd Cincture, naked else and wild
> Among the Trees on Isles and woody Shores. (IX 1115–18)

Death comes upon the earth as Xerxes comes to Greece; death's hosts
are like the Tartar hordes (X 306; IX 431–6). Jacob, Moses, Aaron, and

Tobias are all the subjects of similes designed to connect the prelapsarian world with the later history of God's people and to remind readers that blessedness and virtue must ultimately triumph over the world's evils.

As the historical similes serve to keep simultaneously in the reader's mind great spans of history, so do the invocations serve to bridge time periods. The thematic and poetical importance of the great invocations at Books I, III, VII, and IX, as well as of the momentary voice of the poet at the beginning of Book IV, is quite apparent, but their movement in time has, so far as I know, not yet been related to Milton's handling of time throughout the epic. In the Invocation to Book I, Milton ranges from the Creation through the fall and the Mosaic inspiration to the coming of Christ: for him all those acts are related to his own creative act in 'beginning' the poem. The Invocation to III calls upon the great poets and seers, Orpheus, Thamyris, Homer, Tiresias, and Phineus, all concerned in actual or fabulous history and prophecy, and upon the Muse, who was 'Before the Heavens'. In IV, the brief reference to the Apocalypse recalls both John's act of foreseeing and the sight he foresaw, the end of the world and the ultimate destruction of Satan. In VII, the poet figures himself as returned from heaven to earth ('More safe I sing with mortal voice'), out of Bellerophon's dangers though subject still to the dangers besetting Orpheus. In IX he rejects the standard heroic topic, drawn from the ancient past or from mediaeval Christendom, to turn to his 'higher subject', the fall, from which shall come 'the better fortitude/ Of Patience and Heroic Martyrdom'.

The invocations function as extra-narrative surveys of subject, theme, and symbol; they emphasize the poet's own particular and specific act of continuing creation and they fuse times in still another way with eternity. At the beginning of Book IV, with its picture of idyllic prelapsarian life in Eden, Milton asks for the cry of St John the Divine, 'Woe to the inhabitants on Earth!' to warn Adam and Eve of their coming fall. The reference to Revelations also makes all well: the fall implies salvation. In the same way, in the Invocation to IX, the 'foul distrust and breach/ Disloyal on the part of Man, revolt,/ And disobedience' implies at once its fulfilment in 'the better fortitude/ Of Patience and Heroic Martyrdom'. In I, III, VII, and IX, Milton's own situation is dramatized into actuality – he is before his readers, a poet and a mortal fallen man; he is perhaps too old, born too late, or the inhabitant of too cold a climate to tell his great story as it deserves. In the Invocation to III he is not 'rapt above the Pole', he says, but 'More safe . . . on mortal soil'. In Book VII the reader experiences the Creation after he has experienced the created; he knows with Milton and like every other living man of the long postlapsarian history of the created world; he knows poetically with Adam and Eve the prelapsarian condition. He learns with Adam and Eve from Raphael of the coming into being of the Creation itself. By presenting himself, an unmistakable seventeenth-century man, in the invocation to this book, Milton adds another dimension to the times he presents in the book and has added, psychologically and poetically, another phase of immediacy.

The epic ends on the same sort of fusion. Michael's last words are of the 'New Heav'ns, new Earth, Ages of endless date'; the last words Adam speaks are about time and eternity:

> How soon hath thy prediction, Seer blest,
> Measur'd this transient World, the Race of time,
> Till Time stand fixt; beyond is all abyss,
> Eternity, whose end no eye can reach. (XII 553–6)

As they pass into the historical time for which they have been prepared, the moral obligations and privileges of mankind (i.e., the exercise of free will upon the ground of time) are properly at the forefront of the minds of Adam and Eve. Behind and above their acceptance of their human condition lies their awareness of divine metaphysical truth (i.e., of God's foreknowledge and providence in and from eternity). In this sense one article of the doctrine Milton intended to teach his nation, the inexplicable theological paradoxes of time and eternity, of free will and foreknowledge, is exemplified in the poem's action and demonstrated in its structure. The mysteries of religious truth are not explained in *Paradise Lost*, despite the occasional long explicative passages, for logic cannot explain them. Those mysteries are by their nature contradictory, difficult, and yet inevitable – to be understood they must be, somehow or other, experienced. Through the incredible exercise of poetic tact and strategy, Milton presents these particular paradoxes so that their oppositions are fused and yet made clear. Understanding comes from the poem itself, from the experience of reading it, so that the paradoxes of time and eternity, of free will and foreknowledge, come to seem at the poem's end the natural and proper beginning and end of Christian experience.

NOTES

1. For interesting comments on this point, see Arthur Barker, 'Structural in Pattern *Paradise Lost*', in *Philological Quarterly*, XXVIII (1949) 18; Kester Svendsen, *Milton and Science* (1956) pp. 105–7.

2. Sir Thomas Browne, *Religio Medici*, in *Works* (1686) p. 5.

3. See A. O. Lovejoy, *Essays in the History of Ideas* (1948) pp. 277–95; and articles by Clarence C. Green, in *Modern Language Notes*, LIII (1938) 557–71, and Millicent Bell, in *PMLA* LXVIII (1953) 863–88, as well as Mrs Bell's exchange with Wayne Schumaker, in *PMLA* LXX (1955) 1118–203. The splendid term 'orthodox paradoxes' comes from Ralph Venning's catechetical work of that title, which went into many editions through the mid-seventeenth century. Because of its popularity, its classically paradoxical presentation of the articles of faith, and its convenience, I have cited Venning in several cases instead of the grander paradoxes of the fathers or the scattered paradoxical formulations that fill seventeenth-century religious writing.

4. Venning, *Orthodox Paradoxes* (1650) p. 7: 'God foreknew all things; and whatever he *foreknew* to be, must needs be, and yet . . . God's foreknowledge was not the cause of their being.' Compare Herbert Palmer, *Memorials of Godliness & Christianity* (1657) p. 62: 'He [the Christian] knows God's providence orders all things; yet is he so diligent in his business, as if he were to cut out his own fortune.' See also Milton, *Of Christian Doctrine*, in *Works*, XIV (1933) 65.

5. Venning, p. 2; Marjorie H. Nicolson, *The Breaking of the Circle* (1950) ch. 2.

6. *Of Christian Doctrine*, p. 41.

7. Venning, p. 2.

8. *Of Christian Doctrine*, p. 57: 'So extensive is the prescience of God, that he knows beforehand the thoughts and actions of free agents as yet unborn, and many ages before those thoughts or actions have their origin'; p. 65: 'For the foreknowledge of God is nothing but the wisdom of God, under another name, or that idea of every thing, which he had in his mind, to use the language of men, before he decreed any thing.'

9. Dionysius the Areopagite, *On the Divine Names*, trans. and ed. C. E. Rolt (1951) pp. 72–5.

10. St Augustine, *Confessions*, trans. William Watts (1651) pp. 753–4.

11. Venning, p. 10.

12. Browne, *Works*, p. 27.

13. Venning, pp. 9, 10.

14. In general, orthodox theologians took the view with Augustine that time began with the Creation (see Frank Egleston Robbins, *The Hexaemeral Tradition* (1912) pp. 6–7; Arnold Williams, *The Common Expositor* (1948) pp. 40, 42). Grant McColley, in *Paradise Lost* (1940) pp. 16–17, makes a 'chronology' of the events in heaven before the Creation. On the whole, Milton seems in the poem to speak analogically of time before the Creation (cf. the 'grateful vicissitude' of night and day in heaven; 'Nine times the space that measures day and night') and to distinguish between duration in the natural and supernatural worlds (see *PL* V 580–2; VI 684–5; X 89–90). In *Of Christian Doctrine*, however, he makes plain a crisper view of time, that it could have existed before the Creation and probably existed from the Son (*Of Christian Doctrine*, pp. 181, 189).

15. See F. T. Prince, 'On the Last Two Books of *Paradise Lost*', in *Essays and Studies* (1958) pp. 40, 51; George Wesley Whiting, *Milton and this Pendant World* (1958) pp. 165–200.

16. Cf. *Of Christian Doctrine*, pp. 55, 57, 65, 85–7.

17. Marjorie H. Nicolson, 'Milton and the Telescope', in *Science and Imagination* (1956).

18. One might further note that Uriel, Raphael, and Michael, all of whom in *Paradise*

Lost reveal to the reader supernatural or prophetic events, are among those angels frequently called the 'eyes' of God. They operate as such in the poem, where they constantly present their narrative as from God's point of view. See Merritt Y. Hughes, Introduction to *PL*, in his edition of Milton's *Complete Poetry and Major Prose* (1957) p. 182.

19. Venning, p. 12.

20. [John Salkeld], *A Treatise of Paradise* (1617) p. 250; for further discussion of this point, see William Haller, *The Rise of Puritanism* (1938) pp. 152–3.

21. C. S. Lewis, *A Preface to Paradise Lost* (1944) p. 125.

22. Barker, pp. 17–30; Prince, pp. 38–52.

23. See W. B. C. Watkins, *An Anatomy of Milton's Verse* (1955) pp. 43–4.

24. On Milton's heresies and doctrine see, *inter alia*, Lewis, p. 89; B. Rajan, *Paradise Lost and the Seventeenth-century Reader* (1947) ch. 2; Maurice Kelley, *This Great Argument* (1941); George Newton Conklin, *Biblical Criticism and Heresy in Milton* (1949); A. S. P. Woodhouse, 'Notes on Milton's Views on the Creation: the Initial Phases', in *Philological Quarterly* XXVIII (1949) 211–36.

LAWRENCE A. SASEK

The Drama of *Paradise Lost*, Books XI and XII (1962)

SINCE the eighteenth century, critics have given the conclusion of *Paradise Lost* very little appreciative attention; they have either ignored the last two books, or written patronizingly about them, or criticized them adversely. One recent opinion, typical of even a fairly sympathetic reader of Milton's poetry, is that the two final books have no 'dramatic significance' or 'energy' and constitute 'a languid movement' toward the conclusion.[1] To admirers of Satan, the final dialogue of Adam and Michael merely continues the poetic deterioration that began as early as Book III. Readers more sensitive to the drama of temptation are likely to stop reading with attentive appreciation after the reconciliation of Adam and Eve in Book X and to respond thereafter only to a few beautifully phrased moral precepts in Michael's advice to Adam, besides, of course, the final twenty-five lines, in which the cataclysmic image of the gate of Paradise, crowded with avenging Angels and lighted by the flaming sword, gradually fades away, to be replaced by the quiet movement of the epic conclusion, describing in simple words the mood of Adam and Eve at their departure into the world of sorrow. In numerous studies of the structure, diction, and imagery of *Paradise Lost*, scholars dismiss the last two books with a discussion of the possible reasons for a decline in poetic power, a decline usually assumed without an attempt at demonstration.

To some extent, the universality of the negative reaction to the last two books is its own justification. But not entirely. The revival of enthusiasm for Donne's poetry after more than a century of neglect is one of several available examples of factors in critical appreciation that sometimes unjustly decree long disfavor to unique poetic achievements. Two such factors are misreading and reading with prejudice owing to the preponderance of adverse opinion, which, in literary criticism as well as in politics, sustains a band-wagon psychology. These factors may well have caused the final two books to suffer continual, undeserved neglect or, at least, lack of properly attentive reading. More careful attention may not lead to discovery of outstanding verbal merits in them, but it may quite possibly restore to them something of the force they might logically be expected to have as the concluding sixth part of the epic. Fairly recent efforts at explanation have brought about new appreciation of the drama of Adam and Eve's dissension and reconciliation,[2] and we should, before accepting the theory of Milton's lapse in creative ability at the end of his story, try to explain the content and style of his conclusion as the result of a deliberate working out of his epic plan. One such attempt was made by E. N. S. Thompson, but it apparently failed to influence critical opinion appreciably. Affirming the importance of the final two books in the development of Milton's epic theme, he emphasized the poetic effectiveness of some of Milton's scenes from biblical history;[3] but he apparently failed to convince critics that the last two books were more than a necessary but uninspired conclusion, attaining the poetic intensity of the preceding books only in isolated passages.

Paradoxically, the last two books may have been misread because of the general knowledge of the traditional epic device that Milton was there adapting. Before the decline of classical studies, comparison of the shields of Aeneas and Achilles was a schoolboy exercise that few potential students of Milton escaped and that predisposed them to dismiss Milton's biblical paraphrase as merely an instance of his adherence to epic tradition. Their interpretation influenced even readers who are hardly familiar with these passages of the *Iliad* and *Aeneid* in translation. Perhaps the conclusion of *Paradise Lost* suffers most from having an element in common with the *Aeneid*: a presentation by the poet of the course of history following and arising from the events of his main action. If considered a mere adaptation of the vision of the future that Virgil described on the shield of Aeneas (*Aeneid* VIII 626–728), the vision seen by Adam seems diffuse and over-extended. The future glory of Rome is presented by Virgil in slightly more than one hundred lines, whereas Michael's exposition of the future occupies about 1100 lines. In a similar way, the scenes that Milton modeled on Homer's description of the shield of Achilles (*Iliad* XVIII 478–608) may lead the reader to attribute the same function to the passages in *Paradise Lost* that their analogues have in the *Iliad*. The result is a distortion of Milton's meaning and a disregard of the organic functions of the passages in his epic. What is needed, then, is more emphasis on the differences and unique qualities in Milton's use of a traditional epic device.

Milton's debt, in his final books, to the predecessors whom he mentioned in *The Reason of Church Government* (1641–2) is obvious, but more superficial than is generally realized. From Homer he imitated a few scenes. From Virgil and Tasso (*La Gerusalemme Liberata*, Canto XVII) came the basic notion of a glimpse of the future, including portrayals of the illustrious descendants of the hero. From Tasso, perhaps, came the idea of a commentator. But one cannot be sure how directly the line of influence reached *Paradise Lost*, for Milton was obviously familiar with the use made of these epic models by Du Bartas, in whose *La Sepmaine* Adam is given a revelation of the future by the Archangel Michael. The similarities in Du Bartas' and Milton's presentations of biblical history extend from specific scenes to the general situation, including the removal of Eve from the scene while the Archangel speaks with Adam.[4]

In both epic poems the relevant passages have one function in common: they enlarge the scope of the action. In the *Iliad* the scenes on the shield of Achilles provide a background for the fighting before the gates of Troy; they place the Trojan war in perspective with all of life by showing men at work and at play, in the pursuits of peace as well as of war. That they are intended to present the world as a whole, the cosmic setting of the epic conflict, is clear enough from the fact that the river Oceanus, the sea, which the Greeks believed to encircle the whole habitable world, is engraved around the rim of the shield. The shield of Aeneas extends the *Aeneid* in time; scenes from Roman history and portraits of illustrious Romans place the action of the *Aeneid* in perspective with the whole history of Rome, which, to Virgil and the Romans, was the entire civilized world. The shield of Rinaldo is less comprehensive, but it does extend the significance of the action of *La Gerusalemme Liberata* to Tasso's times, by presenting the illustrious ancestry of the house of Este. In both *La Sepmaine* and *Paradise Lost*, Michael unfolds to Adam a world history which concretely relates the story of the fall to universal history.

But the differences between Milton's biblical pageant and the analogous epic scenes of his predecessors are fundamental. Homer, Virgil, and Tasso used essentially descriptive techniques. The scenes in the *Iliad* are of men in action, but they are presented as pictures on a shield, without narrative quality in themselves and without narrative function in the *Iliad*. Virgil took from Homer the basic device of pictures on a shield, but gave it an even more static quality, in that many of his pictures are merely portraits. Only when the history of Rome is brought to the battle of Actium are scenes of action recounted. The shield of Rinaldo is occupied solely by portraits of Rinaldo's illustrious progeny, a pedigree of the House of Este; stories are told about the figures on the shield, but they are merely commentaries on the portraits and form no narrative sequence. In the *Aeneid* and the *Gerusalemme Liberata*, as in the *Iliad*, the actions on the shield are at most dynamic pictures and have no narrative connection with the action of the epic. At most, the shields send their owners into action with a greater awareness of the significance of their deeds.

Like his predecessor Du Bartas, Milton adapted the epic device by substituting for the shield a coherent narrative sequence. Milton's vision and narrative, his adaptations of the epic device, modify the course of his main plot and are, in fact, an integral part of it, a logical conclusion or outcome of preceding events and a necessary link between them and his ultimate conclusion. But Milton went further than Du Bartas in adding a dramatic quality to the traditional devices. The *Sepmaine* contains no dramatic dialogue; the angel's narration proceeds without interruption, and Adam's reaction is given in one consecutive discourse. However, throughout the vision of Milton's Book XI and Michael's narrative in Book XII, the voice of Adam keeps breaking into the story: questioning, sorrowing, rejoicing. Instead of a mere historical pageant we have a dialogue in which the incidents narrated are selected for their effect on Adam. The angel's tone and mood change with those of his interlocutor. Constantly, three elements – Michael's mission, the story of biblical events, and Adam's state of mind – are linked by cause and effect relationships. The last two books of *Paradise Lost* thus become a study of Adam's development from horror at the thought of leaving Paradise, to shame and despair at the consequences of his sin, to a final understanding of and reconciliation with God's purpose. Adam gradually attains the state of mind indicated by God when he orders Michael to send him from Paradise 'though sorrowing, yet in peace'. And it is on the process by which Adam attains his new, final insight that the attention of the reader should be directed, if the last two books are to be appreciated for their due significance as the end of the drama of sin and promise in *Paradise Lost*. The biblical scenes mean far less in themselves than do their counterparts in the earlier epics.

The organic function of the last two books in the development of Milton's theme has been affirmed by James H. Hanford; however, he stopped with the scene portraying the death of Abel, which, he noted, was the final crisis of the loss of Paradise, for in it death entered the story, excepting by allegory, for the first time.[5] But mere physical death is not the end of the tale, and all that Adam is to learn and to suffer vicariously in the last two books is organic to the poem if we accept Milton's first statement of his argument at face value. Consistently with epic tradition he summarized his theme in the opening lines of the epic: it is to be the story 'Of Mans First Disobedience, and the Fruit/ Of that Forbidden Tree'.[6] By the end of Book x, man's first disobedience has been narrated in full, but the 'fruit' is yet to be described, if we take the word in its inevitable double sense as not only the physical object, but also the result of the action revolving about the forbidden tree; the 'fruit' or fruition of the disobedience is revealed to Adam in the last two books.

Some of the results of sin are shown in Books ix and x, in the familiar passages telling of Satan's humiliation and of the physical change in the created world, but mainly in Adam and Eve's mutual recriminations and final reconciliation and penitence. At the beginning of Book xi, while the son intercedes at the throne of the Father for the repentants, Adam and Eve find comfort in their new reconciliation with each other and with God, taking pleasure especially in the foretold victory of Eve's descendants over Satan. Eve, whose words always reveal less spirituality than Adam's, takes pleasure in the familiar environment of Paradise. But her words fall ironically upon the reader's ear, since they have been preceded by the Father's injunction to Michael to expel Adam and Eve from Paradise. The task of Michael embraces the whole dramatic problem that must be resolved in the last two books. The reasons given for the expulsion are several, and those most commonly noted by readers are the theological arguments that, in themselves, provide no adequate justification of the last two books. Adam and Eve are held to be unfit inhabitants of Paradise because, corrupted by sin, they cannot reside among pure elements. Nor can they be given an opportunity to eat of the tree of life and so become immortal in their corruption. However sound the theological principles expressed in the symbolic argument may be, they are not dramatically effective, for the reader has been made aware of the repentance of Adam and Eve and of their profession of obedience to the divine will. Another reason for the expulsion is more significant, although sometimes over-looked: God notes that Adam's action since the eating of the fruit, action dramatically presented in the epic, makes him unfit to live in Paradise. His fallen nature is not only an abstract theological concept; it is portrayed in his behavior. In spite of his repentance, evident in his manner while he repents is the fact that his heart is 'variable and vain'; his repentance is caused by grace won for him by the son (XI 90–3). The very joy of Adam and Eve at the beginning of Book XI is thus a sign of instability, while Eve's pleasure in the physical environment shows excessive regard for the material, a degree of spiritual blindness. By implication, Michael's task is, in part, to help Adam achieve stability and to give both Adam and Eve a deeper understanding of their sin and a more sober perception of their hopes. Explicitly, Michael is to send Adam and Eve, who are now in a foolish, unjustified state of self-confidence, from Paradise 'though sorrowing, yet in peace' (XI 117), in a state of mind more consistent with their present human lot. To do so, Michael must make Adam apprehend, both intellectually and emotionally, the nature of their sin and cause him to accept the expul-sion as just, yet not destroy hope. To achieve his end, Michael must reconcile, in Adam's awareness, justice with divine mercy. His task is to fulfill conclusively Milton's announced intention in *Paradise Lost*: to 'justifie the wayes of God to men'. Noteworthy is the statement that throughout his discourse with Adam, Michael is to have divine inspiration; he is to be enlightened by God (XI 115). In one sense, the divine inspiration is Milton's credo concerning the truth of the Bible; but, dramatically, it suggests that his words are of unique importance, since they come more directly from God than Raphael's earlier discourses.

Michael's procedure is to announce the dread sentence of expulsion abruptly, prefacing it only with the encouraging promise that Adam will have time to repent and so escape Death. Milton here uses the device of epic iteration, by having Michael repeat the sentence verbatim, as if to emphasize it. Thereafter, the whole trend of Michael's discourse with Adam is to mitigate its harshness, but his opening words are appropriate to his military dress; he repeats the command like a soldier under definite orders. Adam, who had forebodings of unwelcome news when he saw Michael approach, is 'Heart-strook with chilling gripe of sorrow' (XI 264) and unable to speak. Consistently with dramatic decorum, then, Milton has Adam receive his sentence silently, leaving to the woman the commentary, a lamentation that she can utter without impropriety. Although Adam weeps later in the discourse, it is for the misfortunes of others, not because of his immediate, personal tragedy. But Eve greets the news as 'worse then of Death' (XI 268) and speaks a touching lament for the loss of Paradise. In chivalric manner, the angel gives Eve what words of comfort he can, pointing out that she is in duty bound to follow her husband, and that her home, her Paradise, is wherever he dwells. The suggestion that human companionship will mitigate the rigors of life outside Paradise revives Adam's spirits also. Adam's words contrast sharply with Eve's preceding lament; instead of commenting on the material loss, the loss of Paradise, he reveals the proper mood of a penitent, the spiritually-oriented awareness that the greatest punishment and cause of sorrow will be loss of the presence of God and of the chance to serve Him. Adam's speech, then, reveals his moral attitude, contrasts his character and preoccupations with Eve's, and, in addition, motivates Michael's next words. In answer to Adam's question concerning where he can find God if he is removed from Paradise, Michael explains the reasons for the biblical resumé that is to follow. He will show Adam what will befall his offspring so that Adam can learn a vital lesson: 'so shalt thou lead/ Safest thy life and best prepar'd endure,/ Thy mortal passage when it comes' (XI 364-6). That the ensuing action will constitute a moral lesson is clear enough; there is no doubt of its didactic function. But it has been introduced dramatically, and from Adam's varied moods thus far, one can expect that the succeeding revelations will also have a dramatic effect upon him.

From an objective, critical perspective, the purpose of the vision and narrative is not only biblical paraphrase for its own sake, nor merely the instruction and education of the reader, but also the satisfaction of the reader's curiosity concerning the final condition of Adam, the state of mind and soul in which Adam will leave Paradise. Milton preaches, insofar as he does so, dramatically, through his characters. The reader is to follow and learn from the vision by observing its effect on Adam. Whether or not the intention is successfully fulfilled cannot be determined until we learn to read the passage without preconceptions of its purpose and quality. That a mere poetic resumé of biblical history is not intended is clear enough from the principles of selection Milton followed. His inclusion of specific passages is best explained by a consecutive study of their effect on Adam throughout the two books. His omissions may be illustrated by one example, noted long ago by Warburton. The sins of the Israelites, their rebellions during their wanderings in the desert, are omitted, although, as Warburton noted, some incidents 'would have afforded noble imagery'.[7] But they would merely have duplicated impressions of evil which Adam had already received, and at this point Michael's speech was designed to comfort Adam by showing his descendants reaching the promised land. Hence, although the biblical story of the wandering in the desert is full of setbacks, such as the incidents of the golden calf and the rebellion of Korah, Dathan, and Abiram (Numbers xvi), in Michael's account only the establishment of the Mosaic laws is included. Studies which might, in themselves, have provided good subjects for poetry are omitted as inappropriate to the dramatic function of the narrative and inconsistent with its immediate dramatic purpose.

To set the stage for the vision that Adam must be shown, Michael takes him to a hilltop, from which, apparently, the whole world is visible. The succeeding catalogue of place names (xi 388–411) could, perhaps, be justified as a *tour de force* of versification and sound effects, but it also plays a vital part in the story; it enlarges the scope of action from the terrestrial Paradise to the whole known world. A vast stage is set for the playing of the biblical drama, for the portrayal of the causes of Adam's succeeding emotions and utterances. At first the large stage seems to dwarf Adam's significance by reducing the relative importance of Paradise, which for several books has been the locale of all the action; yet, paradoxically, his stature is enlarged from that of one inhabitant of an isolated Paradise to that of the grand progenitor of the whole world of men. His emotions and speeches are now in counterpoise not merely with Eve's, but with the vast, panoramic scenes of biblical history.

The first biblical scene shown by Michael is the murder of Abel. Hanford has called this 'the true climax of the story of the fall',[8] but this estimate of its importance may be an exaggeration. The scene, however, is dramatically significant in that it shows to Adam for the first time the repugnant aspect of the physical death that his sin has brought into the future experience of himself and his descendants. Death, which has heretofore been a dread notion, now becomes a clearly apprehended experience. The sight shocks Adam, but at this point in his education he seems more distressed by the physical pain than by the moral evil of murder. 'Is this the way/ I must return to native dust?' (xi 462–3) is his ultimate query. Michael, in answer, intensifies the horror of the vision by showing a picture of the lazar house, with its inmates in the throes of various maladies. Why Milton enlarged the number of diseases listed from eleven in the first edition to seventeen in the second can only be conjectured, but possible reasons are that he was striving for a more representative, and hence more comprehensive, list of human ills and that he was trying to provide a stronger motivation for Adam's violent reaction. Having seen death in its manifold horrors, Adam loses composure: 'compassion quell'd/ His best of Man', and he weeps (XI 496–7). But consistently with Milton's development of Adam's psychology, the fit of grief changes to a question of God's ways: should not man, made in 'Th'Image of God' (XI 508) be free of deformites? When Michael explains briefly that sin has debased man's nature, Adam, with the words 'I yield it just' (XI 526), accepts, in effect, a justification of the doctrine of original sin. But still concerned mainly with physical death, Adam asks if there is a more pleasant way to die. He is reconciled to his mortal end by Michael's account of the death of a temperate man. But, because he has been developed consistently as a dramatic character instead of a mere symbol in a didactic discourse, he reacts too strongly; he seems almost eager for death. By comparison with what he had feared a moment earlier, a mild and benign death now seems welcome. Only after this dramatic action and reaction is he given a properly balanced view by the Archangel: 'Nor love they life, nor hate; but what thou livst/ Live well, how long or short permit to Heav'n' (XI 553–4).

With line 555 begins a new sequence of visions, designed to teach Adam to recognize evil in various forms. The lesson is necessary because so far, even when Adam saw evil in the murder of Abel, he has been impressed primarily by its physical horror. He has yet to learn that evil may have a bewitchingly pleasing aspect. The first scene of Adam's second lesson is an analogue of Achilles' shield in that it shows the occupations of men at peace: practicing mechanical arts and enjoying music, love, and festivity; but Milton put a similar scene to very different use. Adam, blind to the signs of vanity and lust, reveals his ignorance by showing pleasure in the vision, declaring that 'here Nature seems fulfilled in all her ends' (XI 602). Thus he motivates the necessary instructions from Michael; the explanation that the busy, ostensibly happy cities are the abodes of evil. Adam's reaction is characteristic; as he did after the fall, he attributes the evil to women, and Michael echoes Raphael's early warning (VIII 561–94) as he places the blame on 'Mans effeminate slackness' in allowing himself to be seduced despite his

superior wisdom (xi 634). The dialogue thus reaffirms the early admonition of Raphael and resolves conclusively the mutual recriminations of
Eve and Adam immediately after their fall. The peaceful scene is
supplemented by a vision of warfare, from which one solitary man,
Enoch, is rescued by divine intervention. From the pictures of men at
peace and war, Adam receives the lesson that the arts of men, which
seem fair from the outside, are full of evil within and ever ready to
erupt into war. The just man has little chance to sway the world by his
own eloquence or virtue. Earthly codes of fame and honor are explicitly
repudiated as empty of virtue.

Beginning with line 712, Adam is again shown a world living at
peace. The outwardly pleasant scene appears to be redundant, but as it
leads to the deluge, Adam learns a new lesson. He has already seen the
pervasiveness of evil, the small influence of goodness among men, and
the concern of God for the just; but he is now shown as well God's
punishment for sin. In other words, divine justice is here vindicated. In
the last half of Book xi, Adam has progressed emotionally from his
dismay at the disguises of evil and at its pervasiveness to rejoicing in the
endurance of the just and in God's protection and care of the faithful;
now the covenant of God with Noah, the agreement never to destroy
the world, ends Adam's uncertainty about the mortal future of his
descendants. At the end of Book xi, he has seen death and evil; he has
learned that the pains of death may be mitigated and that evil, although
deceptive in appearance, may be avoided; and he has achieved a
balanced perspective of the evil and good in man's nature. The vision is
not joyful, but it permits hope, and Adam seems ready to face his
natural life, the consequences of his natural acts, calmly and hope-
fully.

As is well known, Book x of the first edition of *Paradise Lost* included
the books numbered xi and xii in the second and subsequent editions.
The only textual change made by Milton at the point of division of
Books xi and xii was the addition of five lines at the beginning of the
new Book xii, saying that Michael had 'paus'd/ Betwixt the world
destroy'd and world restor'd'. He then resumed his narration. The
change can be explained by the disproportionate length of the former
Book x and by other structural considerations.[9] The point at which
Milton chose to begin the new book can be accounted for partly by
Michael's implication that the world was beginning anew (xii 7).
Another explanation is provided by the change in Michael's method of

presentation of biblical history at this point; heretofore he has shown Adam visions, and hereafter he will merely narrate events. This change in technique, however, raises more questions than it answers: for one must wonder why Milton abandoned the vision at this point. The professed dramatic reason is apt enough; one can readily accept Michael's statement that Adam's 'mortal sight' was beginning 'to faile' (XII 9), but it is far from inevitable or conclusive. Aesthetic variety seems to be an inadequate reason, since the reader could go on imagining visions without boredom; in fact, the visions are more imaginative and vivid than the succeeding narration. And Milton's technique in Book XI was flexible enough to allow him to present such diverse scenes as the strife of Cain and Abel, a broad panorama of biblical life, the rescue of Enoch, and the deluge.

A logical explanation of the change in technique may be found in the dramatic relationship of Michael and Adam, which, after the deluge has been shown, enters a new phase. Visions of events were needed to teach Adam the appearance of death, of good and evil actions, and of God's rewards and punishments. When these pictures have been apprehended, Adam has to achieve an intellectual understanding of God's scheme of salvation, including the nature of moral virtue, of the incarnation, and of redemption. At the moment, Adam is yet unaware of the immediate causes of sin among men, of the moral discipline needed to avoid it, and of the basis for hope of salvation. He must be instructed in theological doctrine; and Milton, thinking perhaps of the duty of the preacher, poet, and prophet, who lacks the power of evoking physical visions, causes Michael to adopt the technique of the pulpit. Significantly, Adam's last question in the epic concerns the duty and fate of the clergy XII 480 ff). Furthermore, in Book XI Adam learned lessons which, although new to an inhabitant of Paradise, were familiar enough to Milton's public. The succeeding instructions are aimed more directly, although still through Adam, at Milton's readers.

Michael's first story is of Nimrod and ends in the building of the Tower of Babel. Adam's reaction to it shows a developing conscience, a growing knowledge of moral right, as he denounces the usurpation of power by one man over another (XII 63–78). But Michael must point out to Adam the reasons for tyranny, which is a consequence of Adam's sin, and the justice of God in permitting evil to exist. The lesson may be topical in part, but Milton was certainly aware, as his readers must be, that it could be topical in any age, not in seventeenth-century England

alone. The most important reason for Milton's choice of this episode is
that it provides a needed lesson at this stage in Adam's spiritual development.

The second story of Book XII provides an introduction to theology,
as Michael recounts the election of the chosen people, the reign of the
patriarch Abraham, the exodus of the Jews, and their history up to the
conquest of Canaan. Here for the first time Adam becomes aware
of the full extent of divine mercy; he realizes that his descendants will
be shown greater favor than they have merited (XII 276–9). But,
in accordance with his fallen 'variable' nature, he becomes overly-
optimistic, assuming that the successes of the Jews represent the conclusion of the history of his earthly descendants. He must be recalled by
Michael to awareness of sin among the Jews; and their history is carried
to the appearance of the Redeemer in the line of David. Again, Adam is
too much pleased, and consistently with his human intellect and with
the prophecies that have been given him earlier, he now pictures Christ
defeating the serpent in a physical contest. The pretext is thus furnished
for Michael's exposition of the doctrine of redemption and of the
importance of works of faith and love. The second cardinal virtue,
hope, is in a sense the theme of all the discourses of Michael. The
biblical history ends with the triumphant apocalyptic vision of the final
judgment and the conquest of death.

Adam has now been brought from his first despair at the thought of
death, through a succession of hopes and fears, to a comprehension of
the final victory of good over evil. Remembering the alternation of his
overly-optimistic and ultrapessimistic reactions, one is not surprised at
his comment, 'full of doubt I stand,/ Whether I should repent me now
of sin/ By mee done and occasiond, or rejoyce/ Much more, that much
more good thereof shall spring' (XII 473–6). And one should be reluctant to attribute to Milton any notion of the *felix culpa*, at least without
severe qualification.[10] Adam's speech does not express a reasoned
theological view of the consequences of sin; read dramatically, it
expresses his emotional reaction to news of the final triumph of good,
after he has several times been on the verge of despair. The tale of
misery that has preceded the final triumph and the tale of postbiblical
human history that Michael has yet to unfold, both contradict any
argument that the fall was 'fortunate'. Furthermore, as Diekhoff has
indicated, it is beside the point to say that the saints will eventually
reach a higher level of bliss than Adam enjoyed in Paradise, for Raphael

had explained to Adam that his state in Paradise was not static or terminal.[11] If he had remained faithful, he might gradually have achieved an angelic nature (v 493–503). Now the happy outcome is reserved for a few among many and must be reached through the pain and misery described in Books XI and XII. Although the victory of good separates *Paradise Lost* in mood from the classical tragedies of Greece, it does not, on the other hand, make the poem exactly a divine comedy, if we consider Adam, as man, the principal character. The truth is that Adam is both Lear and Edgar, both Hamlet and Fortinbras, and we cannot forget the defeat of the one while we take comfort in the reassertion of order represented by the other. Although Milton affirms the happiness of the saints, he portrays vividly the expulsion of Adam from Paradise.

Moreover, the words that suggest the concept of *felix culpa* are not Adam's final comment on the human predicament. Following his outburst of joy, he asks Michael what guides the just will have in their earthly pilgrimage, and the answer is a pessimistic survey of the history of the Christian era, including the grim summary and prediction: 'so shall the World goe on,/ To good malignant, to bad men benigne' (XII 537–8). Adam's response, and his final word, is hopeful but almost stoic in its resignation to suffering; he sums up his lesson with the words 'Henceforth I learne, that to obey is best' (XII 561) and 'suffering for Truths sake/ Is fortitude to highest victorie/ And to the faithful Death the Gate of Life' (XII 569–71). Michael's approval of Adam's words is clear enough when he calls them 'the summe/ of wisdome' (XII 575–6). He suggests only adding deeds and virtues to knowledge (XII 581–5).

The long dialogue then concludes with words that, like the preceding, may have universal, didactic application, but that are inextricably part of the dramatic situation. Several lines refer to the approach of the angelic guards, who are to escort Adam and Eve from Paradise. But before and after announcing to Adam that the time for departure has come, the Angel speaks words of comfort, which also could be misinterpreted if taken out of context. The statement, 'then will thou not be loath/ To leave this Paradise, but shalt possess/ A paradise within thee, happier farr' (XII 585–7), may seem, at superficial glance, to be a confirmation of Satan's theological principle: 'The mind is its own place' (I 254); but in context, Michael is merely saying that Adam will be happier with a good conscience outside Paradise than he would be with a bad conscience within Paradise. No comparison is made with his early state of innocence in Paradise; Michael's word is a logical concluding speech.

NOTES

1. R. M. Adams, *Ikon* (Ithaca, N.Y., 1955), pp. 125–7, 207. These views may be compared with the strictures of J. B. Broadbent, *Some Graver Subject: an Essay on 'Paradise Lost'* (1960) pp. 269–98.

2. See E. M. W. Tillyard, *The English Epic and Its Background* (1954) p. 437; and Kester Svendsen, *Milton and Science* (Cambridge, Mass., 1956) pp. 105–12.

3. 'For Paradise Lost, XI–XII', in *Philological Quarterly*, XXII (1943) 376–82.

4. See George Coffin Taylor, *Milton's Use of Du Bartas* (Cambridge, Mass., 1934) pp. 112–24.

5. 'The Dramatic Element in *Paradise Lost*', in *Studies in Philology*, XIV (1917) 185.

6. All citations from *Paradise Lost* are to *The Works of John Milton*, ed. Frank A. Patterson, *et al.*, 18 vols (New York, 1931–8).

7. *The Poetical Works of John Milton*, ed. Henry John Todd, 4 vols (1852) II 531.

8. 'The Dramatic Element in *Paradise Lost*', p. 185.

9. For a thorough discussion of Milton's change from an epic of ten books to one of twelve books, see Arthur Barker, 'Structural Pattern in *Paradise Lost*', in *Philological Quarterly*, XXVIII (1949) 17–30.

10. The argument for Milton's adoption of the notion of the 'fortunate fall' is made at length by Arthur O. Lovejoy, 'Milton and the Paradox of the Fortunate Fall', in *Journal of English Literary History*, IV (1937) 161–79.

11. John S. Diekhoff, *Milton's Paradise Lost* (New York, 1946) pp. 130–1. See also H. S. V. Ogden, 'The Crisis of *Paradise Lost* Reconsidered', in *Philological Quarterly*, XXXVI (1957) 17–19.

WILLIAM G. MADSEN

From Shadowy Types To Truth (1965)

IN recent years critical interest in *Samson Agonistes* has shifted from the question whether the play has a middle to the question of the play's theme and its relation to the other works of Milton's maturity. The terms Hebraism and Hellenism, which once figured so prominently in discussions of the theme, have all but disappeared, and it is now fashionable to speak of this classical tragedy with an Old Testament folk hero as Christian. Its spirit is 'religious and Christian'; it is 'a classical tragedy with a Christian theme and outlook'; it is a 'remarkable blend of Greek form with Christian content'; Samson himself is 'an heroic figure as conspicuously modern, Christian, and Miltonic as it is Hebraic'; *Samson Agonistes* is really *Christus Agonistes*, and the agony of Samson is a 'surrogate for the unbloody sacrifice of the Mass'.[1]

The fact that Milton was an avowed Christian poet obviously gives this view a good deal of antecedent probability; still, *Samson Agonistes* does not read like a Christian play: it is very difficult to transmute the muscular Samson into a Christian athlete, and even more difficult to make Christians of Manoa and the Chorus, from whose mouths proceed all the reflections on the meaning of Samson's tragedy. Critics who are not themselves Christians, or who wrote before Christian orthodoxy once again became intellectually respectable, have felt themselves under no compulsion to Christianize the play. Tillyard saw in it a 'settled ferocity, not very lovely', although he was willing to admit Christian strains alongside the Stoic ones. Hanford went so far as to say that *Samson Agonistes* proves that Milton did not think that Christ's sacrifice was a necessary instrument of salvation; even Christ's example, it appears, might be dispensed with by those who enjoy a direct and special relation with the Divine. More recently Arnold Stein's analysis of the play contains not a single reference to Christ or Christianity. (Stein's, however, is a special case, for his interpretation, as I hope to show, is the most profoundly Christian of all.)[2]

How one relates *Samson Agonistes* to *Paradise Lost* and *Paradise Regained* depends to some extent on whether or not one regards the play as Christian, but there are problems enough in either case. Tillyard sees in it evidence that Milton had regained his faith in action after the quietism of *Paradise Regained*; Maynard Mack sees no conflict but rather a reconciliation of the competing ideals of action and contemplation. Woodhouse does not think a work so divergent from *Paradise Regained* in 'doctrine, temper, and tone' could have been written at the same time and consequently dates *Samson* in 1660-1, the period of Milton's greatest disillusionment. Others, however, see it as a kind of companion piece to *Paradise Lost* and *Paradise Regained* in that it presents a 'pattern-hero' who differs from Abdiel and Christ only in being more fully human and whose regeneration is thus a more compelling example for us fallen sons of Adam.[3]

It is ironic that a work whose simplicity and straightforwardness is often commented on should have given rise to such divergent and even antithetical judgments. There are those, no doubt, who would attribute this fact to the well-known tendency of Milton scholars toward special pleading – the problem of belief seems to arise in an especially acute form when Milton is being discussed – but I would attribute it rather to a failure to realize that *Samson Agonistes is* complex in a special way. I shall suggest that it is both non-Christian and Christian in much the same way as the Old Testament may be considered both non-Christian and Christian; and that it is, or at least may be regarded as, a companion piece to *Paradise Regained* and *could* have been written at the same time, even though it is remarkably different in 'doctrine, temper, and tone'.

The key to an understanding of *Samson Agonistes* is the method of biblical interpretation known as typology. In its narrowest sense the theory of typology states that certain persons, things, and events of the Old Testament are symbolic prefigurations, foreshadowings, or types of certain persons, things, and events of the New Testament. Thus Joshua is a type of Christ (the antitype); the synagogue a type of the Christian church; the sacrifice of Isaac a type of the Crucifixion. Sometimes the antitypes are not limited to the New Testament but extended to the whole Christian church and its members. The exodus of the Jews from Egypt to the Promised Land may be regarded (as it was by Dante) as a type of the journey of every Christian soul from the fleshpots of this world through the wilderness of self-denial and suffering to the Promised Land of Heaven. Some theologians have regarded certain persons and events of the New Testament as types whose antitypes are to be found in the future history of the Church. The method can even be extended beyond the confines of the Bible to encompass pagan history and literature. Dante regarded the Roman Empire as a foreshadowing of the Catholic Church, and Renaissance Neoplatonists were fond of seeing in Hercules a type of Christ and in pagan sacrifices a foreshadowing of the Mass.

Typological interpretation of the Old Testament was universally practiced by both Protestants and Catholics in Milton's day, and it fell into disuse only in the eighteenth and nineteenth centuries. It has recently enjoyed a revival among theologians, although there is nothing like general agreement about how it is to be applied or even about its general validity as a mode of interpretation. Some modern theologians reject it altogether; others would limit the Old Testament types to those explicitly mentioned in the New Testament; a minority feel free to exercise their own critical judgment or ingenuity. We need not concern ourselves here with the technical rules for discovering types laid down by theologians. The following observations, derived from a study of the types commonly accepted by Milton's contemporaries, will be sufficient for our merely literary purpose:

1. A type is a historical person or event, not a mythical person or a recurrent event like the rising and setting of the sun.

2. A type looks forward in time, not upward through the scale of being. The theory of typology is thus firmly grounded in the Judaeo-Christian world of existences and is fundamentally alien to the Greek world of essences.

3. Natural objects may be types, but they are usually such only in special historical circumstances. St Paul tells us that the rock that Moses struck was Christ (the water that issued forth was regarded as a type of the blood and water that flowed from Christ's side when it was pierced by the spear); this does not mean that every rock is a type of Christ.

4. There must be differences as well as similarities between a type and its antitype. (A most important rule for *Samson*, as we shall see.)

5. Neither the actors of a typical event nor the authors of their history understand the typological significance of what they are doing or writing. The Jews wandering in the wilderness did not know that manna prefigured the Eucharist, nor did Joshua know that in leading his people into the Promised Land he was a type of Jesus leading his people into Heaven.

6. Hence, the meaning of a type cannot be known until it has been fulfilled in its antitype.

Although Milton is often credited with a strictly rationalistic theory of biblical interpretation, references to the doctrine of typology may be found in writings from all periods of his life. In *The Reason of Church Government* he says that 'all those sumptuous things under the law, were made to signify the inward beauty and splendor of the Christian church', and he draws an elaborate analogy between the new temple described in the prophecy of Ezekiel and the soul of man, which is God's 'rational temple'.[4] In *Paradise Lost* Michael explains the significance of the Law to Adam in these words:

> So Law appears imperfet, and but giv'n
> With purpose to resign them in full time
> Up to a better Cov'nant, disciplin'd
> From shadowy Types to Truth, from Flesh to Spirit,
> From imposition of strict Laws, to free
> Acceptance of large Grace, from servile fear
> To filial, works of Law to works of Faith. (xii 300–6)

What has this to do with Samson? Critics as different in their assumptions and methods as Hanford, Krouse, and Woodhouse agree that Milton did not present Samson as a type of Christ. It is true, of course, that there are no explicit references to Samson as a type of Christ. How could there be when the words of the drama are confined to Old Testament actors? The meaning of a type cannot be known until the antitype has been revealed, and Samson and Manoa and the Chorus know nothing of Christ. That there are, in fact, implicit foreshadowings of Christ in Milton's Samson I shall suggest in a moment; perhaps it is even more important for an understanding of Milton's conception of Samson, however, to recognize the differences between them, for it is essential to the whole doctrine of typology that the type be different from as well as similar to the antitype.

The major differences between Samson and the Christ of *Paradise Regained* can be summed up as action *v.* passion and letter (or flesh) *v.* spirit (or word).

Just after Harapha leaves, the Chorus exults in the return of Samson's heroic vigor:

> Oh how comely it is and how reviving
> To the Spirits of just men long opprest!

> When God into the hands of thir deliverer
> Puts invincible might
> To quell the mighty of the Earth, th' oppressor,
> The brute and boist'rous force of violent men
> Hardy and industrious to support
> Tyrannic power, but raging to pursue
> The righteous and all such as honor Truth. (1268–76)

Mindful of Samson's plight, however, the Chorus goes on to suggest that his vocation may be that of the patient sufferer:

> But patience is more oft the exercise
> Of Saints, the trial of thir fortitude,
> Making them each his own Deliverer,
> And Victor over all
> That tyranny or fortune can inflict.
> Either of these is in thy lot,
> *Samson*, with might endu'd
> Above the Sons of men; but sight bereav'd
> May chance to number thee with those
> Whom Patience finally must crown.   (1287–96)

The vaguely Christian connotations of the words 'saints' and 'patience' should not blind us to the essentially Stoic quality of the idea of victory over fortune, lot, and chance. Even if one should insist on regarding this passage as Christian, it is clear that Manoa and the Chorus finally regard Samson as an active, not a passive, hero:

> O dearly bought revenge, yet glorious!

Manoa echoes the Chorus's thought:

> *Samson* hath quit himself
> Like *Samson*, and heroicly hath finish'd
> A life Heroic, on his Enemies
> Fully reveng'd hath left them years of mourning.   (1709–12)

Samson's death was of a piece with his life, and his memory will inflame the breasts of the valiant youth of Israel 'To matchless valor, and adventures high' (1740).

One such valiant youth was the young Jesus of *Paradise Regained*. Although he does not mention Samson in his soliloquy in the desert, the example of an earlier deliverer springs readily to mind when he says:

> yet this not all
> To which my Spirit aspir'd; victorious deeds
> Flam'd in my heart, heroic acts; one while
> To rescue *Israel* from the *Roman* yoke,
> Then to subdue and quell o'er the earth
> Brute violence and proud Tyrannic pow'r,
> Till truth were freed, and equity restor'd.   (I 214-20)

These are precisely the terms the Chorus had used in the passage about the active hero quoted above, and Samson too had spoken of his own 'great exploits' (32) and 'mightiest deeds' (638) and of the promise that he 'Should *Israel* from *Philistian* yoke deliver' (39). The similarities, however, only heighten the great and significant difference: the aspiration to victorious deeds is an early stage of Christ's spiritual development; it is, in fact, one of the temptations of Satan, who is the great celebrator of heroic action in *Paradise Regained*. Satan tells the devils that Christ is adorned with 'amplitude of mind to greatest Deeds'; his mind, more exalted than Solomon's, is 'set wholly on the accomplishment/ Of greatest things'. Later he tells Christ, 'all thy heart is set on high designs,/ High actions', and the heroes he proposes for imitation are all men of action: Alexander, Scipio Africanus, Pompey, Julius Caesar, and Judas Maccabaeus, who retired to the desert with arms; we would hardly be surprised if Satan were to add the name of Samson to this list. Satan's understanding of Christ's role as the deliverer of Israel is like Samson's understanding of his own role, and when Satan appeals to Christ's sense of zeal and duty by recounting the abominations inflicted on Israel by the Romans, he too echoes the Chorus in *Samson* when it speaks of 'Tyrannic power . . . raging to pursue/ The righteous and all such as honor Truth' (1275-6).

Samson's inability to rise to Christ's contempt for 'ostentation vain of fleshly arm' (III 387) is underlined by Milton in the Harapha episode. Whether or not we regard Harapha's visit as a temptation, it is clear that Samson's response is seriously flawed. Wholly admirable is his trust in the living God, his willingness to acknowledge that God has inflicted these indignities on him justly; less admirable, at best, is his eagerness to engage Harapha in single combat, his pathetic belief that by clubbing Harapha to death he will demonstrate the glory of God. The language of chivalric combat used by both Samson and Harapha places this encounter at a vast moral distance from the 'great duel, not of arms' in which Christ engages the Father of all the giants of the earth. Samson, it is true, has purified his motives since the time when 'swoll'n with pride' he walked about 'like a petty God ... admir'd of all and dreaded' (529–32). But while purity of heart is a necessary part of the 'wisdom' that vanquishes 'hellish wiles' (*PR* 1 175), it is not enough. After all, some at least of the motives that Satan proposed to Christ were beyond reproach.

A more fundamental contrast between Samson and Christ is comprehended in Michael's lines quoted earlier:

> So Law appears imperfet, and but giv'n
> With purpose to resign them in full time
> Up to a better Cov'nant, disciplin'd
> From shadowy Types to Truth, from Flesh to Spirit.

Throughout his life Milton opposed to the literalism and carnality of the Old Testament the spirituality of the New. It is the basis of his attack on the bishops, whom he calls Judaizers and whose altars and candles at noon he says were 'superstitions fetched from paganism or Jewism'.[5] The Jews of the Old Testament, according to Milton, were content to remain in the letter of the law and did not realize, for example, that the ceremonial vestments were merely typical foreshadowings of the inward purity of Christians.

In *Paradise Regained* it is primarily Satan who represents the fleshly, literalistic Old Testament point of view. Someone has wittily observed that the trouble with Satan is that he cannot recognize a metaphor. The most obvious example is his failure to understand the significance of the Dove. When he was at the baptism, he tells his followers, he saw Heaven unfold her crystal doors and on Christ's head 'A perfect Dove descend, whate'er it meant'. Christ, on the other hand, knows perfectly well what it meant:

> But as I rose out of the laving stream,
> Heaven open'd her eternal doors, from whence
> The Spirit descended on me like a Dove. (1 280–2)

In the temptations that follow, Christ's strategy with Satan is to internalize and spiritualize Satan's terms by turning them into metaphors. And Satan is so literalistic that he can't even understand a metaphor when it is explained to him. To his suggestion that Christ turn stones into bread to relieve himself and others in the wilderness with food, Christ replies, 'Is it not written ... Man lives not by Bread only, but each Word/ Proceeding from the mouth of God ...?' And a little later he contrasts God's word to the words that proceed from Satan's oracles: 'For lying is thy sustenance, thy food'. But Satan returns next morning to appeal to Christ's physical hunger, telling the devils,

> And now I know he hungers where no food
> Is to be found, in the wide Wilderness.

But Christ, we know, is 'fed with better thoughts' and is 'hung'ring more to do [his] Father's will' (II 258–9). When he tells Satan he has no need of food, the arch-literalist is baffled. 'How hast thou hunger then?' he asks (II 321), and proceeds to display his ludicrous baroque banquet. Christ counters with an oblique reference to the Eucharist:

> I can at will, doubt not, as soon as thou,
> Command a Table in this Wilderness,
> And call swift flights of Angels ministrant
> Array'd in Glory on my cup to attend, (II 383–6)

and ends with a contemptuous question,

> And with my hunger what hast thou to do? (II 389)

In the temptation of the kingdoms that follows, Satan clings to his literalistic Old Testament interpretation of the role of the Messiah. Christ tells him, before the temptation is well under way, that he who reigns within himself is more a king; that to guide nations in the way of truth is yet more kingly; and that 'to give a Kingdom hath been thought/ Greater and nobler done, and to lay down/ Far more magnanimous than to assume'. But Satan hears not; he merely shifts his ground from means to motives. He appeals to Christ's sense of glory and then to his zeal and duty 'to free/ Thy Country from her Heathen servitude'. Christ has a conception of spiritual liberty and servitude far beyond Satan's ken:

> Should I of these the liberty regard,
> Who freed, as to their ancient Patrimony,
> Unhumbl'd, unrepentant, unreform'd,
> Headlong would follow, and to thir Gods perhaps
> Of *Bethel* and of *Dan*? (III 427–31)

But Satan persists, suggesting that Christ might ascend the throne of Tiberius and 'A victor people free from servile yoke' (IV 102). 'What wise and valiant man would seek to free/ These thus degenerate, by themselves enslav'd,' asks Christ, 'Or could of inward slaves make outward free?' (IV 143-5). The baffled Satan makes one last effort of the imagination. Christ seems 'otherwise inclin'd/ Than to a worldly Crown', and Satan suggests to him that, as his empire must extend, 'So let extend thy mind o'er all the world', ruling the Gentiles by persuasion. But this is the furthest Satan's mind will stretch, and when Christ rejects the learning of Athens, Satan admits he does not understand whether Christ's kingdom will be 'Real or Allegoric'. The joke is on Satan, as Northrop Frye has shown us, for Christ's kingdom, allegoric to Satan, is the only kingdom that is real.[6]

One way of defining Christ's strategy in *Paradise Regained* would be to call it a purification of the word. 'In the beginning was the Word, and the Word was made flesh.' Milton would add to this formula, 'The Word was made flesh so that flesh might become word.' In *Paradise Lost* when Christ incarnates himself he does not lessen or degrade his nature, but rather raises human nature to the level of divinity; when Satan incarnates himself in the serpent, he merely imbrutes his own essence.

If we turn now to *Samson Agonistes*, we will find no such metaphorical activity; at the most stones are turned into bread, but physical hunger is not transmuted into spiritual hunger. The two major motives of blindness and delivery from bondage receive only a limited metaphorical extension that falls far short of Christ's achievement in *Paradise Regained*.

Samson, for example, has insight enough to recognize that his present servitude is not so ignominious as his servitude to Dalila, and he can see that the Israelites were brought to servitude by their vices and hence prefer 'Bondage with ease' to 'strenuous liberty' (271), but he still thinks it possible 'of inward slaves [to] make outward free' (*PR* IV 145). The insights of the Chorus are on a lower level: they regard Samson's blindness as a 'Prison within Prison' (153), and they suggest that the man who can patiently endure what chance inflicts is the deliverer of himself. Manoa's apprehension is the most earthly and literalistic of all as he pathetically and ironically bustles off to arrange for Samson's ransom. In his final recognition that 'death who sets all free/ Hath paid his ransom now and full discharge' (1572-3) he rises no higher than the pagan conception of death as release from affliction. All these attempts to purify the ideas of bondage and deliverance remain within the limited moral and spiritual vision of paganism and Old Testament Judaism; nowhere is there a realization that because of Adam's sin man is in bondage to Satan and that Christ is his only deliverer, that it is Christ's death alone that sets all men free, and that to the faithful death is 'the Gate of Life'.

In the same manner the theme of blindness receives at most a moral purification. Manoa characteristically hopes for a miracle, the literal restoration of Samson's sight. The Chorus refers to Samson's 'inward eyes' (1689), but they do not suggest that he can tell of things invisible to mortal sight. Samson's insight, like his insight about his bondage to Dalila, is that his present blindness is not so bad as when he 'saw not how degenerately [he] serv'd' (419). When we compare Samson's limited awareness with Milton's exalted spiritualizing of blindness in the invocation to Book III of *Paradise Lost*, are we not justified in assuming that Samson suffers a kind of spiritual, as well as physical, blindness?

The contrast between the old dispensation of the letter and the new dispensation of the spirit is deliberately heightened, I suggest, by Milton's technique of putting into the mouths of the characters words that almost automatically call for a metaphorical interpretation by the Christian reader. One of my students saw in the following lines an oblique allusion to the Crucifixion:

> O dark, dark, dark, amid the blaze of noon,
> Irrecoverably dark, total Eclipse
> Without all hope of day! (80–2)

If that seems too private, more than one commentator has heard Christian overtones in the following lines of Manoa:

> Reject not then what offer'd means, who knows
> But God hath set before us, to return thee
> Home to thy country and his sacred house, (516–18)

and

>   I however
> Must not omit a Father's timely care
> To prosecute the means of thy deliverance
> By ransom or how else. (601–4)

The most obvious example is the Chorus's comparison of Samson to the Phoenix:

> So virtue giv'n for lost,
> Deprest, and overthrown, as seem'd,
> Like that self-begott'n bird
> In the *Arabian* woods embost,

> That no second knows nor third,
> And lay erewhile a Holocaust,
> From out her ashy womb now teem'd,
> Revives, reflourishes, then vigorous most
> When most unactive deem'd,
> And though her body die, her fame survives,
> A secular bird ages of lives. (1697–1707)

The comparison of Christ to the phoenix was a Christian common-place; here, significantly, the phoenix is not even used as a symbol of personal immortality, but only of the immortality of fame.

Alongside such terms, whose Christian significance provides an ironic counterpoint to the literal significance intended by the speakers, we find words that can only be regarded as Old Testament or pagan. The emphasis on revenge at the end of the play is the notorious example; equally pagan is the Chorus's reliance on the concepts of fortune, chance, and lot in the famous passage on patience already quoted. It is hard to avoid the conclusion that Milton, far from trying to Christianize *Samson Agonistes*, was at some pains to maintain the integrity of his Old Testament materials. Instead of collapsing Samson and Christ, he is concerned to measure the distance between various levels of awareness (represented by Manoa, the Chorus, and Samson) possible to those living under the old dispensation and the level of awareness revealed by Christ in *Paradise Regained*.

In what respect, then, is Milton's Samson like Christ? Did Milton simply turn his back on the whole tradition of Christian exegesis of the Samson story? With much of that tradition he no doubt had little sympathy. One cannot think that Milton regarded the carrying off of the gates of Azzah as a type of the harrowing of Hell; or the jawbone of the ass as a type of the Gospel; or Samson's locks as the rays of heavenly contemplation. Certainly no such fanciful resemblances found their way into *Samson Agonistes*. In the list of parallels between Samson and Christ given in Thomas Hayne's *The General View of the Holy Scriptures*, however, there is a significant item which, taken in conjunction with Arnold Stein's analysis of the meaning of Samson's *agon*, fully reveals Milton's intention. The last of Hayne's parallels reads (in part) as follows: 'Christs Divinitie permitting it, he was bound, led to the Judgement hall, mocked. . . .' In the opposite column: 'The spirit of God, which strengthened Sampson, permitting, he was bound, led away, mocked. . . .'[7]

Samson's agonized consciousness that he is an object of scorn and
mockery is a motive that runs all through the play. As early as line 34 he
complains that he has been made the 'scorn and gaze' of his enemies; a
little later he says he is exposed

> To daily fraud, contempt, abuse and wrong,
> Within doors, or without, still as a fool,
> In power of others, never in my own. (76–8)

When he hears the Chorus approaching he thinks it is his enemies 'who
come to stare/ At my affliction, and perhaps to insult' (112–13), and he
reverts to this topic at least twelve more times in the course of the play.
The climax of this theme is reached when Samson refuses to go with
the Philistine officer:

> Have they not Sword-players, and ev'ry sort
> Of Gymnic Artists, Wrestlers, Riders, Runners,
> Jugglers and Dancers, Antics, Mummers, Mimics,
> But they must pick mee out with shackles tir'd,
> And over-labor'd at thir public Mill,
> To make them sport with blind activity?
>
> . . .
>
> Can they think me so broken, so debas'd
> With corporal servitude, that my mind ever
> Will condescend to such absurd commands?
> Although thir drudge, to be thir fool or jester,
> And in my midst of sorrow and heart-grief
> To show them feats, and play before thir god,
> The worst of all indignities, yet on me
> Join'd with extreme contempt? I will not come. (1323–8, 1335–42)

But he does come, and, as Stein so finely says, the man who has failed
as the athlete of God succeeds as the Fool of God.[8] Is Samson himself
conscious of the significance of his new role? Has he finally learned that
it is humiliation that exalts? Earlier he had acknowledged that the
indignities heaped on him by Harapha were inflicted justly by God;
here there is no indication in the text that Samson attaches any moral
or spiritual significance to his willingness to suffer public humiliation
at the Philistine games. On the contrary, he obviously still thinks of
himself as the athlete of God:

> If there be aught of presage in the mind,
> This day will be remarkable in my life
> By some great act, or of my days the last. (1387-9)

And it is as act, not as passion, that Manoa and the Chorus regard Samson's victory. He has revenged himself on his enemies and heroically has finished a life heroic. Only in a few words of the Messenger do we get a glimpse of the Samson who might have been:

> He patient but undaunted where they led him,
> Came to the place . . . (1623-4)

But not to the place called Golgotha. Even in this essential parallel between Samson and Christ we are acutely aware of the difference between the 'faithful champion' who destroys his enemies and the Savior who forgives and redeems his.

The harshness of the contrast between Samson's ethic and Christ's may be mitigated by regarding the destruction of the Philistines as a foreshadowing of God's terrible judgment on evil and of the Last Judgment in particular. Such an interpretation, however, robs Samson of his existential reality and makes of the play a ghostly paradigm. If, on the other hand, we view Samson first of all as a concrete individual living in a concrete historical situation, then we must insist that his significance for the Christian reader lies primarily in his inability to measure up to the heroic norm delineated in *Paradise Regained*. For it is humiliation that exalts, not the ruin of a pagan temple. Although he dimly foreshadows the humiliation of his Savior, Samson remains blind to the spiritual significance of his suffering. He cannot know, nor can Manoa and the Chorus, that they must all remain in bondage until the death of One who will in truth, not in shadow, prosecute the means of their deliverance and return them home to their Father's house.

NOTES

1. Walter Clyde Curry, '*Samson Agonistes* Yet Again', in *Sewanee Review*, XXXII (1924) 351; A. S. P. Woodhouse, 'Tragic Effect in *Samson Agonistes*', in *University of Toronto Quarterly*, XXVIII (1959) 222; Kenneth Muir, *John Milton* (1955) p. 183; E. M. Clark, 'Milton's Conception of Samson', in *University of Texas Studies in English*, VIII (1928) 99; T. S. K. Scott-Craig, 'Concerning Milton's Samson', in *Renaissance News*, V (1952) 46-7.

2. E. M. W. Tillyard, *Milton* (1930) pp. 333-4; James Holly Hanford, '*Samson Agonistes* and Milton in Old Age', in *Studies in Shakespeare, Milton and Donne* (New York, 1952) p. 177; Arnold Stein, *Heroic Knowledge* (Minneapolis, 1957).

3. Tillyard, *Milton*, p. 328; *Milton*, ed. Maynard Mack (Englewood Cliffs, 1950) p. 28; A. S. P. Woodhouse, '*Samson Agonistes* and Milton's Experience', in *Transactions of the Royal Society of Canada*, 3rd ser. XLIII, sec. 2 (1949) 157–8; M. M. Mahood, *Poetry and Humanism* (New Haven, 1950) p. 211.

4. *The Reason of Church Government*, I ii, in *John Milton: Complete Poems and Major Prose*, ed. Merritt Y. Hughes (New York, 1957) pp. 645–6. All quotations from Milton are taken from this edition.

5. *The Likeliest Means to Remove Hirelings*, in *John Milton*, ed. Hughes, p. 865.

6. Northrop Frye, 'The Typology of *Paradise Regained*', in *Modern Philology*, LIII (1956) 231.

7. Thomas Hayne, *The General View of the Holy Scriptures* (1640) p. 218, reproduced in F. Michael Krouse, *Milton's Samson and the Christian Tradition* (Princeton, 1949) facing p. 69.

8. Stein, *Heroic Knowledge*, p. 196.

M. M. MAHOOD
Milton's Heroes (1950)

DRYDEN held that *Paradise Lost*, considered as a Heroic Poem, was a failure: Milton's subject 'is not that of an Heroic Poem properly so called. His design is the losing of our happiness; his event is not prosperous, like that of all other epic works; his heavenly machines are many, and his human persons are but two'.[1]

This indictment is seldom taken seriously. Milton, it is felt, had no need to obey those neo-classical laws which so neatly defined and distinguished the Kinds. But Dryden's censure demands to be taken seriously, for if we dismiss it as irrelevant we must side with the critics who drive a wedge between Milton's purpose and his achievement. It seems to me less detrimental to Milton as an artist that he should have known his aim but failed to hit the mark (which is Dryden's contention) than that he should have intended to write one sort of poem and then, by the intervention of a troublesome Unconscious, produced something entirely different. It is possible to take a third view – namely, that Milton knew what he wanted to do and did it.

Like other humanists of his age, Milton was haunted by the Idea of the Heroic Poem, a work which would present human nature in its fullness of perfection. The lines on heroic verse added to his Vacation Exercise of 1628 mark the beginnings of Milton's long deliberations on the most fitting form and subject for so great an enterprise; and Tillyard, in tracing the course of these deliberations, has shown how Milton was attracted now by the Spenserian and now by the classical form, and how he weighed the rival claims of a Biblical, classical or national hero.[2] These problems are openly debated in *The Reason of Church Government* where the intrusive nature of the theme shows how obsessive had become its grip upon Milton's imagination:

> Time serves not now, and perhaps I might seem too profuse to give any certain account of what the mind at home, in the spacious circuits of her musing, hath liberty to propose to herself, though of highest hope and hardest attempting; whether that epic form whereof the two poems of Homer, and those other two of Virgil and Tasso, are a diffuse, and the book

of Job a brief model: or whether the rules of Aristotle herein are strictly to
be kept, or nature to be followed, which in them that know art, and use
judgment, is no transgression, but an enriching of art: and lastly, what king
or knight, before the conquest, might be chosen in whom to lay the pattern
of a Christian hero. And as Tasso gave to a prince of Italy his choice whether
he would command him to write of Godfrey's expedition against the
Infidels, or Belisarius against the Goths, or Charlemain against the
Lombards; if to the instinct of nature and the emboldening of art aught
may be trusted, and that there be nothing adverse in our climate, or the fate
of this age, it haply would be no rashness, from an equal diligence and
inclination, to present the like offer in our own ancient stories; or whether
those dramatic constitutions, wherein Sophocles and Euripedes reign, shall
be found more doctrinal and exemplary to a nation. (Preface to Book II)

Milton had to wait nearly twenty years before he could fulfil these
ambitions. That he looked upon *Paradise Lost* as their fulfilment is made
clear by a passage in the epic which contains many echoes of the prose
paragraph I have just quoted. There Milton claims to have found a
theme for heroic verse more fitting than any subject of Spenserian
romance or classical epic:

> argument
> Not less but more Heroic then the wrauth
> Of stern *Achilles* on his Foe pursu'd
> Thrice Fugitive about *Troy* Wall; or rage
> Of *Turnus* for *Lavinia* disespous'd,
> Or *Neptun's* ire or *Juno's*, that so long
> Perplex'd the *Greek* and *Cytherea's* Son;
> If answerable style I can obtaine
> Of my Celestial Patroness, who deignes
> Her nightly visitation unimplor'd,
> And dictates to me slumbring, or inspires
> Easie my unpremeditated Verse:
> Since first this Subject for Heroic Song
> Pleas'd me long choosing, and beginning late;
> Not sedulous by Nature to indite
> Warrs, hitherto the onely Argument
> Heroic deem'd, chief maistrie to dissect
> With long and tedious havoc fabl'd Knights
> In Battels feign'd; the better fortitude
> Of Patience and Heroic Martyrdom
> Unsung; or to describe Races and Games,
> Or tilting Furniture, emblazon'd Shields,

> Impreses quaint, Caparisons and Steeds;
> Bases and tinsel Trappings, gorgious Knights
> At Joust and Torneament; then marchal'd Feast
> Serv'd up in Hall with Sewers, and Seneshals;
> The skill or Artifice or Office mean,
> Not that which justly gives Heroic name
> To Person or to Poem. Mee of these
> Nor skilld nor studious, higher Argument
> Remaines, sufficient of it self to raise
> That name, unless an age too late, or cold
> Climat, or Years damp my intended wing
> Deprest, and much they may, if all be mine,
> Not Hers who brings it nightly to my Ear. (IX 13-47)

The startling thing about this passage is its position in the epic. This claim to have found a subject of true heroic magnitude might pass unquestioned if it were made at the beginning of the work, where it could serve as proem to the building of Pandaemonium and the election of the Messiah. It might form an apt introduction to the Heavenly Wars which are described in the fifth and sixth books. But Milton chose to place it at the opening of the ninth book which, far from recounting any heroic deeds, tells of the disastrous weakness of Adam and Eve. Momentous as are the implications of their Fall, the act itself is so trivial that Satan turns it into an infernal comedy to amuse his followers:

> Him by fraud I have seduc'd
> From his Creator, and the more to increase
> Your wonder, with an Apple. (X 485-7)

Can Milton's claim to have found a 'higher argument' be reconciled with the events which follow it? Or is Dryden right in denying to *Paradise Lost* the title of a heroic poem?

In seeking a solution to this problem, we need to bear two things in mind. The first is that Milton, while confronted with a choice between many possible epic subjects, never questioned current literary theory of the Heroic Poem's spirit and purpose. The passage quoted from *The Reason of Church Government* makes it clear that his *magnum opus* is to lay before its readers an heroic pattern of public and private virtues: it is to be at once commemorative and exemplary, setting forth past achievements in order to incite present and future readers to emulation. Secondly, *Paradise Lost*, as the first part of a heroic trilogy, cannot be considered in isolation from the two succeeding poems. The germs of both *Paradise Regain'd* and *Samson Agonistes* are to be found in the *Cristus Patiens* and the *Samson pursophorus or Hybristes, or Samson marriing or Ramath Lechi* of the Cambridge Manuscript, as well as in some lines of *Paradise Lost* which seem to foreshadow the later poems. Milton may not have had any clear concept of his last two poems when he wrote his long epic, but he felt, once *Paradise Lost* was completed, that he still had something to say about the heroic potentialities of human nature.

In the years intervening between the writing of *The Reason of Church Government* and the composition of *Paradise Lost*, Milton all but lost faith in these potentialities. The Parliamentarians, leaders and rankers alike, fell short of those deliriously high expectations which he had expressed in his pamphlet, *Of Reformation in England.*[3] Milton found himself compelled to probe the roots of heroic action to discover why its fruits were so seldom sound, and in consequence the Renaissance epic pattern – 'the history of a great man making good for the instruction of the ruling class of nobles'[4] began to seem an inadequate form of the Heroic Poem. He still held, with other humanists, that the genre should have a didactic aim; but the didacticism of both classical and Romance epic now appeared to him to be superficial, since neither distinguished the false heroism from the true. Milton now sought the origins of heroism rather than its outcome; and he found the source of a spurious heroism in 'Mans first Disobedience' and of a true heroism in 'one mans firm obedience fully tri'd'.

The problem of heroism was an intensification of the humanist dilemma, and in the Fall of Adam and Eve Milton discovered both the source and the symbol of that self-sufficient humanism which perverted the mind from attaining its true heroic magnitude, even while it opened the way to a certain specious grandeur of the kind typified in Satan. On the other hand, Abdiel in *Paradise Lost* and the Christ of *Paradise Regain'd* both exemplify the heroic strength of those natures which remain loyal to their divine origins. Because humanism is his central theme, Milton makes the angel Abdiel a nearly-human being, and in the shorter epic the Saviour is represented as the perfect man, as yet scarcely aware of His divine progeniture. Only when he has thus explored the metaphysical roots of both true and false heroism does Milton attempt a pattern-hero in the character of Samson. Neither Christ nor Abdiel could supply this pattern, since both were untainted by Adam's Fall; but in the Samson story Milton found the material for a drama of regeneration, the return from a false concept of heroism to the understanding of true heroic strength and such an attainment of 'Paradise Within' as Divine Grace placed within reach of all Adam's sons. No work is more characteristic of the Baroque age, when the perennial conflict between a true and a false humanism was intensified by the moral, political and economic individualism of the Renaissance.

There were few aspects of the humanist revolt which Milton failed to observe, but he has most to say on three impulses which were strongly developed in his own nature and may be said to have motivated all his work as a poet and a pamphleteer. The liberty of the human person was the ideal defended in all his polemical writings: in *Paradise Lost* he turns to study the misuse of that liberty in the revolts of Satan and of Adam. The love of fame which spurred him over every obstacle to his career of poet-prophet might be a divine discontent with temporal bounds; but it might also be an infirmity of mind, the camouflage to a gigantic egotism. And stronger than either of these instincts in Milton's nature was the scholar's thirst for knowledge, the passion of the Reason which claimed supremacy over the Passions, at once the noblest and the deadliest of the mind's desires. Liberty and licence, true and false glory, the dangers of a little curious learning and the blessing of real wisdom – such distinctions were especially vital to the seventeenth century as heirs to the damaged estates of Renaissance humanism. They are among the dominant themes of Milton's three major poems.

Satan has more to say about liberty than has any other character in *Paradise Lost*. Many of his pronouncements on the theme prove, however, on a close inspection, to be mere rhetorical flourishes. Milton had heard the name of liberty bandied about a good deal by either side during the Civil Wars; and Satan, in his public speeches, usually makes such propagandist use of the word. Milton takes care that the reader shall not be deceived so easily as the rebel angels. Sometimes he warns us directly that Satan's 'potent tongue' can only utter 'high words, that bore Semblance of worth not substance' (VI 135; I 527–8). At other times the hypocrisy with which Satan uses the word 'liberty' is conveyed to the reader in a more oblique and subtle manner. Thus in addressing his followers before the outbreak of the heavenly war the rebel angel demands to know who

> can introduce
> Law and Edict on us, who without law
> Erre not? (V 797–9)

Milton's 'fit audience, though few' must, I feel, have recognised in these words an echo of the Stuart pretension to Divine Right. The implicit analogy would make it clear that Satan's speech was not to be understood as the protest of the liberator against tyranny, but rather as the tyrant's assault upon liberty's safeguard, the law. In the same address, Satan's revolt against the hierarchical order of Heaven is seen to be rooted in his own pride rather than in a genuine desire for equality, when he accepts the hierarchical order for his followers: 'for Orders and Degrees Jarr not with liberty'. Here liberty is a convenient slogan which Satan can afford to cast aside after the first day's fighting. Once his faction's blood is up, he assures them that they are

> Found worthy not of Libertie alone,
> Too mean pretense, but what we more affect,
> Honour, Dominion, Glorie and renowne. (VI 420–2)

Glory and renown are uppermost in Satan's thoughts when he is alone: we hear nothing about liberty in his soliloquies in Eden.

Yet even when we have disallowed Satan's catch-phrase usage of 'liberty', the fact remains that he and his adherents revolt in the name of Liberty and that they attach some definite meaning to the term. The word's significance in Hell is made clear by Mammon's Pandaemonium speech:

> Let us not then pursue
> By force impossible, by leave obtain'd
> Unacceptable, though in Heav'n, our state
> Of splendid vassalage, but rather seek
> Our own good from our selves, and from our own
> Live to our selves, though in this vast recess,
> Free, and to none accountable, preferring
> Hard liberty before the easie yoke
> Of servile Pomp. (II 249–57)

The kind of freedom which Mammon here describes is a total self-sufficiency. 'Licence they mean, when they cry libertie';[5] the distinction, which was a leading theme of Milton's prose works, is kept throughout *Paradise Lost*. Their true and created liberty seems thraldom to the rebel angels and they replace it with a false liberty in the name of which they enthral themselves. Their minds are too stunted to comprehend the liberality of a Creator who bestows free will upon His creatures, and all their reasoning is built upon the fallacious premiss that liberty and 'creatureship' are incompatible. If they are created, they cannot be free: but they know their wills to be free: therefore they cannot be created. This total self-sufficiency is claimed by Satan during the conclave which precedes his revolt:

> That we were formd then saist thou? & the work
> Of secondarie hands, by task transferd
> From Father to his Son? strange point and new!
> Doctrin which we would know whence learnt: who saw
> When this creation was? rememberst thou
> Thy making, while the Maker gave thee being?
> We know no time when we were not as now,
> Know none before us, self-begot, self-rais'd
> By our own quick'ning power, when fatal course
> Had circl'd his full Orbe, the birth mature
> Of this our native Heav'n, Ethereal Sons.
> Our puissance is our own. . . . (v 853–64)

Many details in the opening book build up an impression of the rebels' confidence in their own 'quick'ning power'. Thus Satan is described as 'impious' – a word Milton always uses in its Latin sense of 'unfilial'; the fallen angels imagine that they have escaped from the burning lake through their 'own recover'd strength' (I 240); and the account of their appearance on earth as false gods serves to stress the self-idolatry behind their revolt. The same self-confidence is heard in Book VI, when Satan claims that his followers,

> while they feel
> Vigour Divine within them, can allow
> Omnipotence to none. (VI 157–9)

He himself has already done much to kindle these feelings by the incendiary speech of the previous book, where he addresses his faction as 'Thrones, Dominations, Princedoms, Vertues, Powers'. The words make a resounding pentameter, but this is not the sole reason for Milton's choice of these five angelic orders. The line's effect of inflation is achieved as much by its sense as by its sound, since the words have associations which give their sequence a movement from the idea of delegated power to that of inherent strength. 'Thrones' are the mere inanimate symbols of authority, 'Dominations' in part conveys the idea of vicegerency, since a 'lord' is given dominion over others by his sovereign, but because *Dominus* is 'the Lord' it also carries the suggestion

of absolute rule; and this ambiguous gap is narrowed in 'Princedomes',
since a prince could be a monarch in his own right. 'Vertues' effects the
transition from the bestowed title to the inherent source of authority,
an inner force or *virtù*; but the word's ethical sense suggests that such
force is still controlled by the moral law. In the final 'Powers' all such
ambivalencies have disappeared, and the word implies unqualified rule
and strength. The line's whole rhythmic force descends upon it, and the
effect is sustained, in the manner of an organ-stop, through the following
lines – an instance of the way that Milton can make his verse approxi-
mate to music without loss of that semantic delicacy which he inherited
from the Elizabethans and the 'late fantasticks' –

> Thrones, Dominations, Princedomes, Vertues, Powers,
> If these magnific Titles yet remain
> Not meerly titular, since by Decree
> Another now hath to himself ingross't
> All Power. . . . (v 772–6)

Abdiel, in his reply to Satan, takes up the word 'Powers' in a way
which suggests that the foregoing interpretation of this line is not so
overstrained as it may appear. He reminds Satan that the Son created all
the angelic orders,

> Crownd them with Glory, & to thir Glory nam'd
> Thrones, Dominations, Princedoms, Vertues, Powers,
> Essential Powers. . . . (v 839–41)

Milton's scholastic training causes him to blend the medieval meaning
of 'essential' with its modern sense of 'intrinsic'; and 'Essential Powers'
suggest a strength which is potential rather than actual, bestowed upon
its user by and for some end outside himself. To the rebel angels, on the
other hand, power is not essential but existential and therefore entirely
at their own disposal.

This trust of the fallen angels in their own self-sufficiency shows itself
in their belief that they can easily reascend to Heaven. Satan's question,

> For who can yet beleeve, though after loss,
> That all these puissant Legions, whose exile
> Hath emptied Heav'n, shall faile to re-ascend
> Self-rais'd, and repossess their native seat? (I 631–5)

is echoed by Moloch when he bids his companions remember

> That in our proper motion we ascend
> Up to our native seat: descent and fall
> To us is adverse. Who but felt of late
> When the fierce Foe hung on our brok'n Rear
> Insulting, and pursu'd us through the Deep,
> With what compulsion and laborious flight
> We sunk thus low? (II 75–81)

But Raphael, a more reliable witness, describes the rebels' fall as precipitous:

> headlong themselvs they threw
> Down from the verge of Heav'n, (VI 864–5)

and the implication is that their flight could not be otherwise than headlong, since in shifting the gravitational centre of their being to their own 'Vigour Divine', they lost the original directive of their ascent.[6] Thus it can be truly said that they threw themselves from Heaven; the Father speaks of them as 'Self-lost' (VII 154) for their self-sufficiency bars their reascent more effectively than any adamantine doors, and long before Satan was driven from Heaven he had made a 'Hell within him'.

Marlowe had depicted a similar inferno of the mind in *Doctor Faustus*, where the hero's rebellious pride is the sole obstacle in the way of his return to grace.[7] Like Faustus, Satan takes refuge in a despair which enables him to picture himself as the victim of an amoral Fate. He insists that it is such a Fate and not Justice, which has given the Almighty the victory; and the poets among his followers complain in their heroic lays 'that Fate Free Vertue should enthral to Force or Chance' (II 550–1). These laments are so persuasive that Milton is compelled to make the Father's initial speech, in Book III, a refutation of such arguments; man and angel, being endowed with freewill, trespass 'without least impulse or shadow of Fate' (III 120). Stoicism is another refuge of a wounded self-sufficiency, and as the poets in Hell are all fatalists, so the philosophers are all Stoics who

> arm th'obdured brest
> With stubborn patience as with triple steel. (II 568–9)

One can scarcely speak of the humanism of angels; but the revolt of Satan and his peers is directed to the same ends as the revolt of a false humanism, and in consequence it displays all the irony of the humanist

dilemma, whereby those who have rebelled in the name of a mis-
conceived liberty end by denying that they have any freedom of action.

Whatever else Satan may lose by his fall, he keeps his wits about him.
His soliloquy at the beginning of Book IV reveals an astonishingly
candid and exact self-knowledge, and this insight into the motives of
his own revolt enables him to judge rightly of the weakest points in
Adam's and Eve's defences. The human fall, like that of the angels, is an
assertion of self-sufficiency; but Eve's action is differently motivated
from that of Adam, according to the psychological differences of their
natures as man and woman.

For sheer energy of dramatic invention, the Temptation of Eve excels
over every other scene in the epic. 'Devil and woman, both, fairly take
your breath away' is the verdict of E. E. Stoll.[8] With subtle dialectical
cunning, Satan works upon the self-confidence that Eve has already
shown in insisting on being left to work by herself, in order to turn it
into a self-sufficiency comparable with his own. Thus he inflames her
amour-propre, already perhaps a little sore from Adam's mistrust, by a
threefold attack, first on her personal vanity, next on her social vanity,
and finally on her intellectual pride. Since Eve is no ordinary woman,
the first two shafts, though they strike home, do her little injury. Satan
is forced to muster all his rhetorical skill for a display of sophistry in the
course of which the idea of divinity is transferred from the Creator to
Eve herself. He begins by speaking of 'God', but by a clever use of the
phrase which accompanied the fruit's interdiction – 'Ye shall be as
Gods' – he shifts to 'the Gods', not in the usual Miltonic sense of angelic
beings, but meaning a plurality of deities:

> The Gods are first, and that advantage use
> On our belief, that all from them proceeds;
> I question it, for this fair Earth I see,
> Warm'd by the Sun, producing every kind,
> Them nothing: If they all things, who enclos'd
> Knowledge of Good and Evil in this Tree,
> That whoso eats thereof, forthwith attains
> Wisdom without their leave? (IX 718–25)

This is such a denial of the Creator as preceded Satan's own fall; and his
argument ends with a similar attempt to transfer godhead to the
created being: 'Goddess humane, reach then, and freely taste'. Eve does
so; and her action is shown to be an assertion of self-sufficiency, a
transference of trust from God to self, when in her next speech she

denies the Creator's omnipotence and omniscience. The gift of knowledge (she argues) cannot be His to give, or it would not thus grow
within reach of Eden's inhabitants – a parallel to the rebel angels'
conviction that they cannot both be free and created – while Heaven is
so high and remote that there is a good chance of her deed remaining
unobserved.

Eve's logic is stumbling and inept after Satan's agile sophistries, and
this contrast is an essential feature of the scene. For Eve's intellectual
pride betrays her into thinking herself the argumentative match for one
able to reason intuitively (as angels do) rather than discursively, as a
human being. Feminine intuition never had a more fatal result. And to
Milton's way of thinking, Eve was arrogant not only in attempting to
follow the course of Satan's intuitive logic, but in daring to debate such
a metaphysical problem in any way at all. The basis of such an attitude
is to be found in the parts of Raphael's discourse which describe the Scale
of Creation ascending from the lowest organisms endowed only with 'vital
spirits' (that is, vegetable life) through those with animal spirits and
then those with intellectual, to the two orders of being which enjoy the
divine gift of reason – men and angels (v 469–90). Because every kind of
being has its inferior and its superior on this ladder, and because woman
was created subsequently to man, Eve's place was a rung below Adam,
and accordingly she has a much smaller share of the reason which unites
him with the heavenly natures, and a much larger share of the passions
that human nature has in common with the brute creation. This
difference is implied when she leaves Adam and Raphael to their
discussion of astronomy, not (Milton is careful to point out) because it
was beyond her understanding, but because she preferred to learn new
facts from Adam who 'she knew would intermix Grateful digression,
and solve high dispute With conjugal Caresses' (VIII 54–6). On this
theory of the sexes Milton bases his concepts of love and lust as they are
expounded by Raphael at the end of Book VIII. Adam has just admitted
that Eve is his inferior in the Scale of Nature:

> For well I understand in the prime end
> Of Nature her th' inferiour, in the mind
> And inward Faculties, which most excell,
> In outward also her resembling less
> His Image who made both, and less expressing
> The character of that Dominion giv'n
> O're other Creatures.

But her beauty causes him to lose this sense of his superiority:

> All higher knowledge in her presence falls
> Degraded, Wisdom in discourse with her
> Looses discount'nanc't, and like folly shewes;
> Authoritie and Reason on her waite . . . (VIII 540–54)

Raphael sees a sign of danger in Adam's words. His passion for Eve may cause him to forget his intermediary position, as a being endowed with reason, between Nature and God:

> What higher in her societie thou findst
> Attractive, human, rational, love still;
> In loving thou dost well, in passion not,
> Wherein true Love consists not; love refines
> The thoughts, and heart enlarges, hath his seat
> In Reason, and is judicious, is the scale
> By which to heav'nly Love thou maist ascend,
> Not sunk in carnal pleasure, for which cause
> Among the Beasts no Mate for thee was found. (VIII 586-94)

Modern readers, with the slam of Nora Helmer's door still resounding in their ears, are maddened by Milton's theory of the relationship between man and woman – 'Hee for God only, shee for God in him' (IV 299). But it is unfair to attribute such lines to the poet's misogyny. His theory of the sexes is based upon that Christian gradualism which is the background to most seventeenth-century philosophy;[9] and he gives special prominence to the idea because it offers an explanation of the Biblical and Augustinian distinction between the motives for Adam's and Eve's falls. Both were impelled by a self-sufficient pride – 'a perverse desire of height, in forsaking Him to whom the soul ought solely to cleave, as the beginning thereof, to make itself seem its own beginning'[10] – and this separation from God breaks the Chain of Being in which man is the vital link between Creator and creation. Eve breaks it by an upward pull, and Adam breaks it by a downward wrench. A less rational nature than Adam, Eve aspires to intellectual equality with angels. He, on the other hand, sins in full awareness of the consequences involved in the act. Passion gains the mastery of reason and he is drawn down by 'The Link of Nature' and 'The Bond of Nature' (IX 914, 956). Eve forces upon a door, Adam slams one to; she claims 'angelicity' and he denies his heavenly nature.

When Adam resolves to join Eve in eating the fruit, and so to die with her, she exclaims

> O glorious trial of exceeding love! (IX 961)

The words supply one of the many significant echoes which combine to give the poem its perfect symmetry; they call to mind the Heavenly Host's praises of the Messiah after His election:

> O unexampl'd love,
> Love nowhere to be found less then Divine! (III 410–11)

This echo gives a double dramatic effectiveness to Eve's cry. In one way the words are an instance of tragic irony, because there is all the difference possible between Adam's sacrifice and that of the Messiah. But Eve's words, by bringing to mind the Son's reconciliation of divine and human natures, sound the hope of man's recovery even in the instant that marks the 'compleating of the mortal Sin Original'. Milton, when he came to write of that promised recovery, chose the Temptation as the symbol of Paradise regained, since of all the events recorded in the Gospels it seemed to him the one best fitted to show Christ as healer of the twofold harm done by Adam and Eve. As Adam broke the chain of being in subjugating reason, the divine faculty, to the passions, so the Saviour's reason overthrows physical and intellectual appetite; and as Eve's reason was easily perverted through the sophistries whereby the serpent 'made intricate seem strait', so Christ's Right Reason confutes Satan's 'weak arguing, and fallacious drift' (*PR* III 4) until the Adversary finds

> the perswasive Rhetoric
> That sleek't his tongue, and won so much on *Eve*,
> So little here, nay lost. (*Paradise Regain'd*, IV 4–6)

The verbal duel of *Paradise Regain'd* represents the victory of Reason over fallacious arguments; and there is little to show how 'Heav'nly love shal outdoo Hellish hate' (*PL* III 298), small demonstration of that 'unexampl'd love' which compels the Son to suffer such an ordeal. Indeed, there can have been few readers of *Paradise Regain'd* who have not echoed the protest made by Tuckney against the ideas of the Cambridge Platonists with whom Milton had much in common: 'Mind and understanding is all; heart and will little spoken of.'[11] But while it is undeniable that, in Milton's faculty psychology, Reason dominates and directs the Will (and it might be said in defence of

Milton as of the Cambridge Platonists that the times had a special need
of Reason's coolness and clarity), many passages in the longer epic make
it clear that he acknowledged the will's conformity with Divine Love
to be an essential part of Paradise Within. Love, rather than Reason,
resolves the seeming contradiction between freewill and a created
condition. 'Freely we serve', Raphael explains to Adam, 'Because we
freely love' (v 538-9).

The loyal angels, and Adam and Eve in their unfallen state, voice this
paradox of love's free compulsion in speeches which are placed in direct
contrast with Satan's outbursts of hatred. Thus the fourth book begins
with Satan's soliloquy, every phrase of which is charged with resentment. Adam and Eve appear; and Adam's first words acknowledge the
Creator whom Satan denies, voice the gratitude which is too burden-
some a debt for Satan to pay, and renounce the merit which Satan
would arrogate to himself:

> Sole partner and sole part of all these joyes,
> Dearer thy self then all; needs must the Power
> That made us, and for us this ample World
> Be infinitly good, and of his good
> As liberal and free as infinite,
> That rais'd us from the dust and plac't us here
> In all this happiness, who at his hand
> Have nothing merited. . . . (IV 411-18)

Eve expresses her gratitude with even greater fervour than Adam, since
hers is a double debt; Adam, as well as the Creator, is a source and end
of her being. She tells of her awakening into life, and of the way in
which she pined for her own reflection until her desire found fulfilment
in Adam. Since, in Milton's Platonic scale, human love is both analogy
and ascent to Divine Love, it is perhaps not too fanciful to see in Eve's
tale an allegory of the human mind turned from its egotism to the love
of God. Milton's clearest and completest pronouncement on true and
false liberty is not, however, made in the philosophic calm of Eden, but
struck out in the white heat of argument which precedes the war in
Heaven. Satan 'on the rough edge of battel ere it joyn'd scoffs at the
loyal angels for their servility and evokes from Abdiel this magnificent
reply:

> Unjustly thou deprav'st it with the name
> Of *Servitude* to serve whom God ordains,

> Or Nature; God and Nature bid the same,
> When he who rules is worthiest, and excells
> Them whom he governs. This is servitude,
> To serve th' unwise, or him who hath rebelld
> Against his worthier, as thine now serve thee,
> Thy self not free, but to thy self enthrall'd. (VI 174–81)

Thy self not free, but to thy self enthrall'd: the phrase is a clue to all the seeming contradictions in Satan's character. Like the human – and humanist – revolt, the revolt of the angels is initially a movement of self-fulfilment, and Satan at first appears completely fulfilled, a being of heroic proportions. Milton gives the devils their due; Satan and his followers have all the virtues of courage, loyalty and pity which had once been highly acceptable in Heaven, and at first their intellectual powers remain undiminished in Hell. But when he compares them to giant trees withered by lightning (I 612–15), he conveys a sense of the utter sterility of all such intellectual and moral qualities divorced from the source of their renewal. Satan's diminution during the course of the poem is the inevitable withering of an uprooted tree. The evil he represents is no productive and active principle in conflict with the Good, but a perversion or negation of goodness, symbolised by his entry into Eden:

> Thence up he flew, and on the Tree of Life,
> The middle Tree and highest there that grew,
> Sat like a Cormorant; yet not true Life
> Thereby regaind, but sat devising Death
> To them who liv'd. (IV 194–8)

By the same process, Satan's claim, made in the opening book of the epic –

> The mind is its own place, and in it self
> Can make a Heav'n of Hell, a Hell of Heav'n. (I 254–5)

is only too well substantiated by that self-enslavement which prompts his outcry in Eden,

> Which way I flie is Hell; my self am Hell, (IV 75)

and by his sober realisation, at a later stage of the action, that

> all good to me becomes
> Bane, and in Heav'n much worse would be my state. (IX 122–3)

Milton's public life had left him with the conviction that there was no radical measure which 'could of inward slaves make outward free' (*PR* IV 145); and from that conviction grew the dramatic and significant contrast, in *Paradise Lost*, between the self-enslavement of the fallen angels and humans and the glorious liberty of the children of God.

The distinction between true and false liberty is sharp and clear to Milton, even if the element of self-portraiture in Satan reveals that he found it no easier than do most people to live by his own convictions. Other parts of the humanist problem were less readily solved. In particular, Milton's fierce ambition for literary fame hampered his attempt to distinguish a true glory from a false. Milton never parted from his thirst for fame; but he gave it a new directive, such as he also gave to his desires for liberty and knowledge. This reorientation of 'that last infirmity of Noble mind' is the central theme of *Paradise Regain'd*.

There were certain periods in Milton's life when his longing for fame became almost obsessive. Such a time was his last year at Cambridge, where the poet had shown enough promise to realise that great things were expected of him. The *Letter to a Friend*, of which the drafts are preserved in the Cambridge Manuscript, admits that he has already felt the promptings 'if not of pure, yet of refined nature' to achieve fame – 'a desire of honour & repute & immortall fame, seated in the brest of every true scholar'.[12] The Seventh Prolusion, composed about the same time as this letter, made Milton's ambitions public:

> I pass over a pleasure with which none can compare – to be the oracle of many nations, to find one's house regarded as a kind of temple, to be a man whom kings and states invite to come to them, whom men from near and far flock to visit, while to others it is a matter for pride if they have but set eyes on him once. These are the rewards of study, these are the prizes which learning can and often does bestow upon her votaries in public life.[13]

Towards the end of that period of intensive study at Horton, which was to equip him to win such renown, Milton's thirst for fame once more became feverish in its intensity. 'My own disposition is such', he wrote to Charles Diodati in the September of 1637, 'that no delay, no rest, no thought nor care for anything else, can divert me from my purpose, until I reach my goal and complete some great cycle of my studies'; and he followed this with another letter admitting all his thoughts to be 'So help me God, of immortality'.[14]

This immortality which Milton so eagerly desired at the outset to his career was of a particular kind. An autocratic temper, joined with a Calvinistic sense of election that outlasted his rejection of Calvin's dogma, made Milton contemn popular praise and seek only the approbation of other elected natures. Fame such as he conceived and sought meant renown among the discerning few during his lifetime and a wider and enduring recognition by posterity. In the same year of 1637 he composed the verses *Ad Patrem*, in which he repays his father's long generosity with the promise that his son's fame shall be of a kind to raise him above the common rout:

> Jamque nec obscurus populo miscebor inerti,
> Vitabuntque oculos vestigia nostra profanos.[15]

Ad Patrem is one of Milton's several trial flights in Latin verse, and since Latin was still *lingua franca* among educated Europeans, it is very probable that at this time Milton intended to use the classical language for his masterpiece. On his tour abroad in 1638 and 1639, his Latin poems served him as a cultural passport among the Italian *literati*. His triumphal progress through Italy certainly strengthened Milton's conviction that he was a Mediterranean man and for the rest of his days he was to feel himself a castaway from Greek and Roman culture. Yet on his return to England he decided to make English his medium and thereby renounced (or so it seemed to him at the time) a European fame for a merely insular reputation. Behind the decision lay a conflict between his ambition and his patriotism which is suggested by an autobiographical passage of *The Reason of Church Government*:

I began thus far to assent both to them [i.e. his Italian friends] and divers of my friends here at home, and not less to an inward prompting which now grew daily upon me, that by labor and intense study, (which I take to be my portion in this life,) joined with the strong propensity of nature, I might perhaps leave somthing so written to aftertimes, as they should not willingly let it die. These thoughts at once possessed me, and these other; that if I were certain to write as men buy leases, for three lives and downward, there ought no regard be sooner had than to God's glory, by the honor and instruction of my country. For which cause, and not only for that I knew it would be hard to arrive at the second rank among the Latins, I applied myself to that resolution, which Ariosto followed against the persuasions of Bembo, to fix all the industry and art I could unite to the adorning of my native tongue; not to make verbal curiosities the end, (that were a toilsome vanity,) but to be an interpreter and relater of the best and sagest things

among mine own citizens throughout this island in the mother dialect.
That what the greatest and choicest wits of Athens, Rome or modern Italy,
and those Hebrews of old did for their country, I, in my proportion, with
this over and above, of being a Christian, might do for mine; not caring to
be once named abroad, though perhaps I could attain to that, but content
with these British islands as my world. (Preface to the Second Book)

The *Epitaphium Damonis* was written while Milton was forming the
resolutions recorded in this prose extract; there also he takes his leave of
Latin verse and resigns himself to a purely national fame:

> O mihi tum si vita supersit,
> Tu procul annosa pendebis fistula pinu
> Multum oblita mihi, aut patriis mutata camœnis
> Brittonicum strides, quid enim? omnia non licet uni
> Non sperasse uni licet omnia, mi satis ampla
> Merces, & mihi grande decus (sim ignotus in ævum
> Tum licet, externo penitusque inglorius orbi)
> Si me flava comas legat Usa, & potor Alauni,
> Vorticibusque frequens Abra, & nemus omne Treantæ,
> Et Thamesis meus ante omnes, & fusca metallis
> Tamara, & extremis me discant Orcades undis.[16]

But while Milton abandoned the learned language with regret, it is
evident from the resonant roll of these geographical names that the high
calling of national poet was a prize that fired his ambition. His first
pamphlet in defence of the Puritan cause ends with the vision of himself
as prophet of the new theocracy:

> There, amid the hymns and hallelujahs of saints, some one may perhaps be
> heard offering at high strains in new and lofty measures to sing and celebrate
> thy divine mercies and marvellous judgments in this land throughout all
> ages. (*Of Reformation in England*, end)

But this ambition was frustrated in its turn. Before many years had
passed, the hymns and hallelujahs of the Saints had turned to a barbarous
noise 'Of Owles and Cuckoes, Asses, Apes and Dogges' (Sonnet xi),
creatures unworthy of the *Arthuriad* which Milton had thought to
compose in their honour. Then, just when it seemed to him that his
sacrifice of an international for an insular fame had been in vain, the
chance came for Milton to win European renown as a Latinist by the
Defensio pro populo Anglico. He set a wildly high store by the work,
seeing himself as a second Demosthenes with the whole Continent for
market-place:

I seem to survey, as from a towering height, the far extended tracts of sea and land, and innumerable crowds of spectators, betraying in their looks the liveliest interest, and sensations the most congenial with my own. . . . Of all the lovers of liberty and virtue, the magnanimous and the wise, in whatever quarter they may be found, some secretly favor, others openly approve; some greet me with congratulations and applause; others, who had long been proof against conviction, at last yield themselves captive to the force of truth.[17]

There was good reason why Milton held this, his least readable work, in such exaggerated esteem; the *Defence* cost him his sight, and for a time it seemed that his highest bid for fame had deprived him of all further hopes. But the mood of passive resignation, when the poet felt that nothing more remained to him except to stand and wait, did not last long.[18] He overcame his disability to the extent of again challenging European Latinists with his *Defensio Secunda* – a much greater piece of rhetoric than the *First Defence* – and of once more swaying public opinion at home by his praise or reproof of the nation's leaders. Again his fame rose and once again, bubble-like, it vanished in an instant. In 1660, *Eikonoklastes* and the *Defensio pro populo Anglicano* were burnt by the public hangman, and there were those who would have been pleased to see Milton share their fate. The royal amnesty left the poet his life, but the Restoration deprived him of what had for many years been his life's ambition – to be the prophet of a free and united nation. All Europe had once talked from side to side of his eloquence. Now, fallen on evil days,

> In darkness, and with dangers compast round,
> And solitude,

he turned to the completion of his long-delayed epic, resigned to the belief that his only audience would be a few choice spirits among his compatriots.

These many vicissitudes in his quest for fame compelled Milton to reflect long and deeply upon the nature of the thing he sought, and to test upon his pulse the truths of current philosophical theories about the value of fame. From the beginning of his career as a poet, he was aware of two ethical approaches to the problem. The first of these was pre-Renaissance. Medieval Christendom had recognised two kinds of fame – the present reputation of the active man and the heavenly reward of the contemplative who renounced all earthly glory; and the Middle Ages were in no doubt over whose was the better part. Langland called his ideal man of action Do-Well, but to his embodiment of the contemplative ideal he gave the name of Do-Bet. The Reformation attack on monasticism and the Renaissance cult of the Aristotelian, active hero, whose magnanimity embraced both private and public virtues, reversed these traditional values by exalting Do-Well over Do-Bet. In a study of 'The Christ of *Paradise Regain'd* and the Renaissance Heroic Tradition',[19] Merritt Hughes has shown the effect on Milton of this ethical conflict:

> From the time when he wrote *Church Government* until he completed
> *Paradise Regain'd* Milton must have been concerned over the conflict of the
> contemplative with the active ideal, and its possible solution by some
> 'heroic' spirit, in art if not in life. In the background was Catholic Christianity,
> standing for the priority of the contemplative principle. Closer to him was
> the Renaissance, with its challenge to the life of action.

Closer still, it might be added, was the great movement of reaction against Renaissance values, represented by Counter-Reformation sanctity in religion, Mannerism in art and Jacobean *contemptus mundi* in literature. This 'Counter-Renaissance' once more exalted Do-Bet over Do-Well by rating sufferance above action and the heavenly fame won through private virtue above the wide glory offered by a public life.

The issue was one which divided the Ancients and the Moderns in their mounting quarrel; and the passage on the incomparable pleasures of a well-deserved fame already quoted from the Seventh Prolusion, suggests that Milton in his Cambridge days was on the side of the Moderns in this as in other matters. But towards the end of that oration, Milton had to forestall the argument, much favoured by the 'Ancients', that the quest for fame was the most fruitless of human activities, now that the world was drawing to its end:

> Ignorance . . . declares that glory is mankind's most powerful incentive,
> and that whereas a long succession and course of years has bestowed glory
> on the illustrious men of old, we live under the shadow of the world's old
> age and decrepitude, and of the impending dissolution of all things, so that
> even if we leave behind us anything deserving of everlasting fame, the
> scope of our glory is narrowed, since there will be few succeeding genera-
> tions to remember us. It is therefore to no purpose that we produce so
> many books and noble monuments of learning, seeing that the approaching
> conflagration of the world will destroy them all.[20]

Fantastically remote from reality as such an argument now sounds, it represents a view widely and seriously held in the early seventeenth century; and Milton, who had once attempted to refute it, in the verses *Naturam non pati Senium*, here accepts the argument in order to turn it back upon his opponent. Even if time is coming to a stop, the Ancients should strive for that heavenly fame which they rightly value above any worldly reputation:

> I do not deny that this may indeed be so; but yet to have no thought of glory when we do well is above all glory. The ancients could indeed derive no satisfaction from the empty praise of men, seeing that no joy or knowledge of it could reach them when they were dead and gone. But we may hope for an eternal life which will never allow the memory of the good deeds we performed on earth to perish.[21]

Thus Milton, at the outset of his career, draws the traditional distinction between the two kinds of fame and gives traditional precedence to that which is laid up in Heaven. As yet there is no conflict in his mind between the two conceptions, because he is never in a moment's doubt of his ability to make his name as a poet and thus both eat his cake and have it. But in 'Lycidas', written some six years later, an inner conflict is felt in the sharp juxtaposition of the two kinds of fame; at some time since leaving Cambridge Milton had experienced the dread that a premature death might rob him of literary immortality. In the face of such a threat, he found it by no means easy to rate the heavenly above the earthly reward; and in the passage on fame in 'Lycidas', the argument that 'Fame is no plant that grows on mortal soil' does not outweigh the bitter energy of his protest against 'the blind *Fury* with th' abhorred shears'. *The Reason of Church Government*, written at a time when Milton's renunciation of a European for an insular fame was causing him to ponder the worth of reputation as an incentive, shows a further stage in the development of Milton's thoughts on this subject. Here he defends 'honest shame', or the desire to be well spoken of, as a sound inducement to acts of virtue and valour. And in *Paradise Lost* the fundamental innocence of this desire is implied when the unfallen Adam declares that shame to be worsted in Eve's presence will make him proof against all Satan's wiles (IX 312–14). 'Yet this', continues Milton in the prose work, 'is but the fear of infamy'. There is a higher motive than regard for the good opinion of others, and that is regard for oneself as the Divine Image:

> But he that holds himself in reverence and due esteem, both for the dignity of God's image upon him, and for the price of his redemption, which he

thinks is visibly marked upon his forehead, account himself both a fit person
to do the noblest and godliest deeds, and much better worth than to deject
and defile, with such a pollution as sin is, himself so highly ransomed and
ennobled to a new friendship and filial relation with God. (*Reason of Church
Government*, II 3)

In this passage, which represents seventeenth-century humanism at its
best and which could be matched by many similar extracts from the
sermons of Caroline divines, Milton is reaching towards a conception of
fame which will reconcile the overt glory of the active man and the
hidden fame of the contemplative. The approbation of God was worth
far more than that of men; but the Candle of the Lord was not intended
to be hid under a bushel, and whoever aspired to fame in Heaven was
likely to make that aspiration known to men by the 'noblest and
godliest deeds'. In fact, Milton's experience compelled him to question
the antithesis between active and contemplative. Like Langland, who
had lived in a time of natural and social calamities as disturbing to old
ways of thought as anything which happened in the seventeenth
century, Milton sought a Do-Best – a way of life which would reconcile the medieval *contemptus mundi* with the Renaissance thirst after
glory. It was in keeping with the Baroque spirit that such a reconciliation should be effected through transcendence rather than through
compromise; and during the years of repeated setbacks in his own quest
for fame which preceded the writing of *Paradise Regain'd*, Milton
evolved a philosophical theory of fame which marked the completion
of a triad built upon the humanists' glorification of the impulse and its
condemnation by the anti-humanists.

This theory of fame is expounded in the third book of *Paradise
Regain'd* which deals at length with Satan's offer to Christ of 'the
authority and the glory'. Milton – who follows St Luke's order for the
three temptations – is not greatly concerned with the first and third
assays by which Satan tries to entice the Saviour into a miraculous
display of His divine powers. They fall outside the scope of his intention
to show Christ as the perfect man. Accordingly, in Milton's poem, the
first temptation merely serves the purpose of bringing the protagonists
together in the sharp enmity that follows their mutual recognition, and
the third temptation, culminating in Satan's fall, is reduced to the
outward symbol of the victory Christ has already won in His abnega-
tion of worldly power. Since Milton is dealing with a humanist
problem he concentrates all the dramatic interest of the work on the

one temptation out of the three which was within the experience of the human mind at its heroic best.

For Milton never ceased to regard the thirst for fame as a weakness, if weakness it were, peculiar to noble minds. In the *Second Defence* he had praised Fairfax for triumphing over 'that flame of ambition and that lust of glory which are wont to make the best and greatest of men their slaves'[22] and these words are echoed when Satan rejects Belial's suggestion, that, to tempt Christ, the devils should 'set women in his eye and in his walk':

> With manlier objects we must try
> His constancy, with such as have more show
> Of worth, of honour, glory, and popular praise:
> Rocks whereon greatest men have oftest wreck't. (II 225-9)

Already Satan has perceived in his opponent that 'amplitude of mind to greatest deeds' (II 139) which distinguished the active Renaissance hero; and Christ's first soliloquy reveals such a temper of mind:

> Victorious deeds
> Flam'd in my heart, heroic acts, one while
> To rescue *Israel* from the *Roman* yoke,
> Then to subdue and quell o're all the earth
> Brute violence and proud Tyrannick pow'r,
> Till truth were freed, and equity resor'd. (I 215-20)

Since Satan thus knows Christ to be proof against all sensual temptations it may at first seem surprising that he should renew his attack by spreading a lavish banquet in the wilderness. But the action shows that he has lost none of the cunning that subverted Eve. He does not expect to succeed with this fresh temptation, nor with the offer of great wealth which follows; both are feints, designed to trap his opponent at the disadvantage of a too easy confidence in his power to resist. At such a crisis, a nature less perceptive of Satan's treachery might well have fallen prey to the subtle rhetoric with which he proffers

> The fame and glory, glory the reward
> That sole excites to high attempts the flame
> Of most erected Spirits. (III 25-7)

But the Saviour parries this, the deadliest stroke of Satan's eloquence, with a speech on glory which claims our attention as Milton's most complete and mature treatment of this long-vexed problem.

Christ's chief argument is that no mortal fame can compare with an
immortal glory won through the approbation of Heaven – an argument used many times before by Milton. But previously it had occurred
in contexts, such as the passage on fame in 'Lycidas', which implied a
conflict between this traditional concept and the poet's own ambition.
In *Paradise Regain'd*, however, the closing words of Christ's speech
suggest an emotional discovery which enabled Milton to imbue an
age-old commonplace with new significance:

> Shall I seek glory then, as vain men seek
> Oft not deserv'd? I seek not mine, but his
> Who sent me, and thereby witness whence I am. (III 106–7)

'Not I, Lord, but Thou': Milton's ultimate feeling about the thirst for
glory is that, like other humanist impulses, it is a divinely-bestowed
quality which can exalt or debase the mind according to whether it is
given a Godward or selfward direction. It becomes a stolen fire only
when man 'thinks to break out into sudden blaze' for his own glory.
Already, in *Paradise Lost*, Milton had pointed a contrast between the
self-seeking ambition of the rebel angels and the loyal angels' indifference to all but the Creator's will. Raphael cut short his story of the
war in Heaven with the words:

> I might relate of thousands, and thir names
> Eternize here on Earth; but those elect
> Angels contented with thir fame in Heav'n
> Seek not the praise of men: the other sort
> In might though wondrous and in Acts of Warr,
> Nor of Renown less eager, yet by doome
> Canceld from Heav'n and sacred memorie,
> Nameless in dark oblivion let them dwell.
> For strength from Truth divided and from Just,
> Illaudable, naught merits but dispraise,
> And ignominie, yet to glorie aspires
> Vain glorious, and through infamie seeks fame:
> Therfore Eternal silence be thir doome. (VI 373–85)

For Milton, man's self-arrogation of this as of other impulses was
symbolised by the Fall of men and angels; so when in *Paradise Regain'd*
Satan, with the occasional stupidity of the very cunning, contends that
the desire for glory is blameless since even God extracts glory from His
creation, he lays himself open to the argumentative thrust which

clinches the debate. To Christ's rejoinder that glory is due to the Creator, but not to that part of the creation which has brought infamy upon itself in striving to wrest that glory from Him,

> Satan had not to answer, but stood struck
> With guilt of his own sin, for he himself
> Insatiable of glory, had lost all. (III 146-8)

The difference between a true and a false glory thus lies not so much in the contrast of the active man's worldly recognition with the contemplative's hidden fame as in the contrast of the theocentric and egocentric directions given to a single desire. On the principle that he who loses his life shall save it, it follows that mortal fame often comes to those who have renounced it. Job and Socrates were two such, and Christ makes use of their posthumous fame to prove that

> so much bounty is in God, such grace
> That who advance his glory, not thir own,
> Them he himself to glory will advance. (III 142-4)

The Saviour himself is to be the greatest exemplar of this advancement, for the stress which Milton places upon His obscurity – 'Private, unactive, calm, contemplative' (II 81) does not imply that the poet had abandoned the Renaissance concept of the good life for the medieval ideal. By means of a romance setting, Milton portrays Christ as a postulant to knighthood, strengthening himself through vigil for the feats of arms that he is to perform. Heroic action, Milton says in effect, has its springs in contemplation, for only there can the mind gain the self-knowledge which will prevent it arrogating to itself the glory of future achievements.

The theme that glory is won in its renunciation reappears in *Samson Agonistes*. Milton's tragedy is a drama of regeneration. Its action (which is all within the hero's mind) follows the descending and reascending curve represented by the three stages: thirst for glory; renunciation of glory; bestowal of glory unsought. Critics have recognised more wounded pride than true repentance in Samson's first speeches, and Manoa finds him

> self-displeas'd
> For self-offence, more then for God offended. (514-15)

Samson in his strength had not claimed the glory of his achievements for himself. He was the champion of Israel and the God of Israel. But the implication of the play's opening act between Samson and the chorus of his fellow Israelites is that the hero had experienced a kind of religious *hubris*, a certainty that his own election made him indispensable to God. The first part of the tragedy, up to the entrance of Dalilah, depicts Samson's gradual submission to 'Heav'ns desertion'. The contest must now be between God and Dagon, since Samson himself renounces all hope of heroic action:

> So much I feel my genial spirits droop,
> My hopes all flat, nature within me seems
> In all her functions weary of herself;
> My race of glory run, and race of shame,
> And I shall shortly be with them that rest. (594-8)

The Chorus for their part conclude the second act with a prayer that Samson's labours may be turned to peaceful end; to them also it appears that action had been finally replaced by suffering. This is the turning-point of the play, the moment when Milton begins to demonstrate his belief that *vincit qui patitur* – 'who best Can suffer best can do' (*PR* III 194-5). In the moment that Samson accepts his own elimination from Israel's struggle, the power is given him to re-engage in the fight.

Scarcely have the Chorus begged 'some source of consolation' for Samson than Dalilah appears. Her entry is a forceful peripeteia, since the resentment and opposition which she, and later Harapha, awaken in Samson help to render his strength of will equal to his regained physical strength. Within a short time the hero who had craved 'deaths benumming opium' is challenging Harapha to single combat; and on Harapha's departure the Chorus celebrate both active and passive heroism as if both were now within Samson's reach. The champion is ready for the promptings of those 'rouzing motions' which impel him to a final act that embraces and transcends the two kinds of heroism. Manoa's words draw the curve of the action into a full circle:

> *Samson* hath quit himself
> Like *Samson*, and heroicly hath finished
> A life Heroic,

and Samson's renunciation of glory wins him an honoured tomb and the finest exequy in the language.

In his Seventh Prolusion, Milton sustains the thesis that 'Learning brings more Blessings to Men than Ignorance' in such terms as these:

When universal learning has once completed its cycle, the spirit of man, no longer confined within this dark prison-house, will reach out far and wide, till it fills the whole world and the space far beyond with the expansion of its divine greatness. Then at last most of the chances and changes of the world will be so quickly perceived that to him who holds this stronghold of wisdom hardly anything can happen in his life which is unforeseen or fortuitous. He will indeed seem to be one whose rule and dominion the stars obey, to whose command earth and sea hearken, and whom winds and tempests serve; to whom, lastly, Mother Nature herself has surrendered, as if indeed some god had abdicated the throne of the world and entrusted its rights, laws, and administration to him as governor.[23]

I doubt if there is to be found anywhere in the writings of the sixteenth and seventeenth centuries an expression of the humanist exultation in knowledge more fervent than this passage of Milton's. By the poet's own admission,[24] his love of learning overrode all other passions, even his desire for fame. 'Milton indeed writes like Marlowe', says Tillyard in his discussion of this Seventh Prolusion, 'and as if the passionate disillusion which blighted those high hopes in the early seventeenth century had never existed'.[25]

Did disillusion ever overwhelm Milton? There are passages and themes in his last poems which suggest that the poet in later life rebuffed, with a harsh obscurantism, the intellectual pride of his youth, that the Hebraistic and anti-humanist strain in his character triumphed ultimately over the Hellenist and humanist elements. The three outstanding instances of this are: Christ's repudiation of Greek culture in *Paradise Regain'd*; the archangel Raphael's replies to Adam's questions about astronomy in the eighth book of *Paradise Lost*; and Milton's choice of the Tree of Knowledge myth as an epic subject. These three rejections of intellectual liberty – if such they are – have also been studied by critics from a somewhat different viewpoint, as the revelation of an unresolved conflict in Milton's mind between allegiance to his declared themes and loyalty to his own deepest convictions. Thus it is usual to regard these three matters either as a conquest of the Renaissance Milton by Milton the Puritan or as the signs of a tussle between these forces which is disastrous to his poetic integrity. But I think it more probable that Milton was keenly aware of the two conflicting views of knowledge – the one that 'Knowledge is but Sorrow's spy', the other that 'God himself is truth; in propagating which, as men display a greater integrity and zeal, they approach nearer to the similitude of God';[26]

and that his choice of the Genesis myth, far from ensnaring him in an
unconscious confusion between the two, represents his conscious
determination to get down to the bedrock of this as of other humanist
problems.

Before we attempt to consider the knottiest of all Miltonic problems,
his handling of the Tree of Knowledge theme in *Paradise Lost*, we may
perhaps glance at his treatment of intellectual appetite in *Paradise
Regain'd*. There, Satan evokes the beauty of Athens' 'sweet recess' of
learning, with an ardour that has aroused the suspicion that here, for
once, Milton must be of the devil's party. But for the situation to have
any dramatic force at all, the temptation must be made really tempting,
as Spenser recognised when he described the Bower of Bliss; and a
passage in the *Areopagitica* suggests that Milton had Spenser's precedent
in mind in writing *Paradise Regain'd*:

> That virtue therefore which is but a youngling in the contemplation of evil,
> and knows not the utmost that vice promises to her followers, and rejects it,
> is but a blank virtue, not a pure; her whiteness is but an excremental
> whiteness; which was the reason why our sage and serious poet Spenser,
> (whom I dare be known to think a better teacher than Scotus or Aquinas,)
> describing true temperance under the person of Guion, brings him in with
> his palmer through the cave of Mammon, and the bower of earthly bliss,
> that he might see and know, and yet abstain.

A more serious difficulty is to be found in Christ's reply, which has
been taken as Milton's masochistic rejection of the intellectual freedom
he had once cherished. But the speech is dramatic, not personal, and
accordingly needs to be considered in relation to its context. Christ
does not reject Greek philosophy out of hand but only the devil's offer
to supply him with that knowledge; and his claim to derive 'Light from
above' is not, I think, meant to imply that Milton, like the sectaries,
relied more on inspiration than on intellect, but that no knowledge
could be more than vanity when it was not built upon the fundamental
revealed truths of human existence, man's creation, fall and redemption:

> Alas what can they teach, and not mislead;
> Ignorant of themselves, of God much more,
> And how the world began, and how man fell
> Degraded by himself, on grace depending?
> Much of the Soul they talk, but all awrie,
> *And in themselves seek vertue, and to themselves*
> *All glory arrogate, to God give none.* (IV 309-15)

I have italicised the lines which seem to suggest that Milton is here drawing a distinction between true and false knowledge, akin to the one he had already drawn between true and false liberty in the characters of Satan and Abdiel, and between a true and false glory at an earlier stage of the *Paradise Regain'd* debate. The validity of all knowledge, Milton here implies, is conditioned by its origin and by its directive. Accordingly, the one school of Greek philosophy which earns his unqualified scorn is that of the Stoic – 'Wise, perfect in himself, and all possessing Equal to God' – whose knowledge began and ended in himself. 'True wisdom', which Milton goes on to distinguish from her 'false semblance', is rooted in a self-knowledge derived from Christian doctrine, and tends wholly to the glory of God; the point is identical with that made in the Seventh Prolusion which Milton had composed some thirty-five years previously:

> God would indeed seem to have endowed us to no purpose, or even to our distress, with this soul which is capable and indeed insatiably desirous of the highest wisdom, if he had not intended us to strive with all our might toward the lofty understanding of those things, for which he had at our creation instilled so great a longing into the human mind. . . . The more deeply we delve into the wondrous wisdom, the marvellous skill, and the astounding variety of [the world's] creation (which we cannot do without the aid of Learning), the greater grows the wonder and awe we feel for its Creator and the louder the praises we offer Him. (pp. 107–8)

The same distinction between true wisdom and spurious learning is implicit in another part of Milton's work which has been taken as proof of his obscurantism: Adam's discussion with Raphael about current theories of astronomy. Basil Willey has shown how Milton's humanism here causes him to identify a presumptive curiosity with the scholastics' inquiry into the 'why' of phenomena, and true wisdom with scientific research into the 'how';[27] he is, in fact, taking sides in the controversy of the Ancients and Moderns on the side of the modern humanists. But the experimental knowledge which Milton approves is not the complete empiricism which Bacon purveys in a sugar-coating of piety. It is 'godly and useful learning'; and for Milton the epithets are not contradictory, since 'useful' means, in his view, not 'utilitarian', but whatever might help man's ascent towards a comprehension of divine things. Once again, Milton's views on the subject have changed little since his Cambridge days; the course of study outlined in his Third Prolusion, 'Against the Scholastic Philosophy', is just such an ascent of the Scale

of Nature as Raphael commends to Adam in Book v of the epic. In
Book VII, Adam plants his foot squarely on this ladder when he begs
Raphael to unfold

> What we, not to explore the secrets aske
> Of his Eternal Empire, but the more
> To magnifie his works, the more we know. (VII 95–7)

Again, in Adam's words as Raphael ends his tale of Creation, Milton
implies the rightness of his insatiable thirst after knowledge:

> What thanks sufficient, or what recompence
> Equal have I to render thee, Divine
> Hystorian, who thus largely hast allayd
> The thirst I had of knowledge, and voutsaf't
> This friendly condescention to relate
> Things else by me unsearchable, now heard
> With wonder, but delight, and, as is due,
> With glorie attributed to the high
> Creator. (VIII 5–13)

Adam's astronomical problems, on the other hand, appear to Raphael
to have no godly or useful purpose. They represent the scholastic
curiosity into the unsearchable causes of phenomena, an attempt to
short-circuit the legitimate course of true knowledge, which lies in the
processes of observation and experiment. Milton's infusion of this
intellectual humility into the humanist faith in scientific method is a
striking example of the strenuous Baroque attempt at reintegration.
Raphael repels Adam's curiosity about the earth's motion because it is
just such an intuitive leap as Eve hopes to make when she is tempted
into eating the apple. And this brings us to the core of the problem:
Milton's handling of the Genesis myth of the fateful Tree.

The by now classical discussion of this matter is that in Basil Willey's
The Seventeenth Century Background, where Milton's treatment of man's
Fall is shown to be a major example of the period's conflict between
pictorial and conceptual thinking:

> Here indeed was a strange situation: Milton, believing, as we have seen, in
> 'Knowledge', and in 'Reason' as choice of good by a free agent cognisant of
> evil, selects as the subject of his greatest poem a fable which represents the
> acquisition of these very things as the source of all our woe. (p. 247)

Professor Willey's demonstration of this conflict is brilliant and
irrefutable; my sole excuse for tampering with the subject here is

that I think some re-examination of the problem may reveal less of
an unconscious confusion and more of a controlled reconciliation in
Milton's thought. The words 'Knowledge' and 'Reason' in the passage
just quoted point to two kinds of possible conflict which are closely
related but which, for the sake of clarity, I will keep distinct. The first is
that Milton, as a scholar and champion of the New Learning, could
not, with any measure of integrity, depict the action of Adam and Eve
as a lapse, since its *result* was the coming of thought into the world:
'Milton was a Promethean, a Renaissance humanist, in the toils of a
myth of quite contrary import, a myth which yearned, as no Milton
could, for the blank innocence and effortlessness of a golden age.'[28]
The second is that Milton, as the militant pamphleteer who scorned a
fugitive and cloistered virtue, must needs approve the *act itself* as a brave
vindication of Reason's freedom to choose: 'Only a being capable of
sin could know the meaning which Milton really attached to the notion
of spiritual freedom; thus the Fall was logically a necessary stage in the
evolution of man'.[29]

The answer to the former of these objections seems to me to be that
Adam and Eve do not, by the Fall, exchange ignorance for knowledge.
It is true that Satan, overhearing Adam speak of the Tree of Knowledge,
takes its interdiction to mean that the first humans are kept in a state of
savage ignorance; but the four books of Raphael's discourse are a
massive refutation of his error. 'Because Adam yet lacked experience',
wrote Campanella in his *Apology for Galileo*, 'all learning was poured
into him'.[30] The apple imparted nothing, since it was not a magical
fruit, but the 'sole pledge' of Adam's obedience (III 95). This was the
traditional interpretation of the myth, and Milton follows St Augustine
closely when he discusses the matter in the *De Doctrina Christiana*:

> The tree of knowledge of good and evil was . . . a pledge, as it were, and
> memorial of obedience. It was called the tree of knowledge of good and
> evil from the event; for since Adam tasted it, we not only know evil, but
> we know good only by means of evil. For it is by evil that virtue is chiefly
> exercised, and shines with greater brightness.[31]

Eve eats the apple in the hope of acquiring, like Faustus, a new source of
the knowledge which, in the usual course of things, she would have
gained from Adam; and she plans to divert such knowledge to her own
use by gaining equality with him or even superiority over him – 'For
inferior, who is free?' And because the relationship between man and

woman was for Milton, as for the poets of many centuries, a symbol or shadow of that between God and the soul, Eve's action stands, among other things, for the human mind's denial of its Creator by perverting the gift of knowledge to its own use. We are back, in fact, at the distinction between true and false wisdom as one of motive, and at Milton's concept of the Fall as a crossroads of the mind at which its love of learning, like its other impulses, takes the wrong direction. The *hubris* and self-awareness which overwhelm Adam and Eve are not the result of any magical properties in the apple; they are an inevitable sequel to the mental processes which lead up to the action.

In thus speaking of the Fall as a psychological experience, we must not forget that for Milton it was also a historical fact. The Tree of Knowledge was an allegory of God; but 'when God allegorises, he does not merely write or inspire parables, he also *causes to happen the events which can be allegorically interpreted*'.[32] Milton's belief in a historical Fall is, I think, the main refutation of the second inconsistency which has been discovered in the poem: that Milton was forced by his own subject to express disapproval of an act he instinctively approved and to commend a state of existence which he would have found quite intolerable. The chief support for such a view is to be found, not in the poem, but in a passage of the *Areopagatica*:

> Good and evil we know in the field of this world grow up together almost inseparably; and the knowledge of good is so involved and interwoven with the knowledge of evil, and in so many cunning resemblances hardly to be discerned, that those confused seeds which were imposed upon Psyche as an incessant labor to cull out, and sort asunder, were not more intermixed. It was from out the rind of one apple tasted, that the knowledge of good and evil, as two twins cleaving together, leaped forth into the world. And perhaps this is that doom which Adam fell into of knowing good and evil; that is to say, of knowing good by evil.
>
> As therefore the state of man now is; what wisdom can there be to choose, what continence to forbear, without the knowledge of evil? He that can apprehend and consider vice with all her baits and seeming pleasures, and yet abstain, and yet distinguish, and yet prefer that which is truly better, he is the true warfaring Christian. I cannot praise a fugitive and cloistered virtue unexercised and unbreathed, that never sallies out and sees her adversary, but slinks out of the race, where that immortal garland is to be run for, not without dust and heat. Assuredly we bring not innocence into the world, we bring impurity much rather; that which purifies us is trial, and trial is by what is contrary.[33]

The crucial words of this famous passage, in its relationship to *Paradise Lost*, are those which open the second paragraph: 'As the state of man now is.' Whether Milton approved or disapproved of Eve's action, whether he would have been bored or happy in his own Eden, are irrelevant queries, because his epic is not a golden dream of the state of innocence; it is an attempt to explain the facts of the human situation. *Paradise Lost* is not an outcry over spilt milk. As the state of man now is, he knows good only by distinguishing it from evil, and Milton condemns all attempts to put the milk back in the bottle by making a private and artificial Eden in cloister or study. A born fighter, he welcomed all hazards which lay before the warfaring Christian; but his relish for the mental fight did not mean that he preferred the state of experience to the state of innocence – which neither he nor any man living knew enough about to be able to judge – but that he acknowledged the Divine Mercy which brought good out of evil by making this sifting of the seeds the highest pleasure of the intellect. 'The end then of learning', he states in his tractate *Of Education*, 'is to repair the ruins of our first parents by regaining to know God aright.'[34] Grace rekindles the light of Right Reason and thus empowers it to accept the good and reject the ill by the process whose happy outcome is foretold in *Comus*:

> Yea even that which mischief meant most harm,
> Shall in the happy trial prove most glory.
> But evil on it self shall back recoyl,
> And mix no more with goodness, when at last
> Gather'd like scum, and setl'd to it self,
> It shall be in eternal restless change
> Self-fed, and self-consum'd, if this fail,
> The pillar'd firmament is rott'ness,
> And earths base built on stubble. (590–8)

Milton, then, believes in a Fortunate Fall; which is something quite different from believing the Fall to be a commendable act. In this belief he is very much of his own time. 'O felix culpa' is a characteristic cry of the century which took the Magdalene as its patron saint. A. O. Lovejoy has traced the historic origins of this paradox of the Fortunate Fall, and shown the popularity which the concept enjoyed in the seventeenth century.[35] Indeed it was an idea highly acceptable to the new optimism of the period which had risen from the ashes of Renaissance humanism. If Elizabethan *fin-de-siècle* melancholy, and its equivalent in the countries of the Counter-Reformation, represented the prodigal son's sojourn in a land of famine, the next age finds him feasting on the fatted calf; and as early as 1612 St François de Sales expresses, with new fervour, the traditional paradox of 'Blessed be the time That appil take was':

> Et tant s'en faut que le peché d'Adam ayt surmonté la debonnaireté divine, que tout au contraire il l'a excitee et provoquee: si que, par une suave et très amoureuse anti-peristase et contention, elle s'est revigoree a la presence de son adversaire, et comme ramassant ses forces pour vaincre; elle a fait surabonder la grace ou l'iniquité avoit abondé, de sorte que la sainte Eglise, par un saint exces d'admiration, s'escrie, la veille de Pasques: 'O peché d'Adam, a la verité necessaire, qui a esté effacé par la mort de Jesus Christ; o couple bien heureuse, qui a merité d'avoir un tel et si grand Redempteur!' Certes, Theotime, nous pouvons dire comme cet ancien: 'Nous estions perdus, si nous n'eussions este perdus.' (*Traité de l'Amour de Dieu*, II v)

Milton's treatment of the problem of knowledge is not, of course, without its inconsistencies; a poet and a layman, he could scarcely be expected to provide a neatly satisfying answer to one of the deepest theological problems. A major inconsistency lies, as Willey has shown, in the fact that Adam's freedom is represented both as a negative freedom from external coercion and as the service of reason or power to sift the seeds of good and evil which really is subsequent to the Fall.[36] Milton cannot solve the difficulty in an entirely rational manner, and his insistence on the Fortunate Fall represents something of a supra-rational, Pascalian leap, an attempt to knot by paradox the strands whose conflicting pull allows no other reconciliation. The idea of a Fortunate Fall is seldom far from Milton's thoughts, and the theme of 'All is best', which concludes both *Paradise Lost* and *Samson Agonistes*, is the final statement of a *motif* integral to the meaning of either work. In the epic, Satan declares, in the first book,

> If then his Providence
> Out of our evil seek to bring forth good,
> Our labour must be to pervert that end,
> And out of good still to find means of evil. (I 162-5)

but Milton adds that

> all his malice serv'd but to bring forth
> Infinite goodness, grace and mercy shewn
> On Man by him seduc't. (I 217-19)

Before the Creation, the angels sing

> to him
> Glory and praise, whose wisdom had ordain'd
> Good out of evil to create, (VII 186–8)

and after the act is accomplished they repeat the theme:

> Who seekes
> To lessen thee, against his purpose serves
> To manifest the more thy might: his evil
> Thou usest, and from thence creat'st more good. (VII 613–16)

After the Fall, the Son brings the contrite prayers of Adam and Eve to the Father, declaring them to be

> Fruits of more pleasing savour from thy seed
> Sow'n with contrition in his heart, then those
> Which his own hand manuring all the Trees
> Of Paradise could have produc't, ere fall'n
> From innocence. (XI 26–30)

At the end of the poem these fragments of the *motif* are gathered up into one final, resonant statement:

> O goodness infinite, goodness immense!
> That all this good of evil shall produce,
> And evil turn to good; more wonderful
> Then that which by creation first brought forth
> Light out of darkness! full of doubt I stand,
> Whether I should repent me now of sin
> By mee done and occasiond, or rejoyce
> Much more, that much more good thereof shall spring,
> To God more glory, more good will to Men
> From God, and over wrauth grace shall abound. (XII 469–78)

Samson Agonistes is also the story of a Fortunate Fall. By ways which, the Chorus stresses, are not man's ways, God brings triumph for Samson and the Israelites out of the hero's 'captivity and loss of eyes'; apparent evil is once more the source of final good:

> All is best, though we oft doubt,
> What th' unsearchable dispose
> Of highest wisdom brings about,
> And ever best found in the close.

These lines are echoed in Pope's effort to vindicate the ways of God to
Man:

> All Discord, Harmony not understood;
> All partial Evil, universal Good:
> And, spite of Pride, in erring Reason's spite,
> One truth is clear, WHATEVER IS, IS RIGHT. (*Essay on Man*, I, end)

But Pope's glib statement has nothing in common with the katharsis
achieved by the conclusion of *Samson Agonistes*. The optimism of
Milton's belief that all is best crowns the endeavour of a lifetime to
recognise and reject the worst. And this faith is accomplished not 'in
erring Reason's spite', but in the exercise of that same Reason through
whose obliquity man fell, and through whose rectitude, by the
Providence that turns all to good, he is also saved.

NOTES

1. From the *Discourse concerning Satire*, in *Essays*, ed. W. P. Ker (1900) II 29.
2. E. M. W. Tillyard, *The Miltonic Setting* (1938) pp. 168–204.
3. *The Student's Milton*, ed. F. A. Patterson (1930) p. 469.
4. Tillyard, op. cit. p. 153.
5. Sonnet XI: 'I did but prompt the age to quit their cloggs . . .'
6. See C. S. Lewis, *A Preface to Paradise Lost* (1942) p. 102: 'That door out of Hell is firmly locked by the devils themselves, on the inside.' It is possible, I think, that Milton was attempting, in describing the ascents and descents of his good and bad angels, a reconciliation between the Thomistic, medieval theories of motion and those held by the modern scientists of his time, like Galileo. For a discussion of the conflicting views of truth behind these theories, see the first chapter of Basil Willey's *The Seventeenth Century Background* (1934).
7. Does Milton take the theme of a Hell within the mind from Marlowe? It is noteworthy that Satan's soliloquy at the beginning of Book IV, in which this idea is prominent, was written before the rest of the poem, and while Milton still contemplated a dramatic form for the work; the verse is here much closer to that of Elizabethan drama than it is elsewhere in the epic. On the other hand, the idea was in the seventeenth-century 'climate of opinion' and is found in the writings of the Cambridge Platonists who have so much in common with Milton. 'Heaven is first a Temper, and then a Place' (Whichcote); 'As the Kingdom of Heaven is not so much without men as within . . . so the tyranny of the Devil and Hell is not so much in some external things as in the qualities and dispositions of men's minds' (John Smith). As Grant McColley has shown – 'Paradise Lost', in *Harvard Theological Review*, XXXIII (1939) 206 – the theory is of medieval origin and is expressed by St Thomas Aquinas and St Bonaventura.
8. *Poets and Playwrights* (Minneapolis, 1930) p. 265.
9. B. Rajan – '*Paradise Lost*' and the Seventeenth-century Reader (1947) p. 66 – has shown how this conception of the relationship of woman to man 'typified one of the deepest and most impersonal feelings of the time'.

10. *City of God*, Book XIV, ch. 13 (Healey's translation). C. S. Lewis (*A Preface to Paradise Lost*, pp. 65–71) has shown the complete accord, in all essentials, between St Augustine's account of the Fall and Milton's.

11. Quoted by Gladys Wade, *Thomas Traherne* (Princeton, 1944) p. 226.

12. *The Student's Milton*, ed. F. A. Patterson, pp. 1127–8.

13. *Private Correspondence and Academic Exercises*, trans. P. B. Tillyard, with Introduction by E. M. W. Tillyard (1932) pp. 112–13.

14. Ibid. pp. 11 and 14.

15. lines 103–4. Cowper translates:
> Henceforth exempt from the unletter'd throng
> Profane, nor even to be seen by such.

16. lines 168–78, thus rendered by Cowper:
> These themes I now revolve – and oh, if Fate
> Proportion to these themes my lengthen'd date,
> Adieu my shepherd's reed! yon pine-tree bough
> Shall be thy future home; there dangle thou
> Forgotten and disus'd, unless ere long
> Thou change thy Latian for a British song;
> A British? – even so, – the pow'rs of man
> Are bounded; little is the most he can:
> And it shall well suffice me, and shall be
> Fame, and proud recompence enough for me,
> If Usa, golden-hair'd, my verse may learn,
> If Alain bending o'er his chrystal urn,
> Swift-whirling Abra, Trent's o'ershadow'd stream,
> Thames, lovelier far than all in my esteem,
> Tamar's ore-tinctur'd flood, and, after these,
> The wave-shorn shores of utmost Orcades.

17. *The Student's Milton*, ed. F. A. Patterson, p. 1138 (from the *Second Defence*).

18. I follow Tillyard's dating of the sonnet *On his Blindness*. See his *Milton* (1930) app. G.

19. In *Studies in Philology*, XXXV (1938) 264–5.

20. P. B. Tillyard's translation, p. 117.

21. Ibid. pp. 117–18.

22. *The Student's Milton*, ed. F. A. Patterson, p. 1151.

23. *Academic Exercises*, trans. Tillyard, p. 112.

24. *Letter to a Friend*, in *The Student's Milton*, ed. F. A. Patterson, pp. 1127–8.

25. Introduction to the *Academic Exercises*, p. xxxvi.

26. Bohn edition of *Milton's Prose Works*, I 236 (*Second Defence*).

27. Willey, *The Seventeenth Century Background*, pp. 261–3.

28. Ibid. p. 255.

29. Ibid. p. 255.

30. Quoted by Grant McColley, in *Harvard Theological Review*, XXXIII (1939) 218.

31. Ch. 10, p. 986 of *The Student's Milton*, ed. F. A. Patterson.

32. Willey, *The Seventeenth Century Background*, p. 239.

33. *The Student's Milton*, ed. F. A. Patterson, p. 738.

34. Ibid. p. 726.

35. 'Milton and the Paradox of the Fortunate Fall', in *Journal of English Literary History*, IV (1937) 161–79.

36. Willey, *The Seventeenth Century Background*, pp. 253–6.

J. B. BROADBENT
Milton's Rhetoric (1959)

SCHOLARS have made us conscious of formal rhetoric as a factor in Renaissance poetry: in Tudor and Jacobean lyrics, in Spenserian narrative stanzas, and even in dramatic blank verse. All three contexts of rhetorical usage – lyrical, narrative, dramatic – are to be found in Milton's poetry; he was the last great practitioner of rhetoric on such a scale before the twentieth century.

There are difficulties and dangers in studying rhetorical practice. Learning a hundred or so figures and remembering them while reading strains the mind and can obscure the poetry. The very names of the figures, as classified by classical and Elizabethan rhetoricians, ring in the head with an exotic hypnotic rhythm – *antimetabole*, *polysyndeton*, *synathroesmus*, *procatalepsis*, *anthypophora*. The terms are out of date; recognizing some of the devices may sharpen our response to the poetry, as recognizing a metaphor and distinguishing it from a simile does; but today we do not judge a poet by his skill at introducing an *antanaclastic epanalepsis* into his pleasantly diversified *prosopographia*. This could be a criterion (subject of course to decorum) at a time when it was much more difficult to write English with mere competence, and when logic and oratory were closer to literature than they are now. On the other hand, a little more terminology than we do have would probably be a help both in teaching people to write sentences and punctuate paragraphs and in discussing special effects. Peacham defines the figure *tmesis* as 'when a compounded worde is parted by the interpolation of another word, and sometyme of many'[1] – 'wind-lilylocks -laced' and 'Miracle-in-Mary-of-flame', for instance. Dr Davie, Mr Bateson, and I discussed these dangers, and some of the advantages, in contributions to *Essays in Criticism* called '16th-Century Poetry and the Common Reader'.[2] A point we overlooked is that for the Elizabethans rhetoric was synthetic, not analytic. A knowledge of the figures and their most appropriate application, learned at school, might help the orator to write his speech or the courtier his poem; it was not intended as a critical or interpretive procedure.

Yet some of the figures I am going to discuss are as important in *Paradise Lost* as the devices we already take into account with ease – meter and rhyme, metaphor and simile, etymology and symbol. And some attention to Milton's use of actual rhetoric may give us a clearer understanding of what we mean by saying, as we do also of Marlowe and others, that his verse is 'rhetorical'.

I will lessen the dangers by omitting those branches of rhetoric which do not have an important, and hitherto unrecognized, effect on the reader:

1. Forensic figures which dispose arguments, such as *antirrhesis* (rejection of erroneous argument) and *procatalepsis* (anticipation of objection), or which manipulate emotion in a merely persuasive way, such as *sarcasmus*, *mycterismus*, and the like. Many of these are used in the debates in *Comus*, *Paradise Regained*, and *Samson* and in the debates in Pandemonium and Heaven and between Satan and Eve, and the flytings between Satan and Ithuriel, Gabriel, Abdiel. But so long as we do recognize these debates as wholly formal, the knowledge that when Abdiel says 'O argument blasphemous, false and proud' (v 809) he is using *epodioxis* is not going to intensify our response; nor do we have to know that 'grant it thee unjust That equal over equals Monarch Reigne' (831) is *concessio* before we recognize it as a common turn of argument.

2. Typically prose schemes, such as *regression* (e.g., 'Judge not that ye be not judged'). Many of the figures occurred originally in prose oratory; the Renaissance rhetoricians, especially Puttenham, applied them to verse by equating lines and stanzas with sentences and paragraphs: John Hoskins[3] takes his English examples of *epizeuxis* and *anadiplosis* from *Arcadia*. But our prose is even more different than our verse from that of the Renaissance; and Milton's own prose is not euphuistic or rich in any rhetoric except of the debating kind.

3. Grammatical and orthographical peculiarities, such as *antisthecon* (e.g. 'brast' for 'burst') and *apocope*. We heard a lot about these in the footnotes of Milton's late Victorian editors (Verity), but they really belong to prosodic and textual study, such as Professor Wright's and Miss Darbishire's introductions to their editions of Milton.

4. 'Imagery' in the modern sense, i.e. mostly metaphor and simile. These have been well enough recognized. Our definition of 'imagery' derives from the imagists, of course, who abandoned non-tropal figures.

5. The generic terms, such as *narratio* (relating an example) and *pragmatographia* (describing an action). Miss Tuve[4] has insisted on their

importance to questions of rhetorical decorum, but it seems to me that
the saving grace of Renaissance rhetoric, its appeal to decorum, was
ineffective and is still least helpful when made from a codified genre,
whether general like epic, or local like these. I might add, though, that
chronographia (description of passing or changing time) is symbolically
important in *Paradise Lost*, especially in Books IV, V, and VIII, where a
series of this figure marks a paradisal day and night at the center of the
poem, and contrasts with the timelessness of Hell (cf. the unreliability
of its climate) and of Heaven.

   6. The vices of style. These are mostly linguistic usages. Two of
them seem typically Miltonic: *cacozelia*, the invention of new words
and phrases 'other then the good speakers and writers in any language,
or then custome hath allowed',[5] including the coinage of 'fine words out
of the Latin'; and *soraismus*, the use of actually foreign words in English
writing. But in fact there are very few neologisms in *Paradise Lost*, and
most of the classicisms had been used recently before by other writers:
e.g., *hyaline* (*NED* 1621), *nitrous* (1601), *opacous* (1621), *stupendous* (1666).
The great majority of apparent Miltonisms belong either to the Middle
Ages or to the great word-forming period of the late sixteenth century:
e.g., *cincture, eternize, implicit, innumerous, pernicious, sciential*. Some look
old but were actually new: *bland* (1661), *florid* (1650), *tube* (1651); but
many more were very old and even dialectal: *lee, meaths, tedded, tine,
tuft, warp*. As for *soraismus*, words like *ammiral, divan, soldan*, dated from
the Crusades and were much less esoteric than Eliot's Sanskrit.

   I include a few of the less familiar tropes, such as *antonomasia* (epithet
instead of name) and *prosonomasia*, and one or two forensic figures
which have a tonal or syntactical effect; but I am mainly concerned
with schemes: that is, non-tropal arrangements of words and syntax
having a prosodic and therefore often a semantic effect. These largely
comprise what Puttenham (ch. 10) classes as 'sententious figures' as
opposed to the 'auricular' (grammatical and orthographical) and
'sensable' (tropal). He calls the schemes sententious 'because not only
they properly apperteine to full sentences, for bewtifying them with a
currant & pleasant numerositie, but also giuing them efficacie and
enlarging the whole matter besides with copious amplifications'. I shall
start by demonstrating the effect these figures have in the structure of
Milton's poetry by examining them in a familiar passage of *Samson
Agonistes*. Then I shall discuss Milton's use of them in general, moving
towards their special importance in *Paradise Lost*; and compare his use

of rhetoric briefly with that of a few poets of his time. I shall define unfamiliar figures in notes, referring to one other case of their use in Milton.[6]

My introductory example is from Samson's first soliloquy:

> Scarce half I seem to live, dead more then half.
>
> 80   O dark, dark, dark, amid the blaze of noon,
>   Irrecoverably dark, total Eclipse
>   Without all hope of day!
>   O first created Beam, and thou great word,
>   Let there be light, and light was over all;

synonymia (same idea repeated); *ploce* ('half'); *antithetical epizeuxis* ('live, dead' adjacent).

ecphonesis ('O'); *epizeuxis* ('dark, dark, dark' adjacent); *brachylogia*   80 (ibid, no conjunctions); *oxymoron* (dark–blaze).

ploce ('dark').

distant *anaphora* (80) and *apostrophe* ('O . . .'); *antonomasia* ('Beam' for God).

ploce ('light').

> 85   Why am I thus bereav'd thy prime decree?
>   The Sun to me is dark
>   And silent as the Moon,
>   When she deserts the night
>   Hid in her vacant interlunar cave.

erotema ('why . . .?').   85

oxymoron (sun dark); *ploce* ('dark').

simile.

prosopopoeia.

traductio prosonomasia (phonetic repetition in 'vacant . . . cave').

> 90   Since light so necessary is to life,
>   And almost life it self, it if be true
>   That light is in the Soul,
>   She all in every part; why was the sight
>
>   To such a tender ball as th'eye confin'd?

prosonomasia ('light . . . life'); *gnome* (scientific necessity of light).

ploce ('life'); *aporia* ('if it be true . . .').   91

ploce; prosonomasia ('light').

climax (light in soul, soul in every part); *erotema* ('why . . .?'); *prosonomasia* ('light . . . sight'); *zeugma* ('is' for light and soul); *rhyme* ('sight' with 'night' at 88).

95   So obvious and so easy to be quench't,
      And not as feeling through all parts diffus'd,
      That she might look at will through every pore?
      Then had I not been thus exil'd from light;
      As in the land of darkness yet in light,

hirmus (parallel construction of 'so . . . so')   95
simile; erotema.
prosopopoeia.
ploce ('light'); *rhyme* ('light' with 'sight' at 93).
traductio ('darkness' from 'dark' at 86, etc.); *oxymoron; antistrophe*
      ('light' ends 99 and 98).

100   To live a life half dead, a living death,

      And buried; but O yet more miserable!
      My self, my Sepulcher, a moving Grave,

      Buried, yet not exempt
      By priviledge of death and burial
      From worst of other evils, pains and wrongs,
      But made hereby obnoxious more
      To all the miseries of life,
      Life in captivity
      Among inhuman foes.

oxymoron (twice); *traductio* ('live . . . life'; 'dead . . . death');
      synonymia (cf. 79); quasi-*refrain* (cf. 79); *alliteration* (on *l*).   100
ecphonesis ('O').
prosonomasia ('self . . . Sepulcher'); *oxymoron* ('moving Grave');
      parison ('my self, my . . .'); *ellipsis* (no verb).
ploce ('buried').
traductio ('burial' from 'buried'); *ploce* ('death').
synanthroesmus (catalogue of 'evils, pains and wrongs').   105
antithesis (not exempt but more obnoxious).
anadiplosis ('life' ends 107 begins 108).

The *similes* are obvious, but actually less important than the prevailing
figures of *oxymoron, traductio, ploce,* and *prosonomasia*.[7] *Oxymoron* is used
to indicate the conflict within Samson as well as the inhuman contradiction of his external circumstances. The iterative figures have several
functions: they represent the circling thoughts of the speaker as, like
Adam in *Paradise Lost*, Book x, he tries to find a way out of his misery
and merely plunges deeper into it, returning in line 100 to the idea he
began with in line 79; they give a lyrical quality to his speech by
chiming on key-words – 'life . . . light . . . sight; dark; buried . . . burial;

dead . . . death'; and, together with *rhyme* and *antistrophe*,[8] the [aɪ]
diphthong keys together the apparently incoherent and spoken structure of the verse, tightening the varying line lengths by similar endings
and co-ordinating the varied stress systems by similar sounds within the
lines.

This speech is chosen for its value as an example. If we were reading it
in context, we might complain that the patterning of the words usurps
their meaning. That is the characteristic peril of the rhetorical style; but
I should be prepared to argue that such an effect is dramatically decorous
at this point in the play precisely because Samson is valuing himself
rather than doing anything. Later, Samson speaks quite differently,
unrhetorically, in dramatic accents:

> My self? my conscience and internal peace.
> Can they think me so broken, so debas'd
> With corporal servitude, that my mind ever
> Will condescend to such absurd commands?
> Although thir drudge, to be thir fool or jester,
> And in my midst of sorrow and heart-grief
> To shew them feats and play before thir god,
> The worst of all indignities, yet on me
> Joyn'd with extream contempt? I will not come (1334)

'Lycidas' also consists of a 'combination of various forms of verbal
repetition – of which anaphora, epanalepsis, and polyptoton are the
most notable'.[9] But, as a whole, 'Lycidas' *feels* more flexible and is less
obviously rhetorical than *Samson* because of the diversity of line length,
rhyme, etc., and because of the wealth of highly tropal figures. Milton's
lyric verse generally, although written closer to the sixteenth century
when rhetoric was in its prime, relies less on rhetoric to convey meaning
and suggestion than does the verse of his major poems. Despite the
elaborate patterning of words and sounds in 'Lycidas' and the lyrical
parts of *Comus*, it is *Paradise Lost* that provides the most and clearest
examples of the chief rhetorical devices – not only line-for-line but
qualitatively: schemes, and tropes other than those we normally
acknowledge to be 'images', show up all the more when rhyme is
absent, when images are few, and when the diction tends to be abstract.
We should therefore expect a great deal of rhetoric in *Paradise Regained*,
but even there it is proportionately less than in *Paradise Lost*; if there
were more, it would be obtrusive. It stands out most clearly in the
third and fourth books:

Thou neither dost perswade me to seek wealth
For Empires sake, nor Empire to affect
For glories sake by all thy argument.
For what is glory but the blaze of fame,
The peoples praise, if always praise unmixt?
And what the people but a herd confus'd,
A miscellaneous rabble, who extol
Things vulgar, & well weigh'd, scarce worth the praise,
They praise and they admire they know not what;
And know not whom, but as one leads the other. (III 44)

The *climax*, *parison*,[10] and other figures seem directed more to constructing the argument than constructing the verse; indeed, the difficulty one has in judging *Paradise Regained* is probably due to its arguments overrunning, as they do here, the structure of the lines. The poem is most like *Paradise Lost* in its rhetoric when Satan is tempting:

If Kingdom move thee not, let move thee Zeal,
And Duty; Zeal and Duty are not slow;

. . .

Zeal of thy Fathers house, Duty to free
Thy Country from her heathen servitude. (III 171)

Here is *anadiplosis-epizeuxis*, but also *epanodos*.[11] *Epanodos* and the other more formal figures are less common in the narrative epic. But on the whole the rhetoric shares in the general muting of style in the poem (as in *P.L.*, Books XI–XII), though it increases sharply in Book IV, reaching a climax with the climax of the action:

560   To whom thus Jesus: also it is written,
       Tempt not the Lord thy God, he said and stood.
       But Satan smitten with amazement fell
       As when Earths son *Antaeus* (to compare
       Small things with greatest) in *Irassa* strove
565   With *Joves Alcides*, and oft foil'd still rose,
       Receiving from his mother Earth new strength,
       Fresh from his fall, and fiercer grapple joyn'd,
       Throttl'd at length in the Air, expir'd and fell;
       So after many a foil the Tempter proud,
570   Renewing fresh assaults, amidst his pride,
       Fell whence he stood to see his Victor fall.
       And as that *Theban* Monster that propos'd
       Her riddle, and him, who solv'd it not, devour'd;
       That once found out and solv'd, for grief and spight

575 Cast her self headlong from th'*Ismenian* steep,
   So strook with dread and anguish fell the Fiend,
   And to his crew, that sat consulting, brought
   Joyless triumphals of his hop't success,
   Ruin, and desperation, and dismay,
580 Who durst so proudly tempt the Son of God.
   So Satan fell. . . .

Note the 'anti-rhyme' of *stood–fell* at lines 561–2; the *ploce* and *traductio* series from line 562 to line 581 on 'fell . . . fall', with an antithetical series on 'stood . . . rose . . . stood', and *prosonomasia* with *foil* and *strook*. The most elaborate example is line 571, with *ploce* on *fell* and *stood*, *traductio-epanalepsis*[12] on 'Fell . . . fall', and *traductio-antistrophe* with line 568 on *fall–fell*.

But in the 10,000 or so lines of blank verse in *Paradise Lost* there are over 100 cases of end-line *antistrophe* (identical rhyme); nearly 100 of *anaphora* (its opposite); about 60 of *anadiplosis*, 50 of *epanalepsis*, and over 40 of *epizeuxis* – all iterative schemes tending to the effect of rhyme. These, together with about 150 cases of actual rhyme of varying intensity, indicate how far Milton used rhetorical devices to decorate the blankness of his verse. The considerable amount of actual rhyme in *Paradise Lost* has often been noted;[13] what nobody has pointed out is that in blank verse rhyme is simply an iterative scheme like *epanalepsis* and *anadiplosis*. Identical rhyme was called, as a figure, *antistrophe*; near-rhyme is *prosonomasia* combined with *antistrophe*; there is also what I call 'anti-rhyme':[14]

   Returned on that bright beam, whose point now raisd
   Bore him slope downward to the Sun now fall'n. (IV 590)

   So dear I love him, that with him all deaths
   I could endure, without him live no life. (IX 832)

It is because of this poetic, even prosodic effect of theirs that I concentrate on the iterative schemes. Quantitatively also they predominate in *Paradise Lost* over all other classes of figure, including tropes, and over individual figures except *ploce* and *traductio*, which outnumber but cannot outweigh them. The distribution is significant. *Ploce* and *traductio* are impossible to count accurately, but Book IX has an overwhelming majority of *ploce* and, proportionate to its length, about eight times as much *traductio* as Book I; Book IX is followed by Books

III, VIII, and X. The more formal schemes, such as *anaphora* and *climax*, are more evenly distributed; but even the schemes which preponderate over the whole poem occur in patches: a third of all cases of *anadiplosis* lie in Books III and IX; Book III has more *antimetabole*[15] than any other book; in it and in Books IV, VII, and IX, most of the *antistrophe*, *epanalepsis*, and *epizeuxis* is concentrated. So, even after adjusting for different lengths, Books III and IX stand as the most heavily endowed with this peculiarly prosodic and verbal kind of rhetoric.[16]

The monopoly of Books III and IX indicates that iterative and verbal figures belong especially to theological contexts. In both books the theology is presented in the form of debate. The debate in Heaven is often linked with that in Pandemonium; but the devils' debate is much more forensic. They apply the rules of disposition and suasion, but their arguments are urging of individual ambitions, manifest in language which is more tropal than schematic. In contrast, the debates in Books III and IX are dialectical. This universalizes the heavenly debates and gives them something of the character of interior monologues, unifying the persons of the Godhead and internalizing the relations between Satan as tempter, Adam, and Eve. These theological contexts are bare of tropes; so we have an essentially abstract and verbal treatment of the poem's central issues.

The issue between fallen-to temptation and proffered salvation is presented by a contrast between the rhetoric that Satan uses in tempting, Eve in falling, and the rhetoric that Father and Son use in planning salvation.[17] Satan's tempting rhetoric is a parody of the Father's:

> Not free, what proof could they have givn sincere
> Of true allegiance, constant Faith or Love,
> Where onely what they needs must do, appeard,
> Not what they would? what praise could they receive?
> What pleasure I from such obedience paid. (III 103)

> Of good, how just? of evil, if what is evil
> Be real, why not known, since easier shunnd?
> God therefore cannot hurt ye, and be just;
> Not just, not God; not feard then, nor obeyd:
> Your feare it self of Death removes the feare. (IX 698)

There seems to be little difference. But the similarities – *erotema* (rhetorical question), *parison*, etc. – are superficial. The Father's speech is less sympatheic, yet obviously more authoritative than Satan's:

greater weight, a preference for formal schemes rather than iterations. The difference is even more obvious when salvation has been arranged and the Father celebrates it with extraordinarily elaborate schemes, the Son with lyrical rhetoric. The Father's schemes symbolize the Logos uttering its ultimatum of rationality:

> So Man, as is most just,
> Shall satisfie for Man, be judg'd and die,
> And dying rise, and rising with him raise
> His Brethren, ransomd with his own dear life.
> So Heav'nly love shall outdo Hellish hate,
> Giving to death, and dying to redeeme,
> So dearly to redeem what Hellish hate
> So easily destroy'd, and still destroyes
> In those who, when they may, accept not grace. (III 294)

It reveals the crudeness of the myth and its bargain; but it has a definiteness which Satan's fluid relativism cannot shift. The contrast is temperamental in Milton; this rhetorical expression of it, though, is to emphasize the redeeming human office of the Son. In combination with his lyricism, it symbolizes 'the strife of mercy and justice', indicating something of the nature of the Godhead and the functions of its persons:

> Father, thy word is past, man shall find grace;
> And shall grace not find means, that finds her way
> The speediest of thy winged messengers,
> To visit all thy creatures. . . .
>
>   .   .   .
>
> Behold mee then, mee for him, life for life
> I offer, on mee let thine anger fall;
> Account mee man. (III 227)

So the Son represents theological grace by grace of prosody, the Father dogma by schemes – although, approving redemption, even he echoes the Son's lyrical figures:

> for I will cleer thir senses dark,
> What may suffice, and soft'n stonie hearts,
> To pray, repent, and bring obedience due.
> To prayer, repentance, and obedience due,
> Though but endeavord with sincere intent,
> Mine eare shall not be slow, mine eye not shut. (188)

All these speeches are based closely on biblical texts. Satan is never
lyrical, rarely schematic: his rhetoric tends to question-begging *parison*
and *traductio* and especially to *aporia* (affected doubt); his figures flicker
with suspicious speed, sentences wind with serpentine ease. As a
forensic display, Satan's rhetoric is often superior to the Father's; but it
is always just off-key:

> One fatal Tree there stands of Knowledge call'd,
> Forbidden them to taste: Knowledge forbidd'n?
> Suspicious, reasonless. Why should thir Lord
> Envie them that? Can it be sin to know,
> Can it be death? and do they onely stand
> By Ignorance, is that thir happie state,
> The proof of thir obedience and thir faith? (IV 514)

The appearance of incisive argument is typically Satanic: it is given by
the neat structure – the *epanalepsis* of 'Forbidden . . . forbidd'n?' for
instance – and by the use of *pysma* (repeated rhetorical questions) to
insinuate agreement without offering anything definite enough to
disagree with. The *pysma*, combined with *parison* ('can it be . . .? Can it
be . . .?') and *asyndeton*, give a speaking tone to the sentences which is
typical of Satan but only at unfortunate moments heard in the speeches
of the Father.

The difference between the rhetorical habits of God and Satan is
paralleled in the speeches of Adam and Eve, according to whose
influence they are under at the time; and in them the difference is
helpfully exaggerated. At the temptation Eve parrots Satan. Even her
lyric to Adam's fallen love is debased by a Satanic note:

> O glorious trial of exceeding Love,
> Illustrious evidence, example high!
> Ingaging me to emulate, but short
> Of thy perfection, how shall I attaine,
> Adam, from whose deare side I boast me sprung,
> And gladly of our Union heare thee speak,
> One Heart, one Soul in both; whereof good prooff
> This day affords, declaring thee resolvd,
> Rather then Death or aught then Death more dread
> Shall separate us, linkt in Love so deare,
> To undergoe with mee one Guilt, one Crime,
> If any be, of tasting this fair Fruit,

> Whose vertue, for of good still good proceeds,
> Direct, or by occasion hath presented
> This happie trial of thy Love, which else
> So eminently never had bin known. (IX 960)

Dramatically, the whole thing is ironic: we know that Eve's humility is false because she has already asked herself whether it might not be better to 'keep the odds of Knowledge in my power Without Copartner? so to add what wants In Femal Sex' (820); we realize that in taking this occasion to affirm his love for Eve, Adam has denied his love for God; we know that the 'dearness' of his love is also the dearness of the Son's sacrifice to be (III 216, 297, 300, etc.). But our present interest is the way in which these more obvious ironies are supported by the peculiarly Satanic notes in Eve's rhetoric: the suddenly conversational cadence of 'whereof good prooff This day affords'; the shockingly flippant *parison*, *prosonomasia*, and *alliteration* in 'Rather then Death or aught then Death more dread' – a flippancy which God's similar figures never suggest; the thoughtless *aporia*, 'If any be'; and the speciously solemn *gnome*, 'for of good still good proceeds'. On the other side, the Son's sacrificial *ploce* on 'mee',[18] which he repeats in Book XI, is used by Adam and Eve as they move towards reconciliation and repentance:

> first and last
> On mee, mee onely, as the sourse and spring
> Of all corruption, all the blame lights due;
> So might the wrauth. (831)

> On me exercise not
> Thy hatred for this miserie befall'n,
> On me already lost, mee then thy self
> More miserable . . .
> . . . me, sole cause to thee of all this woe,
> Mee mee onely just object of his ire. (927)

Similarly, the Father's *antistrophe* on 'prayer, repentance, and obedience due' enlarges to the repeated last paragraph of Book XI, where Adam and Eve

> prostrate fell
> Before him reverent, and both confess'd
> Humbly thir faults, and pardon beg'd, . . .

The critical question is, Can issues presented so formally take effect in a poem which elsewhere appeals strongly to the senses and the imagination? Blake's answer would be No: schematic rhetoric is only another symptom of the tyranny of a life-denying rationality over the fluid and passionate nature of language. A less ethnocentric answer is that Milton was justified historically, as well as temperamentally, in worshiping the kind of rationality celebrated in *Paradise Lost*; that he was justified artistically in using a rational poetic to construct a theodicy with; and that we can learn from this. Where the Metaphysical poets characteristically used tropes to link man with cosmic issues –

> Could I behold those hands which span the Poles,
> And turne all spheares at once, pierc'd with those holes?

– Milton used schemes. When we put against Satan's good-evil and love-hate (e.g., IV 69) *antitheses* and *antimetaboles*, their opposites in the celestial rhetoric, we see the rhetorical structure of the whole poem. It is an *epanodos* on the subjects proposed by the first invocation (hence the Empsonian ambiguities[19] – that is, *prosonomasia* – on 'fruit', 'taste', 'all', 'fall', 'woe', etc.). The method is synthetic, not analytic, demanding *a priori* agreement about the value of its terms. It is not true to the Bible, which is highly tropal. It seems to be new in epic (Virgil, Milton's closest rhetorical model, does not use schemes thematically or dramatically). It prefigures the mechanics of deism. But it is a method which makes it possible to *think* about theology; and it is in this rationality, whether explicit or exemplified by figures, that the poem's uniqueness lies. In any case, its rigidity is softened by Milton's final attitude. Although in the Platonic controversy about good rhetoric and sophistry, Satan represents the latter, it is at the moment of the temptation that Milton presents him like 'som Orator renound in *Athens* or free *Rome*' collecting himself for eloquence in a great cause (IX 667). It is only in the last two books of the poem and in *Paradise Regained* that Milton purges his own practice, as Christ purges his admiration, of oratory. Even there Satan offers the classical rhetors illustriously – 'Those antient, whose resistless eloquence Wielded at will that fierce Democratie' (IV 268); but Christ rejects them as

> herein to our Prophets far beneath,
> As men divinely taught, and better teaching
> The solid rules of Civil Government
> In thir majestic unaffected stile
> Then all the Oratory of *Greece* and *Rome*.

One can argue endlessly about Milton's part in *Paradise Regained*. I think it true, though, that as a poet he came to trust less and less in art, and even that he always had a sense that the poetry does not matter. The last two books of *Paradise Lost*, as well as *Paradise Regained*, dismiss, along with heroics, the elaborate pastoral and the celebratory and argumentative rhetoric for which he had such a *métier*; they leave us in domestic actuality. The 'Nativity Ode' ends its orchestrated virtuosity with a simple cadence. The poet of 'Lycidas', having constructed all that gorgeous artifice, watches a real sun setting and walks out of his own poem. The chorus is dismissed from *Samson*. At the end of *Paradise Regained*, after the mild rhetoric of the angelic choir, Christ 'unobserv'd Home to his Mothers house private return'd'. The difference between these rhetorical patternings of language, and actual life, is acknowledged and approved.

In the examples above, Milton was using rhetoric to expound theology, to distinguish characters,[20] and to choose sides.[21] Another context, also dramatic, in which more than an average amount of rhetoric occurs is the soliloquies of characters in misery. The speech of Samson analyzed at the beginning of this essay is a late example. Satan's miserable soliloquies typify his own attitude with the contradictory figures of *antithesis* and *antimetabole* and the desperate logic of *parison*:

> If then his Providence
> Out of our evil seek to bring forth good,
> Our labour must be to pervert that end,
> And out of good still to find means of evil;

> fardest from him is best
> Whom reason hath equald, force hath made supream
> Above his equals. Farewel happy Fields
> Where Joy for ever dwells: Hail horrours, hail
> Infernal world, and thou profoundest Hell
> Receive thy new Possessor: One who brings
> A mind not to be chang'd by Place or Time.
> The mind is its own place, and in it self
> Can make a Heav'n of Hell, a Hell of Heav'n.

> Me miserable! which way shall I flie
> Infinite wrauth, and infinite despaire?
> Which way I flie is Hell; my self am Hell;
> And in the lowest deep a lower deep

> Still threatning to devour me opens wide,
> To which the Hell I suffer seems a Heav'n.

> So farwel Hope, and with Hope farwel Fear,
> Farwel Remorse: all Good to me is lost;
> Evil, be thou my Good.

antithesis	
parison antimetabole	(I 162)
parison	
antithesis	
antithesis antimetabole	(I 247)
parison	
parison	
parison	
antithesis	(IV 73)
antimetabole parison	
parison	
oxymoron antithesis	(IV 108)

The dominant figures – *oxymoron* and *antimetabole* – have in their syntax a force as symbolic as any metaphor might possess. The one-sided plausibility of Satan's arguments is appropriate to his loneliness, compared with the dialectical strife of mercy and justice in the Godhead. The punctuation of the poem with his ever more constructed soliloquies reveals the crumbling of his intellect and spirit from 'that fixt mind And high disdain' which was his in Hell (I 97). The Father's rhetoric is sometimes unpleasing, but it is constant; Satan's degenerates with his soul from the active determination of 'out of good still to find means of evil' to the collapsed nihilism of 'Evil, be thou my Good'. The process is carried further in Satan's dialogue of misery with the Son in *Paradise Regained*:

> For what he bids I do; though I have lost
> Much lustre of my native brightness, lost
> To be belov'd of God, I have not lost
> To love, at least contemplate and admire
> What I see excellent in good, or fair,
> Or vertuous, I should so have lost all sense.
> What can be then less in me then desire
> To see thee and approach thee, whom I know
> Declar'd the Son of God, to hear attent
> Thy wisdom, and behold thy God-like deeds?
> Men generally think me much a foe
> To all mankind: why should I? they to me

Never did wrong or violence, by them
I lost not what I lost, rather by them
I gain'd what I have gain'd, and with them dwell
Copartner in these Regions of the World,
If not disposer; lend them oft my aid,
Oft my advice by presages and signs,
And answers, oracles, portents and dreams,
Whereby they may direct their future life.
Envy they say excites me, thus to gain
Companions of my misery and wo.
At first it may be; but long since with wo
Nearer acquainted, now I feel by proof,
That fellowship in pain divides not smart,
Nor lightens aught each mans peculiar load.
Small consolation then, were Man adjoyn'd:
This wounds me most (what can it less) that Man,
Man fall'n shall be restor'd, I never more. (I 377)

The extraordinary abundance of rhyme, *antistrophe*, *ploce* and *traductio*, and the final *anadiplosis*, are marks of Satan's factitious pathos. The Son recognizes them.

Second to the debates and temptation, and equal with the miserable soliloquies, in density of rhetoric, are the lyrics in *Paradise Lost*. They represent the most sophisticated accomplishment of the seventeenth-century ambition to paraphrase the Psalms. The angels' Gloria before Creation (VII 182) anticipates the herald angels' gospel to the shepherds, and their hymn at the return from Creation evokes Psalm 24. The last two are simple constructions, bound into the heroic verse by *anaphora* ('Glorie': VII 182–184–187; 'Open': 565–566–569, repeated with *traductio* at line 575). The other hymns are more complicated. Eve's evensong to the seasons in Book IV (actually a hyperbolical affirmation of her love for Adam, hence a true nocturne) has its pastoral materials steadied and heightened for the context of religious epic by rhetorical figures. It consists of a huge *antistrophe*: 'Sweet is the breath of morn, her rising sweet, With Charm of earliest Birds . . . But neither breath of Morn when she ascends With charm of earliest Birds. . . .' Thus two stanzas are balanced about line 650. The first consists of a long *merismus* (the figure is too big to be sure of its identity) in which the beauty of all the seasons is defined by examples in parallel construction: 'pleasant the Sun . . . fragrant the fertil earth . . . and sweet the coming on Of grateful Eevning milde.' In the second, these are all repeated, in the same order,

but negatively, being rejected as not sweet without Adam, thus forming
a kind of *expeditio* (series of short similes dismissed as unequal to the
subject). Repetition on this stanzaic scale is used only once again in the
poem, for the last paragraph of Book x. Milton makes the Puritan
claim that Adam and Eve's morning hymn at v 153 is

> Unmeditated, such prompt eloquence
> Flowd from thir lips, in Prose or numerous Verse,
> More tuneable then needed Lute or Harp
> To add more sweetness. (v 149)

In fact it is a rhetorical paraphrase of the Benedicite, rather as sung by
the Three Holy Children of the Apocrypha. It consists of apostrophes to
representative ranks in the chain of being – angels, sun and moon, air
and water, etc. The apostrophes are linked by extended *ploce* on the
word 'praise': 'sound his praise . . . resound His praise . . . still new
praise . . . still advance his praise', etc. The whole thing is made highly
lyrical by an abundance of *prosonomasia*, rhyme, near-rhyme, anti-
rhyme, and identical rhyme (i.e., *antistrophe*), both within the lines, and
at the ends: 'light . . . Night . . . Night dawn Morn . . . praise climb'st
fallst fli'st flies . . . Light . . . praise rise . . . rise skie . . . praise . . .
blow . . . flow praise . . . praise . . . praise.' Within the elements, the
figure of *auxesis*[22] corresponds with their movement, and with the
general movement of the lyric down the scale of being: of the sun, for
example, 'both when thou climb'st, And when high Noon hast gaind,
& when thou fallst', and of the mists as incense,

> Whether to deck with Clouds the uncolourd skie,
> Or wet the thirstie Earth with falling showers,
> Rising or falling still advance his praise.

This schematic skeleton is clothed with the animating trope of *personification*. Raphael's two speeches on the scale of being in Book v are even
more elaborately formed on rhetorical schemes. One need only point
in the first speech to the *climax*

> of Elements
> The grosser feeds the purer, earth the sea,
> Earth and the Sea feed Air, the Air those Fires
> Ethereal, and as lowest first the Moon. (415)

In his second speech there is again a 'vertical' system of *auxesis* and
climax whereby the syntax, like the elements it describes, interlocks:

> whence the soule
> Reason receives, and reason is her being,
> Discursive, or Intuitive; discourse
> Is oftest yours, the latter most is ours.

But played against this, keeping it fluid, yet reinforcing the escalator effect of what Raphael is saying, there is a 'horizontal' system of phonetic figures, *prosonomasia*, *traductio*, etc., so clear that it can be represented diagrammatically:

```
green      leaves      breathes
    floure                      flours fruit           life
           Spirits                    Spirits aspire
       Reason receives   reason being                  degree
sense whence                      Discursive discourse yours
```

These smooth phonetic shifts do not cloy because there are also sharper and purely verbal transitions: 'breathes . . . aspire' and 'intellectual . . . understanding'. The ornament directs the ear to the argument lying beneath it, especially the fundamental analogue of biological development.[23] In the lyrics of the Chorus in *Samson* both schemes and tropes are abandoned:

> Oh how comely it is and how reviving
> To the spirits of just men long opprest!
> When God into the hands of thir deliverer
> Puts invincible might
> To quell the mighty of the Earth, th'oppressour,
> The brute and boist'rous force of violent men
> Hardy and industrious to support
> Tyrannic power, but raging to pursue
> The righteous and all such as honour Truth. (1268)

Here not David but Isaiah is the original, and the prophetic plainness is drawn into a melody constructed almost entirely out of its own rhythms; trope would weaken its force, a scheme harden its individuality.

In narrative contexts, especially in *pragmatographia*, Milton is very sparing of rhetoric. This accords with rhetorical theory, that in *pragmatographia* the chief figures should be onomatopoetic.[24] Thus Books I, II, IV, and V, consisting mainly of action and scenery, contain less than the average amount of *ploce*, *traductio*, and other iterative schemes. The three occasions when schematic rhetoric is used descriptively, the Hell of Book II, Chaos, and the Limbo of Fools, are not entirely successful.

> The parching Air
> Burns frore, and cold performs th'effect of Fire.
> Thither by harpy-footed Furies hail'd,
> At certain revolutions all the damn'd
> Are brought: and feel by turns the bitter change
> Of fierce extreams, extreams by change more fierce,
> From Beds or raging Fire to starve in Ice. (II 594)

Here we have piled-up half-rhyme, alliteration, *epizeuxis*, *antimetabole*, and *oxymoron*. A little further on there is a *parison* series culminating in Milton's most famous example of *brachylogia*.[25]

> Through many a dark and drearie Vaile
> They pass'd, and many a Region dolorous,
> O're many a Frozen, many a fierie Alpe,
> Rocks, Caves, Lakes, Fens, Bogs, Dens, and shades of death.

The extreme continues with *asyndeton* in Chaos:

> So eagerly the fiend
> Ore bog or steep, through strait, rough, dense or rare,
> With head, hands, wings, or feet pursues his way,
> And swims or sinks, or wades, or creeps, or flyes. (947)

This regression to a hyper-Spenserian rhetoric, as practiced by the Fletchers, indicates that Milton was writing allegorically here, as in the description of Death ('The other shape, If shape it might be call'd that shape had none . . . Or substance might be call'd that shadow seem'd, For each seem'd either') and the Limbo, with its catalogue of 'Cowles, Hoods and Habits . . . Reliques, Beads, Indulgences, Dispenses, Pardons, Bulls, The sport of Winds'. In each case, it is true, the kind of rhetoric used is functional: *brachylogia* and *asyndeton* having a scornful, wearying effect, in which Hell (and Roman Catholicism) are mockingly disposed of; the *parison* and *antithesis* of Death turn him inside out. But these allegories are too thin to bear the physical intrusion of Satan;[26] and the other incident which might have provoked allegorical rhetoric, Sin and Death building their bridge over Chaos, is described in very concrete and heroic terms, with little schematic rhetoric.

A glance at previous and subsequent rhetorical usages will correct any impression my accumulated examples may have given that Milton's rhetoric is overplayed. The general outline of rhetorical usage is clear, anyway until the eighteenth century. It starts in Anglo-Saxon:

Hwaer cwom mearg, hwaer cwom mago? Hwaer cwom maþþumgyfa?
Hwaer cwom symbla gesetu? Hwaer sindon seledreamas?
Eala beorht bune, eala byrnwiga,
eala þeodnes þrym![27]

This version of the *Ubi sunt?* formula may be due to classical influence,
but it is in tone with the rest of 'The Wanderer', a miserable soliloquy
like Milton's. Chaucer and the Scottish Chaucerians used rhetoric
locally, but the technique became general in the late sixteenth century,
overblew in the Fletchers' hands, and, as it ceased to be a school subject,
degenerated into a stock of conscious poeticisms. Pope was wise to use
less rhetoric than Dryden: satire is sharpened by a few figures only, such
as *zeugma, oxymoron,* and *antithesis*; the satirical effect of the heroic
couplet would be blunted by elaborate schemes, and antitheses be
diffused by an accumulation of trope. In later eighteenth-century blank
verse everything Miltonic was copied except, unhappily, rhetoric:

> Hail, Source of Being! Universal Soul
> Of heaven and earth! Essential Presence, hail!
> To thee I bend the knee; to thee my thoughts,
> Continual, climb, who with a master-hand
> Hast the great whole into perfection touched.
> By thee the various vegetative tribes,
> Wrapt in a filmy net and clad with leaves,
> Draw the live ether and imbibe the dew.
> By thee disposed into congenial soils,
> Stands each attractive plant, and sucks, and swells
> The juicy tide, a twining mass of tubes.
> At thy command the vernal sun awakes
> The torpid sap, detruded to the root
> By wintry winds, that now in fluent dance
> And lively fermentation mounting spreads
> All this innumerous-coloured scene of things.[28]

Thomson's iterative schemes – *parison, epanalepsis, anaphora, brachylogia* –
are very loose, and the statements are scattered so that the rhetoric,
instead of unifying the syntax, supporting the sense, and charging the
verse with lyricism as in Adam's morning hymn or Raphael's degree
speech, makes us only more aware of the blankness of the verse. The
familiar faults of eighteenth-century Miltonic blank verse are largely
due to a lack of rhetoric, because the weight of the imitated meter and
the diction cannot be sustained by any ordinary arrangement of

language. The crumpling of rhythm and syntax unsupported by
rhetoric seen in Book XII of *Paradise Lost* was repeated sometimes by
Wordsworth:

> I with him believed
> Devoutly that a spirit was abroad
> Which could not be withstood, that poverty
> At least like this, would in a little time
> Be found no more, that we should see the earth
> Unthwarted in her wish to recompense
> The industrious, and the lowly Child of Toil,
> All institutes for ever blotted out
> That legalised exclusion, empty pomp
> Abolish'd, sensual state and cruel power
> Whether by edict of the one or few,
> And finally, as sum and crown of all,
> Should see the People having a strong hand
> In making their own Laws, whence better days
> To all mankind.[29]

But in the better Wordsworthian blank verse the function of rhetoric is
performed by a strongly individual and conversationally sonorous tone
of voice, and by the counterpoint of sharply differentiated words which
provide sufficient tension. This is similar to Milton's practice in the
chorus from *Samson* quoted above, and it has been the practice of
modern poets in reflective verse. But after Wordsworth the nineteenth
century produced hardly any blank verse of the reflective or abstract
kind in which rhetoric is necessary. The major work in blank verse was
descriptive, with a richness of trope and diction that made schematic
rhetoric superfluous – or dramatic in a colloquially particularized way,
like Browning's monologues. For reflective verse, such as *In Memoriam*,
stanza was used; if it was not, the lack of rhetorical structure led to
confusion, as in Browning.

So Milton was writing at a time when rhetoric had overripened and
was about to fall away altogether for a long time. If we compare him
with his rhetorically minded predecessors, we find that he not only
avoided the more obvious and formal figures such as *symploce* and
collectour[30] – that was largely due to the form of his verse – but also he
was never guilty of that curious high-pitched tone, the exhibitionism,
of the earlier poets. His schemes have structural function, his tropes

significance; they are never used for their own sake. Milton never
descends to this level of *antimetabole*: 'Which still wex old in woe,
whiles we still wexeth new'.[31] He tends rather to

> mazes intricate,
> Eccentric, intervolv'd, yet regular
> Then most, when most irregular they seem (*PL* v 622)

The sense demands *antimetabole*, so the figure is onomatopoetic, its
complexity matched by the diction. The passage analyzed from
Samson, rhetorical as it is, does not approach the artifice of Timias'
comparable soliloquy in the *Faerie Queene*:

> But if to loue disloyalty it bee,
> Shall I then hate her, that from deathes dore
> Me brought? ah farre be such reproch fro mee.
> What can I lesse do, then her loue therefore,
> Sith I her dew reward cannot restore?
> Dye rather, dye, and dying do her serue,
> Dying her serue, and liuing her adore;
> Thy life she gaue, they life she doth deserue:
> Dye rather, dye, then euer from her seruive swerue. (III v 46)

Apart from the lesser structural and iterative figures – *anaphora*,
anadiplosis, etc. – this stanza contains figures rarely used by Milton, such
as *collectour*; and the rhyme makes the *ploce*, *traductio*, and *prosonomasia*
superfluous and heavy. In the *Faerie Queene* such artifice is perhaps not
out of place, especially in a stanza that is a love-complaint that might
easily have been written as a sonnet. But the natural development from
Timias' stanza, which none of Satan's or Samson's soliloquies could
lead to, is nonsense-verse like this, published in 1633:

> New light new love, new love new life hath bred;
> A life that lives by love, and loves by light:
> A love to him, to whom all loves are wed;
> A light, to whom the Sunne is darkest night:
> Eyes light, hearts love, souls onely life he is:
> Life, soul, love, heart, light, eye, and all are his:
> He eye, light, heart, love soul; he all my joye, & blisse.[32]

Milton's predecessors sometimes leaned on rhetoric when they did not
know what to say next or could not otherwise obey the rules of their
own prosody. Spenser uses *anadiplosis* and *antimetabole* to finish a stanza
for him when describing the arras in the House of Temperance:

> In which was nothing pourtrahed, nor wrought,
> Not wrought, nor pourtrahed, but easie to be thought. (II ix 33)

Milton's typical *anadiplosis* is economical, and integrated with the local rhythm and tone:

> though fall'n on evil dayes,
> On evil dayes though fall'n, and evil tongues. (*PL* VII 25)

Spenser will also use *anaphora* to finish a stanza for him:

> The whiles the Championesse now entred has
> The vtmost rowme, and past the formest dore,
> The vtmost rowme, abounding with all precious store. (III xi 27)

Milton can use the figure dramatically, to indicate the tone of a speaker's voice, his indignant breathlessness:

> Know ye not then said Satan, filld with scorn,
> Know ye not me?[33]

This is the *loquitur* technique of the novelist. Milton's anaphoristic phrases are always short; so are his phrases forming *antistrophe*, of which his weakest and most elaborate example is:

> who shall goe
> Before them in a Cloud, and Pillar of Fire,
> By day a Cloud, by night a pillar of Fire. (XII 202)

Rubel (p. 278) quotes three lines by Gabriel Harvey, each ending with the phrase 'in comparison with these', and Verity a fivefold *anaphora* from Tennyson's 'Marriage of Geraint'.[34]

These are negative examples. The positive virtues of Milton's rhetoric can be judged from comparison with the usage of poets whose reputation is today higher than Spenser's or Tennyson's and whose work is not dubbed 'rhetorical'. Shakespeare uses rhetoric dramatically. In plays such as *Richard III* which are rhetorical in the general, Marlovian sense, dramatic effect is anulled because nearly everybody speaks rhetorically; but in *Othello*, for instance, the effect is more dramatic than in *Paradise Lost* because no other character uses the figures so abundantly. 'O now, for euer Farewell the Tranquill minde . . .' is similar in effect to speeches of Satan, Samson, and Timias. Shakespeare's rhetoric chiefly manifests character, of course;[35] but in a good deal of twentieth-century English poetry, rhetoric has again been used structurally: either, following Donne, to dispose and contain argument;[36] or to stiffen freely shaped verse in lyrical and reflective modes, to depersonalize the musings of an individual, and to knit the themes which underlie apparent disorder of meter and meaning in large complicated symbolic poems such as *Four Quartets*.[37] This is the Miltonic usage. Milton abandoned both the tropal richness displayed in his own early verse, and the rhyme until then normal for narrative poems, for the sake of tonal coolness, and intellectual freedom. But he admitted the need then for some 'Adjunct or true Ornament of Poem or good Verse' which shall give 'musical delight' and yet not be 'to all judicious ears, triveal' or to the poet a 'vexation, hindrance, and constraint'. This musical delight 'consists only in apt Numbers, fit quantity of Syllables, and the sense variously drawn out from one Verse into another'.[38] The third element refers not to enjambement only but also to the iterative schemes we have been discussing.

NOTES

1. Henry Peacham the elder, *Garden of Eloquence* (1577 ed.). The second edition (1593) has been reprinted in facsimile by W. G. Crane (Gainesville, Fla., 1954).

2. IV (1954) 117–27, 421–30. Cf. I. A. Richards, 'The Places and the Figures', in *Kenyon Review*, XI (1949) 16–30.

3. *Directions for Speech and Style*, ed. H. H. Hudson (Princeton, 1935); see P. A. Duhamel, 'Sidney's *Arcadia* and Elizabethan Rhetoric', in *Studies in Philology*, XLV (1948) 134–50, for discussion of the prose use of figures.

4. *Elizabethan and Metaphysical Imagery* (Chicago, 1947).

5. Puttenham, *Arte of English Poesie* (1589), ed. G. D. Willcock and A. Walker (1936) p. 251.

6. I mostly adopt Puttenham's terminology, but usage differed widely. I have checked Nicolas Caussin, *De eloquentia sacra et humana*, 3d ed. (Paris, 1643) and Abraham Fraunce, *The Arcadian Rhetoric*, repr. E. Seaton (Oxford, 1950) and Peacham; but see Warren Taylor's dictionary of *Tudor Figures of Rhetoric* (Chicago, 1937; privately distributed by University of Chicago Libraries), which also collates Hoskins, Rainolde, Sherry, and Wilson (whom I have consulted) and Charles Butler, Angel Day and Dudley Fenner (I have not read these). The handiest list is in Veré L. Rubel's *Poetic Diction in the English Renaissance* (New York, 1941), which I have found quite the most lucid, practical, and critical book on the subject. See also D. L. Clark, *Rhetoric and Poetry in the Renaissance* (New York, 1922) and W. G. Crane, *Wit and Rhetoric in the Renaissance* (New York, 1941) and Miss Tuve. I have consulted some studies of other poets' rhetoric, such as Sister Miriam Joseph, *Shakespeare's Use of the Arts of Language* (New York, 1947); but most have been concerned with the rhetoric of argument or logic – e.g. Gladys D. Willcock, 'Shakespeare and Rhetoric', in *Essays and Studies by Members of the English Association*, XXIX (1943) 50–61, and Ruth Wallerstein, 'Rhetoric in the English Renaissance: Two Elegies' (Donne's on Prince Henry and 'Lycidas'), in *English Institute Essays, 1948* (New York). Others deal with

forensic prose, including W. M. Gilman, *Milton's Rhetoric: Studies in His Defence of Liberty* (1939). I am grateful to Miss K. M. P. Burton, fellow of Newnham College, Cambridge, for several suggestions.

7. *Ploce* is the significant repetition of a word or phrase with others intervening; *traductio* the same with a change in the word's grammatical form, often to punning effect; *prosonomasia* is the juxtaposition of almost homophonous words – a quasi-pun.

8. Consecutive lines ending with the same word(s) – i.e. identical rhyme; it may occur internally, though.

9. E. S. Le Comte, *Yet Once More: Verbal and Psychological Pattern in Milton* (New York, 1953) p. 25. His chapter 2 gives an introduction to some of Milton's rhetorical devices under the heading 'Epic Iteration', with examples from the Latin poems, which I do not deal with here. *Polyptoton* is Puttenham's *traductio*.

10. *Climax:* series of phrases in parallel construction, interlocked by syntax to show the interdependence of the elements named (*PL* VIII 145–7). *Parison:* series of phrases in parallel construction neither disjunctive (*asyndeton*) nor dependent on subsequent main clause (*hirmus*) (*PL* I 185–91).

11. *Anadiplosis:* repetition of last word(s) of one line at beginning of next or next but one (*PL* IV 162–4). *Epizeuxis:* words repeated adjacent to each other (*PL* III 171–2). *Epanodos:* expansion of statement by repetition and amplification of key-words (*PL* IX 697–9).

12. *Epanalepsis:* repetition of first word(s) of line at end of that or next line ('Lycidas', 165).

13. By Bridges, who is quoted by Verity (ed. *PL*; rev. ed., Cambridge, 1921) pp. lxii ff; more thoroughly by J. S. Diekhoff, 'Rhyme in *PL*', in *PMLA*, XLIX (1934) 539–43, corrected by J. M. Purcell, 'Rime in *PL*', in *Modern Language Notes*, LIX (1944) 171–2.

14. Cf. *Richard II*, I ii 35 (the end of a speech): 'What shall I say, to safegard thine owne life, The best way is to venge my Glousters death.'

15. *Antimetabole:* repetition of phrase in reverse order (*PL* VIII 160–4).

16. e.g. the average incidence of *anadiplosis* is about 6 per 1000 lines. But Book I has 0 in 800, Book VI has 1 in 900, while Book III has 10 in its first 400 lines.

17. I deal with this more contextually in chapters 4 and 10 of *Some Graver Subject* (1960).

18. The *mee*'s, though spelt emphatically here, derive their emphasis from the rhythm and from the figure of *ploce*, independently of spelling. I discuss this matter in a review of Darbishire's and Wright's editions of Milton's poems in *English Studies* (1958–9).

19. *Structure of Complex Words* (1951) ch. 4, '*All* in *PL*'. The spirit of much modern analytic criticism is rhetorical in a way that joins it to the Tudors and separates it from the Augustans and Romantics, who were much more concerned with sentiment.

20. Cf. A. H. Sackton, *Rhetoric as a Dramatic Language in Ben Jonson* (New York, 1948).

21. I gesture at Kenneth Burke, *The Philosophy of Literary Form* (New York, 1941), where he discusses psycholiterary 'strategies'.

22. *Auxesis:* arrangement of elements in climactic order (*PL* IV 24–6).

23. I discuss the significance of this in chapter 7 of *Some Graver Subject*.

24. See Tuve, p. 97.

25. *Brachylogia:* series of disjunctive single words.

26. See *Some Graver Subject*, ch. 3.

27. 'Wanderer', 92. See Adeline C. Bartlett, *Larger Rhetorical Patterns in Anglo-Saxon Poetry* (New York, 1935).

28. James Thomson, 'Spring', 556.

29. 'Prelude' (1805) IX 518.

30. *Symploce:* combined anaphora and antistrophe; *collectour:* concluding a passage by repetition of preceding key-words (*PL* VII 446–8).

31. *Faerie Queene*, I ix 9. This is one of Rubel's definitive examples (p. 227). My own

illustrations are no more partial to Milton than this to Spenser: Milton simply did not use the figures in this way.

32. P. Fletcher, *Purple Isle*, I 8.

33. IV 827. Cf. the dramatic–descriptive effect of

> To whom thus Jesus: also it is written,
> Tempt not the Lord thy God, he said and stood.

34. Note to *PL* VII 26.

35. Subsequently, as wit and character and with them blank verse lost vitality, rhetoric regressed to mere ornament. Spenser is indeed Dryden's master in these lines from *All for Love*:

> How I have lov'd, you know; how yet I love,
> My only comfort is, I know myself;
> I love you more, ev'n now you are unkind,
> Than when you lov'd me most. (v. Cleopatra)

But the genre is not Spenserian. French dramatic rhetoric is also in the background, but the language is not French.

36. Mainly in the 'academic' poets, as they have been labeled. Many of them are or have been dons (Davie, Prince, Holloway, Wain, Amis) or have read English as undergraduates in a critical climate which used Metaphysical poetry as a criterion of excellence. For examples, see F. T. Prince's 'Soldiers Bathing' (title poem, 1954) and 'Sun' (ibid.) and Thom Gunn's 'Carnal Knowledge' in his *Fighting Terms* (1954).

37. The first paragraph of 'East Coker' has an elaborate rhetorical skeleton; the chief figures are *parison* and *anaphora*.

38. See Arnold Stein, 'Structures of Sound in Milton's Verse', in *Kenyon Review*, xv (1953) 266–77, and chapter 6 of his *Answerable Style* (Minneapolis, 1953). Stein's critical procedures in reading *PL* are fundamentally rhetorical.

WILLIAM HALLER

'Hail wedded love' (1946)

IN the early summer of 1642, on the eve of the civil war, Milton came home from a holiday in the country, bringing with him the sixteen-year-old daughter of an Oxfordshire squire as his bride. The young wife stayed with her husband a few weeks and then returned to her family, promising to rejoin him at the end of the summer. When the end of summer arrived, the civil war having in the meantime begun, she failed to keep her word. About a year after the marriage, Milton published a pamphlet of forty-two pages entitled *The Doctrine and Discipline of Divorce restor'd to the good of both sexes*. Six months later he issued a second edition of this work, extended to twice its original length. At about the same time he put out a second pamphlet on the subject, *The Judgement of Martin Bucer concerning Divorce*, and early in the following year two more, *Tetrachordon* and *Colasterion*. I shall not recount the rest of the story, what little we know of it, how his wife came back to him when the war was over, and how seven years later she died, leaving him blind, with three young daughters to bring up, with the burden of public office, and with great literary ambitions yet unfulfilled. That he fell short of satisfying the standards set for husbands and fathers by later moralists should not, in the circumstances, seem surprising. Nor should it seem strange that the legend that the mighty champion of liberty in the state was a petty tyrant in the home was relished in the hey-day of royalism and disillusion which followed the rule of Puritan saints. With the rise of the Victorian matriarchy, earnest souls, zealous in the cause of woman, found it not easy to be patient with a man who could put into the mouth of the mother of mankind the words, 'unargued I obey'. Biographers, critics, novelists, and vindicators of women's rights have seen in Mary Powell the perfect image of brow-beaten womanhood and in her husband that of the overbearing male caught and laid low by the Achilles heel of sex. Latterly, of course, anybody with a modicum of the new psychology has been able to read John Milton's unconscious mind like an open book.

It is not my purpose to defend him or to explicate his troubles. Let us forget Mary Powell and the wrongs of women and consider what Milton actually said on the subject of divorce. The occasion which prompted him to write was, no doubt, his own misadventure in the choice of a wife, though he nowhere says anything directly about that circumstance. What made him write as he did, what made him think of divorce as the remedy for the predicament into which we suppose him to have fallen, was that he had been thinking in a certain way about love and marriage. He had been thinking about these things, that is, in the way he had learned to do both as an English Protestant and as a Renaissance humanist, idealist, and poet. The divorce tracts reveal the twofold root of that romantic conception of love which fills half of modern literature, which in modern life leads or is supposed to lead us, two by two, to the marriage bureau, and which finally lands many of us, alas, in the divorce court.

When St Paul bade women submit to their husbands, he expressed the patriarchal conception of the family which prevailed in the ancient world. When, however, he bade husbands love their wives, he was probably not thinking that, as a necessary incident to getting married, they should undergo such an awakening and reorientation of the soul as Plato described under the name of love, though without associating it specifically with the attraction that brings men and women together. Paul himself underwent a love which made him a new man, but still this was not the love of woman. So the Church, while admitting sex as the natural basis for marriage, did not regard it as the appointed sphere for a transforming spiritual experience, and in providing for marriage did not neglect to provide as well for persons who remained unmarried. But with the Reformation and the cutting off of religious celibacy, marriage came to be thought of as the one way of life prescribed by the scriptures for every normal person, and the condition of the unmarried to be represented as something to be avoided, pitied, or held in contempt. Hence Milton, who in an earlier age might have lived contentedly enough in the condition of Petrarch or Erasmus, seems to have decided at thirty-four that he should take a wife. He did so, expecting quite consciously and explicitly – does he not tell us how he had read all the best literature on the subject? – to enter into a very special kind of intimacy with the woman he had chosen. Plato had taught the generations how the soul, by seeking beauty upon beauty, might attain good upon good. Ovid had induced them to believe or make believe that falling in love with a woman was something like being born to a new life, as though she were divinity and her beauty the fair face of the good enlightening the heart of her adorer. This worship of beauty in woman, as it first found expression in literature, had nothing necessarily to do with marriage. It was a delightful game or art for those to practise who could afford it, and when it led to earnest, as of course it often did, it might lead to almost anything. It brought Dante to heaven, but Paolo and Francesca it brought to hell. One point, however, is clear; it did not lead Guinevere to ask Arthur for a divorce in order that she might marry Lancelot.

The literature of lady-worship was first brought to England for the entertainment of courtiers, but through the Press and the theater it reached the great popular audience which arose in the sixteenth century. In thus passing from court to city, it underwent a change in accordance with the taste, the moral standards, and the religious convictions of the new public which was being more and more affected by the rise of Puritanism. Exactly when this transition from the *amour courtois* to the *amour bourgeois* was complete, it would be difficult and is not necessary to determine. The effect was to establish the convention that no lover should come courting unless he meant to offer marriage and that no one should marry without first falling in love with the chosen spouse. Hence in Spenser's poem, love which does not lead to marriage is made, but for one exception, to appear evil or absurd, and the love which leads to higher things leads by way of marriage, and the happy lovers in Shakespeare's plays, though they go through the attitudes of courtly love and hang sonnets on the trees, make ready to marry their mistresses before the play is over. Hence, too, when Charles I's French queen revived the old game of lady-worship at court and playwrights took to presenting love too profanely on the stage, the spokesmen of middle-class moral sentiment let their disapproval be known.

Yet the code of feeling and behavior set forth by the Puritan preachers in pulpit and press, while tempering the worship of female beauty, helped at the same time in its own way to promote a more emotional attitude toward women. At an earlier time, the preachers would have been men dedicated to chastity and a celibate life, and they did not now, in deference to St Paul, altogether condemn celibacy. They merely insisted, still on the authority of Paul, that the power to abstain from woman was a gift of God bestowed upon but few men and no more often upon themselves than upon others, indeed, if anything, less often, since, as Satan's special targets, they were more liable to the burning of the flesh. Hence, seeing that marriage was the appointed tactic for defeating the evil one upon this particular ground, the preachers, almost to a man, embraced matrimony as it were their holy rule. The effects of this dedication of churchmen to conjugal life were probably no less important than that of poets to the celebration of love and beauty. The preachers believed that the sphere of religious experience was the breast of the individual and that the decisive event in the life of the soul was the experience of being reborn like Paul in the faith. This teaching, they held, was set down for all to read in the scriptures and for each to confirm by the grace of God in his own mind and heart. The preachers professed to look upon themselves simply as men appointed to expound the word, report its workings within themselves, and persuade others that what had happened to them and to Paul might happen to any man or woman. The primary means of grace was, of course, God's own word in print or spoken from the pulpit, but besides that, all God's works and creatures resounded with vocation to the soul, and obviously no occasion called more compellingly than love and marriage.

Hence the preachers addressed themselves to telling the people how they should feel and act according to the spirit of godliness in these as in other relationships. Their instructions, which found their way into many published commentaries and sermons as well as tracts and treatises dealing specifically with marriage and the family, should be studied by anyone who sets up to tell us what young men and maidens of that age, like John Milton and Mary Powell, learned from their elders concerning – may I say? – the facts of life. One of the earliest books on the subject was Coverdale's translation (1541) of a work by the reformer Bullinger, called in English *The Christen State of Matrimony*. Many others followed before Milton took up the theme in 1643, such as, to mention only some of the leading writers, Perkins' *Christian Oeconomy* (translated into English, 1609), Henry Smith's *Preparative to Marriage* (1591), Dod and Cleaver's *Godly Form of Household Government* (1598), Whately's *Bride-bush* (1617) and *Care-cloth* (1624), Gouge's *Of Domesticall Duties* (1626), and Rogers' *Matrimoniall Honour* (1642).[1] The main body of the Puritan clergy had learned early in Elizabeth's reign that their interest lay, not in directly attacking established law and authority but in preaching the gospel. They did not, consequently, find

fault with the long established laws relating to marriage, and as Henry
VIII settled into his grave, they dropped the subject of divorce. They
devoted their efforts to teaching the people how they might marry and
at the same time turn both the pleasures and the pains of matrimony to
the profit of the soul, to teaching, in other words, how marital relationships might be suffused with religious and hence with greater emotional
significance. St Paul had, to be sure, insisted that the husband was the
head of the wife and that the wife should submit to the husband, and
this lesson did not lack reiteration in the pulpit. But the apostle laid
down the duty of husbands no less emphatically than that of wives.
Though the wife was bound to obey the husband, the husband was
bound to love the wife, and each was to render without restraint or
difference what was named 'due benevolence' to the other. It was this
relationship of love and obedience, reciprocal, inseparable, exclusive,
and unique, which made marriage in truth the image, nothing less, of
Christ's relation to his Church. Much, it is true, was said long before
Milton on the theme, drawn from 1 Corinthians xi 7 of 'he for God
only, she for God in him'. But the preachers seem to have felt less need
for telling their hearers that men were superior to women in the order
of nature than for insisting how nearly women might be expected
through love and marriage to approach their husbands' level and how
desirable it was that they should do so. No one questioned the obvious
truth that the more obedient the wife the more loving the husband was
likely to prove, but – *amor vincit omnia* – the key to the arch was not
obedience but love. For the more perfect the husband's love, the less he
would wish or need to exact that submission which the wife, for the
greater love of him, would freely yield without his bidding. The more
Abrahams, the preachers said, the more Sarahs, the more Sarahs the
more Abrahams. Sensible men that they were, they realized that,
committed as they were to matrimony, their condition would be easier
to bear if they chose congenial women for their mates and depended
more on affection and understanding than upon the assertion of their
God-given authority.

Such was the burden of their teaching. They exhorted the young to
choose helpmeets with godly companionship as the chief end to be
desired and, the more surely to attain that end, to choose as true affection and spiritual attraction prompted rather than appetite or self-
interest. They exhorted parents not to interfere with such promptings
in the hearts of their children. A wife, they said, was to be regarded not

simply as a bedfellow or a servant, but as a spiritual equal and companion. The later preachers especially dilated upon the joys of spiritual
union, sanctifying the union of the flesh, and upon the misery of those
who, coupled in body, were divided in soul. The most enthusiastic
went so far as to say that husbands and wives, in thus communing with
one another, came nearer to communion with God himself. One final
step, however, they did not take in pursuing the logic of their doctrine.
The perfect union of souls was the end to be sought by every married
pair, but if the marriage of true minds failed to come off as expected,
the parties were still yoked in wedlock and must be content to remain
so with no redress save patience and prayer. Choose your love, the
preachers said again and again, but no matter what the event, you must
love or at any rate expect to abide by your choice. It demanded a
stouter spirit, under a sharper compulsion, to carry the Puritan doctrine
of marriage to its extreme conclusion.

That Milton had been well grounded in that doctrine long before
starting to Oxfordshire on the holiday from which he returned a
married man, there can be no question, even though we cannot precisely name his instructors. He had often, surely, listened to the sermons
of Richard Stock at Allhallows in Bread Street, one of the tall pillars of
the Puritan brotherhood. His tutor, Thomas Young, was a pupil of still
another great man of the Puritan pulpit, Stock's friend Richard Gataker.
He passed his boyhood almost within earshot of Richard Sibbes at
Gray's Inn, of Thomas Preston at Lincoln's Inn, and of William Gouge,
author of that exhaustive work, *Of Domesticall Duties*, at St Anne's
Blackfriars. From such men as these, undoubtedly, came Milton's
primary religious and moral training. He at once associated himself
with the members of this group when he returned to London in 1639,
and he came to their support in 1641 in their concerted attack upon
prelacy. There is, therefore, no need to speculate as to what Milton was
taught in his youth concerning such matters as chastity and marriage,
and no need, I venture to say, to speculate oversubtly as to what may
have been passing through his subconscious mind. The well-known
passage in his *Apology*, written just before his own marriage, in which he
recounts his early literary and moral training, should be read in the light
of current Puritan teachings.[2] He says there that 'last of all' – he has been
speaking of his reading of Plato and the poets – 'not in time, but as
perfection is last, that care was ever had of me, with my earliest
capacity not to be negligently train'd in the precepts of Christian

Religion', and that he had had infused into him, 'with timeliest care', 'the doctrine of holy Scripture unfolding those chaste and high mysteries . . . that *the body is for the Lord and the Lord for the body*'. The 'precepts' and 'doctrines' here referred to, if we may judge from the divorce tracts, are substantially the same as those which may still be read, if we take the trouble, in the writings of the preachers. If anything is certain about those writings, it is that they held up no conception of virginity as an end or good in itself, were not concerned with celibacy, associated chastity with marriage, and urged everybody for his or her soul's good to love and marry. If there could be any doubt as to whether Milton entertained similar ideas or not, it should be removed by the essentially Puritan interpretation he puts upon the well-known text in Revelation xiv 4. He has not slumbered, he says, over the saying that the songs of the blessed before the Lamb in Zion are to be heard only by 'those who were not defil'd with women'. Nevertheless, he omits mentioning the phrase, 'for they are virgins', which immediately follows in the Bible, and on the words, 'not defil'd with women', he adds the significant and characteristic comment, 'which doubtlesse meanes fornication: For marriage must not be call'd a defilement'. Neither Milton nor the preachers could believe that married men were to be excluded from heaven. Nor was this the only occasion on which he insisted that the scriptures could not possibly mean what they were commonly thought to say.

Much, however, though Milton learned from his religious teachers concerning chastity and love and marriage, he learned much from another source as well. He also learned about these matters, he tells us in the same outburst of self-revelation, from the poets and philosophers. As a boy, he says, he had read, enjoyed, and imitated the smooth elegiac poets, meaning chiefly Ovid, and what they wrote about, he observes, everybody knows. As he grew older, however, he came to deplore what these writers too often say about women and to prefer 'the two famous renowners of Beatrice and Laura who never write but honour of them to whom they devote their verse'. Then after Dante and Petrarch, he went on to those 'lofty Fables and Romances, which recount in solemne canto's the deeds of Knighthood founded by our victorious Kings'. In other words, he read about love in Arthurian romance but above all in *The Faerie Queene*. Finally, he tells us, 'riper yeares and the ceaselesse round of study and reading' brought him 'to the divine volumes of Plato and his equall Xenophon'.

What Milton learned about chastity and love, that love 'whose charming cup is only vertue', from Plato, Dante, and Petrarch hardly needs to be explained. In his own words, he learned 'how the first and chiefest office of love begins and ends in the soule'. But he did not learn from Plato, Dante, and Petrarch that the love whose office begins and ends in the soul was to be looked for in marriage and only in marriage. The poet who taught him that lesson, better teacher than Gouge and Perkins, but not of a very different doctrine, was Spenser. The influence on Milton of the spirit and thought of Spenser's great poem first becomes apparent in *Comus*, but it has been somewhat misunderstood.[3] Milton, in modelling the Lady of his masque upon the lady knight of chastity in *The Faerie Queene*, gave her all the spiritual self-sufficiency which Spenser names chastity, but he could not, for a very obvious reason, give her Britomart's special status and character as a woman united in spirit to the man of her choice. The understanding of *Comus* and Milton's other early poems on the subject of love has suffered because recent critics and biographers have yielded to the temptation to see in these writings, English, Latin, and Italian, a fairly complete and exact record of the poet's own emotional development and of his efforts at inner adjustment to sexual tensions, repressions, sublimations, and the like. In the interpretation of *Comus*, this has led to the suggestion that Milton was expressing, not simply the moral self-assurance of a young soul which knows exactly what it wants and that what it wants is right, but notions of an ascetic, celibate chastity, clothed with something like supernatural powers and blessings. They have attached great importance to the frequent reference in the poem to 'saintly chastity' and to the use at one point of the phrase

> the sage
> And serious doctrine of virginity,

besides the recurring allusions in *Comus* and other poems to the virgins who hear the singing of the blessed in heaven. (I have referred above to the significant qualifying comment on this text in the *Apology* of 1642.) If such an interpretation is correct, then we can only conclude that Milton, a convinced Protestant if ever there was one, was letting his mind work, on this one occasion, in a manner directly contrary to the whole tenor of the religious and moral training to which he had been subjected and to the ideas which he himself began to set forth so unequivocally in 1642. It is possible, I suggest, that the best of scholars may have been too quick in calling in modern psychology's artful aid. No doubt Milton underwent tensions for which he found relief in expression, but when it comes to sifting his poems for the secrets of his heart, we should remember that he was above all things an extremely self-conscious, passionate, literary artist, one, moreover, who took it to be axiomatic that the forms of his art, each with its appointed subject-matter and style, were fixed in nature and that his business was to master as many of them as he could compass both in theory and through practise. Who then shall say, except as the poet may explicitly make known, when he is unburdening his private soul in these poems and when he is simply practising his art?

It is at any rate to be questioned whether Milton wrote *Comus* in order to get certain private emotions off his mind or simply to oblige his friend, Henry Lawes, with the book of a court-masque to be presented on a particular occasion. The result was obviously the work of an amateur, but an amateur of genius who knew what was called for. The occasion required that he prepare the lines of a formal entertainment, especially including an attractive part for the unmarried daughter, aged fifteen, of the great earl before whom the thing was to be given. He assigned her the role of maiden chastity, assailed but never hurt. Nothing could have been more entirely proper, conventional, and expected. Then he filled her speeches and those of the two young lads, her brothers, with entrancing sentiments and noble ideas concerning virtue, drawn from Plato and Spenser, and this, too, was quite in order. He could hardly, however, in the circumstances, have ventured to bring in the theme of marriage. He could certainly not have made the Lady Alice go coursing about like Britomart in search of the man who was to be her husband and the father of her children. But this surely does not indicate that Milton at twenty-six failed to understand Spenser's meaning, to perceive that what made Britomart so sufficient in herself, so secure, so chaste, was married love. He must have perceived that in her, and in the tissue of stories of which she forms a part, was to be seen the unparalleled poetic expression of the very ideals concerning love and marriage which had been held forth also by his religious and moral teachers.

When Spenser in *The Faerie Queene* comes to the virtues he names chastity and friendship, his poem resolves itself into a fabric of interlacing tales of unmatched, mismatched friends and lovers, sorting themselves out into pairs, seeking each his or her own proper mate and spiritual counterpart. The base souls, though they may begin in seeming amity, conclude in strife and hatred. The nobler spirits, no matter how they begin, all end in love and peace and, with one exception, in the bonds of matrimony. As they intermingle in their encounters and adventures, like joins with like and true and false fly asunder. Thus Florimell, afraid of men, arrives at last in the arms of Marinell, who is afraid of women, and each becoming the other's complement and remedy, they love, marry, and lose all fear. The union of Amoret and Scudamore, endangered by the *amour courtois*, is redeemed by Britomart – until upon second thought Spenser remembers he must not let her steal the show from Arthur – and Britomart is a woman invincible because she is already united in spirit to her true mate and natural lord. She and Arthegall meet first in battle, but when he beholds her, beautiful though perspiring, he can only make religion of his wonder and she can only yield to the greater beauty, 'tempered with sternesse and stout majestie', which she recognizes in him. She is a rather formidable figure, like her Shavian namesake a managing matron of the upper classes, but she is not like Radigund an embattled feminist. She knows her place, as a woman, in the scheme of things, knows like Eve

> How beauty is excelled by manly grace
> And wisdom, which alone is truly fair.

The exception in Spenser's legend of good women is Belphoebe, but she is such an exception as does indeed prove the rule. For when the poet tries to conceive a woman of noble spirit who contents herself with less than marriage, he can conceive of nothing in particular for her to do. She makes a handsome figure in her sporting clothes, but she fades out of the story in a fit of misunderstanding and jealousy which comes about when she catches her single male admirer yielding to a natural impulse she has done too little to allay.[4]

Thus, while the preachers, with the authority of the scriptures to draw upon, depicted the spiritual joys that men were to look for in marriage, Spenser, with the poets and philosophers behind him, also exalted married love. The influences of both Reformation and Renaissance combined to promote that idealistic, quasi-religious, romantic attitude toward marriage to which Milton gave what seems such curious and extreme expression in the divorce tracts. Whether he had expected to encounter a sort of blend of Sarah and Britomart in the person of Mary Powell, one would not dare to say. Nevertheless, the predicament that concerns him is that of the man who has looked eagerly forward to the companionship of marriage only to find himself yoked, not to a fit conversing soul, but, as he says, to an 'image of earth and phlegm', an 'uncomplying discord of nature',[5] 'a loyal and individual vexation',[6] a woman fit to supply nothing better than 'a displeasing and forc't remedy against the sting of a bruit desire'.[7] It is the plight of an innocent and honorable man who has discerned too late 'the unlivelines and naturall sloth' which too often hides under 'the bashfull mutenes of a virgin'. Respecting modesty and believing, as friends tell him, that 'acquaintance, as it increases, will amend all', he has met 'if not with a body impenetrable, yet often with a mind to all other due conversation inaccesible, and to all the more estimable and superior purposes of matrimony uselesse and almost liveles'.[8]

There was, up to a point, nothing new in this picture of the misery that follows upon ill luck in the lottery of marital choice. Time and again the preachers had warned people against such risks. But by the summer of 1642, the revolution in Church and state was in full swing, the prelates had been stripped of their power, and there remained for the time being no authority to compel obedience to the laws of the Church which forbade a man in the predicament described by Milton from seeking the remedy implied by that hope of married bliss he had been led to embrace. He therefore seized the occasion to press to its logical conclusion the doctrine which the preachers had been setting forth in their sermons and tracts and the ideal which Spenser set forth in his poem. He proposed that Parliament, having in effect removed prelacy, should forthwith revoke canon law and authorize divorce by mutual consent of the parties on grounds of 'indisposition, unfitness, or contrariety of mind'[9] – 'thus with one gentle stroking to wipe away ten thousand teares out of the life of man'.[10]

Whether Milton's proposal was the correct solution of the difficulty he had in mind or whether his confidence in the efficacy of an Act of Parliament to assuage unhappiness was well founded is not, of course, the question. The divorce tracts, whatever one may think of divorce, express with peculiar eloquence the idea or, if one prefers, the dream of the good which their author had learned to hope for in marriage. Marriage, he declared, is 'a divine institution joyning man and woman in a love fitly dispos'd to the helps and comforts of domestic life'. Its essence lay in 'conjugal love arising from mutual fitness to the final causes of wedlock, help and society in Religious, Civil and Domestick conversation'.[11] First in importance came 'the apt and cheerfull conversation of man with woman' and only after that – 'a secondary end in dignity, though not in necessity'– 'the purpose of generation'.[12] True, Paul had said (1 Cor. vii 7) that he wished all men might be like himself, saying also that, in recommending marriage, he spoke 'by permission and not of commandment' (1 Cor. vii 6), but for Milton these texts, interpreted as he chose to interpret them, had little practical significance. In the same place the apostle also said that 'every man hath his proper gift of God, one after this manner and another after that', and he declared in another place (1 Tim. iv 1–3) that forbidding to marry was the doctrine of devils. In strict accordance with Puritan teaching, Milton took all this to mean that God did grant to some the ability to remain in the condition of Paul, but the gift was bestowed upon but few while marriage was plainly declared (Heb. xiii 4) honorable for all:

> Whatever hypocrites austerely talk
> Of purity and place and innocence,
> Defaming as impure what God declares
> Pure, and commands to some, leaves free to all.

For anyone, therefore, to abstain from marriage 'who hath not receiv'd the continence' was inexpedient and wicked. One who did refrain, 'not being supernaturally gifted', was 'in a diabolicall sin, equall to that of Antichrist who forbids to marry'.[13] But – and this was the crucial point – it also followed from Milton's premises that Paul's other saying, 'it is better to marry than to burn', could not possibly bear the implication commonly put upon it. Marriage was not intended as a license to the incontinent – 'God does not principally take care for such cattell'. For allaying the mere burning of the flesh, 'strict life and labour, with the abatement of a full diet' should suffice. Paul was speaking of something quite different. He was speaking of that 'inbred desire' to join with 'a fit conversing soul', of that desire stronger than death properly called love, that 'intelligible flame, not in paradice to be resisted', 'that rationall burning that marriage is to remedy'.[14]

Whenever he comes to this theme, the poet who goes hand in hand with the dialectician in the divorce tracts usually takes complete possession of the page. Recollecting the eighth chapter of Proverbs, he declares that the soul of man must have its pleasures and pastimes,

'which as she cannot well doe without company, so in no company so
well as where the different sexe in most resembling unlikenes, and most
unlike resemblance cannot but please best and be pleas'd in the aptitude
of that variety'. God gave man to delight in woman as he himself
delighted, before the world was made, in that reflection of himself,
playing ever before him, which is the eternal wisdom.[15] Nor does
Milton forget Plato and the help which the wise ancients can afford in
the understanding of the scriptures. What Socrates tells of love in the
Symposium, 'the sonne of *Penury*, begot of Plenty in the garden of
Jupiter' makes clear what Moses meant in Genesis by revealing 'that
Love was the son of Loneliness, begot in Paradise by that sociable and
helpfull aptitude which God implanted between man and woman
toward each other'.[16] It is the same love, still burning 'in the proper
meaning of St Paul', the same 'matrimoniall love', waxing or waning
as it meets or misses its true conversing counterpart – 'reflection of a
coequal and homogeneal fire' – which is likened, he says, by ancient
sages to Eros and Anteros. Hence, as we should expect, Milton scorns
Augustine's 'crabbed opinion', that it would have been more becoming
for Adam to have looked for solace in manly friendship rather than
'spend so many secret years in an empty world with one woman'.[17]
Adam had the company of God himself; he had the angels to converse
with and the creatures to delight him; he might have had 'a thousand
friends and brother Adams' created from the same mould as himself.
Nevertheless, the words 'it is not good for man to be alone' mean
nothing but 'alone without woman'. 'Till Eve was giv'n him, God
reckn'd him to be alone.' No creature but woman in no relationship
but wedlock could satisfy that 'rational burning', that solitariness of
soul, which was the first thing in this world 'which Gods eye named not
good'.[18] Moreover, not only is marriage essential for the solacing of
man's loneliness of spirit, but the ministering to that loneliness is the
function of marriage from which all its other uses directly flow. The
coupling of bodies may be accomplished without joining of souls, but
the mere traffic of male and female is not marriage and cannot make
one flesh. Nothing can make husband and wife truly one 'but likenes,
but fitnes of mind and disposition, which may breed the Spirit of
concord, and union between them'. Where that is lacking "tis not to
say, they shall be one flesh, for they cannot be one flesh'.[19] Indeed, those
who are united in spirit, 'where the mind and person pleases aptly', can
more readily forgo the body 'than when the mind hangs off . . . for

there all corporall delight will soon become unsavoury and con-
temptible'.[20]

Yet if the mind does hang off, what then? Milton was incapable of
meeting the distressful ambivalence of man's greatest earthly blessing
with the bland irony of Chaucer, as when Chauntecleer tells Pertelote,
who, being only a hen, understands no Latin, that the meaning of
'mulier est hominis confusio' is 'womman is mannes joye and all his
blis'. Milton was also incapable of taking refuge in the cynicism which
Donne expresses when, in one of his moods, he cries out against

> That loving wretch that sweares,
> 'Tis not the bodies marry, but the mindes

and goes on to exclaim

> Hope not for minde in women; at their best
> Sweetnesse and wit, they are but Mummy, possesst.

He was a man of faith, an idealist, and a revolutionary, an alarming
kind of person always, one who believes that human powers and
human resolution are, by the grace of God, capable of promoting the
good of man here and now. 'Yet if it were sudden & swift,' he says,
speaking of reform, 'provided still it be from worse to better, certainly
wee ought to hie us from evill like a torrent, and rid our selves of
corrupt Discipline, as wee would shake fire out of our bosoms.'[21] He
was not, therefore, like his friends the preachers, the man to draw back
from what seemed to him the necessary practical conclusion to the
doctrine of marriage which they had been setting forth. They had said
again and again that the needs of the spirit should be put before the
demands of the body. In 1642, the very year of Milton's own marriage,
Daniel Rogers, in his *Matrimoniall Honour*, had said it all over again with
egregious unction and exuberance. Nevertheless, for the disappointment
and betrayal of the spirit in marriage, they dared to propose only
spiritual remedies and, adhering to the strict letter of the scriptures,
admitted no just cause for divorce except adultery. William Whately,
more reckless than most, did argue in 1617 that divorce might also be
allowed for desertion, but, prompted by High Commission, he quickly
found reason to recant this opinion. Milton was a man of quite different
mettle. To deny divorce as the proper remedy for the failure of marriage
to perform its spiritual function, while permitting it for breach of
carnal union, was, it seemed to him, to make the spirit and its needs

wait upon the body, and this, he argued in *Tetrachordon*, could not possibly be what the Holy Spirit intended, no matter what the scriptures, misinterpreted, were alleged to say. 'Marriage', he declared, 'is a human Society and . . . all human society must proceed from the mind rather then the body. . . . If the mind therfore cannot have that due company by marriage, that it may reasonably and humanly desire, that marriage can be no human society'.[22] To provide for man's worthiest part is most worthy God's care; to set the body above the mind is contrary to nature. A union in which the mind is denied contentment 'is not of God's institution, and therefore no marriage'.[23]

When he reached this point, Milton had come full circle in the philosophy of love. Plato and the poets had taught him that the office of love begins and ends in the soul. Spenser and the preachers in their several ways had taught him that the love whose office is in the soul must be sealed in marriage. He concluded that in a union where love cannot exercise its rightful office 'there can be left of wedlock nothing but the empty husk of an outside matrimony'.[24] No marriage is possible except it be the marriage of true minds; any other union is a living in sin; the law that would compel a man to sin or forbid him to seek the good that marriage is designed to furnish is no law of God but the tyranny of Antichrist. Thus when it comes about that, in order to save his soul, he who loves must marry and he who is married must love, it follows that, in order to marry and love, a man may have to divorce the woman whom he has discovered to be not in truth part of his soul, his other half.

But, let me repeat, the reasoning which led Milton, in the heat of revolution and the chagrin of personal disappointment, to a conclusion so full, to say the least, of practical difficulties, sprang first of all from an idealistic view of marriage, a view based both upon Puritan doctrine and the historic idealization of beauty in women.

> A nice and subtle happiness, I see,
> Thou to thyself proposest, in the choice
> Of thy associates,

the Almighty says to Adam when the latter has made known his wish for a companion

> fit to participate
> All rational delight

But Adam receives divine assurance that, in forming such a desire, he is expressing the free spirit within him, 'my image', says God, 'not imparted to the brute'. So, when Adam leads Eve to the nuptial bower, the poet exclaims, 'Hail wedded love!' 'Here', about the marriage bed and nowhere else,

> Love his golden shafts employs, here lights
> His constant lamp, and waves his purple wings,
> Reigns here and revels.

But wisdom is superior to beauty, and nothing profits a man, by nature the wiser of the human pair, more

> Than self-esteem, grounded on just and right.

This woman herself well knows. She is a reasonable being because created in the image of man, himself a reasonable being because created in the image of a reasonable God. What Adam is to love in his wife, therefore, is that which he finds 'attractive, human, rational'.

> In loving thou dost well; in passion not,
> Wherein true love consists not. Love refines
> The thoughts, and heart enlarges; hath his seat
> In Reason, and is judicious; is the scale
> By which to Heavenly love thou mayst ascend.

Marriage, thus conceived, stands in the focus of all interest and meaning in *Paradise Lost*. It is the consummation of God's plan of creation on earth. It is the projection of the divine order, of the order of nature and of the soul, into human society. It is the whole of human society in germ, the living microcosm, truly, of family, Church, and state. It is, in consequence, the prime object of Satan's envy, and its disruption the first task to which he addressed himself on this earth. Man's fall ensues when the harmony and order of marriage, the reciprocal rule of love and obedience, freedom and responsibility, reason and conscience, is broken. His redemption is foreshadowed when woman, upon their expulsion from the earthly paradise, declares her renewed loyalty and obedience.

> But now lead on;
> In me is no delay; with thee to go
> Is to stay here; without thee here to stay
> Is to go hence unwilling; thou to me
> Art all things under Heaven, all places thou,
> Who for my wilful crime art banished hence.

NOTES

1. William and Malleville Haller, 'The Puritan Art of Love', in *Huntington Library Quarterly*, V (Jan. 1942).

2. *Works* (Columbia) III 302–6.

3. I find myself, with regret and some trepidation, differing on this point from Denis Saurat, *Milton, Man and Thinker* (New York, 1925); J. H. Hanford, 'The Youth of Milton: an interpretation of his early literary development', in *Studies in Shakespeare, Milton, and Donne*, by members of the English Department of the University of Michigan (New York and London, 1925); E. M. W. Tillyard, *Milton*; and A. S. P. Woodhouse, 'Argument of Milton's *Comus*', in *Toronto Quarterly*, XI (Oct. 1941).

4. In this interpretation of Spenser's allegory, I am indebted to John Erskine, 'The Virtue of Friendship in *The Faerie Queene*', in *PMLA*, XXX (1915) 381 ff, and to C. S. Lewis, *Allegory of Love*.

5. *Doctrine and Discipline of Divorce*, in *Works*, III 400.

6. *Tetrachordon*, in *Works*, IV 205.

7. *D & D of D*, in *Works*, III 492.

8. Ibid. in *Works*, III 394–5.

9. Ibid. in *Works*, III 388.

10. Ibid. in *Works*, III 390.

11. *Tetrachordon*, in *Works*, IV 101–5.

12. *D & D of D*, in *Works*, III 382.

13. *Tetrachordon*, in *Works*, IV 84; see also *Judgement of Martin Bucer*, in *Works*, IV 57.

14. *D & D of D*, in *Works*, III 396–7.

15. *Tetrachordon*, in *Works*, IV 85–6.

16. *D & D of D*, in *Works*, III 398.

17. *Tetrachordon*, in *Works*, IV 85.

18. Ibid. in *Works*, IV 83.

19. Ibid. in *Works*, III 97–8.

20. *D & D of D*, in *Works*, III 391.

21. *Of Reformation*, in *Works*, III 66.

22. *D & D of D*, in *Works*, III 422–3.

23. *Tetrachordon*, in *Works*, IV 87.

24. *D & D of D*, in *Works*, III 402.

Select Bibliography

Poems of Mr John Milton: the 1645 Edition with Essays in Analysis, ed. Cleanth Brooks and John E. Hardy (Harcourt, Brace, 1951).

Milton's Lycidas: the Tradition and the Poem, ed. C. A. Patrides (Holt, Rinehart, 1961).

Milton: Modern Essays in Criticism, ed. Arthur E. Barker (Oxford U.P., 1965).

Rosemond Tuve, *Images and Themes in Five Poems by Milton* (Harvard U.P., 1957; Oxford U.P., 1958).

The Living Milton: Essays by Various Hands, ed. Frank Kermode (Routledge & Kegan Paul, 1960; paperback, 1963).

Anne D. Ferry, *Milton's Epic Voice: the Narrator in Paradise Lost* (Harvard U.P., 1963; Oxford U.P., 1963).

C. S. Lewis, *A Preface to Paradise Lost* (Oxford U.P., 1942; paperback, 1960).

Arnold Stein, *Answerable Style: Essays on Paradise Lost* (University of Minnesota P., 1953; Oxford U.P., 1953).

Joseph H. Summers, *The Muse's Method: an Introduction to Paradise Lost* (Harvard U.P., 1962; Chatto & Windus, 1962).

A. J. A. Waldock, *Paradise Lost and its Critics* (Cambridge U.P., 1947; paperback, 1962; Peter Smith, 1962).

B. A. Wright, *Milton's Paradise Lost: a Reassessment of the Poem* (Methuen, 1962; Barnes & Noble, 1962).

Christopher B. Ricks, *Milton's Grand Style: A Study of Paradise Lost* (Clarendon P., 1963).

Stanley E. Fish, *Surprised by Sin: The Reader in Paradise Lost* (Macmillan, 1967; St Martin's Press, 1967).

Arnold Stein, *Heroic Knowledge: An Interpretation of Paradise Regained and Samson Agonistes* (University of Minnesota P., 1957; Oxford U.P., 1957).

M. M. Mahood, *Poetry and Humanism* (Yale U.P., 1950; Jonathan Cape, 1950).

F. T. Prince, *The Italian Element in Milton's Verse* (Clarendon P., 1954).

Roy Daniells, *Milton, Mannerism and Baroque* (University of Toronto P., 1963).

Barbara Lewalski, *Milton's Brief Epic: The Genre, Meaning, and Art of Paradise Regained* (Brown U.P., 1966; Methuen, 1966).

Milton's Sonnets, ed. E. A. J. Honigmann (Macmillan, 1966; St Martin's Press, 1966).

Robert M. Adams, *Ikon: John Milton and the Modern Critics* (Cornell U.P., 1955).

Notes on Contributors

ARTHUR BARKER teaches at the University of Illinois at Urbana and has written *Milton and the Puritan Dilemma 1641–1660*.

J. B. BROADBENT teaches at Cambridge and wrote *Poetic Love* and *Some Graver Subject*.

CLEANTH BROOKS, is Gray Professor of Rhetoric at Yale and author of *The Well-Wrought Urn*.

MURRAY W. BUNDY, Professor Emeritus of Washington State University, has written *Theory of Imagination in Classical and Medieval Thought*.

ROSALIE L. COLIE, author of *Paradoxica Epidemica: The Renaissance Tradition of Paradox*, teaches at the University of Iowa.

STANLEY FISH teaches at the University of California at Berkeley and has written *John Skelton's Poetry* and *Surprised by Sin: The Reader in 'Paradise Lost'*.

WILLIAM HALLER, Professor Emeritus of Columbia University and Fellow of the Folger Shakespeare Library, Washington, D.C., is the author of *Rise of Puritanism*, *Liberty and Reformation in the Puritan Revolution*, *The Elect Nation* and *Elizabeth I and the Puritans*.

J. B. LEISHMAN, who taught at Oxford until his death in 1963, wrote *Themes and Variations in Shakespeare's Sonnets*, *The Art of Marvell's Poetry*, *The Metaphysical Poets: Donne, Herbert, Vaughan, Traherne* and *The Monarch of Wit: An Analytical and Comparative Study of the Poetry of John Donne*.

WILLIAM G. MADSEN, author of *The Idea of Nature in Milton's Poetry*, teaches at Emory University, Atlanta.

M. M. MAHOOD is Professor of English at the University of Kent; she is the author of *Poetry and Humanism*.

LAWRENCE A. SASEK, who teaches at Louisiana State University, specialises in Milton and sixteenth- and seventeenth-century literature. He has written *Literary Temper of the English Puritans*.

WAYNE SHUMAKER teaches at the University of California at Berkeley and has written *Elements of Critical Theory*, *English Autobiography*, *Literature and the Irrational* and *Unpremeditated Verse: Feeling and Perception in 'Paradise Lost'*.

J. H. SUMMERS, Professor of English at Washington University, St Louis, has written *George Herbert: His Religion and Art* and *The Muse's Method: An Introduction to 'Paradise Lost'*.

ARNOLD WILLIAMS, Professor of English at Michigan State University, has written *The Common Expositor*, *The Characterization of Pilate* and *Drama of Medieval England*.

Index